Second Edition

Methods in Vocational Business Education

By

HARM HARMS, Ed.D.
Head of the Division of
  Business Administration
College of Guam
Agana, Guam

and

B. W. STEHR, Ed.D.
Associate Professor
Department of Business and
  Economics
Marshall University
Huntington, West Virginia

SOUTH-WESTERN PUBLISHING CO.

CINCINNATI 27   CHICAGO 44   BURLINGAME, CALIF.
        DALLAS 2   NEW ROCHELLE, N. Y.

X96

Library of Congress Catalog Card No. 62-12628

H163

Printed in the
United States of America

PREFACE

A good methods course fulfills a necessary and vital function in business teacher education programs. The purpose of this book is to help make the basic methods course in business education as useful and as productive as possible. Many colleges and universities offer only one general methods course, covering both the skills and the nonskills, for the teacher of business subjects in the high school. This volume is designed to meet the needs for a basic book in this course.

Good teaching requires that the teacher possess a sound foundation in at least two areas of professional education: (1) understanding of the purposes and aims of education, and (2) understanding of the psychology of learning. The book has been organized to orient the reader to these two fundamental areas at the beginning—Chapters I and II.

Chapter III is divided into three parts, setting the style for the remaining chapters with the exception of Chapter X. Part I of the chapter presents broad principles; Part II deals with implementation of the principles; Part III cites research and current literature undergirding the first two parts of the chapter. In many instances enough of the original source material has been included so that this book can be readily used as a handbook by teachers already in the field.

Although this book is an outgrowth of the thoughts presented in *Methods in Vocational Business Education, First Edition,* with the exception of a limited number of pages the material in this volume is entirely new. Chapters VIII and IX on the basic business or nonskill courses are new. Chapter VIII marks the transition of the skills teacher to the nonskill business areas. It shows the evolution of the nonskills teacher and lays down broad principles. Chapter IX illustrates actual techniques and devices for implementing the principles stated in Chapter VIII.

iii

In the book we have tried to spell out the means for effective teaching, using our years of experience in the classroom as a basis. We have endeavored to face honestly the realities of teaching in the high school classroom. Teachers are not always able to work under ideal conditions; we have attempted to suggest procedures and materials that can be utilized under most circumstances. Beginning teachers, particularly, are interested in "How can I teach this?" rather than in elaborate theories on teaching methodology. We have attempted to fill this practical need.

After carefully reviewing the literature of business education, we have drawn liberally on the research of leaders in the field and on the work of seasoned classroom teachers. It would be most difficult to give full credit for all the ideas presented in this volume. We want to gratefully acknowledge, however, the help given to us by all the authors and publishers mentioned in the book and by the business education leaders with whom we discussed this material either in person or by correspondence. Special acknowledgment is made to Dr. Pedro C. Sanchez and Mr. John Trace, administrative officers of the College of Guam and Department of Education, Territory of Guam, at the time this manuscript was prepared, for their assistance and helpful suggestions. A special word of thanks should be given to Pauline Harms and Mary Stehr for their patient and efficient assistance with the manuscript.

If this volume will furnish methods teachers with additional material for their teacher education classes, if it will give the experienced teacher a quick review of present-day methods and materials, and if it will make the job of the beginning teacher easier, then the authors will feel well repaid for their efforts.

HARM HARMS
B. W. STEHR

CONTENTS

CONTENTS

v

CHAPTER I

EDUCATIONAL CONCEPTS IN THE SPACE AGE

Sometimes it helps our thinking if we locate our position within the complete scheme of things. Therefore, before dealing with the methods of teaching the business subjects, it might be well to take a brief look at education in general and the place of business education in the total educational framework of the secondary schools of the nation.

This chapter will attempt to crystallize for the business teacher and for those who are planning to teach business subjects guidelines for answering the questions: What is good education? Specifically, what is good business education? Authorities are not wholly in accord as to what constitutes the ultimate in education; nevertheless, there are some trends indicative of sound educational philosophy upon which leading educators in the nation agree in principle.

Trends in American Education

Education in the Not-So-Distant Past. Various attempts have been made in the literature of education to picture the old and the new philosophies of education. The "little red schoolhouse" of the turn of the century is a good example of the old. In penmanship and art, one was taught to copy. In fact, most students never arrived at a stage of schooling involving any creative endeavor. In the little red schoolhouse, pupils learned virtually nothing about physical fitness, and mental hygiene was not yet born. Children ate much but not well of the educational offerings. Facts in school had little meaning, no purpose—just so much to be learned because it was "good for you." Attempts at English composition were so stilted, because of severe criticisms of spelling, grammar, and punctuation, that rarely did anyone dare to strike out on his own. In botany the class was forbidden to talk about anything that was in the least familiar; plants or trees of a domestic nature were taboo. The time was spent on Latin terms that frighten one even now, while the home orchard and flower gardens died for want of knowledge of plant culture.

The class followed Caesar through many a campaign, but failed to learn the meaning of a few of the common prefixes. These students studied the minutest crystals in geology, but they learned nothing to help them appreciate the wonderful outcroppings of the Grand Canyon or even those in the backyard of the school. They learned names of states and their capitols, but they learned not a word about the influence of geography on the lives of people. They learned dates in history, but they found nothing to help them function as economic citizens in a free society.

The Emergence of the "New Day" in Education. The learning process is often anything but logical. Educators frequently retire to a philosophical "mountain top," and after weeks of careful deliberation come forth with an outline or a formula so sound that the casual observer will frequently remark, "Well, I wonder why they didn't think of that in the first place," or, "It looks self-evident. Why didn't they come to that conclusion a long time ago?" So it was that an appraisal of secondary education through much study and research in the early years of this century resulted in more effective evaluative criteria for our high school curricula and gave us a fundamental, abiding philosophy of education; namely, *that our schools shall be a living example of democracy in action.*

We are a sloganized people. No matter how carefully an ideal is worded, almost overnight it becomes a slogan and all thinking about the significant implications of the ideal is lost. What does it mean to have a school be a practical, workable, active, living, dynamic example of American democratic principles in action? The fundamental principle of democracy is one that seeks always to extend the area of *common interest*. The test of the democratic ideal is the manner in which conflicts are resolved. If there is a minority opposition in a totalitarian country, the minority is "liquidated." In a democratic system, however, the minority is heard and its point of view considered. An endeavor is made then to reach a compromise by finding a point upon which all members of the group agree, and from this common ground a workable solution is eventually formulated.

Democracy in action, as related to the school, means that there must be participation by all individuals concerned and that all must to some extent have a voice in establishing the environment in which they are to function. It means a liberal amount of discussion and a majority agreement before a plan is put into action; and that once a plan has been adopted by the group, it is the duty of all to support this action. In such a school program all take part—the parents, the faculty, the students, the administrators, and other members of the community.

The "new day" in education emphasized interest, purposes, needs, activity, meaning, and feeling to enhance the degree to which learning takes place. Leaders in this educational climate, such as Bode, claimed:

> All this is but another way of saying that the school, ideally, is a place where pupils go in order to carry on activities, from which certain reconstructions or reorganizations of experience are expected to result. This emphasis on activities explains why *interest* occupies so prominent a place in the picture. It also explains the prominence given to "activity" programs, especially on the lower levels.[1]

---

[1] Boyd H. Bode, *How We Learn* (Boston: D. C. Heath and Company, 1940), p. 246.

Briggs, on one occasion, stated:

> Education must not only indicate what one ought to feel
> and think and do, but it must irresistibly impel him to do it.
> We may agree with James that whatever other evidences of
> life it manifests, is of no importance—nay, actually, it does
> not exist—unless it makes a difference in the ways in which
> we feel and think and act.[2]

The abiding basic principles of curriculum planning as
formulated by these pioneers of the "new day" all had to do
with one central theme—meeting the needs of the students
to enable them to function well as members of their community and economic groups.

The American Secondary School in the Modern Age.
A change is taking place in education, a change of revolu-
tionary proportions that can be identified as a trend—a general tendency or inclination in a certain direction. The past
half century has been notable for its accomplishments in the
education of the mass population of the United States. Since
October 4, 1957, the date of the Russian Sputnik, the problem of American education has been how to make the most
effective use of the technological and scientific resources of
the nation. We want to sustain and enhance our present
standard of living, yet cope with the Kremlin in the race
for space. The educational system now strives for depth, as
well as breadth, in the total educational development of
youth. They must not only cultivate the ability to earn a
living for themselves and their families, to participate as
members of their communities, but must also become prepared to fit into the total framework of society as free,
independently-thinking and functioning citizens.

Typical of the concern for the direction of education,
particularly at the secondary school level, is the view
expressed by Professor Irwin Widen:

---

[2] Thomas Briggs, *Pragmatism and Pedagogy* (New York: The Macmillan Company, 1940), p. 25.

Recent years have brought tremendous advances in the state of our technology. We have zoomed into the air age and have blasted off for the space age. Yet, as has been wisely pointed out, a rocket ship is no more useful to man than an ox car if he does not know where he wants to go.

As it has to other fields of endeavor, technological progress has come to education. Our school buildings have become more functional, our teaching and administrative practices more efficient, and our public-relations techniques more astute. Still, with education as with transportation, advanced means do not of themselves guarantee the attainment of worthy ends.

What should be the ends of education and what means are appropriate to such ends? These are the basic questions that confront our profession.[3]

Two major philosophical issues in education in the United States today are pointed out by Dr. John H. Fischer, President of Teachers College, Columbia University:

In our society, what is the special function of the school? This is the query which, often unnoticed and ignored, underlies the heated discussions about quality in education. It is pointless to ask whether a school is doing its work well until we have agreed on what its work is.

There is a *second* question on which you will have to clarify your own thinking and be prepared to offer a responsible opinion: How shall we conduct schools so as to nurture most fruitfully the individuality of the students? The implications for schools are broad and deep, confronting us immediately with paradoxes. For one of the principal aims of education is to make people alike. In pursuit of this purpose we teach children their mother tongue, a common alphabet, a system of symbols to express quantitative ideas and mathematical processes. But the coin has another side,

---

[3] Irwin Widen, "By Rocket Ship or Ox Cart—We Must Know Where To Go," *Phi Delta Kappan* (June, 1960), p. 403.

for while the common characteristics of people make a community possible, it is their uncommon qualities that make it better. *Variety, innovation, leadership, and progress come only from individuality.*[4]

A major movement in the secondary school in this modern age has been to take a careful look at the "group progress" concept. "Double-track" and "triple-track" programs are being devised in some systems to let strong students proceed at a free rate of speed while others go more slowly. This is an answer to the criticism that able students have often been insufficiently challenged. The multiple-track system is highlighted in a recent book by Dr. James B. Conant,[*] in which he urges the abandonment of such former curricula as "college preparatory," "vocational," "commercial," and urges that, instead, the differentiation be primarily on the basis of student ability and motivation.

For the most part, those who have carefully reviewed the current educational scene seem to be sincere in their belief that increasingly better ways must be found to educate American youth. Robinson[5] lists statements of a dozen leaders in the United States known for their interest in public education who were recently asked to state what single idea represented their most urgent device for America's schools. In his report, Robinson points out that "the highest common denominator in the dozen responses is the optimism that flows from satisfaction with the past coupled with a determination to achieve even more in the future."[6]

Limitations of space in this volume prevent listing of all of these statements, but because these are expressions by persons exerting considerable leadership influence in the

---

[4] John H. Fischer, "Our Changing Conception of Education," *Phi Delta Kappan* (October, 1960), pp. 16-17.

[*] James B. Conant, *The American High School Today* (New York: McGraw-Hill Book Company, Inc., 1959).

[5] Donald W. Robinson, "Ideals for Tomorrow's Schools," *Phi Delta Kappan* (February, 1960), pp. 227-228.

[6] *Ibid.*

future of American secondary education, the following are
included here:

> *Lawrence Derthick*, former U. S. Commissioner of Educa-
> tion, asserts the need "to guarantee to every child the
> opportunity to develop to the fullest his own gifts and
> talents, for the benefit of himself and of the nation."
>
> *William H. Kilpatrick* reminds us of the need for respon-
> sible democratic education: "Since our existing civilization
> is not perfect, we stress the factors of creative and respon-
> sible citizenship, creative that new and better features may
> be devised to improve our civilization, responsible that each
> new proposal may be reliably tested that it may really make
> for the common good."
>
> *Paul E. Elicker,* former executive secretary of the National
> Association of Secondary School Principals, suggests that
> some strengthening of the schools is in order: "America
> now provides a better education for all its youth than any
> other country in the world, yet its aim should be to improve
> the quality of its education." [7]

Business Education in the Age of the Atom

The twentieth century has also been noted for its
achievements and progress in business and commerce.
Therefore, there has been increased educational effort ex-
pended in training and developing future leaders in business
and economics. The last two decades have seen national
attention focused upon the needs of youth for business and
economic education with the result that increased numbers
of programs in business have been introduced in more and
more schools.

**Implications for Business Education in the Nation's
Schools.** To make a living is a prime desire of man, and
history records the efforts of man and nations to achieve
sound economic status. The ability of the men in business
today to operate and control the large concerns did not

---

[7] *Ibid.*

result from their self-initiative and "bootstrap pulling" alone. This growth in knowledge and ability has been due in large measure to the well-directed programs of business education in both the secondary schools and adult education programs.

The business education programs in the secondary schools and post-high school institutions represent a major expression of the concern of a nation for the economic competence of its youth. Its purpose is manifold. Business education consists of the total activity which is planned, organized, and developed in favor of the preparation of youth for responsible economic participation in the community. It is a program of instruction, counseling, guidance, and service which seeks through a variety of activities to provide for and improve the part that each young person must play in his normal social and economic surroundings. The program is one of developing youth beyond mere skill training.

The business education curriculum is a particular and distinct part of the total school program. It should be viewed as such and developed on that basis. It includes the formal aspects of educational effort as these are developed in the classroom under the heading of instruction; personalized efforts to inform and counsel the individual pupil; and general information and guidance activities developed on a group basis. Implied in the total business education effort is the utilization of all of the learning activities possible for the purpose of providing realistic and functional business education experiences.

The responsibilities that rest on the business curriculum were recently restated and reaffirmed by a major association for the improvement of business education in the high schools, the Policies Commission for Business and Economic Education:

> Business education is concerned with two major aspects of the education of youth:

A. The knowledge, attitudes, and nonvocational skills needed by all persons to be effective in their personal economics and in their understanding of our economic system.

B. The vocational knowledge and skills needed for initial employment and for advancement in a business career.

We believe that:

1. Business education has an important contribution to make to the economic literacy of every high school boy and girl.

2. Business education must provide an adequate program of vocational preparation for those boys and girls who will enter business upon completing high school.

3. Business education courses should be available as electives to those high school students planning to go to college and should be accepted by the colleges and universities as meeting part of the college entrance requirements.[8]

Business Education in the Crosscurrents of Educational Change. There is good reason to believe that extensive activity in business and economic education in the high schools will continue unabated. In addition to the philosophical bases indicated above, a multitude of practical problems in business and industry continue to demand the best effort of those who follow the pennant of business education. The increase of paper records, for example, in the past twenty years, while being expedited through the use of machines, has placed a drain on the available top-level manpower.

---

[8] Policies Commission for Business and Economic Education, *This We Believe About Business Education in the High School*, published in the *Business Education Forum* (May, 1961), pp. 19-30.

It is the present-day climate of thought and need for serious appraisal of educational practices that causes us to study critically the business education curricula of the secondary school age group. If ours is indeed the space age, the school must accept the challenge to contribute generously to the preparation of youth for life in a complex and ever-changing world. Ruben Dumler, past-president of the Mountain-Plains Business Education Association, recently commented on this need:

> Sometimes all of us become very complacent because we feel that everything *at present* is going along very nicely. Actually, teachers are always working in the future, and, above all, for the future; therefore, they must be concerned with the future.[9]

Edith T. Smith, 1961 president of the Western Business Education Association, echoes this point of view:

> With the educational tide definitely "coming in" toward the academic program, business educators must re-evaluate their offerings. In doing so, however, we must not lose sight of the fact that we have an obligation to business to provide competent beginning employees. There is no doubt that business education on the secondary level does prepare students to become adept in a marketable skill, and creates an awareness of the need of certain business learnings to properly conduct personal business affairs. These need careful consideration in the re-evaluation of the current high school program.[10]

Good Business Education. Assuming that business education has a significant place in the secondary school program, what are the elements of a *good* program in business education? One set of evaluative criteria presently

---

[9] Ruben J. Dumler, "The Future of Business Education," *The Balance Sheet* (April, 1960), p. 339.

[10] Edith T. Smith, "The Changing Pattern of Business Education," *The Balance Sheet* (February, 1961), p. 243.

available is a set compiled by Tau Chapter of Delta Pi Epsilon, Teachers College, Columbia University. The following is a summary from that publication.[11] The directions for using these evaluative criteria are:

"N" indicates that the item does not apply to this situation.

"1" indicates that the evaluator considers that practically nothing is being done to meet the requirements of a good situation.

"2" indicates that the evaluator feels that little is being done to meet the standards of a good situation.

"3" indicates that the evaluator considers the item to be met only about half as well as it could be if ideal conditions existed.

"4" indicates that the item is adequately met but there is room for improvement.

"5" indicates that the evaluator considers the item to be fully met and it is not likely that any school or department could do better.

These criteria are intended to give a description of the department, not to produce a single index or single symbol which will indicate an overall rating. Therefore, the evaluator should not average or otherwise combine the individual evaluations given to each criterion to obtain a one-symbol rating for the department as a whole.

---

[11] *Evaluative Criteria for Business Education Departments of Secondary Schools,* Monograph 90 (Cincinnati: South-Western Publishing Company, 1954). (A project for Delta Pi Epsilon by Tau Chapter, Business Education Department, Teachers College, Columbia University.)

EVALUATIVE CRITERIA
for
BUSINESS DEPARTMENTS OF SECONDARY SCHOOLS
SUMMARY EVALUATION SHEET
DEPARTMENTAL PROFILE

Articulation with Other Departments Within the School

1. The business education department contributes to the general education of all students.   N 1 2 3 4 5

2. The business education department cooperates with all other departments.   N 1 2 3 4 5

Club Activities

1. The business education club is a student's organization.   N 1 2 3 4 5

2. The business education club acts as a service organization to school, businessmen, and community.   N 1 2 3 4 5

Community Resources

1. The business education department becomes familiar with the community through surveys.   N 1 2 3 4 5

2. The business education department recognizes and utilizes existent community resources.   N 1 2 3 4 5

3. The business education department enriches its curriculum with business materials and resources of the community.   N 1 2 3 4 5

4. Business education classes visit local offices, factories, and stores.   N 1 2 3 4 5

5. The business education department and the community share their facilities for mutual benefits.   N 1 2 3 4 5

6. The business education department serves the community in an advisory capacity.   N 1 2 3 4 5

7. The business education department cooperates with the community in the area of publicity.   N 1 2 3 4 5

8. The business education department and the faculty are encouraged to participate in and evaluate both community and school activity.   N 1 2 3 4 5

Curriculum

1. The business curriculum is based on community needs and interests.   N 1 2 3 4 5

2. The business curriculum is developed as a result of careful planning and group cooperation.   N 1 2 3 4 5

3. The business curriculum is concerned with the overall development of each pupil.   N 1 2 3 4 5

4. The business curriculum develops vocational competency.   N 1 2 3 4 5

5. The business curriculum has the same standing in the school and community as other subjects.   N 1 2 3 4 5

6. The business education department is an effective part of the community's adult education program.   N 1 2 3 4 5

Equipment and Its Utilization

1. There is a definite policy and plan for the purchase and replacement of equipment.   N 1 2 3 4 5

2. There is a record kept of all equipment.   N 1 2 3 4 5

3. There is a definite repair service or upkeep policy.   N 1 2 3 4 5

4. Teachers teach the care and use of equipment.   N 1 2 3 4 5

5. Equipment is representative of equipment being used in the community.   N 1 2 3 4 5

6. Business department rooms are properly equipped.   N 1 2 3 4 5

7. Proper safety precautions are taken.   N 1 2 3 4 5

Guidance Practices

1. The business education department uses consultation services available for special problems in the guidance of students.   N 1 2 3 4 5

2. The business teacher has access to and makes use of records of information about pupils.   N 1 2 3 4 5

3. The business teachers engage in guidance activities.   N 1 2 3 4 5

4. The staff of the business education department has access to adequate information for job guidance.   N 1 2 3 4 5

5. Guidance is a part of the orientation of pupils entering the business curriculum.   N 1 2 3 4 5

6. Guidance is a part of the learning activities of pupils in the business education department.   N 1 2 3 4 5

7. An effective business education guidance program helps pupils evaluate progress.   N 1 2 3 4 5

8. The results of the guidance program of the business education department show their value.   N 1 2 3 4 5

Instructional Material—Visual and Auditory

1. The business teacher is acquainted with the instruction materials before presenting them to the class.   N 1 2 3 4 5

2. The business teacher selects effective materials and resources.   N 1 2 3 4 5

3. The business teacher uses the instructional materials effectively.   N 1 2 3 4 5

4. The business teacher has access to and use of supplementary materials of instruction. N 1 2 3 4 5

Library Materials and Facilities

1. Library facilities are available for the business department needs.   N 1 2 3 4 5

2. The business education department is allotted funds to meet the needs for library services for students.   N 1 2 3 4 5

3. The library has professional materials for business teachers.   N 1 2 3 4 5

Placement and Follow-Up

1. There is an organized plan for placement of students.   N 1 2 3 4 5

2. The placement program gives individuals assistance in finding job opportunities.   N 1 2 3 4 5

3. The placement office cooperates with existing employment agencies.   N 1 2 3 4 5

4. Implications of the placement office's follow-up studies are used as a basis for curriculum change when desirable.   N 1 2 3 4 5

Qualifications and Professional Growth of Teachers

1. The business education department has a qualified staff.   N 1 2 3 4 5

2. The school encourages its business teachers to become more competent through professional activities.   N 1 2 3 4 5

3. The business teachers increase competencies through in-service activities.   N 1 2 3 4 5

4. The business teachers are members of professional educational organizations.   N 1 2 3 4 5

5. The business teachers participate actively in business education organizations.   N 1 2 3 4 5

6. The business teachers are members of local business and civic groups.   N 1 2 3 4 5

7. The business teachers keep up to date by reading current business education periodicals.   N 1 2 3 4 5

Supervisory Practices

1. The business education department's supervisory program is cooperative and democratic.   N 1 2 3 4 5

2. The business education department has a well-organized supervisory program.   N 1 2 3 4 5

3. The business education supervisor has an adequate visitation program.   N 1 2 3 4 5

4. The business education supervisor helps the teachers in their work.   N 1 2 3 4 5

5. The business education supervisor is evaluated.   N 1 2 3 4 5

6. The business education supervisor makes good use of research.   N 1 2 3 4 5

Teaching Methods

1. The business teachers teach in steps of progressive difficulty.   N 1 2 3 4 5

2. The business teachers' methods are adaptable to individual needs, interests, and rates of learning.   N 1 2 3 4 5

3. The business education teachers use effective means of evaluation.   N 1 2 3 4 5

Work Experience

1. The business education department provides a work-experience program for those who need and can profit from it.   N 1 2 3 4 5

2. The work-experience program is supervised
   and coordinated by a business teacher.   N 1 2 3 4 5

3. There is a definite tie-up between the
   work performed and school instruction.   N 1 2 3 4 5

4. There is a definite method of selecting and
   securing the cooperation of the business in
   the community.   N 1 2 3 4 5

5. The business education department selects
   good work stations.   N 1 2 3 4 5

6. There is a continuous evaluation of the
   work experience and the work-experience
   program.   N 1 2 3 4 5

   OVERALL DEPARTMENT RATING   N 1 2 3 4 5

The Role of the Teacher in the Space-Age School

We cannot explain precisely how great minds arise, whether in science, in music and literature, in art, or in business leadership; but we do know that the schools are the agency through which the avenues can be opened. That is why schools exist. That is why teachers teach.

The teacher plans the experiences or activities in which the pupils will take part. He then leads them through these experiences. The teacher plans the learners' experiences so that they will lead as quickly as possible to mastery of desired skill and knowledge. By this means, the amount of trial-and-error effort by the learners is reduced to a minimum. The teacher guides the learners through planned experiences in such a way that the ones who are learning make steady progress in perfecting the skills or understandings being taught.

It is often taken for granted that a person who knows a subject is at once prepared to teach it to others. A man who has become a highly skilled accountant, for example, may feel that he can readily instruct others in the skills of his profession by showing learners how he does the work and by explaining to them the ideas and purposes which are involved. It is only after he attempts to teach this way and discovers later how little his pupils have learned that he realizes the need for reconsideration of how learning takes place.

As the authors of this volume, we are concerned that the business teacher, whether a rank beginner or one with years of experience, should know important factors about the *educational* situation in which he finds himself. Current interest in and efforts to improve high school curricula suggest a need on the part of business teachers to understand the place of the business curriculum within the framework of the general school program and to utilize to the maximum methods and materials of instruction that will do the best job possible of preparing those enrolled in the business courses. Competence in teaching, particularly as applied to new teachers entering the field, is a crucial factor. A significant statement regarding efforts to increase this competence was made recently at a conference held for a state unit of the Association for Student Teaching:

Competence results from:

1. A depth and breadth of knowledge related to teaching responsibilities.

2. A knowledge of children and young people and the ability to work with them in developing the best learning situation possible.

3. A knowledge of current curriculum methods and the opportunity to work with them.

4. A knowledge of the duties and responsibilities inherent in the whole teaching situation.[12]

---

[12] Genevieve Starcher, from an address given before the West Virginia Association for Student Teaching, Marshall University, Huntington, West Virginia, November, 1962.

In short, a teacher-to-be, or one who aspires to rise to greater heights, must know the direction of education today and its problems; must be aware of his place in the total picture; and must be familiar with the means and methods to achieve the goals set forth.

SUMMARY

This chapter is, in effect, a summary in itself. We have attempted to set forth the trends in secondary school education through the use of historical perspective. The past speaks well of business education in the United States. The future is beset by challenges and opportunities for the business teacher to meet and use for the advancement of vocational and basic business understandings.

How successful the teacher's classroom experiences will be will depend greatly on his insight into the learning process, to follow in Chapter II, and on the assimilation and implementation of sound methods in teaching, which are the subject matter of this book.

SELECTED BIBLIOGRAPHY

Aiken, Wilford M. *The Story of the Eight-Year Study.* New York: Harper and Bros., 1942.

American Council on Education, American Youth Commission. *What the High Schools Ought to Teach.* Washington, D. C.: American Council on Education, 1940.

Arensman, Ray W. "A Re-examination of the Businessman-Business Teacher Relationship," *The Delta Pi Epsilon Journal* (February, 1962), 2-9.

Bell, Robert P. "The Place of Business Education in the Secondary Schools," *Business Education Forum* (January, 1960), 3-5.

Blackman, Mildred Russell. "Let's Not Bridge the Gap," *Educational Administration and Supervision* (May, 1954), 313-318.

Blackstone, Bruce I. "Changing Manpower Needs for Office Positions," *Secretarial Education with a Future,* American Business Education Yearbook, Vol. 19, 1962, pp. 28-48.

Bode, Boyd H. *How We Learn.* Boston: Houghton Mifflin Company, 1940.

Boynton, Paul M. "Business Education at the Crossroads," *American Business Education* (March, 1958), 132.

Brubacher, John S., *et al. Modern Philosophies of Education.* Chicago: Fifty-Fourth Yearbook of the National Society for the Study of Education, 1955.

The Changing Business Curriculum, American Business Education Yearbook, Vol. 4, 1947.

Douglass, Harl. *The High School Curriculum.* New York: The Ronald Press Company, 1947.

Evaluative Criteria for Business Departments of Secondary Schools, Monograph 90. Cincinnati: South-Western Publishing Company, 1954.

Fletcher, C. Scott. "The Great Debate in Education," *Crucial Issues in Education,* Revised Edition. New York: Henry Holt and Company, 1959.

General Education in a Free Society. Cambridge: Harvard University Press, 1945.

Gwynn, J. Minor. *Curriculum Principles and Social Trends.* New York: The Macmillan Company, 1960.

Kilpatrick, William H. *The Educational Frontier.* New York: D. Appleton-Century Company, Inc., 1933.

Klausmeier, Herbert J. *Teaching in the Secondary School.* New York: Harper and Bros., 1958.

Lomax, Paul S. "Business Education and the Conant Report," *Journal of Business Education* (March, 1959), 234-235.

Perdew, Philip W. *The American Secondary School in Action.* Boston: Allyn and Bacon, Inc., 1959.

Robinson, Donald W. "Ideals for Tomorrow's Schools," *Phi Delta Kappan* (February, 1960), 227-228.

Spaulding, Francis T. *High School and Life.* New York: McGraw-Hill Book Company, Inc., 1939.

CHAPTER II

PSYCHOLOGICAL PRINCIPLES FOR THE BUILDING OF SKILLS

We generally concede that it is of primary importance to have before us a plan or pattern of action before starting a job. Architects prepare a complete set of blueprints, including detailed specifications, before they begin to build. Aircraft engineers work for many months, even years, in the planning and designing of a new type of plane. So it must be in creating the situation for learning. Considering that a plan is essential when dealing with raw materials that are inanimate, which can be fabricated and shaped in whatever mold the designer or builder wishes, think how much more necessary it is when dealing with the human mind.

How Learning Takes Place

Before a teacher can intelligently begin to build this plan for learning experiences, it is necessary for him to understand certain basic concepts that underlie the process by which a human being learns. Educators have defined learning as any activity that develops the individual and makes his later behavior different from what it otherwise might have been. This is sometimes referred to as a desirable change in the behavior of the human being. We are not always sure just what this "change in behavior" means or how to "make it happen." Bernard attempts to define desirable learning in this way:

. . . We may say that learning is the *modification of behavior*. This process involves many changes in perception and behavior. Improvement is usually involved.

21

. . . In this respect two observations are pertinent. First, not all modification of behavior is learning. Without learning anything new, one may be able to lift heavier weights because of muscular development. One may, however, *learn* some "tricks" in lifting without acquiring stronger muscles. The loss of an arm modifies behavior, but the loss itself is not learning. The person, though, may *learn* to compensate for the loss of his arm.

Second, modification does not necessarily result in improvement—at least in terms of values. Pupils may learn to dislike school, but their adjustment is not improved thereby. Criminals learn to violate accepted legal and moral codes and may become experts at it, but their behavior is, in terms of values, not improved. With these limitations in mind, we may now define learning as *the modification of behavior through activity and experience which improves modes of adjustment to the environment.*[1]

This statement by Bernard indicates that a change in behavior *can*, and probably will, be effected by the teacher, but not necessarily in the right direction. Nor do we find that even when a desirable change in behavior has somehow been accomplished that it will become permanent. Just when it seems that students are in full command of a process and can apply it with ease, they seem to slack off and forget whatever it is they apparently "learned." Gates and his associates find in their studies that this is a common occurrence and refer to it as *the intent to learn:*

Since learning is such a complex process, it is not surprising that it takes place most surely when one *intends to learn and remember.* We are often able to recall, of course, many of the things that have been in margin, rather than the center, of attention. But this kind of *incidental* learning is not trustworthy. The results are too accidental and un-

---

[1] Harold W. Bernard, *Psychology of Learning and Teaching* (New York: McGraw-Hill Book Company, Inc., 1954), pp. 121-122.

reliable. Sometimes only passing reference or casual observation will be sufficient to learn; more often they will be ineffective.[2]

Organizing the Learning Situation

Because of this existing situation of "intent to learn" and its primary importance, the unorganized learning situation and the unguided lesson cannot be depended upon to result in more than minimal and incomplete learning. The formal learning process is essential in the education of youth. This is what we call instruction. It is formal, not in the sense of being stiff and inflexible, but in that it is guided by a teacher, that it provides *selected* facts and *essential* principles, that it takes into consideration motivation, which is basic to the intent to learn, that it suggests and works toward *desirable* changes in behavior, and in our case, as business teachers, that it recognizes the basic principles of skill building. Some years ago, and this is still true, Professor Bode became concerned because educational reference sources were swamped with "ready-made" formal approaches. He cautioned that teachers carefully examine the direction in which instruction would be launched in the classroom:

> It is likely that teachers generally have a less clear conception of what learning is than they had a century ago. The average teacher tends to adopt different features of different theories without being aware that they do not harmonize with one another and without even clearly realizing that he is proceeding eclectically. The problem of learning must be explored, partly to enable the teacher to straighten out his own thinking and partly to enable him to understand the confusion that prevails in present-day education.[3]

---

[2] Arthur I. Gates, Arthur T. Jersild, T. R. McConnell, and Robert C. Challman, *Educational Psychology* (3rd ed.; New York: The Macmillan Company, 1948), p. 298.

[3] Boyd H. Bode, *How We Learn* (Boston: D. C. Heath and Company, 1940), p. 6.

There are vast implications in this statement for the teaching of business. The aims of business education are to provide essential skills and basic knowledge, to assure the formation of sound attitudes relative to these skills and knowledge, and to secure desirable behavior on the job and in the personal activities as a member of the community.

For these reasons, it is for the teacher to direct the classroom situation which provides the basic conditions for learning and affords the best possibilities for accomplishing desirable aims of education, and particularly, in our case, business education. It is not implied that the classroom is at all times to be found within the school building when we speak of a learning situation. Far from it. The psychology of learning implies that the group is being instructed and guided by the teacher, that an organized situation exists, and that procedures have been planned. That the classroom may be found outside the schoolroom, and quite possibly some distance from the school itself, must be recognized.

Basic to good instruction is a need to know "where we are headed." Reed lists several psychological guideposts that can be of help in our daily evaluation of progress:

> The learning process involves three major phases: a goal, a method, and a content. The first condition of effective learning is a goal, or a group of objectives to which it is directed; the second condition is a method or technique or group of techniques by which it works toward the goal; and the third condition is something to work on—content material, or curriculum. The psychology of learning is primarily concerned with the second phase, the method of learning, but it cannot ignore the other two. If the goal is blind, there is no learning; and if it is beyond the capacity of the learner, there is much wasted effort. Similarly, if there is no content, there is no learning; and if it is too difficult, too easy, or useless, there is wasted effort.[4]

---

[4] Homer B. Reed, *Psychology of Elementary School Subjects* (New York: Ginn and Company, 1938), p. 3.

Psychological Guides to Learning

The needs, interests, attitudes, and capabilities of pupils are of fundamental importance. To ignore them is to provide a classroom exercise, or "performance," that will be certain to result in indifference by the pupil and frustration on the part of the teacher. To implement learning, good teaching is required. Good teaching is based on sound psychology. A reasonable understanding of how persons learn has been established by psychologists through constant study and experimentation. The 30 psychological guides to good teaching developed and compiled by Columbia University Professors Mort and Vincent represent one of the most complete references to the place of psychology in teaching and learning. Research on a wide scale would tend to repeat item after item of this basic listing:

1. *No one learns without feeling some urge to learn.* It may be fear, need, inborn drive, curiosity, mystery, challenge, importance, or personal attachment—or any other motivating force. The force has to be there, and the more the force wells up out of the person himself, the more the person will learn of his own accord.

2. *What a person learns is influenced directly by his surroundings.* If you want a person to learn something, make that thing a part of his environment so that he may see it, live with it, be influenced by it.

3. *A person learns most quickly and lastingly what has meaning for him.* The pupils do not always see the meanings the teacher sees. An act takes on meaning from its outcome—what the act produces. To produce a thing he wants or can see the value of, a person is likely to master the skill necessary.

4. *When an organism is ready to act, it is painful for it not to act; and when an organism is not ready to act, it is painful for it to act.* This means that some time must be

spent in preparing learners to learn, that physical action is as much a part of school as mental action.

5. *Individuals differ in all sorts of ways.* When you get a group of people together to do anything, some will be better than others. It is easy to see that some people are taller than others, less easy to see that in dozens of abilities that relate to success in learning any class will show a vast range of difference.

6. *Security and success are the soil and climate for growth.* No one can learn well when he doesn't belong—any more than a plant can grow without roots in the soil. No one can succeed on failure.

7. *All learning occurs through attempts to satisfy needs.* What people do, consciously or not, they do because of need; and as they do, they learn what to do to satisfy need.

8. *Emotional tension decreases efficiency in learning.* Before the skills and facts of teaching come friendliness, security, acceptance, belief in success. Without these, tensions are procured. Constant, monotonous attention to any one thing is also a producer of tension.

9. *Physical defects lower efficiency in learning.* A sound mind in a sound body. For greatest efficiency in any kind of teaching, physical health comes before mental vigor.

10. *Interest is an indicator of growth.* We don't teach to get interest, but if interest isn't present, the teaching isn't prospering.

11. *Interest is a source of power in motivating learning.* When you are interested in a thing, you are in it and feel a part of it. A teacher who doesn't hook his teaching to whatever pupils feel they are already a part of is not making the greatest use of the powers he has at his command.

12. *What gives satisfaction tends to be repeated; what is annoying tends to be avoided.* Practice makes perfect

only when it is the right kind of practice. Learning is efficient if the pupil tries to master what fits his abilities and gives satisfaction.

13. *The best way to learn a part in life is to play that part.* This is the apprenticeship idea. Upon leaving school, the parts in life which pupils play are not completely new to them if they have practiced those parts in school.

14. *Learning is more efficient and longer lasting when the conditions for it are real and lifelike.* Attitudes, habits, skills for life are best learned when the activities of school are like those of life. Methods of teaching should be as much as possible like those one uses in actual living.

15. *Piecemeal learning is not efficient.* We learn facts and skills best when we learn them in a pattern, not as isolated bits of subject matter. The facts and skills that we learn become part of a pattern when we learn them in relation to their use—as part of a project, job, or other enterprise.

16. *You can't train the mind like a muscle.* There is no body of knowledge that is the key to "mind-training." There is no set of exercises that will "sharpen the wits" as a grindstone will sharpen steel. This means: don't isolate the things you want to teach from the real setting in which they belong.

17. *A person learns by his own activity.* He learns what he does; he gains insight as he learns to organize what he does. Within certain limits, the more extensive a learner's activity, the greater will be his learning.

18. *Abundant, realistic practice contributes to learning.* Learners need much practice in the many intellectual, creative, and social acts which we want them to master.

19. *Participation enhances learning.* Participation is essential to any complex learning. Complete participation is important—from planning to checking results.

20. *Firsthand experience makes for lasting and more complete learning.* Learners need experience between read-

ing and hearing about something secondhand and the kind of knowledge and insight that come from firsthand experience.

21. *General behavior is controlled by emotions as well as by intellect.* Far more than a place to train only the mind, the modern school is concerned with training the emotions, too.

22. *Unused talents contribute to personal maladjustment.* Not only are unused talents a waste to society; they form a core of dissatisfaction to the individual. Frustrated talent can lead to many kinds of neurotic symptoms.

23. *You start to grow from where you are and not from some artificial starting point.* It is unrealistic to assume that pupils can move through the grades of school like taking the steps on a ladder jumping from step to step. It is impossible to move a pupil on from some point or grade standard that he has not yet achieved.

24. *Growth is a steady, continuous process, and different individuals grow at different rates.* It is impossible for a class of first-graders to move along all together until they come to the twelfth grade. Each individual learns, but at his own rate. His growth is steady; he does not leap from grade to grade.

25. *It is impossible to learn one thing at a time.* It is impossible to turn everything else off while learning two times two. The learner as a whole responds to his setting as a whole and takes in many things besides two times two. Learning by problems, topics, and projects, replacing learning by bits, makes capital of this fact.

26. *Learning is reinforced when two or more senses are used at the same time.* One-cylinder learning sticks only to reading or only to listening. Pupils learn better if they see with the eyes, touch with the hands, hear with the ears, heft with the muscles, at the same time they are seeing with the mind's eye.

27. *The average pupil is largely a myth.* Grade standards are an average which every pupil is expected to achieve. But any standard that you can set will be too difficult for some, too easy for others. The achievement of a group scatters over a wide range—only a few are at the "average" point. A far greater number are scattered above and below the average.

28. *If you want a certain result, teach it directly.* Your pupils are not born with the skills you want them to have; nor can we always depend upon other teachers to teach pupils to our satisfaction. If your pupils do not know what you want them to know, the most efficient thing to do is to teach it to them.

29. *Children develop in terms of all the influences which affect them.* Not only the 180 days of school, but the 365 days of living in school, home, and community go to make a person what he becomes.

30. *It has been said that a person learns more in the first three years of his life than in all the years afterward.* However this may be, it is certain that the early years of home life are very important. Accordingly, to improve its effectiveness, a school must do what it can to improve the educational setting of the home.[5]

According to Mort and Vincent,[6] these guides can be used in a number of ways: to judge the *variety* of the teacher's practice, to judge the psychological *validity* of his practice, to *test* new practices, and to *justify* his practice.

Setting the Stage for Teaching and Learning

If business education is to be effective, the conditions of learning must be favorable, and the aims of the program must be clearly recognized. Curiosity must be aroused

---

[5] Paul R. Mort and William S. Vincent, *Introduction to American Education* (New York: McGraw-Hill Book Company, Inc., 1954), pp. 303-330.

[6] *Ibid.,* p. 306.

(motivation), appropriate information provided for the students (proper lesson planning), and pleasurable or satisfying practice conditions made possible. Given these primary bases of approach, the efforts of the teacher will bring tangible results of great value to the pupils and a justifiable sense of satisfaction to the teacher. It is to basic factors in each of the three areas mentioned above that we now direct our attention.

MOTIVATION

The ability of the human being to absorb and use knowledge is in itself no reason for doing so. We see this reflected in many instances when pupils derive relatively high scores on entrance examinations and other testing for placement, yet they fail to participate to the limit indicated by the test scores and placement devices. Intelligence alone does not assure the acquisition of knowledge. It is *motivation* that provides the key to learning. Gates points to this necessary element in the learning process when he says:

> Motives which are significant in the educative process include interests, attitudes, needs, and purposes. Such factors as these energize behavior, make it selective, and direct it toward certain ends. Learning is most efficient when the activities to be performed are the means of satisfying needs or attaining important goals.[7]

Because "education" is an abstraction for the pupil, he is rarely motivated by it. Emphasis upon doing for the sake of making a "contribution to the community" might as well be avoided by the teacher. The idea of business skills and knowledges for the sake of *accomplishment,* however, is understood by the adolescent and gives him reason for the instruction that is being offered.

---

[7] Gates, *et al., op. cit.,* pp. 319-320.

In this sense, business education enjoys an advantage not always characteristic of other subject areas. The tendencies of the pupils to use a skill such as typewriting for *immediate* purposes, to be able to fit bookkeeping skills into club and organizational activities, for example, provide springboards from which to leap into the study of the business subjects. The successful teacher exploits these motives to advantage. The problem of meeting both individual and group needs is simplified if the teacher understands these facts in planning for effective teaching.

If desirable conduct is to follow from the teaching that is a change in behavior which we call "education," the instruction must be *ego satisfying*. This means that the interests and drives of pupils must be recognized and used to advantage through emphasis of the most appropriate devices and approaches. The teacher must use incentives, sometimes dramatically, sometimes subtly, but he must use them if motivation for positive behavioral changes is anticipated.

The fact of individual differences in the youth suggests the need for various motivational devices. Certain incentives are required in order to get a high degree of enthusiasm and to enhance the intent to learn. They are necessary also to inspire standards of accomplishment which are consistent with the abilities of youth of the same general age group but with widely differing needs and drives. At any level, the positive approach is an essential to good learning conditions. To suggest values and satisfaction that students understand and can apply to their limited experiences is to obtain positive reaction. Use of a negative approach—to imply fault or punishment—will invite negative responses. How important motivation is in the conduct of classroom teaching is, of course, not always recognized by teachers. Klausmeier attempts to illustrate the significance of this factor in learning in this statement:

Motivation within the learner is essential to an effective learning situation. A student may have any of many motives for learning and usually more than one motive leads to a particular response. Three of the principal motivational forces in human beings are the need to secure mastery over some aspect in the environment, also referred to as the achievement motive; to secure social approval, which if interpreted broadly is also achievement; and to satisfy curiosity, referred to frequently as the exploration motive.[8]

Grambs and Iverson speak of motivation as the "extra push that impels young people toward the hard work of education."[9] They also set up what appears to be an excellent guide to achieving a high degree of motivation:

The *first means of motivation* is *recognizing* students' needs. Here the teacher draws upon all he knows of adolescents in general and those in his class in particular. He identifies those needs relevant to *his* course content and experience.

A *second means of motivation* is making students aware of their needs. Creating such an awareness in a psychologically sound manner means that the teacher has a medium for widening the experience field of the student. If a teacher wishes to interest students in bettering their oral skills, he may provide motivation by recording several job interviews and then asking the class to judge who would get the job— and why. Thus, he provides a springboard into concentrated practice in self-improvement.

We can state the *third means to motivation* as conveying enthusiasm for learning. It is obvious that the teacher will need to sketch in for the students some of the reasons why a study has important implications for them, but unless these reasons take root in student acceptance, no problem unit can eventuate.

---

[8] Herbert J. Klausmeier, "Characteristics of an Effective Learning Situation," *The Teachers College Journal* (October, 1956), pp. 2-6.
[9] Jean D. Grambs and William J. Iverson, *Modern Methods in Secondary Education* (New York: The Dryden Press, 1952), p. 91.

A *fourth means to motivation* is setting goals important to students. Too often the real thing a student works for is a grade. Actually, this is motivation, too—students can and will work very, very hard to get a good grade. But the result is low-level learning. The student actually is not concerned with *what* he is learning or even *how,* but only with a status label. Good motivation establishes goals that in themselves are important.

A *fifth means to motivation* is relating the goal to the student's range of abilities. Setting a goal too difficult or too easy to achieve will destroy a good job of arousing interest. Aspiration levels commensurate with student abilities can be identified through variations in assignments. Students enjoy working hard at tasks in which they can gain personal satisfaction from a sense of being actually *able* to do it.

The final means of motivation that we shall discuss in this section is ensuring a reasonable amount of success to students. This means is closely allied to the preceding one. There we said that the students should be challenged toward goals that lie within the range of their ability. Here we are pointing out that a task remains challenging so long as the student is fairly certain he can do it and do it with some pride in accomplishment. Success must taste good, must not be too cheaply won, and must leave important resources for further learning.[10]

It is around these central points concerning motivation that psychologists and educators seem to agree. It is around these points that business teachers should build skill-building procedures.

Individual Differences as a Factor in Motivation

Perhaps the most challenging thing about teaching is that there are no two students exactly alike and no two classes exactly alike. What happens to the students under

---

[10] *Ibid.,* pp. 91-93.

these existing facts depends upon the effectiveness of the teacher in reaching every student, to a high degree at least. If we were to believe the critics of American education, then it is time that we consider more effective ways of accomplishing this aim. Pupils differ from one another in looks, interests, ability, likes and dislikes, understanding, and rate of accomplishment. Therefore, in planning activities that provide the optimum of motivation, we need to recognize that individual differences stand out as a critical factor.

Rather than attempt to avoid the challenge of individual differences, we should accept it as a major factor of teaching. Dr. Willard C. Olson, Dean of the University of Michigan School of Education, feels that individual differences should be recognized and encouraged:

> Individual differences in children should be cultivated, not cured or tolerated. Wide variations exist in children the world over and are equally prevalent regardless of the method of teaching employed. Literally, the more you teach children, the more unlike they become.[11]

The limits of achievement for different persons vary greatly. A limit that one may reach in a week, in typewriting for example, another pupil may not reach in a month. Not all members of a class will reach the same point of understanding at the same time. The ability to grasp a situation and work out a satisfactory solution may be "duck soup" for some pupils because this element is part of their native equipment. To others, the situation may become a difficult and burdensome task and may never be solved. Teachers must know how to evaluate these differences and make the fullest use of them in classroom teaching and planning. Some pupils have ability in bookkeeping

---

[11] Quoted by Willard C. Olson, Dean, The University of Michigan School of Education, in the *Phi Delta Kappan* (November, 1958), p. 77.

but come equipped with little capacity for typewriting complicated statistical reports. Others may have the ability and capacity for filing and routine clerical tasks but have little inclination toward high-level proficiency in shorthand and transcription. These differences, whether inherited or acquired, suggest that high school teachers arrange the jobs as nearly as possible on an individual performance basis if high classroom morale is to be expected. The course of study, or the lesson plan, can be arranged so that each learner has the opportunity to progress as rapidly as his capacity will permit.

When the teacher is faced with a group of students who have a wide variance of background of experience and knowledge, as in advanced typewriting classes, he may group the pupils in such a way that one or two less capable members can draw on the better-qualified pupils. Definite examples are given in the following chapters on how the advanced students can be of help. As time and facilities permit, the teacher can devote additional time to the slower group until he has brought them more nearly to the general level of the class.

From the standpoint of human behavior and reaction to surroundings, the teacher should know that there may be just as great a difference in emotional reaction between members of his class and the teacher as there is difference in height or weight or intelligence. The teacher's comment or action toward one student may have an opposite effect on another. Or, the reaction of a pupil to certain conditions may be just the opposite of that expected by the teacher. One student will enjoy "digging out" of a difficult problem situation, but another student will sink into despair if he does not have help soon after he gets into a tight spot. One student will be orderly and neat at his machine or desk, while another will always tend to have an unsightly work station.

Individual students vary in their reactions. Therefore, the wise teacher will study each member of his class so that his instructions may secure favorable reaction from the greatest number—all of them, if it is possible. By associating the pupils' interests with success in attaining the objective, a feeling of satisfaction is created. This feeling of satisfaction will promote more learning and in this way be the motivating stimulus.

The greatest single factor in this motivation-creating consideration is that individual differences must be recognized and each pupil assigned to work in the direction of his greatest potential. That we, as teachers, have not always recognized this factor, or have been unable to fully develop the concept in our teaching, is evident as we look at the drop-out rate in many schools. The important thing, however, is to keep trying. Hagen comments on this necessary effort:

> We frankly admit that teaching is an art, much more than it is a science, largely learned in the crucible of experience, and refined through trial and error in the classroom. Fortunately the child is by nature endowed with a need to learn and with the ability to adjust to the average teacher's blunders without too much harm to himself.[12]

Goal Setting

To set goals requires considerable judgment if this is to be significant. Goals set by students themselves are more effective, but students need guidance in fixing goals. The atmosphere of teacher-student cooperation is in great part created by the adroit direction of the teacher. Teachers sometimes lose class cooperation and fail to supply that needed stimulus because they do not take time to understand those whom they teach. To achieve top-level interest,

---

[12] Arnold J. Hagen, "S-R Bonds," *Phi Delta Kappan* (June, 1959), p. 389.

students must be encouraged to take an active part in constructing the plan of action for the course. Too many complications? This is perhaps true, but it depends on whether a teacher is interested in setting up "good-looking" course outlines and in developing a model "paper" course or in helping pupils to learn. In other words, the teacher's plan should be tentative; the final plan for class direction should be developed by both the students and the teacher.

The classroom teacher who attempts this kind of learning situation must be sold on this approach, which, if successfully carried out, achieves a better quality of classroom control and motivation. The teacher's role is to help the class see what alternatives there are, to analyze them, to help the class see the consequences of the choices, and then to outline a plan together. For example, Rainey points to a definite increase in interest in basic economics courses through the use of an "Inventory of Business and Economic Concepts" in which even the poorest students can volunteer information and opinions.[13] (See Chapter IX for details.) Through the use of this plan, the students play an active part in the direction of the class, which results in a feeling of contribution and satisfaction necessary for learning to take place.

In the approach set up by Rainey, the teacher deliberately created a procedure where choice was needed. He did not himself care how the students attacked the actual economic concepts. He knew that every contemporary social activity has its economic roots; so he saw no reason why the students could not choose the topic approaches. Similarly, they could easily see what more needed to be learned—with his guidance. Planning of what content to study—within the limits set by the course and by the teacher—involved the students in an important activity. For them the subject matter became alive.

---

[13] Bill G. Rainey, "Stimulate Economics Students with Supplementary Aids," *Business Education World* (May, 1958), pp. 26-27.

In a great many cases teachers have found that students also get a greater sense of genuine participation in the conduct and direction of their learning if they are permitted to help judge their own accomplishments, that is, "How are we doing?" This implies that teachers accept suggestions of the pupils, permit the class to try them out, and assist the group in deciding which suggestions are really worthy for class use. This teacher-pupil approach to evaluation of progress is time-consuming, at least to the inexperienced teacher, and requires careful consideration. However, the rewards tend to outweigh the apparent disadvantages. Here is a significant incentive for individual pupils to follow through on what the *group,* not the teacher, has agreed upon as a desirable evaluation procedure. Not infrequently teachers will observe that students will give themselves more severe punishment and often more difficult assignments if *they* had a part in setting up sound standards. Moreover, the group becomes a functioning *unit,* instead of a group of disparate individuals, each heading in a totally different direction.

Incentives

Occasionally, of course, a "shot in the arm" is necessary. Unfortunately, some of the incentives are negative rather than positive in motivational response. A negative approach, or method, is one that causes a student to desire to set a high mark for himself in a given activity, not because of the activity itself, but because of a penalty for noncompliance. Penalties of various kinds, including low marks, ridicule, sarcasm, reports to parents, and various other punishments, are almost certain to arouse in the student a dislike of the subject, albeit he *does* finally wind up with a respectable grade. It can almost certainly be concluded that he mutters to himself, "Whooie, I made it; but *never* again." In the interim of completing the course, it is true that he may try to improve, at least enough to escape further penalties; but he associates the subject with penalty and comes to dislike the very thought of that particular area of study.

Good motivation is positive and psychologically sound. Grambs and Iverson point out instances of negative conditions created by teachers through "orders" that have little place in the well-managed classroom:

> If you don't do this well, you will have ten additional problems.
>
> We'll have a test tomorrow if you waste this study period.
>
> We can't stay on this topic all semester; you'd better start studying harder or you'll flunk the course.
>
> Since you did so badly on that last test, we'll have to spend more time on this material.[14]

In general, it seems to be important that the teacher use as many incentives as seem applicable to the situation. Whether these incentives are better if they are intrinsic rather than extrinsic has not been fully determined. In fact, there seems to be a question on the part of psychologists as to whether a real disparity exists. The 49th yearbook of the National Society for the Study of Education defines these incentives and presents the question of real difference:

> The relationship between goals and learning tasks related to them may be described as intrinsic and extrinsic, depending on the logical relationship between the task and the goal. The relationship between the task and the goal may be said to be *intrinsic* if the incentive conditions are functionally or organically related to the activity. Thus the satisfaction derived from hearing a program over a self-constructed radio set is a satisfaction derived from putting the radio to its intended uses. This is an intrinsic satisfaction because the goal is inherent in the successful completion of the task of construction.

---

[14] Grambs and Iverson, *op. cit.*, p. 93.

The relationship between the task and the goal may be said to be *extrinsic* if the incentives are artificially or arbitrarily related to the task. Thus, if a prize is to be awarded to the first boy to complete his radio, the desire for the prize is extrinsically related to the task of radio building.

Because motivational situations are complex, the relation between the task and the goal is often at once intrinsic and extrinsic.[15]

No incentives really act in themselves. They are a part of the total learning situation itself and should be applied as conditions indicate. For example, rewards, or extrinsic symbols, seem to be more effective with less skillful or less able students, while avoidance of criticism by the teacher, or a simple comment made privately, seems to be effective with the superior student. To provide a combination of the two to meet each particular situation seems to be the best approach. A suggested list of incentives that have proved to be practical and applicable are:

1. Individual progress records, charts, graphs.

2. Assignment of responsibilities of work in connection with group effort, for example, "office manager" or "class secretary."

3. Prizes, medals, certificates.

4. Competition in exercise completion, contests, exhibitions.

5. Teacher compliments or comments on student accomplishment.

6. Permitting selection of goals and objectives by students.

Accommodating Goals to Students' Ranges of Abilities

The schools of the nation are bulging at the seams. Colleges, secondary schools, elementary schools—all are faced

---

[15] *Learning and Instruction, The Forty-Ninth Yearbook of the National Society for the Study of Education*, Part I (Chicago: University of Chicago Press, 1950), p. 39.

with the problem of increasing numbers. Because of compulsory attendance requirements, many students are in school who otherwise might have dropped out. The resulting situation is a standard classroom full of pupils with mixed abilities to learn. Quite frequently this is a major motivational problem. A haphazard approach in planning learning materials for such groups will inflate the ego of some pupils and neglect others.

It is the teacher's task to help pupils make adjustments to their learning problems and to refrain from assigning projects, tasks, and performances beyond their abilities, or to make work so general that the superior students lose interest. In either case the result is a feeling of frustration for all. A student will often strike out in an attempt to ward off this frustration, resulting in a possible disciplinary problem. The process of growing up is not easy, particularly in the adolescent years. The classroom teacher represents authority; the judicious use of this authority in the classroom is underscored by Young in her study of delinquency problems:

> All delinquents are trapped in their painful and dangerous conflict over authority. In brief, they treat the world as they have been treated. When adults use their superior strength to break the will and spirit of a child, rather than support and direct that life force toward maturity, the child has only two alternatives: to submit and be crushed, or to fight blindly, bitterly, and destructively.[16]

Motivational Factors in Physical Surroundings

The student lives in the school for a considerable period of his total life span. To him the atmosphere of physical surroundings should be as conducive to work and play as the

---

[16] Leontine R. Young, "Delinquency from the Child's Point of View," *The Presidio* (November, 1960), p. 16.

real home. How important this is to good learning is described in some detail by Grambs and Iverson:

> Just the way a classroom looks does much to build or weaken good management. Even if the classroom is not the most modern, if it is clean and neat, it will help set the tone for businesslike performance.[17]

Klausmeier has made an intensive study of the significance of the physical surroundings on the degree to which learning takes place:

> The physical environment in which the learning takes place is probably as important to efficiency as are the physical conditions in a factory or a bank to success of such ventures. The many desirable features of an environment conducive to learning and familiar to most instructors (are):
>
>> An environment for the original learning which is the same as that in which it will be used later improves learning. Careful examination of the proposed learning tasks is needed to identify excellent environments outside the classroom which will arouse interest, make the activities more real, and encourage retention of what is learned.[18]

The necessity of finding out what the varying capacities of pupils are has been mentioned. The details of these differing abilities will be registered in the physical surroundings in which they work.

The Importance of Success in Motivation

To be successful, students must experience a feeling of accomplishment. It is the teacher's responsibility to see to it that they do succeed—in some phase of their study. We learn by our successes. Somewhere in the planning of courses should be definite procedures that will permit the poorest student to be able to say to himself: "Today I was

---

[17] Grambs and Iverson, *op. cit.*, p. 252.
[18] Klausmeier, *op. cit.*, p. 4.

able to ...." The psychological soundness of this is demonstrated through the well-known and well-established "law of effect" of Thorndike:

> When a modifiable connection between a situation and a response is made and accompanied or followed by a *satisfying* state of affairs, that connection's strength is increased; when made and accompanied or followed by an *annoying* state of affairs, its strength is decreased.[19]

More will be said in later chapters about this crucial element of the learning situation as it applies specifically to lesson planning.

SOUND PROCEDURES IN LESSON PLANNING

The success of teaching is embodied in a situation with a maximum of motivational impetus. Granting that such a situation is provided for, sound lesson planning procedures that include provisions for the motivation must follow.

It is the planning of the teacher in a manner which anticipates the opportunities for the guidance of pupils as they learn through actually doing things which we call *method*. The classroom that is a "beehive of activity" does not necessarily reflect real learning. Such a situation may instead be a reflection of confusion and wasted time and effort that result from lack of teacher control and direction. On the other hand, the "beehive of activity" which follows from careful teacher planning, and preferably teacher-pupil planning, which gives evidence of controlled pupil activity in which pupils are exercising imagination and initiative, experimenting, and working cooperatively in an orderly fashion, is a most desirable situation.

This kind of classroom atmosphere does not just happen. It is the result of careful thought and many hours of soul searching. The specific objective of this textbook is to pro-

---

[19] Edward L. Thorndike, *Educational Psychology* (New York: University Press, 1913), Vol. II, Ch. I.

vide assistance to beginning business teachers in proper lesson-planning techniques; and the chapters that follow are written for this purpose.

PRACTICE GUIDED BY APPLICATION OF PSYCHOLOGICAL PRINCIPLES

The third area of major concern in providing the best learning atmosphere is the proper application of practice, the "doing" of a skill or the application of a knowledge. Adequate opportunity for *correct* practice is essential in the learning of a skill. It is necessary, however, if valuable time is to be conserved, that the teacher understand the principles of learning as related to practice. Because of their repetitious nature, many drill activities become monotonous and decrease in their educational value because the procedures used extend beyond the span of ability of the pupil.

Principles of Practice

Various approaches to practice are used. Some of the most frequently applied are:

1. Trial-and-error.
2. Review of previous work.
3. Extensive practice.
4. Intensive practice.
5. Short periods of practice.
6. Learning by the part method.
7. Learning by the whole method.
8. Practice of new with the old.
9. Point of diminishing returns.

The relatively short span of the formative years dictates, at least in our modern society, that random trial-and-error learning must be avoided if more efficient procedures are available. Kingsley and Garry emphasize the necessity of recognizing the role of the school in eliminating much of this lost motion. They maintain that:

It is evident that learning is a process and an activity which engages a major portion of every individual's life. It is a process so important to the successful survival of human beings that the institution of education and the school has been developed as a procedure for making learning more efficient. The tasks to be learned are so complex and so important that they cannot be left to chance. Nor can it be said that the tasks which human beings are called upon to learn are "normal" to human development and growth, for adding, multiplying, reading, using toothbrushes, lacing shoes, operating typewriters, and a host of other skills are not activities that normally would be learned. In fact, many of the routines to be learned by children and adults are those which do *not* come naturally.[20]

Kingsley and Garry have outlined what appears to be a well-defined and authoritative approach to the principles of productive practice:

> The effectiveness of practice will depend largely upon the manner in which the practice is conducted. From the great amount of work done on this subject, it is possible to state a few generalizations that should be helpful to one who desires to secure the best possible returns for the time and effort expended.
>
> 1. Conditions under which practice should be conducted. Practice should be conducted under conditions similar to those which will attend the use of the skill and the procedures practiced should be those in which the skill is desired. One learns what one practices.
>
> Older methods of drill for students of typewriting called for a great amount of drill on nonsense syllables. . . . It was thought that since these movements were used extensively in actual typewriting, the dexterity acquired in this would be readily transferred to the writing situation

---

[20] Howard L. Kingsley and Ralph Garry, *The Nature and Conditions of Learning* (2nd ed.; Englewood Cliffs, New Jersey: Prentice-Hall, Inc., 1957), pp. 4-5.

in which they would be used. Modern methods call for
the student to start practice on sentences just as soon as
the keyboard is learned.

2. Speed against accuracy.

Effort should be applied in the direction of speed and accuracy according to the requisites of proficiency. On some
skills where quality of performance is far more important
than speed, the effort in practice should be directed toward doing the task as well as possible. Where speed is
an important factor in the skill, practice at as rapid a pace
as possible is desirable. When both speed and accuracy
are important, as in typewriting or handwriting, effort must
be directed in such a way as to secure advancement in
both.

3. Distribution of practice.

For the more difficult and complex skills, practice should
be liberally distributed. The length of the practice period
should be short when new motor tasks are being introduced for the first time. Many motor skills not only involve complexity in the physical movements involved but
also depend upon complex mental processes which increase
the learning difficulty, thus augmenting the need for
spaced practice.

4. Rhythm.

The development of motor skills involves both spatial and
temporal coordination of movement. Rhythm is an aid in
establishing temporal coordination. The playing of music
with lively rhythm will help speed up the slow worker.
Since it operates to reduce tensions in the muscles not
directly used in the task being practiced, rhythm tends to
lessen the fatigue effects of practice. The rhythm of music
can be used to advantage in pacing stroking for typewriting drills.

But to secure the advantages of rhythm, one must know
at what stages to use it. A reasonable familiarity with the

task, ability to make the various movements, and proper form are essential prerequisites to the use of rhythm drills. A young teacher who had been working in her first position for only a few weeks complained that she could not keep her pupils together in group drills in typing because they had to stop to look for the keys. Students will not be able to type rhythmically until they have learned the position of the keys.[21]

We know from a host of personal experiences that efficiency of response does not come from going through the motions of a skill or necessarily from the amount of time spent in practice. Efficient methods applied to practice sessions can cut the required learning time in half. Smith outlines two points for achieving the most from time spent in learning a skill:

1. Advantages of distributed practice.

   In any learning situation the amount of study time available is limited. What is the best way to use it? This is a hard question to answer. There is evidence that for most learning activities, a certain amount of practice spread over a period of time is much more effective than the same amount of time crammed into a short period of time. In learning motor skills such as typewriting far better results are obtained through spreading a few hours each week for a number of years than by spreading five times as many hours per week in one-fifth the same number of years. And the effectiveness of the more gradual learning seems to persist for a longer time after the practice has ended. However, if sufficient motivation is present, and if the child does not become tired of the task, he will obviously achieve more learning in 30 minutes than in 15.

2. The influence of mental set.

   An active intent to learn is much more likely to result in success than is mere passive attention. Students approach

---

[21] *Ibid.*, p. 314.

their study in different ways. One decides to study a lesson for two hours; merely putting in the time becomes his primary objective. His attention focuses more on the clock than on the lesson. Another has a specific purpose to accomplish during his study. He is searching for questions that may be asked the next day, or he is attempting to condense the material into his own words. The mental set of the latter is far more conducive to effective learning.[22]

Hollingsworth cites an interesting example of learning which he has called "The sorrows of an unguided pupil." It is the report of a man who taught himself how to typewrite when he was 30 years of age. The next 20 years of his life were spent at the typewriter. During that time he had occasion to write 25,000 pages of material, mostly from written or printed copy. He learned to type simply by copying from printed materials, looking to find the keys and then back to the copy. At the end of the 20 years he was still looking at the keys and was typing only about 25 words a minute. At 300 words to the page, this man had completed a practice assignment of 7,500,000 words.[23]

Whole Learning and Part Learning

The primary consideration in teaching is the conservation of lost time resulting from unguided practice. Learning a skill is not simply the doing of one action or two; it is a combination of a number of factors which can be referred to as the "whole." Laird and Laird, who have gained the reputation of practical business psychologists through their many studies of job performance, refer to the significance of the "whole":

---

[22] Henry P. Smith, *Psychology in Teaching* (2nd ed.; Englewood Cliffs, New Jersey: Prentice-Hall, Inc., 1954), p. 276.

[23] H. L. Hollingsworth, *Educational Psychology* (New York: Appleton-Century-Crofts, Inc., 1933), pp. 292-294.

If one single part of a job is learned, then another single part, the second, is likely to set back the learning of the first. A task is done differently when it is part of a sequence than when it is done by itself. Many new co-ordinations and timings have to be learned when two things are combined.[24]

This represents the point of view of the Gestalt school of learning, which is described by Washburn:

Those views of the Gestalt school hold that the whole, the configuration, is most important, that learning comes best from analyzing the whole rather than by attempting to add parts to make it a unified pattern. The whole is more than the sum of its parts.

From the Gestalt viewpoint a pattern is destroyed when it is broken up into its constituent parts. If a task or form to be learned is too complex to be grasped as a whole, two psychologically sound courses are open to the teacher:

1. The form may be simplified so far as this is possible without sacrificing its characteristic contours and without ignoring its characteristic setting.

2. Presentation of the form may be postponed until the maturation and experience of the learner insure its comprehension as a whole.[25]

In relation to significant practice, then, we are interested not just in making the keys of the typewriter go, but will achieve a higher degree of skill by understanding the whole process. Laird and Laird relate the example of a Chinese student who got a typewriter and methodically learned the touch system. But there was a constant interference between her newly-learned English and her typewriting skill. The English she wrote in longhand was perfect, but her type-

[24] Donald L. Laird and Eleanor C. Laird, *Practical Business Psychology* (2nd ed.; New York: Gregg Publishing Division, McGraw-Hill Book Company, Inc., 1956), p. 122.

[25] John N. Washburn, "Viewpoints in Learning," *Educational Psychology*, Charles E. Skinner, Editor (New York: Prentice-Hall, Inc., 1945), pp. 313-314, 324.

written letters were filled with errors. Her typewriting was perfect, but not her English on the typewriter, until she practiced the necessary combination of a skill and its application for half a year.[26] How reminiscent this is of students who complete a practice set in bookkeeping letter-perfect but who later, on the job, cannot make a simple trial balance comparison from uncomplicated records.

Whether the whole or the part method is the answer to skill learning is debatable. Evidence rendered by leading psychologists tends to stress the Gestalt approach again and again. Symonds reports the findings of a study he made which emphasizes the whole method as superior in most respects to other patterns, with a word of caution to the teacher in the utilization of the method:

1. The whole-method has proved itself to be superior in memorizing.
2. The whole-method becomes less efficient when the passage to be memorized becomes too long or difficult.
3. The whole-method becomes increasingly effective with increasing practice in using the method.
4. The whole-method, or a progressive part-method, leads to superior learning of acts of skill.
5. With material of a given level of difficulty, the mentally more mature individual can profit more from learning by a whole-method.
6. The whole-method is superior when there is a distribution of learning over several practice periods.
7. One should consider wholeness not in terms of the totality of what is to be learned, but in terms of the degree of integration of the unit to be learned.
8. Learning is most efficient when one first grasps the meaning and organization of the whole, and then proceeds to give attention to the parts and the relation of each part to the other parts and to the whole.

---

[26] Laird and Laird, *op. cit.*, pp. 122-123.

9. Learning is more efficient when the material to be learned is meaningful and rich in associations.

10. One should attempt to learn only that which he understands and comprehends. If material to be learned is beyond the comprehension of the learner, it should be simplified or broken down into meaningful parts.[27]

Just what constitutes a "whole" is not too clear. However, Wanous and Russon attempt to assist the teacher in presenting a working definition and how this concept is best applied:

It would seem . . . that in the matter of whole vs. part learning of typewriting, the teacher might experiment with the individual class to determine the proper size of unit which, to that class, would be considered a "whole." The class could then practice that unit as a whole and give attention to repetitive practice on the parts which might be difficult enough to make such practice necessary.[28]

Learning Plateaus

The teacher should recognize and adjust teaching procedures to "learning plateaus" as these occur. It is not unusual that periods in learning occur in which no apparent progress is taking place. Loss of interest, disgust, failure to complete a minimum of work are probable results. Or, on the other hand, overconfidence and satisfaction with the present state of affairs, with no apparent incentive or inclination to move ahead, can also indicate a plateau. Plateaus are a common component of learning, though not always necessary. All learning curves are not identical; but they generally do present the common characteristic of rising

---

[27] Percival M. Symonds, "What Education Has to Learn from Psychology," *Teachers College Record* (March, 1957), pp. 332-333.

[28] Allien R. Russon and S. J. Wanous, *Philosophy and Psychology of Teaching Typewriting* (Cincinnati: South-Western Publishing Company, 1960), pp. 129-130.

rapidly at the beginning and then gradually leveling off, then rising again, and so on until the level of approximate maximum learning or maximum skill development has been reached.

Plateaus were first described in connection with a study of learning curves by Dr. William L. Bryan, a psychologist at Indiana University. Laird and Laird report significant findings of this study in relation to this "leveling-off" tendency in learning:

1. Learning does not progress smoothly—it has ups and downs; there are good days and poor days.

2. Learning is rapid during the first few practice periods; then it slows down as the ultimate skill is approached.

3. There is a *plateau* in learning, a time when the learner does not seem to improve; he may actually slump downward.[29]

Laird and Laird [30] tell the story about this standstill in the life of Paderewski at the age of 25, already a well-known concert pianist. He was on a plateau of no progress, bogged down in his usual practice methods. Finally, he threw the practice sheets out the window and started over again, practicing elementary finger exercises and scales. This change in practice routine corrected his errors and enabled him to break through the plateau with a greater skill than ever before.

A plateau means that, at least for the present time and present method, the limit has been reached. It takes more than additional practice; there must be another approach used. We are also concerned with the causes for this period of stagnation. Psychologists and educators who have made studies of the plateau point to such causes as improperly graded materials, intensive practice before hand and finger

---

[29] Laird and Laird, *op. cit.*, p. 120.
[30] *Ibid.*

movements become well coordinated, and inability to relax. Some authorities, such as Watkins, tend to point to poor drill procedures as a cause:

> In the past there has been much routine drill work on learnings for which the pupils had no immediate need—drill that pupils considered so much drudgery to be done under the compulsion of a teacher-task-master.[31]

From the research that has been completed in the matter of overcoming the plateau when it exists, there appears to be evidence pointing to the need for increased, *but directed,* effort by the pupil at this point. A falling off of interest, emotional reaction against the subject, and lack of confidence all contribute to the downward slump that is to be avoided. It is said that Paderewski once commented, "If I miss one day's practice, I notice it. If I miss two days, the critics notice it. If I miss three days, the public notices it." An early study in the learning of motor skills points to the necessity of considering the whole approach in attempting to eliminate the plateau from learning. Kao[32] found no plateaus when using wholes: "Plateaus do not appear when the learner can and does attend to the whole complex throughout the course of learning." Clem, in a recent study on typewriting, reinforces this older study with the comment: "The Gestalt school exploded some of the old psychological theories, and the plateau was one of them."[33]

The present-day documentation of this phenomenon of the learning process places emphasis on the fact that the plateau can and does occur in the learning of a skill or a task. Specific mention will be made in the following chapters of methods to overcome this stumbling block.

---

[31] Ralph K. Watkins, *Techniques of Secondary School Teaching* (New York: The Ronald Press Company, 1958), p. 90.

[32] Kju-Lih Kao, "Plateaus and the Curve of Learning in Motor Skill," *Psychological Monographs,* No. 219, 1937, p. 79.

[33] Jane E. Clem, *Techniques of Teaching Typewriting* (2nd ed., New York: Gregg Publishing Division, McGraw-Hill Book Company, Inc., 1955), p. 236.

SUMMARY

When one attempts to teach another, the situation of *intent to learn* is immediately posed. Do the pupils really want to learn, or are they forced into the situation by the society in which they live? It is entirely possible that they may prefer to be doing something other than school work. If so, how can we, as teachers, go about changing these preferences, that is, to create an atmosphere for learning?

All of the reliable background on the education of youth indicates that learning takes place when there is a desire to learn. It is the task of the teacher to raise his sights above the mechanics of lesson planning to look at the more fundamental factors of what makes the human organism react and change behavior in a way that we deem desirable. Learning takes place when pupils understand, enjoy, and are interested in the activities with which they are confronted.

The business teacher girds himself for this challenge by a purposeful study of the following factors, particularly as related to the teaching of skills:

1. *Motivation.* The many factors involved in the motivation of learning have the purpose of creating a dynamic urge that will irresistibly impel the learner to *want* to learn and to translate this desire into action. The major factors to be considered in creating adequate motivation are: (a) to recognize and provide for individual differences; (b) to set realistic and attainable goals, determined through teacher and teacher-pupil planning; (c) to provide incentives, whether intrinsic or extrinsic, the major point being that they help achieve the goals of the course; (d) to recognize the effect of physical surroundings upon the human organism in a learning situation; and (e) to know that success is what "makes the world go 'round" for the student. A student needs to experience success as an encouragement for further experimentation and goal-seeking.

2. *Sound procedures in lesson planning.* Once the stage is set by providing the motivation, well-planned lesson materials and procedures must follow. Many descriptions of "what to do" are given in the following chapters.

3. *Practice.* It has been stated often that practice does not necessarily make perfect. The practice must be of the right kind and based on the best we know about psychology applied to practice. Techniques of successful practice involve: (a) understanding the principles of practice applied to skill—this includes conditions under which practice should be conducted, speed and accuracy, distribution of practice, and the effect of mental set; (b) consideration of the factors of whole learning and part learning; (c) recognition of learning plateaus and making adjustments to meet apparent lack of progress. Plateaus are a common occurrence and can be overcome readily in most cases if the teacher is familiar with the causes and common characteristics.

The principles outlined in this chapter constitute a list on which there is almost universal agreement in education. Many of these principles pertain especially to skill development and should be considered a "must" in the teaching equipment of the business teacher.

SELECTED BIBLIOGRAPHY

Bode, Boyd H. *How We Learn.* Boston: D. C. Heath and Company, 1940.

Clem, Jane E. *Techniques of Teaching Typewriting,* Second Edition. New York: Gregg Publishing Division, McGraw-Hill Book Company, Inc., 1955.

Frandsen, Arden N. *Educational Psychology.* New York: McGraw-Hill Book Company, Inc., 1961.

Gates, Arthur I., Arthur T. Jersild, T. R. McConnell, and Robert C. Challman. *Educational Psychology,* Third Edition. New York: The Macmillan Company, 1948.

Grambs, Jean D., and William J. Iverson. *Modern Methods in Secondary Education*. New York: The Dryden Press, 1952.

Kingsley, Howard L., and Ralph Garry. *The Nature and Conditions of Learning*, Second Edition. Englewood Cliffs, New Jersey: Prentice-Hall, Inc., 1957.

Klausmeier, Herbert J. "Characteristics of an Effective Learning Situation," *The Teachers College Journal* (October, 1956).

——————. *Learning and Human Abilities*. New York: Harper & Bros., 1961.

Laird, Donald L., and Eleanor C. Laird. *Practical Business Psychology*, Second Edition. New York: Gregg Publishing Division, McGraw-Hill Book Company, Inc., 1956.

Learning and Instruction, The Forty-Ninth Yearbook of the National Society for the Study of Education, Part I. Chicago: University of Chicago Press, 1950.

Mort, Paul R., and William S. Vincent. *Introduction to American Education*. New York: McGraw-Hill Book Company, Inc., 1954.

Mouly, George J. *Psychology for Effective Teaching*. New York: Henry Holt and Company, 1960.

Russon, Allien R., and S. J. Wanous. *Philosophy and Psychology of Teaching Typewriting*. Cincinnati: South-Western Publishing Company, 1960.

Smith, Henry P. *Psychology in Teaching*. Englewood Cliffs, New Jersey: Prentice-Hall, Inc., 1954.

Symonds, Percival M., "What Education Has to Learn from Psychology," *The Teachers College Record* (March, 1957).

Thorndike, Edward L. *Educational Psychology*, Vol. II. New York: Columbia University Press, 1913.

Washburn, John N. "Viewpoints in Learning," *Educational Psychology*, Charles E. Skinner, Editor. Englewood Cliffs, New Jersey: Prentice-Hall, Inc., 1945.

Watkins, Ralph K. *Techniques of Secondary School Teaching*. New York: The Ronald Press Company, 1958.

CHAPTER III

TYPEWRITING—PART I

BASIC PRINCIPLES AND CONCEPTS

Introduction

The teaching of typewriting is more than just giving timed writings! A foreign student doing graduate work was forced to learn how to type because he could not find an American typist who could do the job that his thesis required: German, Latin, Greek, etc. He took a standard university-level course in typewriting. Upon his return to Germany, he wrote a letter commenting on his educational experiences. "Of all the subjects I took," he wrote, "I acquired the most from my typing class. I learned much about English, of course, but I also received an insight into the way American business operates, its economics, its office procedures, etc." The teacher who taught the class was just doing the routine job he had always done. A letter like this would raise the sights of many a typing teacher.

At a business teachers' convention in Chicago, a teacher from a small midwestern high school made this remark: "Typing is the only business subject offered in our high school. It is the only classroom contact our students have with the world of business. In teaching this typing course, I feel I have a privilege and a responsibility."

There are many interesting things that could be written about typewriting. Russon and Wanous, Blackstone, Lamb, and several others have devoted entire volumes to the subject. Since this is a methods book and since we have very little space, the material presented here will have to do for

57

the most part with the _how_ of teaching typewriting. Although this chapter is aimed particularly at the beginning teacher, experienced teachers might find this material useful for a quick review. Teachers of methods courses might also want to use these suggestions as a springboard for their discussions on typing.

There was a time when school boards thought that they had fulfilled their responsibility if they erected a glass partition between a "regular" classroom and the typing room. The teacher thought he had done his job if he succeeded in preventing wholesale bedlam and preventing sabotage of the machines. Slowly over the years the idea evolved that typewriting, too, had to be taught—and taught vigorously. Recent statements in the literature of business education are indeed a far cry from the old glass partition days. Erickson, for example, comments as follows:

> A study of student success in typewriting indicates that there is no substitute for good teaching. Good teaching in the typewriting classroom should alter many forms of behavior: ways of doing assigned tasks, attitudes and interests, patterns of skill reaction, relations with others, and the like. It can and should help develop in the student an "intent to learn" and then aid him in the process of learning by such things, for example, as goal setting, or making provision for appropriate reinforcement of the learning.
>
> Someone has said that "awareness is the fourth dimension in living." Awareness might also be called the fourth dimension of good teaching. The typewriting teacher needs a generous portion of an awareness of what it is that typewriting students need if they are to gain skill rapidly. There is more to the teaching of typewriting than a simple call of "Come and get it." Good teaching is more than having a "bag of teaching tricks" or a series of "gimmicks" to use in the typewriting classroom. Not only must the teacher have a keen awareness of the typewriting process, but he must be the catalytic agent who shows the students how to put into prac-

tice those things that are basic to the development of type-writing skill.[1]

Typewriting is the most popular business subject in the high school curriculum. The time may yet come when type-writing will be a required subject for *all* students in the high school—a part of the general literacy program. However, to do that we may have to change our thinking and our procedures. Anderson gives a hint of what may be coming. (See III-1.)[*]

This chapter is divided into three parts: Part I states the general principles, Part II presents techniques and procedures for implementing the principles stated in Part I, and Part III calls attention to research studies and writings supporting the material in Parts I and II.

BASIC PRINCIPLES AND FACTORS ESSENTIAL TO THE TEACHING OF TYPEWRITING

Other authors have compiled their own lists of principles. See III-2 for a list by Douglas, Blanford, and Anderson, and III-3 for one by Tyler of Stanford University. Even though there is some overlapping, it helps to look at these basic concepts from several different angles. It helps, too, to see that most of the authorities are pretty well agreed on the teaching of typewriting. The first fifteen principles have to do with beginning or first-year typing; the others, with advanced typing.

Although it would be difficult to hold the point of view that there is one best way of teaching any subject, there are certain basic facts regarding presentation and procedure that psychologists and research workers have discovered and validated. These the typing teacher simply cannot afford

---

[1] Lawrence Erickson, "A Look at Typewriting," *Business Education Forum* (November, 1959), p. 7.

[*] A reference such as III-1 refers to Part III, item 1; III-4, to Part III, item 4.

to ignore. It is with this in mind that the following basic principles and factors are presented.

I-1   First-Day Procedures

It is recommended that the typing teacher have a first-day procedure with which he is familiar, one that is psychologically sound, and one that he knows will get results. Such a lesson plan should contain provisions for the following:

1. Some type of work to occupy the class until everyone gets in his assigned place and the group settles down to business. If the first day is somewhat chaotic, the teacher should not plan to do anything other than organizational details: books, seating arrangement, supplies, etc.

2. During this period students should actually operate the typewriter, producing meaningful copy.

3. There should be vigorous demonstration on the part of the teacher to set the mood and pattern for the day. (See II-1 on how to make a demonstration table during one class period.)

4. Before the end of the period students should be typing meaningful copy in good rhythm at 40 wpm or better. (Refer to II-2 to see how this is done.)

5. During rest intervals on this first day, the teacher should sell the subject of typewriting. Students need to realize the tremendous significance of typewriting in the modern business office. A good typist (Clerk II or IV) can get a job practically any time and any place.

6. Students should leave the first class with a feeling of excitement over the experience. They should be eager for more. They should have the feeling that typewriting is easy and that they are going to enjoy learning it. The technique outlined in II-2 goes a long way towards accomplishing this objective.

7. The teacher should make no attempt to keep the students from looking at the keys. He might praise those who, toward the end of the period, can write the exercise in good form with complete independence of the machine, that is, without taking eyes from the copy when stroking, returning the carriage, etc.

8. Nothing whatsoever should be said about making errors. Emphasis should be on good work habits, rhythm, correct stroking, proper placement of hands, relaxed position of the body, and manipulation of the carriage throw. No attempt should be made to learn the parts of the machine that do not enter into the presentation.

9. All typewriters should be in good working condition. Margins should be uniformly set. The teacher should attend to such things before class time. The teaching period on this first day is too valuable to devote any of it to machine adjustments or repair.

I-2   Transition to Text

Since under the authors' method the textbook is not used the first day, the teacher should have a definite procedure to take care of the transition from the first-day exercise to the text. The teacher may tie in the "if-it-is-in-the" approach with any standard keyboard method. (See II-3.)

I-3   Mixed Classes and Individual Differences

A class in which all students are absolute beginners is quite a rarity. Even though the subject is listed as Typing I, or Beginning Typewriting, the experienced teacher knows that he will not only find students who are approaching the keyboard for the first time, but also those who already know the keyboard and many who type quite well. It is the teacher's job to so organize the class that the real beginners will not be discouraged and the others will not be bored. Even if the class is quite homogeneous at the beginning, it will not stay that way very long. The factor of individual differences is always with us. (See II-4 for systems of handling several groups in one class.)

I-4   First-Year Typing Objectives—Standards

There are only two basic sets of objectives the teacher needs to keep in mind: (a) objectives for beginning typewriting, and (b) those for advanced or production typing. There was a time when a great deal of space was devoted to delineation of specific objectives for personal-use typing. Now it is generally agreed that any good course in introductory typing will also meet the needs of those who wish to use the skill for personal use.

The objectives of first-year typing should be live, meaningful, and accepted by both teacher and student. When introducing new teachers to beginning typing situations, department heads find it helpful to go over the course outline with them carefully. Considerable time might well be spent on the section marked "objectives" to make sure that these objectives are not just so many words, but that the teacher sees them as guide lines or road markers which will help him steer his course throughout the term. The teacher should go over these objectives occasionally with the students so that they, too, may see where they are going, what they have to do to get there, and why the route they are taking is the best route.

Just as students want to know how they are getting along, so the typing teacher wants to know how *he* is doing. Because of the many variables both in objectives and in local circumstances, it is difficult, and perhaps not even desirable, to have a nationwide set of absolute standards. Such standards would discourage some, for they would present unrealistic aspiration levels; for others, it would mean doing less than they might if they taught to the limit of their capabilities.

In Part II (II-5) a general set of objectives is outlined, and in Part III (III-5) some specific sets of standards from various parts of the country are given. From these the teacher can set up his own set of standards to meet his own particular situation.

I-5 Motivation and the Desire to Learn

The teacher's job is one of motivation, building up energy-packed capsules of desire, then directing that energy effectively to accomplish worthwhile student-accepted objectives. He should not be afraid to use every ace in the deck if necessary to create the desire to learn. In World War II the federal government capitalized on the value of using awards and rewards in order to motivate factory workers to higher achievement. Why should we do less in our typing classes?

If he is going to learn to type, the student must *want* to learn. Through any motivation device at his command, intrinsic or extrinsic, the teacher must create a desire on the part of the student to want to learn. This flame should be kept burning brightly through a variety of interest-stimulating devices. (See II-6 for devices.)

I-6 Knowledge of Progress

The teacher should provide a continuous answer to the question "How am I doing?" Knowledge of progress is one of the essentials of skill building. Without the knowledge of where he was yesterday and where he is now, how can the student possibly be interested in where he is likely to be tomorrow? (See III-6 for an example of a progress chart.)

I-7 Realistic Typing Goals

The teacher should help her typing students to set realistic immediate and long-range goals. The aspiration levels of students differ. Good students are likely to underestimate their abilities; poor students usually attempt too much. This leads to failure, failure leads to frustration, and frustration means no learning. The matter of goal-setting is closely related to the item of success to be discussed in the next paragraph.

I-8   Success Is Crucial

Obtainable goals having been established, the teacher should set the stage so that every student in the class experiences success in reaching these goals. All students should succeed in *something*. There is no better stimulus to skill building than success. SUCCESS IS CRUCIAL! A teacher reports that a student in one of his classes was most discouraged, for she was at the bottom of the class. The teacher was hard pressed to give her something in which she could succeed. The key came entirely by accident. One day the teacher noticed that the girl had developed expertness in returning the carriage. She was asked to make a special demonstration. From that day on she was a new person; her progress was rapid. She, too, had found something in which she could succeed.

I-9   Speed and Accuracy Development

The techniques involved in building speed and the methods that produce the best accuracy results are two different things. Speed and accuracy cannot be stressed in the same breath. While pressing for higher speeds, the teacher might temporarily forget about accuracy; when working for accuracy, he should forget about speed. *As typing power develops, the two will finally merge into one.* (See II-7 for some speed-building programs that have been effective. III-7 lists several other excellent speed and control development techniques.)

Here are some points that should be taken into consideration when trying for higher speeds and for better control:

1. On straight-copy typing, speed scores are reliable. At any time, any place, dependable scores are usually obtainable.

2. Accuracy scores are not reliable. They differ from time to time and from place to place. No single test is dependable.

3. In a speed development program, it is best not to say anything about accuracy in the beginning. Introduce this factor gradually.

4. The most important factor in the speed-building program is the will or the intent to learn. We practice because we *want* to learn; we do not necessarily learn because we practice.

5. Eliminate all unnecessary details. Concentrate on one thing at a time. If you don't need it, don't use it.

6. Always work with meaningful wholes. These should be as close to the professional level as possible. The most meaningful situations are generally the most natural and the most businesslike.

7. The teacher should keep hold of the reins at all times in order to regulate the intensity of the practice effort.

8. Warm-up drills are as essential in typing as they are in sports or in any manipulative activity. The organism needs time to adjust itself both mentally and physically.

9. Developing any skill requires a great deal of practice. Champions training for contests often write whole books, musicians often practice from four to eight hours a day. Typing students might make some progress just by thinking about it—it has been done in some cases—but by and large, to make worthwhile improvements, the students have to do a great deal of typing.

10. Remember that forgetting is normal. Plan for it; review accordingly.

I-10   *Learning Plateaus*

"Plateau" is a polite word for "rut." Plateaus should be avoided if possible and dealt with vigorously when they do appear. Plateaus can often be avoided by anticipating their causes early in the program.

Inexperienced teachers sometimes introduce the "i" and "e" one after the other, thus setting the stage for juxtaposition troubles later on. They often pay little attention to correct techniques in the beginning, thinking that they can fix those things up later on. They talk a great deal about accuracy and use all sorts of special "accuracy building" drills. We now know that such drills do very little good in the first place, and they can do much harm in developing tension plateaus. If it were possible to set up the perfect learning situation and to put into operation all the psychological principles of learning, no doubt we would have a progress curve closely resembling the normal learning curve —no plateaus whatever.

I-11   *The Magic Holding Power Formula*

The real test of a typing teacher's ability comes in connection with an adult evening program. High school classes are usually captive audiences; students usually have no other choice. In adult evening programs, it is different. If they like it, they stay; if they don't, they leave. Some evening class teachers hold almost all of their students to the very end; other teachers lose from 50 to 75 per cent of their students each term. Students reasons for dropping may be something like these: "Oh, I am having my mother give me speed tests." "I couldn't see that I was getting anywhere." "It's not worth the long drive." "At first I came only when I thought the teacher would give us something new; finally, I quit altogether."

Something new! That's the magic word. The magic formula for holding students is nothing else than to give them something new, something that they won't want to miss, *each evening*. This will, of course, involve careful planning, but perhaps that's just the difference between the superior teacher and the average teacher.

I-12   *Evaluation in Beginning Typewriting*

The teacher should have a sound plan for evaluating (grading) his students. The evaluation technique ought to have a direct tie-in with the objectives of the course. When students share in setting up the instrument by which they are to be evaluated, the entire procedure acts as a powerful motivating force. If a student is surprised by the mark he receives at the end of the term, it may be an indication that the lines of communication between teacher and student have broken down. (See II-8 for an evaluation plan that has won considerable acceptance. Also see III-8 for a suggestion on cutting down paper work.)

I-13   *Handling of Papers and Materials*

Office managers in charge of the flow of work put much emphasis on proper placement of paper and supplies. First-semester typewriting is an excellent time to teach effective handling of materials. At the first opportunity this matter can be investigated as a class project, and by experimentation a plan can soon be found that is most efficient for the job at hand. Modern typing texts give specific directions concerning the proper way to insert paper, handle envelopes when addressing, the best carbon paper technique, etc. The teacher should see to it that there is provided a standard place for textbooks and for supplies (paper, erasers, etc.) so that they may be distributed quickly at the beginning of the period and assembled quickly at the close of the period.

I-14 Quality of Typing

What constitutes good typing? Many office managers have been irritated by letters that are just good enough to pass inspection but not poor enough to be rewritten. Such supervisors find it hard to criticize because the office worker himself has not been trained to distinguish between the finer shades of typewritten copy. Too often a sheet of typewritten material, which contains no errors (wrong letters), loses its effectiveness because of uneven intensity of stroke, capitals that are above the line of writing, fingerprints, keys that need cleaning, faulty alignment, poor syllabication, uneven lines, smudgy erasures, and because the material is not well arranged on the page. Typing teachers should, therefore, make sure that they themselves observe good typing standards.

Scrapbooks containing samples of excellent typing done by experienced operators can be used as classroom reference material. Rating charts similar to the well-known handwriting scales can be posted. The letters on such a scale would range from very bad to very good. The poorest is usually characterized by these defects: poor placement (the message is usually crowded near the top of the page, leaving over three fourths of the sheet blank), the lines are uneven, letters are out of alignment (especially the capitals), the touch is uneven (some impressions dark, others hardly visible), the page gives clear evidence that keys need cleaning, some errors have been corrected by smudgy erasures, and there are many strikeovers. A letter of this type may be of very poor quality and still not have a single error of the kind usually checked in typing classes. Teachers themselves should be able to recognize good typing and should be able to demonstrate the technique by means of which such results may be obtained. The last letter on the scale should be a model of neatness, of beauty of design and arrangement, and of rhythm. Students should be asked to rate their daily work by means of this scale and label their work according to the numbers on this chart before handing in their typewritten material.

Another important objective of beginning typing is to develop in the student a sense of what constitutes good form in typing. The student should be able to arrange the material on the sheet attractively. The typing should be clear and even, and the entire job should have an appearance of neatness. Such basic work habits will provide a foundation upon which advance skills may be built. One businessman reports hiring a secretary who could type "well up in the 60's." Her only fault was that her capitals were out of alignment. He called this to her attention, assuming that a day or so would eradicate the trouble. Finally, after weeks of admonition, she was transferred to another department because she seemed unable to eliminate this difficulty. An elaboration of the word "form" by the teacher will often help to inspire students toward better design.

I-15 Classroom Organization

In the introductory chapter reference was made to a philosophy of education which suggested that schools be a living example of democracy in action. Typing teachers should provide opportunities for experience in democratic procedures by effecting a proper classroom organization. Not only will proper organization help students to experience the meaning of democracy, but it will make the whole job easier for the teacher. The typing teacher is the expert who points out right directions, timesaving devices, proper techniques, and who builds enthusiasm. He is the coach, standing on the side lines directing the work of the class in the most efficient manner possible. Early in the term students should be given an opportunity to elect officers: a chairman, a secretary, and various assistants. The librarian should be given charge of books and typing tests to facilitate handling of papers, tests, and the like. If this becomes burdensome, the librarian can have several assistants. There should be a class statistician to check attendance, and a person whose duty it is to supervise bulletin boards. There might also be a supervisor of maintenance —a person whose special duty it is to see that classroom property is protected, that waste is cut to a minimum, and that the room is properly lighted and ventilated.

The class as an organization can pass on many things to be done during the semester. An agreement as to the methods to be used and standards to be achieved will make the term's work a student project. The typing teacher should be familiar with several good classroom organization systems and then choose a plan that best meets the needs of the class. Whatever the details, the student should not be deprived of the opportunity to exercise his initiative —to show that he is dependable and to demonstrate his poise by taking an active part in the work of the class.

It is only by setting the stage so the student may take the first step that the teacher can hope to lead his student toward more difficult objectives. Acting as chairman of a classroom organization may give the student confidence to try for an office in some social organization, which again may lead to class presidency, and later on, perhaps, to leadership in a business organization.

I-16 The Typing Assignment

Typing assignments should correlate with the course objectives. The nature of the assignment will depend on the local situation. If all the work is done during the typing period, and if everything is completed in the teacher's presence, the assignments are of necessity brief and simple. If the class meeting is short in comparison with the total practice time (adult evening programs for example), the assignment must be more specific. An introduction to the work might well be given in class before the students are left to go on their own initiative. (See III-10 where Tate and Ross ask some pertinent questions about the assignment.)

SUMMARY FOR BEGINNING PORTION OF PART I

"As a man thinketh in his heart, so is he." Unless the student feels deep down in his heart that he wants to learn to type, the teacher labors in vain. If the student has taken the first step, that of really wanting to learn the subject, then, to be successful, he must have, or the teacher must create within him, a host of other wants or desires: he must *want* to write with good rhythm, to have good control, to acquire advanced speeds, to be neat, to produce good quality, to learn those factual details without which his speed will do little good, and he must want those basic techniques that the expert has found to be essential.

Having made sure of these wants, the teacher needs but to show him the way and provide the right guidance, encouragement, and materials to make it possible for him to do the job.

ADVANCED TYPEWRITING

Introduction

"Now they are on their own. I have taught them all I know," said one typing teacher with pride as she completed her work with a first-year group of typing students. This is all too common a concept: that we do our real teaching in Typing I, that we have done our job if we have brought the class up to 50 or 60 wpm on straight copy. Many, however, would differ with the above statement and say that when we get to this point, our work is only just beginning. Canfield, for example, comments as follows:

Applying basic skill to practical typewriting problems is generally referred to as production typewriting. Some educators use a variety of terms—practical typewriting, problem-solving exercises, typing application, applied skill practice, and office-application typewriting—to describe production typewriting.

Since the main reason for developing skill is to use it, the typewriting course should be just as concerned with applying typewriting skill as with building it. This is not to say that production typewriting is something separate and distinct from basic skill practice; it is instead just the continuation of it. And, production typewriting requires the same thorough teaching, including demonstration, that basic skill development demands. . . .

There should be a positive relationship between the speed achieved on straight-copy writings and that on production work. Every effort should be made, therefore, to assist students in the development of production rates that are in line with their straight-copying rates. Two suggestions for accomplishing this are to give students plenty of practice on all new types of problems and to time their efforts frequently.[2]

We agree with Miss Canfield. There *should* be a positive relationship between achievement on the routine speed tests and on production, but, alas, such is not the case. Valid research seems to point to the opposite; at least the correlation is not what one would expect it to be. It is only when we *do* something about it, when we use the powers suggested by raw scores of good straight-copy typists and by a period of intensive training convert these abilities into problem-solving dynamos that we have a product able to generate a sustained drive in production. (See III-11 for results of West's study on relationship between straight-copy typing ability and the ability to do production.)

---

[2] Mary Canfield, "Production Typing Must Be Taught Too," *Business Education Forum* (March, 1957), p. 26.

Just as in recent years more and more emphasis is being given to transcription as compared with basic shorthand, so the literature of business education seems to indicate that straight-copy typing without the ability to *do* things with the machine is of relatively little value. Crawford, one of the nation's outstanding exponents of production typing, says:

> Typewriting can no longer be considered a skill alone. Instead, it must be viewed as skill *plus*; and it is to the plus quantity that teachers must give serious thought. . . .
>
> Actually, the role of speed and accuracy in typewriting tends to be significant primarily in terms of the ability of typists to apply those qualities to the solving of problems. The speed factor alone, the accuracy factor alone, or both of them in combination, are relatively unimportant; they gain importance, however, as typists learn to apply the two competencies in problem typewriting. The extent to which typists are capable of applying speed and accuracy to problem solving determines the real value of basic skill in any program of typewriting instruction.[3]

(See II-9 for Crawford's suggestions for handling problem situations.)

We make the same admonition here that we make in transcription where we recommend that the student learn basic shorthand just as rapidly as possible, then take plenty of time with transcription. In typewriting we thoroughly agree with Crawford to take our time when handling production. Our motto is: Use every available pressure to build straight typing speed up to 50 to 60 wpm (can be done in one semester), then take all the time necessary to really learn to do things with the typewriter.

---

[3] T. James Crawford, "Problem Solving—Typewriting's Third Dimension," *Business Education Forum* (April, 1957), p. 20.

In beginning typing the student struggles to master the know-how of the situation. He obtains considerable satisfaction if after much time and effort he can produce *one* letter that is mailable, a form that is usable. In advanced typing, however, such things are taken for granted. Now the slogan is, "How efficient is the operation?" How many acceptable letters can the candidate produce in an hour? How many copies can he turn out? How many pages of a certain manuscript can he do in a given amount of time?

Most of the learning principles mentioned in connection with beginning typewriting also apply to advanced typing. There are, however, some factors that are associated more particularly with the advanced levels. A few of those have been singled out for treatment here.

I-17 Independence of the Machine

One of the earmarks of an advanced typist is that he is completely familiar with his machine; he can make the typewriter talk. Just as a musician must know the notes and a dancer the steps before any thought can be given to interpretation, so the typist must have complete mastery of his machine before he can really tackle advanced-level typing projects. The building of this proficiency, if the student comes lacking in it, is one of the first duties of the teacher of advanced typing.

An example in point: A typing teacher noticed a student using the space bar in connection with a rough draft tabulation project. In reply to the question, "Why don't you use your tabulator stops?" she said, "I never feel sure of myself with them. This has to be just right."

I-18 Multiple-Job Efficiency

"The average new employee," commented office manager Elmer Rule of the Nationwide Insurance Company at a NOMA meeting one time, "does well if you keep her on a certain job for a long time. She soon learns that operation and becomes quite proficient at it. But, if you interrupt her routine typing work and ask her to do something special, there is usually a great deal of fumbling around before she gets going. Assignments which should take only about ten minutes may take as much as a full hour." (See II-10 for a sample five-minute-limit multiple-job project.)

I-19 Factual Information

A student on a cooperative office training program became disturbed over her employer's impatience with her many questions. He had just told her that at the rate she was interrupting his work with questions which he thought she should be able to answer, he ought to be getting half of her pay. Her remark was, "Well, does a typist have to know *everything?*" "No," she was told, "but you should know how to spell the NOMA list, know basic punctuation, know something about word usage, know fundamentals of artistic design and page format, know enough about English to catch routine slips of the boss, and you should know the hundred and one little things in connection with capitals, underscoring, use of footnotes, and so forth." "My," said she, "isn't that just about everything?" Well, if it is, then the typist has to know everything. The ability to type 60 wpm is of little value if much time is lost while scouting about the office for the answer to some little detail that should be a part of one's basic fund of knowledge in office procedures.

I-20 Typing on Printed Forms

There have been many studies endeavoring to find out just how a typist spends her time when on the job in an average office. These lists sometimes contain a score or more of daily activities. Straight-copy typing, when listed, usually comes near the bottom. Typing on some style of business form comes near the top. More will be said about this in connection with office practice. Suffice it to say here that the typist should be familiar with a large number of business forms, know their purpose, and be able to use them in on-the-job situations.

I-21 Letter Typing

Another type of activity that comes near the top of any list of duties is that of typing letters from some basic form. For the most part, the fill-ins or changes that have to be made are of routine nature; however, they can become quite involved. Here is an area that furnishes excellent opportunities for production typing. Letters-per-hour standards are easy to establish. The teacher might want to begin his letters-per-hour projects by having the students do straight copy work from a duplicated set of standard-length letters in order to ascertain the number of mailable copies a student can produce in an hour's time. After the students become familiar with this practice, the problem can be made more realistic by having them fill in addresses, prices, etc., on a letters-per-hour basis.

A class agreed to do a thousand letters for a local civic club charity drive, provided their executives would check the letters for mailability. This they willingly did—and did carefully. The letters that were returned as not mailable were then posted on the bulletin boards. One exceedingly rapid typist did 60 letters. Over half of her letters were returned. No comments were necessary. This did more to improve quality of output than anything else the class might have attempted. Such experiences are the type of thing needed in connection with production typing: much repetition, careful supervision—all in an atmosphere of business-like meaningfulness.

I-22 *Evaluation of Advanced Typing—Standards*

A ninety-year-old gentleman celebrating his birthday made this remark: "I've got one foot in heaven. I'm still enjoying things here on this planet, but I've got my eyes on the next." Students who have reached the advanced stage of training in typing may still have one foot in the classroom, but the other is already in the office. For months they have been hearing their teachers say, "This is the way it is done in the modern office." Films and field trips have conditioned them to what they may expect. It is only logical, therefore, that when we think of typewriting standards and evaluation, we should think in the terms of the businessman. Harlan B. Miller, of the Institute of Life Insurance, for example, has this to say:

> How does a businessman look at typewriting? To put it succinctly, he looks at the typed material which is placed on his desk with just two questions in mind: (a) Is it clean and accurate? (b) How long did it take the typist to complete the job? The first question probably carries more weight than the second since the speed with which a manuscript or letter is typed has no significance unless it meets the quality standards which apply to that particular job.[4]

Advanced typing is a time for realism. It is here that students make the transition from routine straight-copy typing to production and problem solving. Except in rare instances in which a rough draft is all that is required, the office typist will make all the necessary corrections as she goes along. She will proofread material before taking it out of the machine and thus be able to make further immediate corrections if necessary. It is at the advanced typing stage, therefore, that erasure tests should become the rule. (See III-12 for a variety of standards—excellent material to help teachers with their grading and evaluation problems.)

---

[4] Harlan B. Miller, "A Businessman Takes a Look at Typewriting," *Business Education Forum* (November, 1959), p. 9.

I-23 100 Per Cent Dependability in Proofreading

Students and beginning office workers need a shock of some kind before they catch the full significance of this statement, which was seen in a New York office:

ARE YOU POSITIVE IT'S CORRECT? SOMEONE IS GOING TO MAKE SOME PRETTY IMPORTANT DECISIONS TOMORROW ON THE BASIS OF WHAT YOU TYPE TODAY!

The joint meeting of the board of regents and the budget committee of a certain university was about to start. The chairman called the meeting to order. One of the businessmen, used to dealing with figures, startled everyone by saying, "Gentlemen, we might as well go home. There's a mistake here someplace. These figures don't jibe. This throws everything off." The originals from which the typist had worked could not be obtained immediately. The chairman had to call for an adjournment until the discrepancies could be cleared up. The whole matter was carefully investigated. Everything was traced to some careless typing and haphazard proofreading. (See II-11 for information about proofreading.)

I-24 Composing at the Machine

One day the authors visited an executive who is a good typist and uses the typewriter extensively. The executive was writing something in longhand. "Have to make a speech," he said. "Yes," was our reply, "but why the longhand?" "You know," said he, "I've just never learned to think at the machine. As soon as I touch the keys, my thoughts leave me. Just can't get going." "Come to our typing class for a week," we told him, "and we guarantee you will be able to think as you type."

Ability to compose at the machine does not correlate with straight-copy typing skill *unless something is done about it.* How, then, does one learn to think at the machine? (See II-12 for details.)

I-25 Tricks of the Trade

Even though it has been said (and correctly so) that the teaching of typewriting is more than dishing out a bag of tricks, nevertheless, there are many tricks of the trade that add to the efficiency of the typist. True, these "tricks" are by no means the cornerstone of a typing course, but once a good foundation has been laid, many of these little short cuts can be thrown in along the way as interest-getting devices without hampering the overall training program. In learning a foreign language, one limits himself at first to the simple way of saying things; but later on, when he "feels his oats" so to speak, he can begin using delightful local idioms, which add color to the language. So it is with these efficiency or short cut techniques—they add spice to the day's work. (See III-13 for a few office short cuts compiled by NOMA.)

I-26 TV and the Typing Teacher

Practically all of the business subjects in one form or another have been taught successfully by television. The procedures are too new and our space too limited for a complete analysis of all the problems. The important thing to recognize is that here is a technique that requires specific training. (See III-14 for a delineation of some of the difficulties involved.)

SUMMARY FOR PART I

As a summary for Part I, Hoskinson's "Ten Rules for the Beginning Typewriting Teacher" crystallizes many of the points already discussed:

1. Provide a pleasant atmosphere in which students can learn to typewrite.
2. Enter the classroom with plans for the day's work.
3. Utilize as much of the learners' time as possible.
4. Stress the development of good techniques and satisfactory skills on the part of the students before developing their production abilities.
5. Develop speed and accuracy in accordance with psychological principles of skill-building.
6. Employ in the typewriting class only those drills which have meaning to the students.
7. Encourage students to set individual goals toward which to work in developing their typewriting skill.
8. Evaluate the students' work only after they have had an opportunity to develop the skill or technique to be learned.
9. Provide an opportunity for the integration of skills in office-like situations as a terminal stage of typewriting instruction.
10. Be professional.[5]

---

[5] Robert E. Hoskinson, "Ten Rules for the Beginning Typewriting Teacher," *Business Education Forum* (January, 1957), pp. 26, 27, 32.

TYPEWRITING—PART II

TEACHING TECHNIQUES AND PROCEDURES

In Part I we discussed fundamental principles of teaching typewriting. In order that the reader might get the overall picture as quickly as possible, little time was spent in illustrating how these concepts might be put into action. That will be the function of Part II.

II-1   Demonstration

Vigorous demonstration is now an accepted part of the teaching of typewriting. Now and then there are excuses for not demonstrating. "I have tried for two years to get a demonstration stand for our typing room," complained one teacher. To show teachers how easy it is to build a good demonstration stand, we usually make one right in the classroom in connection with each typing methods class. On one occasion we found an old discarded table top. From this we cut two square pieces, one 15 x 15 inches and another 20 x 20. One student bought four swivel casters at the dime store. A 4 x 4 from a nearby woodpile supplied the upright. We nailed the square blocks to the top and bottom of the 4 x 4. Then we put the casters in the four corners of the larger block. The entire operation took less than a class period; the cost was about one dollar.

II-2   First-Day Procedures

The following detailed procedure has been found effective and in accordance with the psychological principles of good skill building mentioned in Chapter II.

After the students are seated and have been supplied with paper, the teacher gives a brief demonstration of how to put the paper in the machine and how to take it out. Classmates are usually eager to help those who have difficulty. The position of the hands on home row is briefly illustrated.

The teacher now writes the word "if" on the board and asks students to feel for the right keys. Classmates help to see that the right fingers are used. At the movable demonstration table, the teacher writes the word, setting both the visible and the sound pattern. Cardboard instead of paper in the teacher's machine will help accentuate the sound. Right thumb is mentioned in spacing. After a few moments of practice on "i-f-space," members of the class are asked to demonstrate how nearly they can approach the quick, flash-like pattern established by the teacher.

After the word "if" has been developed, the word "it" is placed on the board. Since the students are already familiar with "i," the "t" is the only new element. There is sufficient contrast not to cause confusion. Other words are written in like manner until "if it is in the" have been introduced. By the end of the first period students will be writing this phrase rapidly and in good style. On the second day this phrase can be reviewed together with a formal introduction to the text. The sound-and-word-pattern techniques may be continued regardless of the particular approach suggested by the text. This introductory procedure is suggested here simply to assure good basic typing techniques with a snappy, quick, get-away stroke right from the beginning. It is important that the mental process back of the physical manipulation be conditioned to act quickly.

If the first day of typing has been properly utilized, students will go home with a satisfaction of having actually typed something. They await eagerly their next experience. How different this procedure is from other methods where the students sit before a covered typewriter while the teacher spends most of the period in explanations and references to the history of typewriting.

After an initial good beginning, the alert typing teacher continually seeks better answers to such questions as, "How may I best achieve these objectives? Are our objectives still sound? Do we still want to do what we planned in the beginning? Can our skill-building techniques be improved? In mathematics, history, and science, solutions themselves determine the correctness of the method; but in skill subjects a student may use a wrong technique day by day without being aware of a shorter path. It is the duty of the teacher, therefore, to help the students find the best methods of attaining their objectives. Here the teacher is a technician, a specialist called in to serve in the capacity of an efficiency expert.

As soon as the class is in action and things are running smoothly, it is time to check on details. Is the table high enough to enable the student to lower the wrist to secure the correct, comfortable position illustrated in the typing text? (As mentioned in connection with equipment, the table is a relative proposition. It is more often too low than too high.) Are students using the right fingers? Is the stroking executed with a snappy, get-away touch? Is the carriage returned quickly with proper technique?

The whole method of learning would indicate that the keyboard should be learned as quickly as possible. Some teachers introduce students to the entire keyboard the first day; others take as long as four weeks. The average time, however, is ten to twelve class periods. Most textbooks introduce words, phrases, and sentences in the first few lessons. Context material in short paragraphs may be used for timed writing practices by the end of the first week. By this time the class routine is fairly well established, and plans for the semester organization can get under way.

Lessenberry, Crawford, and Erickson give the following suggestion for the first period:

Teaching the Lesson. The students want to get their fingers on the typewriter and make it work. Don't let class organization, clerical work, or interruptions keep you from beginning to teach as soon as the students are assembled. Omit explanations that can be given as appropriately in the next lessons. Reserve the "pep talks" and the motivating examples until a later time. Demonstrate everything you want to do; capitalize on their initial enthusiasm, and keep them typing—and they won't be able to resist learning to type.[6]

II-3 Transition to Text After "If It Is In The" Drill

Some teachers using the "if-it-is-in-the" approach follow up with the three-letter words given below. These words can be used in connection with the "if-it-is-in-the" group in meaningful phrases and sentences and so continue the pattern established during the first two days. One teacher reports excellent results by using rhythm records in 4/4 time for the three-letter words. The drill would then be "f-u-r-space," etc. After a week or two of this type of thing, the basic concept of rhythm in typing should be established.

There are, of course, many different opinions when it comes to teaching the keyboard. All agree that it should be covered in a relatively short time. Tonne, Popham, and Freeman comment as follows:

> Some authorities in the typewriting field introduce the entire keyboard in one period. Others contend that such a procedure causes confusions in responses that prevent development of techniques; they feel it is better to present one or two keys a day and let the students approach expert performance on them. One widely used textbook introduces the keyboard in five lessons, another in six, and a third in nine. In training service personnel, instructors introduced the keyboard in two to six clock hours, by using twenty-six

---

[6] D. D. Lessenberry, T. James Crawford, and Lawrence W. Erickson, *Manual for 20th Century Typewriting* (8th ed.; Cincinnati: South-Western Publishing Company, 1962), p. 36.

three-letter words that included every letter: *fur fun gun gum guy buy but hut jut jug vug jim dim kid red cue my, lot sit wet tex co. fat pat zip qt.*[7]

II-4   Handling Different Groups in One Class

Of the many millions of people who inhabit this globe, there are no two exactly alike. To be different, therefore, is the normal state of affairs. "I am so used to having different levels of ability in my typing classes," said one typing teacher, "that I do something about it the very first time the class meets." Assuming that all machines are in good working condition and margins set, the authors recommend the following:

1. Absolute beginners, those who do not know the keyboard or are so rusty they need a review, are seated in the front of the room.

2. If space is available, it helps to have a vacant row of seats separating the beginners from the others. The non-beginners are now given a 5-minute timed writing. They are instructed to check their papers as soon as they finish. This allows about ten minutes of uninterrupted time to spend with beginners on the "if-it-is-in-the" approach.

3. After ten minutes of intensive work with the teacher, the beginners are far enough along that they can continue on their own for a few minutes, which allows time for a quick appraisal of the 5-minute test results. From this information the next step is planned.

4. Generally, a half dozen or so of the nonbeginners stand out above the rest. They are ready for some form of production work. If there is an out-of-the-way corner available, that's the place for the production workers. A problem that needs very little explanation is all ready for them. In a minute or two they are busy at work.

---

[7] Herbert A. Tonne, Estelle L. Popham, and M. Herbert Freeman, *Methods of Teaching Business Subjects* (2nd ed.; New York: Gregg Publishing Division, McGraw-Hill Book Company, Inc., 1957), p. 107.

5. The remainder of the nonbeginning group now take another timed writing to see if they can do better. The real reason for this second writing is to provide time for the teacher to work with the beginners. There are now three groups: beginners, advanced, and the rest which we will call intermediates. All this in a "beginning" class!

6. The beginners are now far enough along for the teacher to help them with various phases of technique. After all those in the front of the room thoroughly understand the assignment for next time, they work by themselves for the remainder of the period.

7. The beginners are busy with their next day's assignment, and the intermediates are selecting the better of the two tests they have just taken. The teacher then visits the advanced group and goes over the objectives for the term and with the students decides on a specific job for next time. A special short job keeps them "gainfully employed" until the end of the period.

8. The intermediates are now next in line for final attention. With the teacher they decide on a good place to start in the text—letter writing, for example.

9. The opening and closing remarks are always to the group as a whole. After the first few sessions, there are many exercises on which all three groups can work at the same time: short one-minute tests, warming-up exercises, discussions on office procedures, factual information, and so forth. By working together as a group at the beginning and at the end, there is a feeling of class unity, even though the students are working at different levels.

Of course, the teacher always breathes a sigh of relief when the first class is over, and no wonder. It is a most challenging experience. To keep three distinct groups happy and usefully busy every minute of the time for the very first time they come together is no mean accomplishment. From then on the teacher will have to study carefully the needs of each group and come to class with definite plans and materials to take care of these needs.

II-5 Objectives

The objectives of beginning typewriting might well be summarized as follows:

1. ATTITUDE—the *desire* to want to be a good typist.
2. GOOD WORK HABITS—right position at the machine, proper stroking, efficient handling of materials, proper spacing of attention and effort, neatness, and a minimum of lost motion.
3. KNOWLEDGE FACTORS—the proper "know-how." A part of typing efficiency is the ability to exercise quick and accurate judgment in connection with the many writing details. The proper procedure here is simply *to know* what leading authorities have decreed as the best practice.
4. QUALITY AND CONTROL. It is during this stage of his development that the student should formulate a concept of what constitutes good typing, should subscribe to an acceptable standard, should overcome the usual inhibitions, fears, and indecisions which so often hamper proper control.
5. SPEED. Although basic speed patterns are emphasized from the very first day, nevertheless, speed is here placed near the end in this list of objectives. Without the foregoing four objectives, a speed building program is not likely to succeed.
6. PERFORMANCE—the ability to do. Producing practical results with the typewriter, especially on a production basis, should be reserved as an objective of advanced typing. Nevertheless, by the time students have completed the first half of their typing program, they should be able to set up simple letters from printed copy, should be able to arrange copy attractively on different size forms, should be able to do some composing at the machine, . . . and should be able to do simple tabulation.[8]

---

[8] Harm Harms, "Standards for Beginning Typewriting," *The Journal of Business Education* (February, 1945), p. 23.

II-6   *Interest-Generating Devices*

Devices and "teaching tricks" are in disrepute. This has come about, perhaps, by the fact that many teachers do not have a clear concept of what constitutes a good teaching device. Too many devices are in the nature of busy work or just "having fun" exercises. A good device is one that stirs the imagination, generates additional interest, heads directly towards the target, and inspires a host of concomitant learnings along the way. When students have progressed to the point where they can handle problem situations, the teacher will have no difficulty in finding an interest-creating exercise if the text does not supply the needed material. Actual work exercises brought in from the community are sure-fire interest-getting devices.

II-7   *Accuracy*

Speed and accuracy are two important component factors in achieving our typing objectives. As indicated by Clem, business educators have come a long way since the day when the teacher with an eagle eye insisted on absolutely perfect copy with no erasures. The new attitude is more in harmony with actual conditions. The modern typing student emulates the good work habits of efficient stenographers and typists. Certainly they erase, but they maintain a proper balance. Too many erasures destroy efficiency. Accuracy is still of great importance, but it cannot be achieved by overemphasizing it to beginning students any more than one can achieve happiness by telling a person to go out and be happy without making it physically possible for him to do so.

The concept of accuracy should be introduced gradually. First, it might be suggested that the student do as well as he can; next, that he work on his exercise until he is satisfied with it. Carefully and adroitly the teacher can instill higher standards so that the students themselves will not be satisfied with copy containing more errors than necessary at their present stage of development. As a further step, papers having few errors may be placed on display—the teacher need not wait for perfect papers to do this. A desire for accuracy can also be introduced by having the students type five successive one-minute timed writings in an effort to see how many out of the five they can type with one or no errors. Each one-minute timed writing represents a new challenge.

The word "control" is gradually being substituted for accuracy. The aim is to help the student to so direct his energies that he can manipulate the typewriter with relatively few unintentional and undesirable results, actions, or responses. When the will is capable of exerting this influence with effective measures, the typist is said to have control.

Good control involves more than striking the right keys. Errors in technique are frequently more serious and attended with more far-reaching ill results than errors involving the wrong keys. Blackstone is thinking of such errors when he says:

> Of course the student may, by slowing down, type a word correctly. That word needs additional practice too. To mark such words for technique practice, the student may strike the diagonal key after every word that slows him down. After typing the exercise through, he should practice each word that was incorrectly typed and each word that was slow.[9]

Few experienced typists type with perfect control. Errors do creep in. The perfect copy requirement for beginning students is giving way to a more natural situation in which the student does the best he can about accuracy while striving for rapid stroking with good form and with relaxation.

---

[9] E. G. Blackstone, "How to Speed Up Typewriting Instruction," *The National Business Education Quarterly*, XII (December, 1943), p. 65.

Simply to tell the student, "Don't be tense—relax," is about as useful as telling the groom not to be nervous or the young applicant that he must have poise. Something must be done about it. To secure relaxation the typing teacher must help the student by positive means. Relaxing is not so much physical as it is mental. Relaxation and poise go together. Poise is the result of anticipating conditions—familiarizing one's self with coming experiences and the elimination of the element of fear. In order to help him relax, the student should know exactly what is expected of him. The job must be easy enough so he can do it without great difficulty. The student should bear in mind that results from the very beginning are not so important. All that is desired just now is a bundle of good work habits: comfortable position at the machine, quick, snappy stroking, skillful carriage return—all with an air of confidence that permits daring and encourages speed.

The word "tense" as here used refers to that type of nervous condition which produces cold hands, overly taut muscles—a general condition associated with fear and not the tension mentioned by Dvorak and others, where tension is discussed as a readiness of the body to meet the problem at hand. "The new situation of struggling with a typewriter which you desire to operate is bound to heighten the tension of your muscles somewhat, so that you are ready to act. What is called your 'interest' is simply the degree of this bodily tension." [10]

Lessenberry [11] admonishes teachers to talk less about making errors and more about improving technique.

Blackstone and Smith state their opinions concerning accuracy in unequivocal terms in stressing the modern attitude toward this subject:

---

[10] August Dvorak, Nellie L. Merrick, William L. Dealey, and Gertrude Catherine Ford, *Typewriting Behavior* (New York: American Book Company, 1936), p. 89.

[11] D. D. Lessenberry, "The Teaching of Typewriting," *Sixth Yearbook of the National Commercial Teachers Federation* (1940), p. 455.

. . . perfect accuracy requirements are comparable to some of the torture devices of the days of the Inquisition. Modern teachers have a different attitude toward accuracy They strive to have their students improve in accuracy rather than expect them to achieve it at the beginning of the course. Recognizing that the beginner's muscles are imperfectly controlled as yet, and that he is more or less confused by the large number of keys to be struck correctly, the teacher does not criticize the number of errors that the student makes on the first attempt, but urges him, if there are too many errors, to try to do better the next time. Thus, if the student makes thirty mistakes the first time, and only twenty-four the second time, the enlightened teacher does not (as the other type of teacher might) tell him that both papers are total failures; rather, he praises the student for having made progress, which he has certainly done. Thus, the teacher may be able to lead the student toward the goal of perfect accuracy, without the development of fear, discouragement, and failure.[12]

Dvorak, Merrick, Dealey, and Ford have based their conception of accuracy on the time and motion studies of Gilbreth and Gilbreth:[13]

The brilliant insistence of the Gilbreths on standard motions at standard speeds first, with quality of the output second, seems inevitable as soon as motion study is substituted for traditional complacency. Well over a decade ago the Gilbreths successfully put to rout the reverse view hitherto generally accepted. Their photographs concretely show that the paths of correct, fast motions are different from slow motions. Their minutely timed, slow-motion pictures preserve the form of these correct motions. Why seek to justify a continuing of slow motions in any capable beginner? If you agree that correct motions should be taught from the start and that these can be clearly demonstrated, what happens

[12] E. G. Blackstone and S. L. Smith, *Improvement of Instruction in Typewriting* (Englewood Cliffs, New Jersey: Prentice-Hall, Inc., 1949), pp. 151-152.

[13] F. B. Gilbreth and L. M. Gilbreth, *Applied Motion Study* (New York: The Macmillan Company, 1919), p. 112.

to slow typing motions? Wouldn't you push them out of the typewriting-class picture as fast as a first impulse might be to put them in? Of course, your speed should be as near as is reasonably possible to that of the expert. Naturally, to meet variables in yourself, correct motions are taught ahead of fast line rates. Practice fast motions fitted together at your best rate, without forcing. *Work rapidly, regardless of much worthless work at first*; let accuracy seem to go by the board.[14]

An indication of how far the pendulum swung was given by Clem in quoting SoRelle in 1929:

> Much has been written on the subject of speed in typewriting, but the less said about it to the beginner in the art, the better, unless it be that he should be warned to let speed alone until he has acquired habits of accuracy in technique. Accuracy is of first consideration. Speed is necessary, of course, but it is something that must be built on the solid foundation of accuracy.[15]

But that was in 1929. Ten years later Clem [16] reported in *The Business Education World* to the effect that new methods and old philosophies are proving to be fallacies or are being given new interpretations. Metronomic rhythm has been replaced by a new conception of rhythm. Rhythm is now interpreted to be a flow of writing in which the easy combinations are typed faster than the hard combinations. Erasing is now taught as something to be learned and skillfully used. It is now recognized that typewriting tests should test all phases of a typist's work—his knowledge as well as his skill. Relaxation is now stressed. Tenseness

---

[14] Dvorak, *et al.*, *op. cit.*, pp. 299-300.
[15] Jane E. Clem, *The Technique of Teaching Typewriting* (New York: The Gregg Publishing Company, 1929), p. 139.
[16] Jane E. Clem, "New Trends in the Teaching of Typewriting," *Business Education World* (April, 1939), pp. 629-31.

limits the progress of the student so that his learning cannot possibly reach the skill stage.

Blackstone and Smith [17] devote an entire chapter to devices, many of which can be used effectively for promoting accuracy. [The price of accuracy is first of all a desire on the part of the student to achieve such a mark. This often means low speed, more attention to techniques, more practice time, error analysis, and corrective drills.]

The Page Club as an Accuracy Builder. The literature of business education contains many devices intended to promote accuracy. The following is one device that can be used in almost any typing class. The daily lesson material may be used for copy.

Any student writing a page without a mistake during a fifteen-minute segment of the regular typing period becomes a member of the Page Club. His name is placed on the membership scroll. Since it will be some time before many in the class can do this, a preliminary chart is set up showing the greatest number of consecutive perfect lines (seventy spaces) each student has been able to write. Line by line they thus progress toward Page Club membership. Members of the Page Club are eligible to try for the Page Club pin—five consecutive perfect pages. The student may start over as many times as he wishes during the fifteen-minute period. Persons holding the Page Club pin are eligible to try for the guard. This also requires a perfect page on each of five consecutive days, only in this instance students are not permitted to start over. This device is flexible and can be used in connection with almost any material. Other awards may, of course, be substituted. In actual practice office workers need not labor under such a strain, since erasures may be made when necessary. However, the ability to write a paragraph or page with a high degree of accuracy

---

[17] Blackstone and Smith, *op. cit.*

is often quite an asset. For example, the Ohio Civil Service test in typing is a test to see how many perfect lines the candidate can write in a five-minute period.

II-8   Evaluation

See pages 95 and 96 for sample evaluation summary sheets.

II-9   Problem Solving

Crawford recommends the following principles to insure an effective program for developing power in solving problem:

1. Problem typewriting experiences must consist of a great deal more than routine copying. . . . Specific training must be provided in techniques and procedures for identifying and defining the exact nature of problems encountered.

2. Problem typewriting should include much repetitive practice of a meaningful nature.

3. Problems assigned should be completed under the pressure of time.

4. Measurement of problem typewriting should require total performance. All activities involved in completing problems should be included in problem testing. Handling directions, organizing materials, adjusting equipment, making computations, proofreading, making corrections, and the like should be considered part of the testing experience and test results should reflect ability in those functions.

5. Problem typewriting measurement should place practical, realistic responsibilities on the typist. The responsibility for complying with directions, adopting satisfying procedures, verifying content, exercising options, producing satisfactory volume, and for appraisal of completed work must be accepted by the typist. . . .

Name_____   Date_____

EVALUATION SUMMARY SHEET
Beginning Typewriting

This evaluation is made in consideration of the following course objectives:

Acceptable speed and control: 50 to 60 wpm gross, 5-minute test, one error
    per minute.
A solid foundation of good typewriting techniques: stroking, complete com-
    mand of machine, rhythm, manipulative techniques.
Factual information: knowledge of format and design, basic punctuation,
    word usage, spelling, and other such factors.
Foundations of production: letter styles, stencils, masters, manuscripts,
    business forms, etc.
Quality: neat appearance, well-balanced page setup, strikeover, erasures,
    clean type.
Work habits: work station organization, attitudes, operational efficiency.

This is not what is required to pass the course, but what is expected of a
    good typewriting student.

ITEMS AFFECTING FINAL TERM GRADE   SCORE POINTS

Gross speed: average of best 3 out of 5 trials on 5-minute
    tests, based on competency achieved during last month of
    term _____x 2   _____
Control: average errors a minute on the above 3 tests
    (0-.5=100; .6-1.0=80; 1.1-1.5=60; 1.6-2.0=40)   _____
Typewriting technique: (teacher's estimate, percent of 100) _____
Typewriting technique: (student's own estimate)   _____
Factual information: average of tests taken during term   _____
Factual information: score on final examination   _____
Quality: score based on bulletin board scale
    (Samples on display range from 20 to 100)   _____
Work habits: teacher's estimate
Preproduction items--20 points for each classification
    of items completed up to standard.

                Letters, two basic styles   _____
                Stencils   _____
                Master   _____
                Rough draft   _____
                Tabulation, simple   _____
                Tabulation, complex   _____
                Form letter project   _____
                          TOTAL
Summary score of other special items during term   _____

                     TOTAL SCORE FOR TERM   _____

LETTER GRADE FOR TERM_____

Name_____   Date_____

EVALUATION SUMMARY SHEET
Advanced Typewriting

This evaluation is made in consideration of the following course objectives:

Acceptable speed and control: 60 to 70 wpm gross, 5-minute test, one error
    per minute.
Good techniques are assumed. If deficiencies are not corrected during the
    first month, penalty involved.
Factual information: same standards as beginning typewriting. If defici-
    encies are not corrected during the first month, penalty involved.
Quality: since only usable copy will be considered, it is expected that the
    quality will be in keeping with standards in a modern office.
Production: this is the principal objective of the course.

This is not what is required to pass the course, but what is expected of a
    <u>good</u> typewriting student.

ITEMS AFFECTING FINAL TERM GRADE   SCORE POINTS

Gross speed: average of best 3 out of 5 trials on 5-minute
    tests based on competency achieved during last month of
    term. (Tests with more than one error a minute will not
    be considered, except in speeds above 60 wpm.) _____x 2
Number of mailable letters per hour (130-150 words) _____x 10
Number of pages of manuscript (without footnotes) per hour,
    double spaced _____x 10
Number of invoices per hour _____x 10
Number of 5-minute projects in an hour _____x 10
Other projects _____x **?**

OUTPUT FOR TERM

Total output in mailable letters during term _____x 5
Number of 5-minute projects successfully completed _____x 5
Other production achievements _____x ?

- -

Score made on National Business Entrance Typing Tests
    (Teacher will make subjective evaluation.)
Rating on major projects: outside business jobs, for example

TOTAL SCORE FOR TERM

LETTER GRADE FOR TERM_____

Further, the development of problem-typewriting ability requires time; and attempts to achieve desirable results in short-term, abbreviated courses appear to be questionable, indeed. The maturation factor understandably plays an important role in building strength in problem typing; and while teachers may reasonably expect growth in any given semester, they should not expect mature behavior until sufficient time has been invested. Competence demands experience; and experience implies the need for reasonable time.[18]

II-10   Five-Minute-Limit Multiple-Job Projects

The idea of this project is to train students to move quickly from one job to another with a minimum of confusion. One booklet * that more than meets the needs of the most enterprising teacher contains 130 projects. If the booklet is not readily obtainable, the teacher can easily make up her own problems. Care should be taken to make them short so that the average typist can do each job in five minutes or less. Listed below are a few suggestions, each of which can be done easily in five minutes by a student whose gross speed is 40 wpm or more.

1. Type a message on a postal card, address it, and put it in the mail.
2. Same job, but use a double postal card with proper information.
3. Type a short letter from a form letter, making necessary fill-ins.
4. Same job, but make carbon, address envelope, put letter in mail.
5. Type a Ditto master, double space, half page of material.
6. Take above master and run off ten copies; file master.

---

[18] T. James Crawford, "Problem Solving—Typewriting's Third Dimension," *Business Education Forum* (April, 1957), pp. 20-23.

* Ruth I. Anderson and Leonard Porter, *130 Basic Typing Jobs* (Englewood Cliffs, New Jersey: Prentice-Hall, 1960).

7. Type stencil, same length as above Ditto—same message can be used.

8. Run off ten copies of above stencil, file stencil.

9. Type invoice of six items, extend, and total.

10. Check figures of ten invoices done by other students.

11. Arrange work station for project involving carbons, letter-heads, envelopes, etc.; get everything in working order.

12. Make five actual phone calls telling date of certain meeting.

13. Choose partners to help, then proofread two pages of material, checking dates and figures with original.

14. Take a short letter from dictation, transcribe, one carbon, place on teacher's desk for signature. Dictation time not included in the five minutes.

(This, of course, is for those who are in transcription.)

15. Take a message to the principal, get a reply, be back in five minutes.

There is practically no end to projects of this kind. Problems of this nature tie in nicely with what happens to be in the school news at the moment, for example, school party, dance, fund drive, and so forth. When these projects are first introduced, it is well not to say anything about a five-minute limit. Record the time it takes each student to do the job assigned. There is great satisfaction for both teacher and student to see a half-hour job shrink to fit the five-minute schedule. It is not unusual to have a student cut her time down from 45 minutes to the standard five minutes. One teacher referred to minutes as "man-hours" and then tabulated the man-hours saved each day.

II-11 Proofreading

The authors had occasion to watch some typists at work in a local office. "Would you give me a hand, Lucy?" said Betty. Without hesitation, Lucy stopped her work and went

over to Betty's desk. Betty handed Lucy the material she
had just typed. Lucy followed the script carefully while
Betty read from the original. This was not a hasty, let's-
get-this-thing-over type of operation. Each one was very
serious. When they came to figures, important names, or
unusual constructions, Betty read them to Lucy; then Lucy
read back again from her copy. On one occasion Lucy said,
"Doesn't make sense to me, but maybe it's okay." Betty
pushed the intercom button: "Is this really what you
want?" Evidently it was, for they went on with their proofreading. When the job was done, Lucy went back to her
desk and continued her work. Not a moment was lost.
That this was not a new operation could be determined by
the routine which indicated that each one knew just what
to do. The girls had established a technique of helping
each other when it came to the important job of proofreading.

In our typing classes we often let proofreading go without careful checking. Students take a quick look to check
their errors, and that's it. Some have learned not to check
too carefully. "Why penalize yourself?" said one who evidently knew the score.

We need an entirely different approach. For a change
we might not consider the errors at all but have the student's grade depend on his proofreading ability. This type
of thing should be preceded by some drill in *how* to proofread, what to look for, etc. Does it follow the copy? Does
it make sense? These are the two basic considerations.
Names, dates, and figures are particularly important. When
it comes to grammar, punctuation, spelling, and word usage,
it is not so much a matter of following copy as it is to have
the transcript follow good standard usage. There should be
one person in every office who is an authority on such matters. Such persons often win quick recognition. Teachers
should encourage their students to aim for such a mark.

II-12 *Composing at the Machine*

Russon uses the following system for teaching composing at the typewriter:

> Composing at the typewriter may be introduced at any stage of the typewriting course after the keyboard has been learned and a week or two of skill-building lessons have been presented.

> I shall ask you several questions. You number your statements the same as I number my questions, but you make your answers as short as you can. I'll give you an example. Suppose I ask, "What is your full name? Your answer, Sally, would be 'Sally Smith.'" . . .

> From five to ten questions might be asked, such as the following:
> 1. What is your full name?
> 2. What is the make of your typewriter?
> 3. What is the day of the week today?
> 4. What is your grade in school?

> The next day, the "think-as-you-typewrite" lesson would continue. This might be a simple word-association exercise. You would explain that today's drill would also be a short-answer response, but that the students were to typewrite the first word that entered their minds when they heard the cue word spoken by the teacher. As an example, you might say, "Tom, what word do you think of when I say 'sky'?" [19]

Russon then goes on to more and more difficult exercises until the students are writing short compositions.

Another beginning technique is to start the students on a sentence, an idea, or a paragraph and then let them finish it. For example: "I think the party last night was wonderful. I——" "As soon as I leave school this afternoon, I plan to——" In this connection it is best not to check on the typing for quality, spelling, or English. It's the *ideas* that count.

---

[19] Allien R. Russon, "Memo for the Future: More Thinking and Typewriting," *Business Education Forum* (November, 1960), pp. 15, 16.

TYPEWRITING—PART III

RESEARCH AND OPINIONS OF EXPERTS

In this part of the chapter we consider some of the research and some opinions on a variety of aspects of the subject of typewriting. As in other chapters, it is difficult to choose what quotations to use, particularly when several educators express themselves forcefully on the same subject. The compilation begins with a reference to something that has been in the news for a long time—typewriting for *all* students. It may be a pattern for the future.

III-1   Typewriting for All Students

When the new high school was being planned at Wayland, Massachusetts, it was generally agreed that every student in the high school should learn to type. How to accomplish this goal was described by Edward Anderson in the November, 1960, issue of *Business Education Forum.* The program involves the use of large classes—and portable typewriters. When these machines are not being used in the classroom, they are moved about the building wherever there is typing to be done. They are checked out much like books. Anderson concludes his article with the following statement:

> While it is true that the large-group method of teaching typewriting may be somewhat novel, ample evidence has been gathered which adds confidence to the faculty's ability to proceed with the proposed large-group program with a high degree of assurance in its success. One striking feature during the whole of the planning has been the desire of everyone to offer typewriting for all students. The students, the community, and the faculty have accepted typewriting as a normal and necessary part of the school's program and they have not considered it to be something which should be eliminated. Since all people involved are agreed to the

advisability and necessity for all students to learn to type-write, it now remains for the school to provide the instruction in the most efficient and economic manner possible.[20]

III-2 Basic Principles

Douglas, Blanford, and Anderson present the following list of basic psychological principles to be observed in the teaching of typewriting:

Principle No. I. All unnecessary stages that do not serve a useful purpose in the act as performed on the expert level should be entirely eliminated.

Principle No. II.   Possibilities for the development and exercise of all or as many as possible of the elements to be perfected in the entire learning process should be included in the set-up of the learning situation from the beginning.

Principle No. III.   Possibilities for each learner to progress at his own learning rate should be included in the learning situation at all times.

Principle No. IV.   When practice is given on any single phase of the learning process, the element being practiced should be presented in a natural rather than an artificial situation.

Principle No. V.   The teacher should regulate the intensity of the effort being made by the learner.

Principle No. VI. The learner should be working toward a goal that is reasonably easy of attainment.

Principle No. VII.   As the learner approaches the goal toward which he has been striving, a new goal should be set up so that he still has an incentive to work carefully. This should however, in no way detract from the satisfaction obtained from achieving the first goal.

Principle No. VIII.   The repetition necessary for the acquisition of skill should be discontinued as soon as it ceases to be effective.

---

[20] Edward J. Anderson, "Typewriting for All High School Students," *Business Education Forum* (November, 1960), pp. 11-13.

Principle No. IX. Ample opportunity should be provided by the learning set-up for relearning in a successive practice period what has been forgotten since the previous practice period.

Principle No. X. Learners should not be required or in fact allowed to practice when they are disgusted with their practice.

Principle No. XI. The learning period should be broken up into short units, since shorter learning periods are more effective than longer ones.[21]

Tyler uses a somewhat different approach in his set of nine principles:

1. Proper motivation is imperative. The learner learns what he is thinking, feeling, or doing.
2. The learner is stimulated to try new ways of reacting when he finds the old unsatisfactory.
3. The learner must have some guidance of the new behavior which he tries in seeking to overcome the inadequacy of previous reactions.
4. The learner must have appropriate materials on which to work.
5. The learner must have time to carry on the behavior, to keep practicing it.
6. The learner must get satisfaction from the desired behavior.
7. There must be a good deal of sequential practice of the desired behavior.
8. The learner must set high standards of performance for himself.
9. If learning is to continue beyond the time when a teacher is available, the learner must have means for judging his performance to be able to tell how well he is doing.[22]

---

[21] Lloyd V. Douglas, James T. Blanford, and Ruth I. Anderson, *Teaching Business Subjects* (Englewood Cliffs, New Jersey: Prentice-Hall, Inc., 1958), pp. 122-125.

[22] Ralph W. Tyler, "The Teaching Obligation and Typewriting," *Business Education Forum* (November, 1960), pp. 9-10.

III-3 Individual Differences

The handling of individual differences is perhaps one of the most persistent of the plaguing problems of the beginning teacher. Many teachers have worked out their own solutions. Scutro, for example, has found the following to be effective:

> I found a definite need to institute a system that would provide for individual differences in Typing I classes. This need becomes obvious after a few weeks of typing instruction. By the system that I devised, the class is divided into three groups, and material is presented at different levels of progression.
>
> Group I. The presentation of new keys is primarily concerned with the correct fingering.
>
> Group II. The presentation of the new keys progresses at a slower rate.
>
> Group III. The presentation is somewhat analytical so that students can take time in assimilating the new presentation.
>
> Group I. A group I student will spend a minimum amount of time on remedial work in typing. After the remedial work is completed, the student will allocate his time to the typing of two letters.
>
> Group II. A group II student will spend more time on remedial work. After the remedial work is done, the student will type one letter.
>
> Group III. A group III student will spend a good deal of his time on remedial work. More time is spent on typing a letter.[23]

Keffer combines a recognition of individual differences with production:

---

[23] Thomas F. Scutro, Jr., "Utilizing the Group Method in Typing I," *The Balance Sheet* (February, 1952), p. 257.

When a job is assigned and the student has had no previous training or experience in the technique for executing it,
the teacher demonstrates to the student the proper techniques
and methods of executing the job. This demonstration is
usually given to only one student at a time, since the demonstration is given when the student is ready to learn the
techniques required for the job. . . .

With this type of classroom organization, the time allocations of a typical daily lesson plan could be as follows:

    10 minutes   Warmup: exercise in textbook
    15 minutes   Ten-minute timed exercise in textbook
    25 minutes   Production work

This is a method of individualizing instruction in typing
in which all students are *taught* the *basic skills* simultane-
ously. Each student is given an opportunity to *develop these
skills* at his own rate within a planned block assignment.[24]

III-4 Standards for Basic Typing

The following might be of help to a teacher who would
like to know what might be expected of students in beginning straight-copy typing at the end of 18 weeks and at the
end of 36 weeks. These figures do not represent what we
would like to see, but rather what is happening in one
particular case:

A study has been undertaken at the State University of
Iowa for the purpose of determining the speed and accuracy
scores of first-year typewriting students. This study was
started in 1952, and has been continued to the present time.
The number of participating teachers, and the number of
students included in the study, have increased each year.

Copy was sent every six weeks to each of the participating teachers throughout the state. The teachers gave two
timings on the unfamiliar copy and reported the better

---

[24] Eugene R. Keffer, "Individualized Typewriting Instruction," *The
Balance Sheet* (November, 1960), p. 119.

writing of each student. These results were summarized for each six-week period. Condensed summaries for two periods are given in Table 1 and Table 2.

TABLE 1.—ACHIEVEMENT SUMMARY OF 2200 BEGINNING TYPISTS
AT THE END OF 18 WEEKS [a]

	Speed Scale			Accuracy Scale	
Percent	NWAM	*Grade*	*Percent*	*Errors*	*Grade*
Top 7	37-62	A	Top 7	0-1	A
Next 24	26-36	B	Next 24	2-4	B
Mid 38	15-25	C	Mid 38	5-7	C
Next 24	3-14	D	Next 24	8-13	D
Low 7	0-2	F	Low 7	14-up	F

[a] Students were given two 5-minute timings on identical copy which had a syllabic intensity of 1.30. The better writing of each student was recorded in net words a minute. Median speed: 21 NWAM; median errors: 5 in 5 minutes.

Table 1 shows that 31 percent of the typists were typing less than 15 net words a minute at the end of the first semester. Is this a usable skill? One-half of the students were typing only 21 net words a minute or less. Is this speed adequate, even for personal use?

TABLE 2.—ACHIEVEMENT SUMMARY OF 1800 BEGINNING TYPISTS
AT THE END OF 36 WEEKS [a]

	Speed Scale			Accuracy Scale	
Percent	NWAM	*Grade*	*Percent*	*Errors*	*Grade*
Top 7	51-79	A	Top 7	0-1	A
Next 24	39-50	B	Next 24	2-4	B
Mid 38	27-38	C	Mid 38	5-7	C
Next 24	14-26	D	Next 24	8-13	D
Low 7	0-13	F	Low 7	14-up	F

[a] Students were given two 5-minute timings on identical copy which had a syllabic intensity of 1.40. The better writing of each student was recorded in net words a minute. Median speed: 33 NWAM; median errors: 5 in 5 minutes.

Table 2 shows that one-half of the typists were writing only 33 net words a minute or less at the end of one year.[25]

---

[25] Cleo P. Casady and William J. Masson, "Realistic Standards for Beginning Typewriting," *Business Education Forum* (May, 1960), p. 25.

Of course, Casady and Masson say that we should not be satisfied with such results. One teacher brought a class of junior high summer school students up to 40 wpm in eight weeks just to see if it could be done. The 40 wpm represents class average gross on a five-minute straight-copy test with not more than one error a minute. There were 30 students in the class. We must develop basic speed as rapidly as possible—up to 50 or 60 wpm—so we can get into production and problem solving with basic skills that we can really exploit.

Russon and Wanous [26] give us the following straight-copy standards:

> The Tallahassee, Florida, guide uses the three-minute test and permits more errors if the student types at higher speeds. The scale is as follows: (First semester)
>
> 40 gross words, not more than 1 error a minute
> 50 gross words, not more than 2 errors a minute
> 60 gross words, not more than 3 errors a minute
>
> The Los Angeles scale specifies that there should not be more than five errors on a five-minute test. Timed writings in which there is an average of more than one error per minute are not used for marking purposes. Gross words a minute:
>
> | 40 or more | A |
> | 35-39 | B |
> | 25-34 | C |
> | 20-24 | D |
>
> The standards recommended for Baltimore City Public Schools, based on a study of the teaching experiences of Baltimore typing teachers and on a survey of requirements and recommendations of governmental agencies, business firms, and authors of typing textbooks are as follows: (5-minute tests)

---

[26] Allien R. Russon and S. J. Wanous, *Philosophy and Psychology of Teaching Typewriting* (Cincinnati: South-Western Publishing Company, 1960), pp. 51-52.

First semester of 4-semester course—25 NWAM
First semester of 6-semester course—20 NWAM

Students who do not achieve these standards should not receive a passing grade, *regardless* of the quality of their other class work.

Florida State Department of Education sets up the following scale for the second semester on a five-minute test:

50 gross words, not more than 1 error a minute
60 gross words, not more than 2 errors a minute
70 gross words, not more than 3 errors a minute

Connecticut guide provides the following goal: To be able to type unfamiliar matter for 10 minutes at a minimum rate of 25 words per minute with not more than 5 errors.

At the end of the first semester of college typewriting, the following scale may be used: (5 minutes, gross, 1 error a minute)

45 or more	A	37-40	C
41-44	B	33-36	D

The speed levels at the end of the second semester of college typewriting are as follows: (5 minutes, NWAM, not more than 3 errors)

60 or more	A	46-52	C
53-59	B	39-25	D

For a complete discussion of standards with suggestions of all kinds, the reader is urged to consult Chapter II of Russon and Wanous.

III-5 Knowledge of Progress

Tonne, Popham, and Freeman [27] offer the following suggestion for indicating knowledge of progress in typewriting speed and control:

---

[27] Tonne, *et. al.*, *op. cit.*, pp. 96-97.

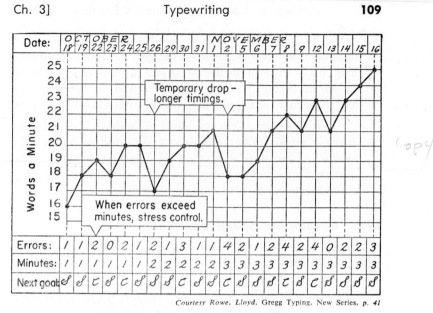

Date:	OCTOBER										NOVEMBER											
	18	19	22	23	24	25	26	29	30	31	1	2	5	6	7	8	9	12	13	14	15	16
Errors:	1	1	2	0	2	1	2	1	3	1	1	4	2	1	2	4	2	4	0	2	2	3
Minutes:	1	1	1	1	1	1	2	2	2	2	2	3	3	3	3	3	3	3	3	3	3	3
Next goal																						

Temporary drop – longer timings.

When errors exceed minutes, stress control.

Courtesy Rowe, Lloyd, Gregg Typing, New Series, p. 41

TYPEWRITING PROGRESS RECORD

Daily Speed Record

Recording Progress. The illustrated record form shows one student's achievements on his timed writings. Each day he selected his most successful, longest timed writing and recorded—

1. The Date. He wrote the date on the top line of the form, as the illustration shows.

2. Words a Minute. On October 18 he typed 16 words a minute. He showed this by putting a large dot where the 16-wam (horizontal) line meets the October 18 (vertical) line.

3. Errors. On October 18 he made 1 error on the writing that he recorded. So he showed this by inserting 1 in the first box below the dot, on the line opposite *Errors.*

4. Minutes. In the box below the number-of-errors entry, he inserted each day the number of minutes he had been timed. His 2-minute timings began on October 26.

5. Next Goal. After comparing his number of errors and number of minutes, he selected the goal he would emphasize in all his practice in the next session. On October 18 he wrote "S" in the bottom box, opposite *Next goal*, to show that he had selected *more speed* for his practice efforts on October 19.

The next goal is always speed (S) *unless the number of errors is greater than the number of minutes. Whenever the number of errors is more than the number of minutes, the next goal must be for surer control* (C), *with stress on typing more accurately instead of more rapidly.*

III-6   Developing Speed and Control

Speed and Accuracy Are Two Different Things—Require Different Methods. When we are typing to build speed, we should concentrate on speed, using all the know-how at our disposal to do the job; when it is control we are after, then we should put our control-getting devices into action. Later, at a less intense level, the two can be blended into a "cruising speed" operation. West compared typing straight-copy skill with performance-on-the-job type of activity and found the following:

> The characteristically near-zero relationship between speed and errors in straight copy work for those at intermediate levels of skill suggests that the factors that account for fast stroking are different from those that bring about accurate stroking—a finding which suggests that any attempt to build stroking speed and reduce errors at the same time will meet with limited, if any success. The two features of performance are apparently based on different underlying factors.[28]

West discovered another interesting fact. [Errors are unpredictable.] A person may make many errors on one

---

[28] Leonard J. West, "Some Relationships Between Straight-Copy Typing Skill and Performance on Job-Type Activities," *The Delta Pi Epsilon Journal* (November, 1960), p. 18.

test and few on another. He may make few errors today
and many tomorrow. The errors a person makes on any
given single timed writing may or may not be an indication
of his typing control. However, speed measured at one
time is likely to be as good an index of this person's true
speed as speed measured at some other time. "Gross stroking speed is the only measure of straight-copy proficiency
with genuine stability and predictive power." [29]
West also says:

> ". . . The low reliability of error scores, it may be added,
> is another reflection of the great complexity of the factors
> that have to do with straight-copy accuracy and suggests,
> as well, that practically everything we have at present by
> way of accuracy-development materials and procedures is of
> doubtful value." [30]

Control Techniques. The authors feel that something
can be done about accuracy and control even though some
of the symptoms are hard to nail down. Russon and
Wanous comment as follows:

> Formerly, the skill-building program in typewriting was
> based, in the main, on timed writings, ranging in length
> from one to fifteen minutes. Accuracy was the keynote of
> these writings. Its virtues were extolled by all early teachers
> of the subject. "Get accuracy," said they, "and everything
> else will take care of itself." The teacher spent most of his
> time getting his students ready for writings, starting and
> stopping his students, and checking papers. The modern
> trend is toward observing students at work. Today's teacher
> stresses curved fingers; quiet arms and hands; quick, sharp
> stroking; and continuous, rhythmic typing. He uses a variety
> of drill materials to bring technique elements into focus, and
> he spends far less time checking papers for errors and record-
> ing them. Instead, faulty stroking and operative techniques

---

[29] *Ibid.*, p. 21.
[30] *Ibid.*, p. 22.

are checked and corrected. The ultimate result of this new emphasis is higher speed *with* control. The skill-building program is said to be "technique centered." A host of modern psychologists support this trend.[31]

Rhythm. Rhythm is still an important factor in the development of typewriting speed and control, although few teachers still insist on metronomic rhythm. A typist working for the Nationwide Insurance Company and noted for her day-by-day output said it this way: "When I have just a small job to do, I usually dash it off without much attention to rhythm or to any definite pattern of operation; but when I have a job that is going to take me all day, then I usually establish a pattern of action based on an easy-flowing rhythm, something that I can keep up for hours. This is usually about ten wpm slower than my spurt speed. Since I usually spurt at 70 or 80 wpm, I would guess that my cruising speed would be about 60 or 65."

Tonne, Popham, and Freeman comment as follows:

> As early as 1890 experts knew that in order to type rapidly it was necessary to write many words or combinations within words as wholes—to type at the *combination* level rather than at the *letter* level. They have automatized the combinations that, for them, bring the quickest responses. Experiments have been conducted by which the length of time elapsing between strokes of expert typists were measured. Conclusions indicate four things:
>
> 1. Experts use a similar pattern in successive writings of any given word.
> 2. The contest exerts considerable influence on the pattern.
> 3. The individual pattern is peculiar to the typist, but agrees in general for those using the same fingering methods and operating at approximately the same speeds.

---

[31] Russon and Wanous, *op. cit.*, p. 25.

4. The pattern usually involves fast combinations of letters rather than whole words, although short common words such as *the* and *and* may form a pattern. The operator speeds up when automatized combinations occur and drops back to the letter level when difficulties are encountered.[32]

The Pipe-Organ Method for Numbers. Much has been said about the "pipe-organ" method of stroking the number keys. Until we have further evidence, however, we may teach the number keys the way we have always been teaching them, or we can use the pipe-organ method. It seems to make little difference. Garabedian reports:

> A total of eight critical ratios for speed were computed. All eight of the critical ratios favored the control group (finger-reach method); one was significant at the 1 per cent level; one was significant at the 5 per cent level; and six were not significant.

> Nine critical ratios were computed for accuracy, and all nine favored the experimental group (pipe-organ method). None was significant.

> While the finger-reach method was superior in terms of speed and the pipe-organ method more accurate, no significant differences can be attributed to either method.[33]

Speed-Building Program. Some teachers swear by one speed-building program, some by another. If the program is based upon sound psychological principles of skill building, if it is simple and easy to operate, if the students like it, and if they feel that this is the one that will do the job for them, then the teacher should feel free to use it. Douglas, Blanford, and Anderson suggest:

---

[32] Tonne, *et. al., op. cit.,* p. 100.
[33] Lilyan Garabedian, "An Experimental Study of the Pipe-Organ Method Versus the Finger-Reach Method of Teaching the Number Keys in Typewriting," M.S., University of Southern California (Los Angeles), 1959, 65 pages. As reported in *The National Business Education Quarterly* (Fall, 1960), p. 30.

A student should never be told to type as fast as he can regardless of errors. Such a procedure results in incorrect techniques and often completely destroys the student's ability to type with control even when this is his objective. The student will find when he attempts to type as fast as he can without considering errors that his fingers "become thumbs." He will clash the keys, have light and dark letters in his typing, irregular spacing, and other typing errors that are signs of poor technique.

What procedures should be used to build the typing speed of the students? Lloyd has made five suggestions which every typing teacher needs to observe:

1. Use copy that is easy until the student has made notable gains. Then use copy that is of average difficulty.
2. Each student should have a specific and immediate goal.
3. The practice should be timed in order to force concentration of effort.
4. Every practice effort should be repeated immediately.
5. The length of the practice effort should be gradually and slowly built from 1 minute to 5 minutes.[34]

The Right Kind of Practice. Tonne, Popham, and Freeman caution against putting students on their own too soon in typewriting practice:

Recently a class of beginning typists was observed at work. During the first half of the period they worked under close direction of the teacher. Their technique was superior. During the second half of the period they typed individually on exercises to be handed in for grading. The rapid deterioration in technique was amazing. They did not type rhythmically or keep their carriages moving; they snatched the paper out of the machine and started over when they made mistakes. They looked up at the end of the lines—and often in the middle of the line if they thought they had made errors. They violated most of the principles of good typing that they had displayed five minutes earlier. Why?

---

[34] Douglas, *et al., op. cit.,* p. 140.

The teacher had shifted objectives too soon and had relaxed his control of the learning situation. Students were trying for a grade, not for typewriting skill. Early in the course, learners need to work on short units with the teacher until they learn how to practice effectively; and even later in the course, the teacher should continue frequently to emphasize effective practice procedures.[35]

III-7 A Speed-Building Device

On March 1, 1943, a student at the Vocational Arts Center, Columbus, Ohio, volunteered to try a special technique known as guided writing (developed by Lessenberry) to see how much improvement in speed could be made in one month's time. The routine consisted of a daily series of five-minute timed writings followed by considerable non-timed Kimball Contest Copy. Five interval timers were used. The first was set for one minute, the second for two, the next for three, etc. The copy was marked to indicate where the student wished to be at the end of each minute. Goals were set at the beginning of each day's work. Frequently it meant slowing down on a particular test and the establishment of higher goals on the next try. By using this device exclusively, the student increased her speed from 61 words a minute to 111. On the 96-word level several tests were written without errors. The highest record of 111 gross words a minute on a five-minute test contained 1.2 errors a minute.

The Skyline Drive. There is no magic or secret formula for increasing typing speed. A review of the training routines used by champion typists indicates that the program is made up of: warming-up drills to secure independent, individual finger action, timed writings in which the candidate always seeks higher levels, and much practice.

---

[35] Tonne, *et al.*, *op. cit.*, p. 129.

The literature of business education contains many devices helpful in a speed development program. The device illustrated on page 117 has been named "The Skyline Drive." It consists of an individual chart for each student. These may be posted on the bulletin board or kept by the typist. In the illustration the uppermost line is the Skyline Drive. It represents the maximum speed at which the student is able to manipulate the typewriter. Any drill material that makes for maximum speed is used. The home-row exercise has been found useful. The typewriter is set for a seventy-space line. To compute their speed, students simply count lines—fourteen words for each line. The next line on the chart (No. 2) shows the results of one-minute timed writings on easy, familiar material with no error limit. Line No. 3 represents the results of one-minute timed writings with a control of one error a minute. The bottom line indicates the speed of five-minute timed writings with an accuracy standard of one error a minute.

Such a chart gives the student a whole series of incentives. The upper line proves to him that he can move his fingers fast enough to write at the speed indicated. With a little effort he can write sentence material, as indicated by line No. 2, at that speed also. In like manner the speed of line No. 3 can be brought up to that of line No. 2, etc. This entire speed-building routine need take no more time than fifteen minutes of the class period. A little additional time may have to be allowed for scoring.

Speed drills	2 min......	(The Skylines)
3 one-minute, no error limit	3 ⎫	Student selects the best out of three trials and records results on his Skyline Drive Speed Chart.
3 one-minute, 1 error a minute	3 ⎬	
1 five-minute speed test	5 ⎭	
Free time	2	
	$\overline{15}$ min.	

Local conditions will determine whether to have this fifteen-minute speed-building program at the beginning or

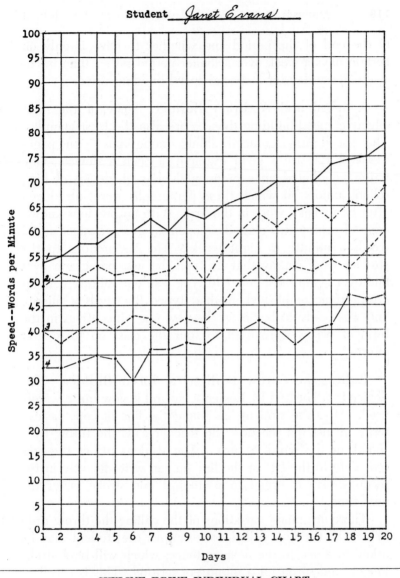

SKYLINE DRIVE INDIVIDUAL CHART
A four-week program to increase speed in typing.

KEY
1. Skyline Drive
2. One-minute timed writings—no error limit
3. One-minute timed writings—one error per minute
4. Five-minute timed writings—one error per minute

at the end of the period and whether to have it only on certain days a week over a longer period rather than intensively every day for a special speed-building drive.

A Speed and Accuracy Builder. Some of the most effective speed-building devices are also the least complex. The speed-and-accuracy-building paragraphs [36] on pages 119 and 120 are a good example of such a device. One writer conducted an experimental class, made up of high school juniors, in which these paragraphs were introduced after two weeks' work in the text. With no previous knowledge of typing this class developed an average speed of 42 words a minute in eight weeks. The instructions to the student were simply that he type the first paragraph over and over again until he could type it in one minute without error. If accomplished, he had typed 25 words a minute and was ready to begin on the next one. Incentives in the form of prizes were used to spur the class on to greater efforts.

Calling-the-Throw Drill as a Speed Builder. This device is advocated by Lessenberry and is now quite widely used. After the student has found the line of copy he can write in just ten seconds, the teacher calls the throw by a signal, or the word "return." The student places the current date to the left of the line he can write fluently in ten seconds. He is urged to write just one stroke faster the next time.

There are many variations of the calling-the-throw drill. When the throw is called, for example, the student may be asked to move to the next sentence, which will be a stroke longer, and so on for a minute of writing. This is excellent for establishing control. Another variation is to have a

---

[36] The origin of the drill paragraphs is not certain. The authors have used them for years, changing the content frequently to include items of local interest.

25 Words

You can build speed and accuracy at the same time if you will just give all the time to drill asked of you by your teacher.

30 Words

Each day you are to give, at the very least, five minutes of practice to these lines; all the extra time you can give now will count much for you.

35 Words

You are required to type this set of drill lines every day until you can type the entire group of lines with no errors. Give every bit of spare time to this sort of typing.

40 Words

As soon as you can type accurately and within one minute the lines on which you are now working, you are to proceed to the next drill. This drill has five more words than the one you have just written.

45 Words

By the use of this easy program you will not fall into any habit of slow, lazy stroking. You will be trying each day to raise your stroking rate. You will also be striving for good typing that is free of mistakes of all kinds.

50 Words

In typewriting, as in other skill subjects, you must keep right at it. There are no short cuts in learning to type well. You may be sure I would have found them if they existed, for I am a firm believer in doing things with the least possible physical effort.

55 Words

You may have noticed by this time that fewer and fewer easy words are being used in these special lines. The stroke intensity is made higher in each drill. You know, of course, that we find the stroke intensity by dividing the total number of strokes by the actual number of words in the drill.

60 Words

If you can possibly do so, type these special drills outside of the regular class period in the typing room. As you write in your class period, strive to maintain a smooth, continuous rate. Do not permit your stroking to lag as you type your assignments, such as letters, manuscripts, or legal papers. Keep your typing rate at its best.

65 Words

It has been said that the only reason for the existence of this machine of keys, cogs, and levers known as the typewriter is its power to increase speed in the writing of business letters and all sorts of legal and business papers. That statement is quite true, but there must also be added to this factor of speed the valuable quality of accurate typing.

70 Words

As simple as this paragraph drill may seem to you, it is most effective. It is a strange fact that we mortals seem to believe that any exercise must be difficult if we are to accomplish anything through its use. That belief is far from the truth. Actually, a simple exercise on the typewriter, repeated over and over, is one of the most effective ways of building speed and accuracy.

75 Words

At any time during your typing you find yourself making certain types of errors, do not fail to give special attention to the stroke combinations or words that cause you difficulty. Remember that it is just about ten times as easy to form a bad typing habit as it is to overcome that habit. That is something to think about whenever you are tempted to become careless and to neglect practice on difficult stroke combinations.

80 Words

A fact not often recognized is that a limited understanding of word meanings and syllable-division rules can cause a delay in the typing of letters or straight copy. As a general rule, the more difficult the copy, the slower the typing rate. Copy containing many words with double letters is spoken of as very "slow" copy. Not even an expert can type much over seventy words a minute on double-letter sequences, no matter how much he may drill.

85 Words

I once heard a young man who had reached the sixty-word rate in typewriting. He found that he was hopelessly "stuck" at between sixty and sixty-two words a minute. Drill and type as he would, he seemed to be unable to get beyond this speed level of sixty words. In despair he appealed to an expert trainer of typists. The expert gave him a series of simple paragraphs which progressed gradually in length, just as do these paragraphs you are typing.

90 Words

In two months he built up his rate to a speed of one hundred words a minute. He was able to write the hundred-word paragraph accurately in one minute. The expert also gave the young man many special timed writings and forced him to write each business letter at his very best rate, timing him on every letter. On the advice of his teacher, the boy entered the amateur class of the state typing contest. This young typist won his event easily, typing more than eighty words a minute for fifteen minutes--without a single error.

95 Words

Each day this young man typed away at the sixty-five word copy. He wrote for at least five minutes, timing himself on each writing of the drill. It was not long before he wrote the paragraph accurately within one minute. He then took the next copy of seventy words and typed it each day from five to ten times. Finally, he was able to write the seventy words in one minute. All this special speed writing was done during the daily practice period, along with other forms of typing.

100 Words

When you reach this speed, you are far above the average in your rate and typing ability. Careful study and thoughtful checking of thousands of typists have pretty well shown that the average student will be able to type at least sixty words a minute; that is, if he stays with his daily practice until he reaches the approximate limit of his stroking ability. When you are able to type this paragraph of one hundred words within one minute, you will have pretty good evidence that you can type between seventy and eighty net words a minute for ten minutes.

CALLING-THE-THROW DRILL

Return carriage every 10 seconds.

		WPM
1.	Avoid waste motions.	24
2.	Know your typewriter.	25
3.	You must try to learn.	26
4.	Keep your wrists level.	28
5.	Relax and you can write.	29

6.	Keep the carriage moving.	30
7.	Try to write with fluency.	31
8.	Keep your eyes on the copy.	32
9.	Check your errors carefully.	34
10.	Avoid excessive wrist motion.	35

11.	Never linger on the space bar.	36
12.	Avoid glancing at the keyboard.	37
13.	Analyze your own typing problem.	38
14.	Keep both feet flat on the floor.	40
15.	Throw the carriage; don't push it.	41

16.	Don't sit too close to the machine.	42
17.	Keep your elbows close to your body.	43
18.	Type steadily; avoid jerks and stops.	44
19.	Speed and accuracy are both essential.	45
20.	Type for accuracy as well as for speed.	47

3/1 — 20.

21.	Take your fingers from the keys quickly.	48
22.	Sit as far back in the chair as possible.	49
23.	Never practice doing anything incorrectly.	50
24.	Strike the keys with a quick, light stroke.	52
25.	Concentrate on the material you are writing.	53

3/2 — 22. *3/5* — 24.

26.	Type only as fast as you can type accurately.	54
27.	Do not let your thumb linger on the space bar.	55
28.	Strike the space bar with the right thumb only.	56
29.	Do not erase over the center of your typewriter.	58
30.	Learn to follow directions quickly and precisely.	59

3/15 — 29.

31.	Do not take your eyes from the copy while writing.	60
32.	Listen for the bell to ring at the end of the line.	61
33.	Know how to insert your paper quickly and correctly.	62
34.	Do not let an error upset your feeling of confidence.	64
35.	Learn the use of every feature on the machine you use.	65

3/17 — 32. *3/19* — 34.

36.	Take an interest in typing if you expect success in it.	66
37.	Use your little fingers as pivots to hold home position.	67
38.	No pupil ever learned to type by merely wishing he could.	68
39.	It is as easy to fix good habits as it is to fix bad ones.	70
40.	Insert paper with the left hand; turn it in with the right.	71

3/21 — 36. *3/23* — 38.

paragraph typed for five minutes but to call the throw at the end of each minute. The student will return the carriage and start to type the paragraph over from the beginning each time. One teacher uses five time clocks, setting them at one, two, three, four, and five minutes. As each bell rings, the students start over from the beginning.

Other Speed-Building Plans. Blackstone and Smith list devices as helpful in speed-building:

1. The teacher has students practice for high speed on drills made up mostly of common words.
2. The teacher has the students practice for high speed on speed sentences.
3. The teacher has the students write a short paragraph and determine the net rate per minute. Then he tells the students to practice this paragraph until they can write it five words a minute faster.
4. The teacher uses progressively faster dictaphone records, if such records are available.
5. The teacher should occasionally give long tests (for instance, of thirty minutes' duration) rather than three-, five-, or fifteen-minute tests.
6. If students are having difficulty, encourage them to keep a little speed in reserve; that is, have them typewrite a little slower than their top speed.
7. The teacher dictates single words or sentences and has the students write each word or sentence as many times as they can before the next ones are given.
8. The teacher uses alphabetical sentences, warming-up exercises, and finger gymnastics.
9. The teacher keeps a daily record of speed.
10. The teacher encourages students to write automatically.
11. The teacher gives rapid calculations, oral drills, and questions that must be answered as the students type; this device is used for the development of automatization.
12. The teacher pairs off students and has them maintain conversation as they type.[37]

---

[37] Blackstone and Smith, *op. cit.*, pp. 221-22.

Clem lists the following as being essential to the development of speed in typing:

1. Physical fitness.
2. Correct posture.
3. A knowledge of the keyboard.
4. Proper technique.
5. Smooth, even stroking.
6. Quick, snappy, but precise key stroke.
7. Efficient fingering ability.
8. Continuity of writing.
9. Ease of operation.
10. Ability to relax.
11. Elimination of waste motions.
12. Mental control.
13. Co-ordination of mind and muscles.
14. Motorized vocabulary.
15. Willingness to work.[38]

George Hossfield, many times world typing champion, gives five essentials for developing speed:

1. Accuracy.
2. Posture.
3. Rhythm.
4. Elimination of waste motions.
5. Sufficient practice.[39]

In a series of articles in *The Business Education World*, Harold H. Smith sets up a training routine for typists. Many of these suggestions can be used to good advantage.[40]

Sometimes the viewpoint of the psychologists can be of assistance. James L. Mursell discusses speed problems in *Business Education World* and sets up the following points:

---

[38] Jane E. Clem, *Techniques of Teaching Typewriting* (2nd ed.; New York: Gregg Publishing Division, McGraw-Hill Book Company, Inc., 1955), pp. 223-229.

[39] George Hossfield, "Five Essentials for Speed in Typewriting," *The Journal of Business Education* (October, 1950), pp. 17-18.

[40] Harold H. Smith, "Training Routine for Typists," *The Business Education World* (December, 1939), p. 290.

1. Acquiring the action pattern.
2. Slow practice and concentration.
3. Control includes movement.
4. Easy practice needed.
5. Changes in movement patterns.
6. Systematize the handling of make-up work.
7. How slow is slow?
8. Set up challenges.[41]

Lamb [42] devotes two chapters to skill building.

III-8   Evaluation

Stewart lists the following suggestions for handling paper work in typing. These have been rephrased to save space.

1. Check students at work rather than the work of the students.
2. Collect only a small percentage of papers for grading.
3. Evaluate some papers with the students during the class hour.
4. Have students proofread and check many of their own papers.
5. Save time in marking and recording work by checking one major detail at a time on all papers.
6. Systematize the handling of make-up work.
7. Sample student papers instead of doing them all.[43]

III-9   Quality in Typewriting

In a study made at Ohio State University, Fleser found the following concerning quality:

Businessmen tend to agree that the following four errors are serious and cause a letter to be unmailable: letters in a

---

[41] James L. Mursell, "The Problem of Speed," *Business Education World* (May, 1942), pp. 753-56.

[42] Marion M. Lamb, *Your First Year of Teaching Typewriting* (2nd ed.; Cincinnati: South-Western Publishing Company, Inc., 1959). Chapters 4 and 5.

[43] Jane Stewart, "Managing Paper Work in Typewriting," *Business Education Forum* (November, 1960), p. 17.

word slightly out of line, failure to space between words, in-correct division of a word at the end of the line, and presence of spaces within a word. Business teachers agreed with the businessmen that these four errors were serious.

Businessmen considered these four errors as minor errors: uneven left-hand margin, crowding of letters, inconspicuous strikeover, and too many spaces between words.[44]

III-10　Assignments—Priming the Pump

An assignment well made is a lesson half learned. Tate and Ross favor priming the pump:

> As four semesters of typewriting are cut to three or two, a great deal of production projects will have to be done outside regularly scheduled classes. . . . Did it ever occur to us that perhaps the practice of outside work in typewriting fell into disrepute because we did not handle it right? Did we plan our classwork so that students were adequately briefed to do such assignments effectively? Did we assign them problems, or did we assign them so many perfect lines of this and that? Did we really habitualize sound techniques before we gave them the responsibility of doing outside projects? Did we explain to them that proper work habits are just as necessary for homework as for classwork? Did we follow up with production tests in class? [45]

III-11　Production

The first edition of this book advocated building basic speed rapidly so that there would be as much time as pos-sible for production and problem solving. Since then we have had some research to support such a concept. West reports his facts in no uncertain terms:

---

[44] Clare Honaker Fleser, "The Effect Upon Mailability of Ten Type-writing Errors as Judged by Businessmen and Business Teachers," M.A., The Ohio State University (Columbus), 1959, 74 pages. Reported in *The National Business Education Quarterly* (Fall, 1960), p. 28.

[45] Donald J. Tate and Kenton E. Ross, "College Teachers Take a Look at Typewriting," *Business Education Forum* (November, 1959), p. 19.

In summary, about a quarter of the factors that underlie straight-copy proficiency are also those that bring about speed at job-type activities. Three-quarters of what it takes to be a rapid typist on job activities are not measured by straight copy scores and, by inference, are not being trained for when the training is devoted to straight copy skill. . . .

At best, none of the three measures of straight-copy performance shown accounts for more than five per cent of the variability in quality scores on the real job activities. Whatever it takes to prepare real typing tasks correctly is not being measured by straight copy skill and, again, is not being trained for when training is devoted to ordinary skill building. . . . Straight copy proficiency has, in general, no relationship at all with the *quality* of work on job-type activities.[46]

What should we say then, eliminate timed writings? Hardly. It simply means that we must recognize that timed writings are not ends in themselves. They are tools to an end—basic typing power, and control, and speed. When we have that, our job has just begun. Then we must go to work on the real job of getting our students ready for the office, and this takes much production and problem-solving activity. Speed in connection with one activity, according to West, does not appear to have much in common with speed required for any other type of activity. It is apparent that each activity requires its own special training. The old idea of transfer of training is applicable only in so far as we associate common elements with job activities and definitely train for such transfer.

III-12   Realistic Standards in Evaluation

What Does a Typist Do? What Is Expected of Her? Here is an executive secretary who gives us her answers. K. Takei states that the following skills are extremely important:

---

[46] West, *op. cit.*, p. 23.

1. The ability to compose at the typewriter.
2. The ability to set up tables.
3. The ability to punctuate properly.
4. The ability to proofread.
5. The ability to continue work after interruptions.
6. The ability to operate the electric typewriter as well as the manual typewriter.
7. The ability to get along with fellow workers and to face each job with the right attitude.
8. The ability to typewrite rapidly, with accuracy and intelligence.[47]

Erasure Tests vs. Customary Speed Writings. In commenting on the shortcomings of various systems of scoring speed writings, Humphrey gives us the following:

> The simplest solution to most of the problems seems to be to use copy tests upon which students are required to erase and correct errors. This procedure has been used at Iowa State Teachers College and observations during the years of experimentation seem to indicate that (a) students who "blow up" on nonerasure writings and become so tense that errors pile up seem to do better on erasure writings; (b) the slowest typists seem to relax and typewrite with greater fluency and accuracy when erasing is allowed; (c) the student who delights in the simplicity of the timed writing and resents any complication of the skill is the only one whose efficiency is apparently impaired by having to erase, and that in these cases, the score is a better indication of typewriting stability than the nonerasure, and (d) even though students seem to dislike having to erase, they achieve better rates than on "net rate" writings.[48]

Speed Tests Not Valid for Grading Purposes. Goldsmith says that timed writing results should not be used *at all* when grading intermediate and advanced students:

---

[47] K. Takei, "An Executive Secretary Takes a Look at Typewriting," *Business Education Forum* (November, 1959), p. 11.
[48] Katherine Humphrey, "Let's Use More Erasure Tests!" *Business Education Forum* (May, 1958), p. 25.

We can all agree, then, on the importance of timed writings on straight-copy matter. However, *they should be eliminated as a basis for grading.* They offer no indication at all of the typist's capability by business standards. . . . However, for the measurement of actual performance, there is really only one important consideration: Is the student able to accomplish a definite amount of work in a certain period of time with acceptable copies? . . .

We know that the disparity between straight-copy performance and production (based on business standards) is astounding. Students are able to type from straight copy at 30 wam, net, with little difficulty. Yet they generally type letters at 10 to 15 wam, or less. This inconsistency applies to all other projects of a business nature. Many surveys taken during the past few years indicate that accuracy requirements of the schools do not match business standards at all. Why? Because the emphasis has been on timed writings with certain error allowances; there has been little concern with *timed production* with the objective of usability in its strictest sense. Students have been taught to think of passing with a 60 or 70 per cent accuracy rating. . . .[49]

Goldsmith's grading plan is based on production. It contains the following elements:

1. The student's grade depends *entirely* on what he is able to accomplish in his class projects.
2. The classwork projects are *timed,* beginning at the earliest possible stage—preferably with the second semester.
3. It is extremely important that the classwork projects be based on both quality and quantity.
4. The student cannot pass the course unless he has demonstrated his ability to type successfully a minimum of two or three straight-copy timed writings. These are not counted in the computation of his grade; they simply constitute a course requirement that he must meet.[50]

---

[49] Samuel Goldsmith, "A Simplified Typewriting Grading Plan," *Business Education World* (April, 1959), p. 14.
[50] *Ibid.,* p. 15.

Production Standards Related to Student's Straight-copying Rate. Most typing methods books and introductions to regular typing texts give detailed sets of standards. Some indicate a certain letter grade if the student makes a given number of words a minute on a test. Recently in connection with production work there has been a tendency to relate the output standard to the student's basic typing speed.

Douglas, Blanford, and Anderson use the following in relating output to basic typing speed. The following standards are suggested for various types of production jobs:

a. Typing letters	2/3 to 3/4 the basic typing rate
b. Address envelopes	50 per cent of basic rate or minimum of 2 envelopes a minute (120 to 150 an hour)
c. Typing rough drafts	40 to 50 per cent of basic typing rate
d. Manuscripts with footnotes	40 to 50 per cent of basic typing rate
e. Manuscripts without footnotes	60 to 75 per cent of basic typing rate
f. Tabulations	25 to 50 per cent of basic typing rate
g. Stencils	4 single-spaced stencils an hour
h. Transcription from voice recording machines	25 words a minute
i. Typing form letters with envelopes (medium length)	10 an hour [51]

Things My School Didn't Teach Me. Forkner quotes a young office worker and lists all the things she wishes the school had taught her. Here are a few of them:

---

[51] Douglas, *et al., op. cit.,* p. 179.

1. The Use of Previous Reports. I wish I had learned to take that previous report, place it in the typewriter, set my tab stops according to the plan of the report, and then typewrite my report.

2. The Importance of Proofreading. I wish I had learned the importance of it while in school.

3. The Importance of Number Competency. I wish I had learned how to typewrite numbers at a better rate than I was able to do.

4. The Skill of Reading, Editing, and Correcting Material. Another job I have had to do for which I felt I should have had better preparation was the job of typewriting materials from rough draft and at the same time being expected to make sense out of what I was typewriting.

5. The Importance of Erasing Skill. It was suggested to me on the job that I could turn out a great many more letters in an hour if I did not take time to make corrections on the carbon copies.

6. Proper Organization of Materials. I guess one of the most bothersome problems I had to solve when I took this job was how to arrange the materials on my desk so that I would not lose time in assembling papers for typewriting.

7. Acceptable Production Standards. My supervisor pointed out to me that I had addressed less than one envelope a minute, whereas an experienced operator could do 120 to 180 an hour. I needed to analyze the steps I took in addressing each envelope and see if I could improve my rates.

8. How to Analyze a Typewriting Job. I think I would have been spared some embarrassment and certainly I would have been a higher producer if my typewriting teachers had insisted that I analyze each problem I had to do in a step-by-step procedure.

9. Problem-Solving Experiences. I believe teachers teach too little real thinking in typewriting classes. I find I

am continually thinking now about whether I can find a better way to do what I have to do.

10. The Value of Repetitive Practice. One final suggestion—would it not be possible for advanced typewriting classes to have more outside work so that students would get more experiences on actual work that someone is going to use? [52]

III-13 *Tricks of the Trade*

Every generation should not have to build from scratch. Each succeeding generation of office workers should be better equipped because of the experience know-how discovered by those who have gone before. From many sources these "tricks of the trade," or "Practical Office Shortcuts," as the National Office Management Association calls them, are handed down to us. NOMA has compiled a lengthy list of these shortcuts. Here are a few samples.

Shortcut No. 604. Common Practice: Transcription department typists read completed letters and correct their own errors, or rewrite the letters if necessary to meet the high standards of appearance required.

Idea: All finished letters given to others to correct or rewrite, after reading and marking by department supervisor. Usually given to extra girls or beginners in department.

Shortcut No. 606. Correction of manuscripts which have covers. Common Practice: The staples or fasteners are usually removed; then the sheets are corrected and refastened.

Idea: Feed a sheet of paper into the machine in the usual way until the edge appears above the paper fingers. Without removing the staples or fasteners, insert the sheet to be corrected between the paper and the cylinder and turn back the platen until the point where the correction is to be made is reached, then make the correction.

---

[52] Hamden L. Forkner, "What I Wish I Had Learned About Typewriting," *Business Education Forum* (November, 1958), p. 7.

Shortcut No. 609. Feeding of Several Sheets at the Same Time. Common practice: Common practice of average operator in feeding several sheets is to even them up before inserting around the platen, and then, after the insertion, to attempt to even them all up by pulling the paper release; but this never assures the middle sheets being even, takes time, and if they happen to be ruled forms, very often the items typed may be a half space too high or too low on the copies, so that it is hard to tell to which item they refer.

Idea: Roll a sheet of paper around the platen leaving the top edge projecting about one inch, and insert the copies or forms in the flap thus formed. If the sheets or forms you insert are even before you start, they will always come through even and trouble is eliminated and considerable time saved.[53]

III-14 Typewriting and TV

"Teaching by television," says Johnston, "requires training. The teacher who intends to make the transition from classroom to studio methods should be exposed to a minimum of six to eight months of extensive training." [54] The following quote will give the teacher who is thinking of going into this field an idea of what is involved:

Now, let me invite you to put yourself in my shoes, and you'll get an idea of what to expect.

You started promotional activities well in advance of the first telecast. You helped prepare newspaper releases, letters, and promotional films for the TV station. (Incidentally, an allowance of at least four weeks should be made for promotional work. High schools should be notified of such a course. Often a high school will agree to set up a class to view a televised course, thus offering an excellent opportunity for the teacher to have regular contact with the telestudent.)

---

[53] *Manual of Practical Office Shortcuts,* Compiled from ideas sent in by members of the National Office Management Association (New York: McGraw-Hill Book Company, Inc., 1947).

The success of this lesson was not accidental. Your show had the necessary ingredients: extensive training and mastery of subject matter on your part, plus the teamwork of the cameraman, floor managers, and director—and you.

Every lesson was carefully planned, practiced, discussed, and timed well in advance of air time. The lesson planning involved a listing of the objectives, activities, reviews, and assignments. This format was then presented to the director; he in turn decided the camera shots for every activity of the lesson. (It is not the responsibility, nor the desire, of the director to tell the teacher what to teach; how it can be most effectively taught *in terms of television* is his only concern.) The director must transplant the instructor from a familiar environment to a completely foreign one. The instructor should not attempt to direct the lesson. The necessity for mutual understanding, for an aura of teamwork, in this aspect of educational TV cannot be overemphasized. The director is a specialist in the field of directing; the teacher is a specialist in the field of teaching. Each must respect the other's competence in his field.

The time required to prepare for an educational TV program can be determined with a fair degree of accuracy by the ratio of one to twelve—that is, for every hour of air time, twelve hours will be required for preparation.[54]

SELECTED BIBLIOGRAPHY

Blackstone, E. G., and Sofrona Smith. *Improvement of Instruction in Typewriting.* Englewood Cliffs, New Jersey: Prentice-Hall, Inc., 1949.

Business Education Forum, November Issues, Typewriting, 1947 to date.

Curriculum Patterns in Business Education, The American Business Education Yearbook, 1956.

Clem, Jane E. *Techniques of Teaching Typewriting,* Second Edition. New York: Gregg Publishing Division, McGraw-Hill Book Company, Inc., 1955.

---

[54] Chester E. Johnston, "What the TV Typing Teacher Should Know," *Business Education World* (November, 1959), pp. 28-30.

DeHames, Dorothy Jean. "Speed and Accuracy Standards for First-Year Typewriting," *The National Business Education Quarterly* (Fall, 1957).

Erickson, Lawrence W. "Teaching the Number Row," *The Journal of Business Education* (October, 1956).

Kamnetz, Harvey. "The Relative Importance of Emphasis on Speed and Accuracy in Beginning Typewriting," *The National Business Education Quarterly* (Fall, 1956).

Kessel, Robert M. "The Teacher's Role in Selecting Typewriting Drills," *Business Education Forum* (October, 1957).

Lamb, Marion M. *Your First Year of Teaching Typewriting*, Second Edition. Cincinnati: South-Western Publishing Company, 1959.

Lloyd, Alan. "Typewriting Classroom Management," a series of three articles in *Business Education World* (February, March, and April, 1955).

Logan, William B. "Non-Projection Techniques," *Enriched Learning in Business Education*, The American Business Education Yearbook, 1953.

Rahe, Harves. "Review of Research in Typewriting," Unpublished Doctoral Dissertation, University of Indiana, 1955.

Rainey, Bill G. "Emphasizing Composition in Typewriting II," *Typewriting News* (Spring, 1957).

Russon, Allien R., and S. J. Wanous. *Philosophy and Psychology of Teaching Typewriting*. Cincinnati: South-Western Publishing Company, 1960.

Skinner, Charles E., and others. *Essentials of Educational Psychology*. Englewood Cliffs, New Jersey: Prentice-Hall, Inc., 1958.

Tonne, Herbert A., Estelle L. Popham, and M. Herbert Freeman. *Methods of Teaching Business Subjects*, Second Edition. New York: Gregg Publishing Division, McGraw-Hill Book Company, Inc., 1957.

Wanous, S. J. "The Need for Motivation in Typewriting," *Business Education Forum* (November, 1957).

CHAPTER IV

SHORTHAND—PART I

TWENTY-THREE BASIC PRINCIPLES

"There won't be any shorthand tomorrow," said a dictation-transcription machine salesman twenty years ago. The echoes of that prediction have continued until today. Gibson, for example, says:

> The teaching of shorthand will be affected, too. . . . Most dictation will be done on dictation machines of one type or another. . . . But of even greater consequence to typists and stenographers, and to accountants and bookkeepers, may be the growing practice of sending paper and magnetic tapes, cards, or other media by mail in place of a printed copy.[1]

It seems that in 1889, Thomas A. Edison predicted that the end of shorthand was not far away because of the invention of the phonograph.

But there are other points of view. Tonne says:

> It would be not only unwise but contrary to all the evidence to assume that shorthand will drop to a negligible subject in the secondary schools. All the evidences of job needs as found in the newspapers and employment agencies and the eagerness with which even marginally competent stenographic students are hired indicates the contrary.[2]

---

[1] E. Dana Gibson, "Automation and Business Education," *Business Education Forum* (January, 1960), p. 13.

[2] Herbert A. Tonne, "The Present and Future of Shorthand," *Business Education Forum* (October, 1960), p. 11.

Zoubek [3] lists survey after survey to show the desperate need for shorthand writers. Wanous quotes the *Wall Street Journal* stating that the shortage of stenographers and secretaries is one of the most serious manpower problems faced by American business today.[4]

For the most part, teachers are doing a good job in the teaching of shorthand. For the most part, also, at one time or another, about everything that needs to be said to enable a teacher to do a good job has been said. Now and then, however, the experienced teacher does not apply the knowledge that is available, while the beginning teacher has not yet had an opportunity to digest and use the materials that are available.

The purpose of this chapter is, therefore, to give a quick review of the old war horses, the time-tested principles and techniques of good shorthand teaching—psychologically sound and philosophically in line with desirable objectives. The reader will no doubt agree with all of them. The authors once compiled a bibliography of 600 references on shorthand and transcription. A sampling of 100 readings from this list showed that approximately 95 per cent, either by direct statement or by the tone of their writings, indicated that they favored the 23 principles listed in this chapter.

If the teacher uses these, he can't go far wrong in teaching shorthand. If he follows these, he need not fear a supervisor or visitor who might wish to observe his class. There are a thousand details that the perfectionist might want to consider—one can never learn them all—but any teacher can shape his teaching to conform to the basic principles listed in the following sections. Should he omit very many of these basic guide lines, it doesn't matter how many details

---

[3] Charles E. Zoubek, "Shorthand on the Way Out, Hardly!" *Business Teacher* (November, 1960), p. 3.

[4] S. J. Wanous, "Let's Break the 'Egghead' Stranglehold on Business Education," *The Balance Sheet* (November, 1960), p. 104.

he does right; he will still be wrong. If he *does* conform to these principles, he will, in our opinion, do a good job of teaching shorthand.

In Part I of this chapter, the 23 principles will be presented as briefly as possible. In Part II, teaching techniques will be given with examples of how these principles might be put into operation. Part III calls attention to research and opinions of experts. These items give additional information and document the material presented in Parts I and II.

I-1   Successful Teaching in Shorthand (As in Any Subject) Requires an Enthusiastic Teacher

Some people are naturally enthusiastic. It matters not what the subject, they have that effervescent urge to say something, and they want the world to know it. People often make fun of a person who rides a hobby, who is forever talking about the merits of his subject-matter area. We may have to tone him down at a faculty meeting and make him settle for half of his original demands, but he is liked. It is easy to whittle down a man's enthusiasm, but it takes dynamite to build it up in a person who does not have it. A teacher must have enthusiasm. A shorthand teacher should not be afraid of overselling his subject. Sharpe, to quote just one of a hundred who have written on the subject, says, "Few things promote success in the teaching of shorthand more than enthusiasm and interest on the part of the teacher." [5]

One can clearly hear the ring of enthusiasm, for example, in the following statement:

The shorthand teacher must have the drive and enthusiasm necessary to motivate his students to their best efforts

---

[5] Hollie W. Sharpe, "A Few Essentials for Teaching Shorthand and Transcription Successfully," *Business Education Forum* (October, 1956), p. 17.

at all times. A skilled teacher soon learns that his classes are quick to respond to his own mental and physical condition. If he enters the classroom tired and despondent, the class soon senses this atmosphere, and the students become sluggish in their reactions that period. If the teacher enters the classroom promptly, full of enthusiasm and energy, the class tends to respond in an alert, vigorous manner.[6]

If an administrator notices that a teacher who was enthusiastic is daily becoming less and less so, he should begin to look around. Dwindling enthusiasm, like a falling barometer, is a sure sign that something is wrong. "It could be," a University of Maine graduate student once remarked, "six classes, a study hall, two committees, a club, a ticket taker at basketball games, those never-ending duplicating jobs, parent-teachers' meetings, and—enthusiasm, did you say? Why, I'm thankful if I can drag this carcass from class to class!"

I-2 Know Your Shorthand Well Enough So That You Can Demonstrate and So That Your Chalkboard Writing Will Inspire Confidence

A foreman once remarked to a student who was working his way through college, "Why do you pass yourself off as a carpenter when you can't saw a straight line?" No person has a right to pass himself off as a shorthand teacher if he can't write shorthand and write it well. Many of the techniques recommended in this chapter presuppose that the teacher can read and write shorthand fluently. If a teacher is not satisfied with his writing ability, we suggest that he work through a set of tapes or other recorded dictation.[7] Better still, he should work through the series and

---

[6] Lloyd V. Douglas, James T. Blanford, and Ruth I. Anderson, *Teaching Business Subjects* (Englewood Cliffs, New Jersey: Prentice-Hall, Inc., 1958), p. 201.
[7] Mary Ellen Oliverio, "Selected Aids for Shorthand and Transcription," *Business Education Forum* (January, 1958), p. 29.

write the copy on the chalkboard, thus learning the shorthand and developing the ability to demonstrate at the same
time.

Many teachers suffer through years of inadequate presentations when they could be masters of the situation by
several months of concentrated effort. The teacher who
knows his shorthand can take his nose out of the book and
enjoy teaching.

Douglas, Blanford, and Anderson sum the matter up as
follows:

> The beginning teacher must possess three very important
> qualities to be successful in teaching shorthand. First, he
> should be highly skilled in shorthand. He should not only
> thoroughly understand the shorthand system that he plans
> to teach, but he should also be highly skilled in reading and
> writing that system. It is not enough for the shorthand
> teacher to tell the students how to write shorthand or even
> to write isolated outlines on the board. He should be able
> to demonstrate to his students the art of taking dictation.
> The teacher who is able to meet the same standards that he
> expects his students to meet will find his students will both
> respect and admire him.[8]

I-3 A Transcriber's Shorthand Does Not Have to Be Perfect to Produce a Mailable Transcript; Therefore, Why Be a Perfectionist?

Mistakes are a natural part of the shorthand classroom
experience. "Nontechnitis" applies to both the teacher and
the student. A teacher in this frame of mind will expect
his students to make certain deviations from the standard
book shorthand. Research has established that a person can
make a 95 per cent correct transcript from 71 per cent correct shorthand notes. Perfect shorthand is not an absolute
must in doing a good job. In a teaching atmosphere re-

---

[8] Douglas, *et. al.*, *op. cit.*, p. 200.

flecting this point of view, students will be encouraged to call attention to irregularities in the teacher's chalkboard shorthand. The teacher should welcome students' comments and center the discussion around some "do's" and "don't's" of correct shorthand. It might be said, however, that a teacher's shorthand should not be sloppy and should, perhaps, deviate not more than 5 per cent from the norm. This has to do with contextual material; words and phrases and preview material should, of course, be accurate. If the teacher is relaxed and enjoys teaching, the students will relax and enjoy learning.

I-4 The Teacher Should Create a Classroom Atmosphere That Is Free From Fear

It does not help much if we tell our students, "Relax, don't be nervous!" and then proceed to do the very things that cause tension: overemphasize grades, test when we should be teaching, dictate new material without proper preview, show by our actions that we are tense ourselves (not properly prepared, perhaps), maintain a hard-boiled, you-get-this-or-else expression throughout the period. There are hundreds of other ways to create tension, but failure to have a proper appreciation of Principle No. 3 is perhaps the greatest fear developer of all.

I-5 Make Students Want to Learn Shorthand

Volumes have been written on motivation. All this material points to the same conclusion: Unless a student really *wants* to learn a certain subject, our best efforts are likely to be in vain. As shorthand teachers, we need to pull all the stops to create enthusiasm for shorthand and an urge to learn it. We can create a desire to learn shorthand by having some of our graduates visit the class and talk about their work; we can point to ads in the newspapers, listing good jobs for shorthand writers; and we can show them what a joy it is to be able to write shorthand as we make frequent demonstrations on the board. But by putting into practice the basic principles of good shorthand teaching and learning, the teacher will have done all that is generally necessary to keep the fires of enthusiasm burning at full blast.

I-6 Tell Them and Show Them How Easy It Is to Learn Shorthand

The often-used first-day statement of the "tough" instructor, "Students, you are not going to find this course easy. In my classes I expect————," has no place in a shorthand class. Our purpose is not to show the students how much we know and how little they know; rather it is to show them that with the usual amount of study and practice in a brief time they, too, will be writing as well as we do. If the teacher sets the stage so that the students go home from the first lesson actually writing more rapidly than they can in longhand, he has won the first round. See II-1 for the story of a class that went home after the first session of shorthand bragging that they had written 60 wpm.

I-7 In Order for Students to Succeed in Writing Shorthand, They Must Experience Success in Writing

A shorthand teacher once had the diabolical urge to see what would happen to a new class if he arranged matters so that not a single student would experience success during the first meeting of the group. It was a night-school course in transcription—stenographers and secretaries from downtown who had come to the university to brush up their shorthand. The teacher took a letter from some text, a letter that had been used to illustrate *what not to use* in the early stages of transcription. There were over 50 error possibilities in the letter. The material was dictated at about 100 wpm. "After all," said the teacher, "this is an advanced class, the office is paying you for writing shorthand, so one can assume that you know *some* shorthand."

The bell rang before they completed their assignment and, incidentally, before the teacher could tell them it was just an experiment. A more depressed group would be hard to find. "Oh, well," thought he, "I'll fix it up with them when they come on Thursday. Then I'll give them something they *can* do, brag them up, everybody will be happy, and we'll go on from there." The trouble was that, even though they had paid their fees, only half of the class came back. Phone calls and explanations were of no avail. The damage was irreparable!

It is the teacher's business to so set the stage that each student will experience some measure of success, without which there can be but little progress. "Nothing succeeds like success" is a trite expression, but many of us have learned from experience that *success is crucial!* How the teacher can make sure that every student finds some degree of success will be shown later in Part II.

Success does something to the human organism. It turns the pessimist into an optimist. It changes the frown to a smile. It throws into the blood stream of the tired, listless person a new supply of energy and produces effects that are often startling. In United States Steel, Andrew Carnegie paid Charles M. Schwab one million dollars a year to manage the business because Schwab had that peculiar ability to bring out the best in people. He recognized their successes in little things, and soon they were able to achieve success in big things. The clever teacher, the good teacher, knows how to tap this reserve.

I-8 Read, Read, Read, and Then Read Some More

Another principle that has been documented almost to the point of excess is that reading in shorthand is *most important.* (III-4.) What shorthand teacher is not familiar with the "reading approach" introduced by Leslie! Current practice differs as to the amount of class time that should be given to it, but all agree that in the learning of shorthand, reading *is* important. There are cases showing that shorthand was learned almost entirely by reading alone. Businessmen are requesting shorthand writers who can read back fluently because more and more revision work is being done while the material is in the shorthand stage.

How the teacher can get his students to do homework in reading and how he can check the reading of an entire class in three minutes and yet have each person read are taken up under techniques in developing good reading habits in Part II. (See II-3.)

I-9 In Some Manner or Other, the Teacher Must Make Certain That All Students Are Learning, That All Are Making Progress, No Matter What the Level and How Mixed the Group

It is not unusual for an instructor who is teaching an adult evening class in shorthand for the first time to exclaim, "There are some students in this class who have had shorthand before! I thought these were supposed to be beginners! What shall I do?"

In his 20 years of post-high school shorthand teaching one of the authors has had only one class in which *all* the students were absolute beginners. At all other times—college, business college, adult vocational programs, day, evening—the classes were mixed. Whether teachers like it or not, this seems to be the *normal* state of affairs. If a teacher of an adult shorthand group should happen to have a homogeneous class, he should consider it a bit of heaven and then get ready for the next inning in which he will most certainly have to have effective techniques that will enable him to handle two and even three groups at the same time and do a good job. (See II-4.)

I-10   New Material Is Learned More Easily, Retained Longer, and the Job Is Accompanied With Greater Satisfaction If the Words Are Presented in Contextual Form

The cruelest thing a teacher can do to a shorthand class is to give the students a list of words, tell them to "learn them," and dismiss the class. It is the teacher's job to make learning easy—students can do it the difficult way without the teacher. The teacher's knowledge of psychology should make him an expert on how the human organism learns to recognize and write new words. He should be eager to organize his class so that a given body of material is learned with the least effort, in the shortest time, and is retained the longest. In shorthand it means learning brief forms and other new words in context. (III-6.)

In the section on techniques, illustrations are given showing how this can be done. In addition, these very techniques can help to boost shorthand class morale, help the students with their English, give variety and interest to the program because the dictation material used has to do with the things that are current and of interest to the student. See II-5 for techniques on presenting brief forms in context.

I-11   Provide a Constant, Day-by-Day Answer to the Question "How Am I Doing?"

The growth in shorthand power is often so gradual that the student is not aware of the progress he is making. He becomes discouraged and has a feeling that he isn't getting anywhere. It's like riding in an airplane. It is difficult to realize while soaring at 35,000 feet in a jet that the plane is traveling at 600 miles an hour; but when the jet comes in for a landing, and we see the trees and houses whiz by, we become aware of speed. So it is with shorthand. We need to give our students landmarks by which they can estimate their speed, by which they can tell the progress they are making. (III-7.) Only by knowing where he is now can the student set proper aspiration levels for himself for tomorrow.

In Part II-6 a procedure is outlined whereby it is possible for a teacher to check the progress of his students in such areas as fluency in reading, speed in taking dictation, knowledge of new vocabulary and brief forms, and the quality of the students' shorthand notes. The motto is: Check-up daily, but test only when necessary.

I-12 Accelerated Final Learnings Are Usually Obtained at the Expense of Terrific Effort

Learning takes time to jell. New material can be learned thoroughly the day it is presented, but at the expense of terrific effort; however, this same material can be learned with much less worry and pressure if learned partially the first time and then reviewed for several days until the new vocabulary becomes a foundation that the student can use for the next assignment.

How often do teachers become exasperated on a Monday when the students seem to have forgotten everything taught them on Friday! At such times it is difficult for teachers to realize that this forgetting, too, is normal. Like it or not, that's the way the human organism works. Just as the same dress often looks new because of a different collar and accessories, so the same vocabulary will sparkle with new interest when presented on another occasion in context with a different theme.

I-13 Encourage Students to Use Their Own Shorthand

To be effective, learning must have real, experiential meaning to the student. In the discussion of contextual learning, the use of the student's own material for dictation purposes is suggested. To add additional interest and to underscore the idea that shorthand is something he can use in daily living, the student should be encouraged to take advantage of his own shorthand whenever possible: Use it to outline assignments or duties to be performed during the day, to make up grocery lists, to keep a diary, and to take class notes. The fact that these notes will be partly in longhand does not matter. As time goes on, the longhand will disappear.

I-14 Eliminate Learning Blocks

It is indeed a fascinating sight at a football game to watch the blockers take out the opposition so that the runner may have an open path for his touchdown drive. The effective shorthand teacher removes all possible learning blocks in order that the student can proceed at the most efficient rate to his touchdown—to become a good shorthand writer.

In his zeal to do a good job, or because of a lack of knowledge of how the organism learns, a teacher may often block the student's progress and cause many additional, unnecessary drives. In some cases he may prevent the touchdown altogether. We are referring to such learning blocks as fear and tension, too much emphasis on accuracy, too much attention to unusual words, drawing versus fluency in writing, too difficult dictation material, poor work habits and poor handling of writing tools, much criticism and little praise, and in general allowing the students to form patterns not tolerated by the professional—habits the student will have to break when he reaches a certain level of proficiency or be content to remain on a mediocre plateau.

We are fortunate that it is the nature of the human organism to grow, to mature, to learn, to develop. If left alone, if no impediments are placed in its path, learning follows a curve about like that pictured on the next page.

If a block is allowed to remain in the path of a learner, the block will tend to slow the curve from its natural devel-

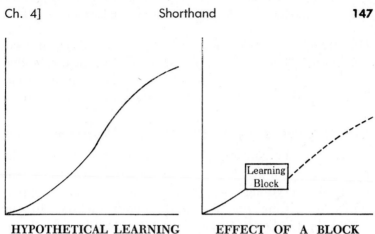

HYPOTHETICAL LEARNING   EFFECT OF A BLOCK
         CURVE   ON LEARNING CURVE

opment. It is the duty of the teacher to anticipate blocks
and to eliminate them before they do damage.

I-15   *Provide An Effective Daily Classroom Procedure Pattern*

In business and industry each day's work is somewhat
different, but the working pattern remains the same; that
is, until new research establishes a better way of doing
things. In the classroom the student should be familiar
with the way things operate so that he can get down to
business as quickly as possible. There should be no question as to the "machinery" of the skill-building lesson.
(III-9.)

A teacher should be able to justify every minute of his
classroom teaching time. Each three- five- or ten-minute
segment should do a specific thing, and the teacher should
know what it is he wants to do with that time. See II-7 for
a sample lesson with justification for each segment of the
period.

No matter what the plan of operation used in the
classroom, the keynote to remember always, according to

Himstreet,[9] is participation, stimulation, variation, and co-operation. These four words, with all the meanings that have been attached to them, in the hands of an enthusiastic and vitally alive teacher are certain to produce results.

I-16   Provide a Democratic, Efficient Classroom

In a well-organized classroom, students share in the responsibility to get the work done. A teacher who insists on doing everything himself robs his students of an opportunity of getting practice in democratic action. In one school the teacher had placed an extra desk in a front corner of the room. Each week a different student took his turn at being chairman for the week. Sitting at this desk gave the student an idea of what it might be like to hold an important secretarial position. In addition, this teacher appointed a class secretary. The chairman and secretary assisted with the routine work of the classroom.

I-17   Assignments Should Be An Important Part of the Daily Classroom Plan and Should Tie in With the Major and Minor Objectives of the Course

An assignment that does not clearly make a contribution to the basic objectives of the course as the student sees them is apt to cause resentment. The student has a right to know where he is going and that all the energy he is asked to expend is helping him to get where he wants to go. Therefore, the assignments should not only be clear and meaningful to the student—in writing on the board, if possible—but should also show how this work will contribute to the next day's work.

An interesting variation is to have the students themselves make the assignment. On such occasions students are

---

[9] William C. Himstreet, "Shorthand Can Be Taught in Less Time," *Business Education Forum* (October, 1954), p. 17.

likely to challenge each step with "Is that necessary?" or "Why do we have to do that?" If the questions cannot be answered, the work has no part in the assignment. On the farm in the winter time it is customary to pour some water in the top of the pump to get it started. This is called "priming the pump." In shorthand, too, we need to "prime the pump"—an assignment that starts the students on their work for tomorrow, gets them in the mood, and makes a valuable contribution to the learning demands for the next lesson.

I-18   Spelling in the Beginning Will Pay New-Word-Initiation Power Later On

Although it may be difficult to find the exact psychological principle undergirding this concept, there seems to be something in the spelling aloud of shorthand words in the beginning stages of the course that conditions the organism to the fluent writing of sounds according to certain principles found later on in the course. This spelling builds an association between the sound of the word and the kinesthetic action required in writing. What actually goes on, we do not know. We do know that spelling aloud in the proper setting, with the proper associations, does facilitate the writing from sound and does pay dividends later when the student is required to take new-material dictation. See III-12 for opinions of others about spelling as a shorthand learning technique.

I-19   Wherever Possible, Use the Gestalt Approach. Give Students the Experience of Discovering the Part From the Whole, the Letter From the Word, the Word From the Sentence

A photographer once took a picture of a lady in a blue dress. When he showed her the finished product, her remark was, "There's something wrong with your camera.

That's not the color of my dress. Why, look at that collar, it looks pink; it should be white." She was thinking of the dress as it appeared to her in the mirror. When the picture was taken, she was standing near a bright red door. The dress "borrowed" some of the red from the door. So it is with shorthand. Every character taught borrows something from its surroundings. Whenever possible, the teacher should give the character the "setting" it will eventually have. Then, if the student wishes to remove the letter from this setting for a minute to give it careful scrutiny, all well and good; but the beginning and end should find the new letter in a suitable environment. The letter "A," for example, should not be presented just as "A," but as it looks in "Mary," or better still, in "Mary made a cake."

I-20   Have a Systematic First-Day Procedure for Starting a New Class

All lessons should be well planned, but the first-day outline should involve some extra-special planning. Everything used should be sure fire. This is no time for experimenting. The method a teacher wishes to employ on the first day depends, of course, on his belief regarding the various approaches. If he believes in an extreme version of the reading approach, his first lesson will perhaps follow quite closely the suggestions given by Leslie; if he believes that reading and writing should go hand in hand right from the start, then he will need a different first-day plan for his class. A sample first-day lesson plan that might be of help to the reading-and-writing approach teacher is presented in II-8.

I-21   Care Must Be Used in Selecting Material for Dictation

Almost any material found in textbooks today is suitable for reading purposes, provided it is used in the lesson for which it is intended. Great care, however, must be used in selecting material for dictation. At this stage, it should be familiar, easy, meaningful to the student, and well previewed. An observing teacher will be constantly on the alert for anything that might act as a brake to fluent writing. Generally speaking, the most frequently used words should be introduced first. Most textbook writers have taken this into account in the organization of their materials. The teacher should not be tempted to introduce uncommon words of his own just because they happen to illustrate the principle being used at the moment.

In his first attempt at teaching shorthand, a teacher located all the words he could find illustrating the "ulate" principle. The list was a dandy. He was proud of it. He was happy, too, to see the principal when he came in. He was well prepared that day. That is, he *was* happy until the principal said, "Even if they all live to be a hundred, they still won't use all those words!" How quickly the principal had put his finger on a weak spot in this man's teaching.

I-22 Don't Teach Rules for Rules Sake: Use Them As a Support, if Necessary, for the Words Being Presented

At a recent convention a veteran business teacher told this story: "When Dad sold the old home place, he asked me to get a trunk which dated back to my high school days. In it I found evidence of the method my teacher had used in shorthand many years before. I found two notebooks: one labeled *Rules*, the other, *Dictation*. It seemed that I had failed miserably in the part of the course having to do with *Rules*, whereas I did fine in *Dictation*. I also found the final examination paper. The section having to do with rules was marked 'F.' On the back of the paper was the following comment by the teacher: 'I am passing you in this course, although perhaps I should not. In ability to take dictation you are good, very good; and your transcription, I must say, is also good; everything else, however, is bad, very bad.' "

Gregg himself once said, "When I first taught shorthand, I, too, made much ado about rules. Then gradually I began doing less and less with them. The less I did, the more fluent became the writing of my students." For many years now the authors have said little about rules. When a student asks a question where a statement of a rule will help, it is given. When the rule will help tie together a list of words on the board, there is no objection to using the rule. If a student is having difficulty and a rule will help, the rule is used.

I-23 When Evaluating Student Progress, Make Sure That the System Used Has the Approval of Your Students and That It Ties in With the Objectives of the Course

In adult classes, some of the best students are often the auditors. They have no grade to worry about; they simply want to learn to write shorthand. They usually reach their objective and are happy about it. Most school systems, however, require teachers to give each person a mark of achievement for the course. This is not too difficult if certain principles of evaluating progress are kept in mind.

Testing should do as little harm as possible to student progress (II-15). Students should be learning and reviewing even while being tested. Testing should be in terms of the objectives set up for the course. Business teachers, as well as those in the general academic area, have often been accused of pointing their teaching toward one objective and then testing for another. Formulating a fine set of objectives is easy; even teaching in the hope of attaining these objectives is also relatively easy; but evaluating these higher-level learning outcomes is often difficult. It has been said that the more important the outcome, the more difficult it is to measure or evaluate. Perhaps that is why we often concentrate on trivia when it comes to evaluating our work. Results of tests should, therefore, be weighed in accordance with the importance of the element in question. For example, a score on a word list is of less importance than ability to take dictation and transcribe.

Students should have a share in planning the evaluation procedure. An example of an evaluation procedure and justification for each part is given in II-9.

SUMMARY FOR PART I

Yes, that's all there is to it. Follow these principles and you will be on the right road, if your goal is to be a good shorthand teacher. Easy? Maybe. A supervisor in one school system made the following comment: "I once had a student who could list all the good teaching principles; she could even elaborate in detail when called upon to do so. When I visited her class, however, I found her teaching the way she had been taught and not according to the above principles. She overemphasized word lists, spent much time in having a single student read aloud, disregarded spelling, gave her class the list of brief forms 'to take home and learn for tomorrow,' failed to prime the pump, dictated material that was too difficult for her beginning class, did little or no previewing, frightened her students to death, used no praise, criticized often, and—well, I could hardly believe that this was the person who did so well in my methods class."

Therefore, in a further effort to make the foregoing principles a part of the reader's actual modus operandi, Part II of this chapter presents examples of how to put into practice the principles presented in this part.

SHORTHAND—PART II

PROCEDURES AND TECHNIQUES

II—Introduction

There are many ways to teach shorthand effectively. Some methods suit one personality; some, another. Condon and Wellman say, "Probably the one best method for all teachers will never be devised. A really enthusiastic shorthand teacher can get good results with any approach or method." [10]

There are many ways in which the principles presented in Part I can be applied. In Part II we shall illustrate some of these basic principles and, on some occasions, give specific examples of the way or ways in which they can be applied. The reason we present our way rather than pick one from the hundreds that are available in the literature on shorthand teaching is that we have used and refined particular techniques and know from years of experience that they work. These techniques are based on sound psychological foundations; therefore, we do not hesitate to recommend them.

II-1   Shorthand Is Easy

"Some time ago, my daughter Alice registered for a course in shorthand at the university," said a lady of our acquaintance. "All week long Alice was in a nervous stew. She *knew* she wasn't going to be able to learn it. Everybody told her that shorthand was difficult. Last night she came home from her first class. She was thrilled. 'Imagine, mother,' said she, 'I wrote 60 words a minute in shorthand. I actually did! It's so easy.'"

---

[10] Arnold Condon and Rowena Wellman, "A Challenge to Some Commonly Accepted Shorthand Teaching Practices," *Business Education Forum* (October, 1954), pp. 9-11.

Would you like to hear about this first-day class, the one Alice was talking about? We have all the facts; we know the teacher. This experienced teacher tells how he starts a class of beginners:

> I have a few minutes of small talk and chit chat about the weather or the headlines. I tell them what a fascinating subject shorthand is. I tell them about the famous men in history who have used it. I tell them about Leslie's statement that anybody who can learn to write longhand most certainly can learn to write shorthand. Then with a few illustrations I show how cumbersome longhand is and how simple shorthand is.
>
> "Would you like to see how shorthand is written?" Many nod their heads. That is my cue to put on a show. On this particular evening I used the poem "The Ship of State." I like to write poetry in shorthand. The meter and the rhyme seem to blend in with the rhythm involved in writing the characters. I write as I talk: "Thou, too, sail on O ship of state; sail on O union strong and great. Humanity with all its fears, with all the hopes of future years is hanging breathless on thy fate."
>
> "Before you leave this room tonight," I tell them, "you, too, will be writing like that." Then I erase what I have written and continue, using this paragraph:
>
> > Good evening. Here I am, and here you are. I can write shorthand. Mary here (pointing to Mary) said, "I would like to write shorthand. I would like to read shorthand. I would like to read and write shorthand." "See," said Mary, "I can write shorthand. I can read shorthand. My, my, I can read and write shorthand. What fun it is to write shorthand."
>
> After I have written this on the board, I read it to the class, pointing to each word as I read. Next the entire class reads the paragraph in unison. We read it several times. I ask for volunteers to read it. Soon everyone in the class can

read it. Then we start to analyze. We spell the word "Mary, M-a-r-y." We learn the letters and learn how they make words. We pick out other words and characters. It becomes a game. Everyone is amazed to find out how much he already knows, just by being able to read the paragraph. I often change this paragraph to tie in with some event that has made the news.

Then we start to write. They have been chafing at the bit to write. Now we are going to give them that thrill. I demonstrate in large letters on the board "good evening," etc. I show them how I make the "g" dig itself into the line. I show that some characters are short and some are long. Soon everyone is writing "good evening" fluently. I insist that they keep up with me as I write on the board. In like manner we work through the entire paragraph. Students help one another with their shorthand penmanship, but we make no effort at refinement at this time—it is the fluency that counts.

We are now ready to take the paragraph from beginning to end. When they get tired, we analyze. Soon they know all the characters in the exercise. By the end of the period most of the members of the class are writing at 60 wpm or better. I have had some beginners who have written up to 100 wpm on the first night, using this very same paragraph.

What have these students learned during this period? They have learned, partly (as all first-time material should be), the following:

Brief forms: can, go, I, write, would, and, it, is, like

Letters: e, a, h, r, d

Special forms: shorthand, fun

The technique of putting sounds and letters together to make words.

The most important thing of all: the fact that shorthand is written fluently and that it is fun. Nothing can stop us now.

II-2 Success Is Crucial

In Part I-9, the importance of taking care of the individual student's needs was stressed. The best way to make it possible for every student to achieve some measure of success is to have a classroom organization that is conducive to the "success for all" principle.

There was a time in the history of business education when contests were sweeping the country. Teachers often neglected the rank and file of their students in order to have a few champions shine at a contest. Consequently, a few students experienced a great measure of success; the rest, none at all.

A classroom organization and procedure that makes it possible for almost all to have success must emphasize, among other things, the importance of growth. When progress is pictured on a growth chart, the poor student will often show a greater gain than the one who starts out with a good record. There should be a variety of aspiration levels. Goals should be reasonable, not only for the class as a whole but also for each individual. If an individual reaches the goal set for him, he is successful regardless of what the others are doing. As will be mentioned later, dictation should be of such a nature that every student at sometime or other during the period will get all the dictation and will therefore experience his portion of success.

II-3 How to Handle Reading Effectively

In Part I-8 we made the statement that a teacher can check the reading of an entire class, regardless of size, in three minutes. The process is simple: The students work in pairs and are designated as "Student A" and "Student B." First A reads to B. B checks the reading in the *Student Transcript* and prompts A when necessary. At the end of exactly one minute, time is called. From the transcript the student determines the speed per minute at which A has been reading. If there were any errors or if promptings were necessary, he deducts five words for each error or prompt and immediately records the net speed on a sheet provided for that purpose. This done, the process is reversed and B reads to A. In not more than three minutes all students in the class have read, and the reading speed of each student for the day has been recorded.

In doing their homework, students are asked to give first priority to reading. Reading homework will therefore have a purpose. The students will try to read as fluently as possible, for they know that a daily check-up is made of their reading.

To the casual observer visiting a reading check-up of this kind, it may seem like sheer bedlam, but it works; and after a few days students accept it as a part of the skill-building pattern and actually look forward to showing what they can do. This type of reading program lends itself to a friendly spirit of competitiveness in the classroom.

In the beginning, as a "success incentive," the students may choose the letters to be used for the next day's reading check-up. Later on, the material for reading may be picked at random from the lesson for the day. A demonstration by an experienced secretary, showing how she and the boss work to improve a letter when it is still in shorthand, often helps to give the students a better appreciation of the importance of reading back fluently from shorthand notes.

II-4   How to Provide for Individual Differences

This fall we scheduled our usual course in beginning shorthand. On the first day of class we found that of this group of 20 students, only 12 were absolute beginners. The other eight had completed Volume I of *Gregg Simplified* or the equivalent. The class was therefore divided into "beginners" and "intermediates." The intermediates agreed to use Volume II of *Gregg Simplified*. Since the room is large, the intermediate group was seated around a table in the rear of the room; the beginners, in the front. After a brief introduction, the intermediates were left to themselves to work on their lesson for the next day. Full attention was then given to the beginners, using the first-day procedure outlined in II-1.

The next day and the days that followed the teacher worked back and forth, first with one group and then with the other, making sure that all members of both groups were working at top capacity at all times. In some exercises, like reading, both groups work together, each at its own level. At other times, while the first group is checking some material just dictated, the teacher works with the second group. By constantly going back and forth from one group to another in short blocks of time, the show is kept going. We never apologize for the set-up. Each group is constantly challenged by setting goals to be achieved while the teacher is working with the other section.

It takes a little practice to become adept at this sort of thing. When we have a new teacher who is not trained in handling a mixed class, we usually work with her the first day, divide the class for her, and help her get started. Even then it doesn't always work. In one instance we came back to visit a class only to find that the teacher had moved group B to the adjoining room. "You told me to divide my time between the two groups," she said, "so I put one group in this room and one in the other. I spend half an hour with the first group and then go to the second group." Obviously, she had not caught the spirit of the thing. When we went to the first group to find the teacher, the students said, "We don't have a teacher. She is in the next room." The secret is to keep moving from one group to the other, have *all* students working all the time, insist that the administration furnish the necessary record players, tape recorders, and any other mechanical equipment necessary for the teacher to handle this type of class. Often we have a tape recorder at each section and have the material needed taped in advance.

"The best job I ever did, judging by the progress of my students," said one teacher experienced in this type of thing, "was the year I had *three* groups of about ten each in one large room. I had to give the situation every ounce of energy I had, but we got results." In any multiple-section-class-in-one-room situation, class organization is extremely important. This is discussed under "Classroom Organization" in connection with Principle No. 16.

II-5   How to Present New Material in Contextual Form

We think it might be of interest to have a detailed description of an actual class taught by a teacher with considerable experience in handling situations of this kind. Here is a description of his nine o'clock class:

> This is Tuesday, December 20. The assignment for today was Lesson 65 in Volume I of *Gregg Simplified*, Second Edition. We have completed the usual work for today having to do with this lesson. The students have done a good job in preparing their assignments. The average score in most of the brackets—reading, vocabulary, brief forms, comparison, and speed—went up today. Everyone is in a good mood. This is the last week before Christmas, and the yuletide spirit is in the air. I have written the new words I want to introduce on the board.
>
> I say to the class in a jovial tone of voice, "What'll we talk about today?" "Let's talk about Christmas," they shout in unison. "All right! Let's get going." The students know by this time that the "dessert" of the class meal is preparing the contextual paragraph containing the brief forms and other key words to be learned in tomorrow's lesson. Many hands go up. All want to say something about Christmas. All have made up a sentence including one or more of the words on

the board. I hold their enthusiasm in check until we are pretty well decided what it is that we want to say about Christmas. Then we go to work. As the students dictate, I write on the board in shorthand. When the paragraph is completed, we work it over and improve the English. No matter how poor the grammar, no one ever makes fun of it. We welcome the opportunity to correct the sentence. When the paragraph is polished up, we put in the punctuation marks in color.

This is now their own dictation material. They have a right to be proud of it. It is their speed paragraph for the next day. The paragraph is read several times from the board to make certain that all can read it fluently. Then the students copy it carefully in their notebooks. If time remains, the paragraph is dictated several times to "prime the pump" for the next day.

According to this teacher, the paragraph mentioned above will be a part of the standard work for the day, an item on which the students will be checked for speed. It will be dictated at 40, 60, 80, and 100 wpm. As in the case with reading, a careful day-by-day record is kept of the student's progress.

If the teacher wishes, he can make a wall chart showing the weekly improvement of the class in speed. Some students like to keep their own progress charts in the back of the book, using a special form for that purpose.

II-6   How to Provide a Constant, Day-by-Day Answer to the Question "How Am I Doing?"

We recommend that students be checked daily on four factors: reading, vocabulary, general quality of their shorthand notes as compared with book shorthand, and the speed at which they can take dictation. The first three minutes is usually devoted to reading. How this may be done has already been explained. A quick spot check on the new vocabulary words or on brief forms, or both, may be taken at the beginning of the lesson. The procedure consists of simply dictating 11 of the words usually given at the beginning of the lesson. Students have had drill on these words the day before as a pump-priming exercise and have reviewed them at home. The first error is not counted. Students who get all words right get the same grade as those who get only ten correct. With that system most of the students usually get a score of 100 per cent on vocabulary for the day. Brief forms are chosen at random from those that have been learned at this stage in the course. Such a check-up usually takes about three minutes.

By a show of hands it can be determined how the class has done on vocabulary. If the class scored 90 per cent or better, it can be assumed that there is no difficulty with the new vocabulary. The teacher may proceed with the next step which is known as "comparison." In the assignment given the previous day, the teacher indicated a certain letter as the comparison letter. Students then know that this letter will be dictated in class and their notes will be checked with the book shorthand. It is not a speed letter; it is dictated so that everyone can get the take.

After all have completed the dictation, the students pick up their red pencils and check their shorthand with the book shorthand. Minor slips and phrasing are not counted as errors. Again students total their errors. The first five errors are not counted—a technique that helps reduce tension and fear. After the first five errors, it's five points off for each mistake. Students who have done some degree of homework usually get a good score. The class is then asked to make little five-word sentences with the words that caused them trouble. Usually the class scores 80 per cent, or better, which is all right. If a student should score low, for example, 50 per cent, the teacher should work with the student to discover the difficulty.

The final check for the day is for speed in taking dictation. The exercise used is the special paragraph which was developed the previous day. This is again placed on the board. The class chairman for the week usually has it written before the bell rings. Students read in unison and improve the chairman's shorthand where necessary. The teacher may then dictate it slowly—usually 40 wpm. If a student can read it back fluently from his own notes, he is entitled to put down a score of 40 wpm for the day; those who do not get 40, get 20 for trying. The same procedure is followed for the 60 speed, the 80, and the 100. Toward the end of the year some may want to take it at 120. As the students gain power and a definite fluent pattern of writing is established, book material is gradually introduced for dictation.

The papers containing the scores on the four factors are then passed to the class chairman, who, with her assistants, records the results on a master blank provided for that purpose.

The period is now half over. The students have been reading and writing shorthand every minute. They have been learning, and at the same time both they and the teacher have obtained an accurate record of their progress. The remainder of the period is devoted to the assignment for the next class, previewing, priming of the pump, and taking dictation from the material in the day's lesson.

II-7   How to Set Up An Effective Daily Classroom Procedure

Class organization and procedure go hand in hand. To keep in operation any given procedure requires a classroom organization that will make such a procedure possible. Every class, including shorthand, should make its contribution to student growth in an understanding of democratic group action and should give the student practice in developing such personality traits as initiative, resourcefulness, poise, and ability to speak before a group—just to mention a few.

The procedures outlined below assume a chairman and a class secretary who automatically take over when the teacher is not there. There may be other assistants if the class is large enough to warrant them. Where possible, a special desk might be set aside for the class chairman to give him prestige. These class officials will be referred to from time to time in the procedure discussions.

It takes a few minutes for the student to adjust himself when he comes to one class after having left another. A preacher was once asked, "What's the most difficult thing about being a preacher?" He answered without hesitation, "Going from one mood to another. Take today for example: I was at a boy scout picnic this morning; I had a funeral this afternoon; and tonight I have a wedding." Students who have just come from a lively discussion in a social studies class will find it difficult to get down to business in a skill class without some time to adjust. A few minutes given to routine matters will give the class a chance to settle. The experienced teacher can sense when the class is ready to get down to serious business.

It is a good thing to divide the class time into teaching blocks; then know just what you want to do in each block. For variety, these blocks may be juggled about. Teachers usually expect students to do homework and check to see that this work is done. Therefore, the first part of the period is given over to a quick check-up on reading, vocabulary, comparison of the student's notes with book shorthand, and speed. How this is done has already been discussed. Every minute of this check-up time is also making its contribution to shorthand learning. The results of the check-up are given to the class chairman who, with his assistants, sees to it that the results are recorded. At stated intervals the teacher computes the average to date. It is a good thing to check the papers carefully now and then to make sure that all scores recorded are authentic. These averages come in handy when it is time to make an evaluation at the end of the term. Scores during the last two weeks are, of course, more significant than those made near the beginning. This check-up portion of the lesson is known as Block No. 1.

Block No. 2 consists of the assignment and the "priming of the pump." Here the students are actually started on their homework for the next lesson. The assignment is written on the board, off to the side. The basic items in the assignment are the factors involved in the daily check-up. To get ready for the vocabulary, the words are written on the board; teacher and students go through the quick customary drill—not to learn the words, but just to get familiar with them. Attention is called to the "comparison" paragraph for tomorrow. The main feature of the assignment is the development of the speed paragraph, a technique for presenting brief forms and new words in context. This procedure has already been described in detail under "contextual learning."

The pump well primed, the teacher then goes on with Block No. 3. This is dictation with books open, not for speed, but for practice in taking semi-familiar material. Students already know how to read this material fluently—demonstrated in the check-up at the beginning of the period. Every portion of class time has been used effectively in reading and writing shorthand.

A classroom-procedure pattern is different from a daily lesson plan. The procedure pattern is the framework into which the daily lesson plan fits and to which it must adjust itself. The classroom-procedure pattern, once carefully worked out, is generally not changed during a term, while the activities within the framework are moved about and changed frequently.

THE SHORTHAND RECTANGLE
(A student-teacher project on procedures)

ACTIVITY   TIME

Warm up.................................... 2 minutes
    Students write memorized material on
    blackboard or in notebooks. They start
    as soon as they enter the room.

Check-up on Reading Speed................... 3 minutes
    Students work in pairs; read to each
    other from the day's lesson for one
    minute; record score.

Daily Brief Form Check-up................... 3 minutes
    Students compose paragraph using the
    brief forms under consideration. They
    take this material from dictation, check-
    ing key words.

Word List Check-up.......................... 3 minutes
    This is used on days when there are no
    new brief forms. Same procedure.

Preview on Today's Dictation................ 3 minutes
    This is today's lesson, the material
    introduced yesterday.

Dictation on Today's Lesson.................10 minutes
    Students can read this material flu-
    ently; have had preview and review.
    Good average speed; no undue pressure.

Presentation of Tomorrow's Lesson........... 4 minutes
    Here the Leslie technique is used--
    spell, spell, spell; also special pre-
    view of tomorrow's speed letter.

Today's Speed Letter or Paragraph..........10 minutes
    Students have prepared this material
    especially for speed building. This is
    an intensive drive for maximum speed.

Dictation for Transcription................. 3 minutes
    In early stages, taken from today's
    lesson; later, on easy new material.

Transcription.............................. 7 minutes
    All students transcribe one short exer-
    cise; good students do additional work.

Closing Activities......................... 2 minutes
    Time clock rings two minutes before
    regular bell to give students time to
    set room in order.

TOTAL TIME.................................50 minutes

"Operation Rectangle" on page 166 is the result of the working of the entire class on the project. This is how they preferred to spend the period. It may not be perfect in every respect, but it is how they wanted to use their time.

II-8   How to Evaluate in Terms of Objectives

Just as the skill-building machinery should be definite, well organized, and accepted by the student, so the evaluation techniques should follow a consistent pattern, should be accepted by the student, and should stress those factors which form the foundation of the course. These techniques should cause as little interruption as possible to the normal progress of learning. It is doubtful if any test or examination given for the purpose of establishing marks, except as it shows the student how he is getting along, actually helps him to learn shorthand, or helps him to increase his speed. What then is a good mid-term or end-of-term evaluation device? The following is a suggestion. It has been developed over the years and has been reviewed by many graduate school classes for its psychological soundness. Each new group should accept it before it is put into operation.

The mid-term and the final evaluation are made up of two parts: the daily averages, with emphasis placed on the near-the-end-of-term scores, and the mid-term and final examinations. All these scores are placed on the student's evaluation sheet, a sample of which is shown on the following page. Part I is simply an average of those factors, which were checked on at the beginning of the period throughout the term. The second part is a formal test on these same factors during the final examination.

As can be seen on the evaluation sheet, the much-discussed word list forms only a small part of the total score. Ten per cent of the student's errors are not counted. If the student is too far down in his ability to write words correctly, however, it is a sign of weakness, and it should

EVALUATION SHEET FOR BEGINNING (FIRST YEAR) SHORTHAND
First Semester

The purpose of this form is to provide a systematic plan
and worksheet for determining the student's grade for the
semester. The shorthand curriculum is divided into two
major parts: 1. Beginning shorthand, two semesters.
2. Advanced shorthand and transcription, two semesters.
Beginning shorthand is again divided into two parts:
(a) basic shorthand, and (b) speed building and introduction to transcription.

OBJECTIVES FIRST SEMESTER

1. To write shorthand fluently in good form, fine
   distinction between length of lines and size of
   circles. Minimum cruising speed* during semester
   on easy, familiar material, 60 wpm.
2. To be able to read back fluently dictated and text
   material.
3. By the end of the semester the student should know
   all of the brief forms and should be able to take
   dictation fluently on brief form material.
4. Should know vocabulary covered with 85 per cent
   accuracy.
5. Should become progressively more fluent in initiating outlines not specifically given in text but for
   which principles have been established.
6. The quality of student's shorthand should compare
   favorably (in principle) with material in text.

GRADE SUMMARY SHEET

(Summary of accumulated daily averages)

Reading: Actual speed per minute _____ x ½   _____

Brief Forms: Actual score in terms of 100
   per cent   _____

Vocabulary: A 90 per cent accurate paper equals
   score of 100 per cent   _____

Quality: 85 per cent accuracy on general con-
   formity with text required (After that, 5
   points off for each error)   _____

Dictation speed: Material dictated at 60, 80,
   100 wpm (Fluent reading back required)
   Score = speed x 2   _____

TOTAL SCORE ON DAILY WORK   _____

FINAL EXAMINATION (Or Midterm)

Reading: Actual speed per minute _____ x ½   _____

Brief Forms: Actual score in terms of 100
      per cent   _____

Vocabulary: A 90 per cent accurate papers equals
      score of 100 per cent   _____

Quality: 85 per cent accuracy on general con-
      formity with text required (After that, 5
      points off for each error)   _____

Dictation speed: Material dictated at 60, 80,
      100 wpm (Fluent reading back required)
      Score = speed x 2   _____

          FINAL OR MID-TERM TOTAL   _____

          GRAND TOTAL DAILY AND EXAM   _____

          FINAL GRADE FOR THE TERM   _____

---

* Since students write 60 wpm beginning with the first class period,
it is assumed that they will maintain this basic minimum speed as the
material becomes progressively more difficult. After a few weeks, the
daily speed takes will range from 60 to 100 wpm.

have something to do with his score. Brief forms are
checked in the same way. Here a greater degree of accuracy is expected. The reading score is the speed made on
a one-minute reading test—the better of the trials. So that
not too much weight is given to reading, the speed is
divided by two in order to obtain the reading score for
evaluation purposes. Quality of shorthand is also a factor.
Here the first 15 per cent of errors made are not counted.
Two letters are dictated at a moderate speed. The students
check the better of the two. With all these advantages in
his favor, if a student still makes a low score, one may be
sure that he is not doing satisfactory work.

The most significant factor of the evaluation plan is the
ability to take dictation and transcribe it. Again, as can be
seen from a study of the evaluation sheet, the speed at

which the student is able to take dictation is the score, only in this case the score is doubled. A student who can take and transcribe at 80 wpm merits a score in dictation of 160. Since we are talking about beginning shorthand, the material used should be familiar; therefore, the dictation used for the test is taken from the daily speed paragraph. Selections are chosen at random. One is dictated at 40, another at 60, another at 80, and one at 100—and even 120, if there is demand for that speed.

If the class is made up of different ability levels—some who have had previous shorthand, some who have not—a handicap system similar to that in common use in bowling or golf can be used. The students understand this and readily accept it. It does away with the resentment often found among beginners when forced to compete on even terms with those who entered the class with previous training in shorthand.

The importance of objectives mutually established and cooperatively achieved can hardly be denied. What do student-teacher-formulated objectives look like? The following is a copy of the list of objectives agreed upon in a class in second-semester shorthand at an eastern university. It will serve as an illustration. "Be it hereby agreed," said the class, "that by the end of the term we want to reach these goals, and we want to do the things which are listed below:

1. Write shorthand so that we can read it back fluently. Remarks made by graduates now working, quotations from executives, comments heard at a meeting, all put together have convinced us of the need for this skill.

2. Practice reading shorthand outside of class; we think this will help us read back more fluently and will help us with our shorthand.

3. We would like to be able to take dictation on new matter, not *too* difficult, at about 100 words a minute.

4. Those of us who could write some shorthand when we came would like to develop speeds as high as possible, maybe 120 or so.

5. We would like to do a little transcription each day so as to give us a good start for the regular transcription course next fall. It will help us to get jobs. Some of us do not plan to return to school.

6. We are still a little rusty on brief forms. We think we should take up again the brief form paragraphs as we used to do (context brief form matter).

7. We think we did better when you tested us now and then on words, especially since these tests did not affect our grades.

8. We think the speed-building drive should be harder and longer. Sometimes we stop just when we are getting warmed up.

9. Since some of us are planning to become teachers, we should like more experience in writing on the blackboard."

These are the objectives, then, that guided the efforts of teacher and student in this particular class. Whether or not these objectives are valid is for the moment beside the point. The important thing is that in the light of their present understanding, both teacher and class agreed that *this* is what they wanted to accomplish during the coming term. Having established what the class wanted to accomplish, the next step followed quite logically—how should these goals be accomplished?

Since the students are the ones who have to do the work, they should have a share in establishing the procedures by means of which these objectives are to be accomplished—with the help and guidance of the teacher. Usually an objective can be accomplished by one of several different routes. If the class likes the "scenic route" best, it should be taken, even if there is a small detour.

Teacher and students should work together in planning the best way to evaluate learning outcomes in the light of mutually established objectives. How well have we done that which we mutually agreed we wanted to do and have done by mutually developed procedures? Pupil-teacher planning in this area is relatively rare. The first step is to make the transition from the "I" to the "we" attitude. It is not so much a matter of how well did I do as a teacher or how well did the student do, but rather, how effective have *we*, the student-teacher combination, been in realizing our objectives? After much discussion and frequent revisions, the following plan was agreed upon by class and teacher as the best and fairest method to evaluate the work of the period and to translate such evaluation into the necessary school marks.

```
          FIVE-PART GRADING PLAN FOR SHORTHAND
         (A teacher-pupil project in evaluation)

  ITEM                                            SCORE

     Reading
         One-half student's actual reading speed.  If
         student reads 240 words a minute, his score
         will be....................................... 120

     Brief Forms
         Actual per cent of key words given in
         context.  If a student misses one out of
         20 words, his score will be.................  95

     Word Lists
         Only 85 per cent accuracy required.  If a
         student writes 80 words out of 100 correctly,
         his score will still be.....................  95

     Dictation Speed
         The score is double the dictation speed.
         If a student takes dictation at 110, his
         score will be............................... 220

     Transcription
         A USABLE transcript merits 100 points.
         Five points are deducted for each error.  If
         a student makes two errors, his score will be  90

  TOTAL SCORE IN POINTS.............................. 620
```

A student-teacher grading committee can be quite helpful in preventing misunderstandings in the area of evaluation. Such a committee usually consists of three members;
the teacher and two students, usually a boy and a girl.
The students are elected by the class. It is the business of
this committee to assign grades on the basis of the pattern
outlined above. Students are urged to bring any complaints
directly to the student members of this committee and then
if necessary to the teacher. There are very few complaints
and still fewer that need the attention of the teacher.

SHORTHAND—PART III

RESEARCH AND OPINIONS OF EXPERTS

III—Introduction

In Part I of this chapter, 23 principles of good shorthand teaching were stated; in Part II, some illustrations of
how these principles might be put into operation were presented. In the final portion, Part III, we should like to
undergird the principles stated earlier with pertinent research or opinions of experts working in the area of shorthand.

III-1 Shorthand Does Not Have to Be Perfect to Be Functional

Tonne, Popham, and Freeman join others in stating that
the stenographer can do a good job of transcribing even if
her notes are not entirely perfect:

> Phillips and Saunders, King, Lockwood, and others found
> that notes only 71 per cent accurate would produce transcripts
> that are at least 95 per cent correct. In other words, extreme

attention to the accuracy of notes, which has been emphasized very greatly in the past, is hardly justified. Of course, the teacher should not forget that when a person is taking dictation, his notes will be as accurate as they are during practice periods and that a much higher degree of accuracy must be required at the practice level in order to attain 71 per cent accuracy of notes under dictation conditions.[11]

We need to be better in practice under ideal conditions than we are required to be for the job-getting test. This is as true for accuracy as it is for speed. If the job requirements are 100 wpm, we make sure that our students can take 120 wpm with ease. They need that extra margin. Recently we sent a girl to take a civil service test for a job with the Navy. The requirements were that she take 80 wpm. She was taking 100 wpm regularly in class; yet she failed the test. Why? "Too fast for me," she said.

III-2   Students Should Write Rapidly, Fluently, Right From the Beginning

We have already stated that it is possible for a class to write 60 wpm or better at the beginning of the course, in fact, at the end of the first class period. Condon and Wellman, for example, give us the following:

> How they write is more important than *what* they write. Development of fluent writing habits is of prime importance. Students must not be allowed to begin with slow, plodding initial writing habits; once such slow habits are established, it is extremely difficult to change them. . . . One should be sure, therefore, that the first writing the student does is fluent writing. Do not worry about proportion, slant, and other details. Precision will come later, as is true in all skills.[12]

---

[11] Herbert Tonne, Estelle Popham, and M. Herbert Freeman, *Methods of Teaching Business Subjects* (2d. ed.; New York: Gregg Publishing Division, McGraw-Hill Book Company, Inc., 1957), p. 141.

[12] Condon and Wellman, *loc. cit.*

III-3 The Human Organism Needs Success to Develop Normally

Presidio, a magazine published by the Iowa State Prison, quotes *School and Society,* September 27, 1958, in the article, "Were the Starkweather Murders Necessary?" Starkweather was the young man from Lincoln, Nebraska, who committed a long string of murders before he was finally apprehended and later executed. There was much discussion as to the why of it. This article concludes with:

> Any school that succeeds in making a child feel he really belongs as a respected member of his group reduces the number who grow up to become criminals. Good schools provide learning experiences in which all children achieve a degree of success. Not only does success help to make good citizens, it helps to do the job we need to do in the classroom.

III-4 A Good Reading Program Is Essential to Skill Development in Shorthand

Concerning the importance of reading, Rowe has this to say:

> The reading of shorthand plates is the best avenue to familiarity with correct, well-proportioned outlines. Most plate writers emphasize proportion and fluency in outline construction. The more shorthand reading the student experiences, the better outlines he will write—in terms not only of proportion and fluency, but of accuracy as well.[13]

Tonne, Popham, and Freeman give some standards as to the speeds we can expect our classes to attain in reading:

> The teacher can grade her timed readings on the class average, or say that near the end of the first semester students

---

[13] John L. Rowe, "The Four Arts of Shorthand Teaching," Part 2, "The Art of Previewing," *Business Education World* (December, 1959), p. 25. (Other articles in the series: "Dictating," October, 1959; "Testing," January, 1960; "Grading," February, 1960.)

should be reading around 100 wpm and near the end of the
second semester around 200. Or she may wish to use the
suggested timings for reading plates given in the 1955 Functional Manuals.[14]

III-5   Students Vary in Their Ability to Learn Shorthand

From the classroom, from business and industry, and
from employment agencies come indications of the wide
spread of individual differences even in a single class.
Whitaker states:

> It is surprising to observe the ability or the lack of ability
> of students who have "completed" business education pro-
> grams. Recently, we had an applicant who had just com-
> pleted high school. She could take dictation at 120 words a
> minute. However, one of her classmates took the same
> examination and she was unable to take dictation at 60 words
> a minute or to typewrite at 30 words a minute.[15]

The question of what to do with the slow learner comes
up frequently in methods classes, as is noted by Young:

> It is believed that there is no difference between the
> learning procedures (the way learning takes place) of slow
> students and that of the average or superior students—the
> difference lies in the rate of learning. The superior student
> naturally learns at a "superior" rate, the average student
> learns at a so-called "normal" rate, while the slow student
> learns at a rate slower than the other two groups.
>
> It is also believed that the procedures used in teaching
> these three kinds of students are quite similar, the materials
> used in teaching them are similar, but the amount of material
> covered and the rate of speed at which it is covered differ
> greatly. In all three cases, the teacher should take care to
> utilize to the maximum extent the abilities of all of the

---

[14] Tonne, *et al., op. cit.,* p. 154.
[15] Joseph C. Whitaker, "Manpower's Testing Program," *Business Education Forum* (May, 1960), p. 24.

students. This will necessitate being alert to individual differences as well as knowing how to organize and teach classes so that this aim will be realized.

Care should be taken not to give the slow learner too much material (for which he will be held responsible) at first. Perhaps it would be wise for the teacher to feed him small amounts of material at a time and as rapidly as circumstances will allow. He will need, as a general practice, more repetition than other students. However, as repetition can be harmful as well as meaningful, the teacher should take care to use repetition only when warranted and not just for the sake of repeating.

There are several worthwhile techniques which may be employed when teaching the slow student to read for understanding. Care should be exercised to ascertain that no one technique is used too frequently. Some techniques which may serve are:

1. Teacher may read to students in early shorthand learning. In this way the students will get the sound of fluent reading.

2. Individual students may be called on to read aloud. (This is a test of the student's ability to read fluently.)

3. Pupils may be allowed to read in unison so as to help establish confidence in their ability to read.

4. Teacher may make reading assignments and ask questions on material read.

5. Teacher should teach the student how to use the key. This will enable the student to discover the meanings of unfamiliar outlines with the least delay and effort.[16]

The student *must* feel that reading shorthand is as easy as reading longhand. He must feel that it is not a burden.

---

[16] William M. Young, "Slow Learners: A Challenge to Shorthand Teachers," *The Journal of Business Education*, XXVI (February, 1959), pp. 256, 263.

But it's not only the slow learner that needs special attention; those at the other end of the scale need help, too. Timm uses the tape recorder to good advantage:

> Hardly a year goes by when you do not have at least one boy or girl in second-year shorthand who is far ahead of the rest of the class. The question arises: What can be done to give the fast writer a chance to become even faster? The tape recorder can be a solution to the problem of the fast writers.
>
> Should students work without supervision? As long as the group using the recorder remains small and its members know the purpose of what they are doing, you will have no difficulty.[17]

III-6　In Teaching Shorthand, Go From the Whole to the Part

Some teachers are by nature Gestaltists. It is natural for them to look first at the whole, then try to fit in the parts. It irks them in a committee meeting to have some committee members start in on some little detail as soon as the discussion starts without first taking a look at the whole problem. Once this is done, they don't mind concentrating on a minor portion that needs attention. Such teachers like to take a look at the entire lesson before discussing individual parts. In shorthand, they like to go from the paragraph or letter to the sentence, to the word, to the letter, if necessary. The following writers seem to follow the Gestalt pattern.

Nelson quotes several well-known psychologists before coming to this conclusion:

> Shorthand theory should be presented to the students in the form of short, easy words comprising phrases or easy

---

[17] Gerald Timm, "Put Your Fastest Writers on Tapes," *Business Education World*, XXXVII (May, 1957), p. 15.

sentences in order to build immediate word recognition of the shorthand characters. Since meaningfulness of material is of major importance to the whole method, short sentences are preferable to isolated words.[18]

In connection with the use of the "Gestalt" speed-building paragraphs, we advocate dictating them several times, until all members of the class have reached the maximum peak of the take. Some have objected to this repetition. Condon and Wellman, however, go along with it:

> Shorthand skill, like typewriting skill, is developed through repetition. The opinion of some teachers is that repetition is monotonous and should be avoided—that it is better to read and copy large sections of shorthand plate where some repetition occurs as a matter of chance. But do teachers follow such procedure in typewriting? Do they get basic repetition through sustained or lengthened timed writings? Such procedure has been widely discounted in typewriting instruction and has been discontinued in many classes. Why, then, continue the practice in shorthand? There is no reason why short repetitive drills in shorthand should be more monotonous than are the short repetitive drills in typewriting. Whether any practice is monotonous depends upon the students' mental outlook, which in turn is determined by motivation.[19]

Cronbach [20] defends this type of learning in developing skills: "Using a response in the context of a significant problem is a superior form of practice."

John Dewey was a strong advocate of the "whole" approach:

> To grasp the meaning of a thing, an event or a situation is to see it in *relation* to other things; to note how it

---

[18] Roger H. Nelson, "Psychological Principles Applied to Shorthand Instruction," *Business Education Forum*, Vol. XII, No. 1 (October, 1958), p. 11.

[19] Condon and Wellman, *op. cit.*, p. 10.

[20] Lee J. Cronbach, *Educational Psychology* (New York: Harcourt, Brace & Co., 1954), p. 377.

operates or functions, what consequences follow from it, what causes it, what uses it can be put to. Since all knowing aims at clothing things and events with meaning, it always proceeds by taking the thing inquired into out of its isolation. Search is continued until the thing is discovered to be a relative part in some larger whole.[21]

III-7   Students Should Compare Their Own Notes With the Well-Written Shorthand Found in the Plates

By constantly looking at the Great Stone Face, Earnest, himself, became the man of renown for which the village had been waiting. In shorthand, we have advocated that students make it a practice to compare their notes with well-written models. Tonne, Popham, and Freeman say:

> The teacher who thinks that there is no paper checking will find that the quality of shorthand that his students write will rapidly deteriorate unless he has some standards to which he holds them. He should not try to regulate the size of notes written, but he should check to see that straight lines are straight, that curved lines are curved, and that circles are correctly turned.[22]

III-8   The Teacher Should Remove Blocks to Efficient Learning

Strony mentions a few of these blocks in the following paragraph:

> The diet that brings discouragement with accompanying low morale and heavy drop outs is usually chuck full of memorization of rules and insistence that nothing but dictionary outlines be written. It is heavy, too, with the writing of lines and lines of words and monotony develops from spending days on each lesson. Other diet faults come from

---

[21] John Dewey, *How We Think* (Boston: D. C. Heath & Co., 1933), pp. 137-138.
[22] Tonne, Popham, and Freeman, *op. cit.*, p. 174.

reading back all the students' notes (which is often most painful in the beginning stages), dictating new matter too soon and without a preview, or frequent testing with most discouraging results.[23]

On the other hand, Strony says, "The classroom diet that pays off is one in which the greater part of the period is spent on reading and dictation—dictation of connected matter rather than isolated word lists." [24]

Cronbach admits that poor teaching methods, or students left entirely by themselves, might accidentally hit upon a method that will produce good results and do no damage, but such persons are betting against terrific odds.

> Skills can be developed by unaided trial-and-error, but ordinarily it is better to assist the learner by showing him the correct response. This saves some of the time he might spend in discovering it, although no one can "show him" the muscular cues and co-ordinations that make the response effective. The person who is left to himself may stumble upon a faulty response pattern instead of the best one.[25]

III-9   A Well-Organized, Psychologically Sound Classroom Procedure Is Imperative

The shorthand program outlined by Brown and Frerichs is too long to be presented here, but it has in it many desirable features. Concerning having a good framework within which to operate, they suggest that a teacher might do well to study thoroughly several good, well-balanced shorthand teaching programs, evaluate each, then pick the one that best fits his needs, or, if he desires, take the usable parts from each and build a program of his own.[26]

---

[23] Madeline S. Strony, "Streamlining Shorthand Instructions," *Business Education Forum* (October, 1954), pp. 12-14.

[24] *Ibid.*, p. 13.

[25] Cronbach, *op. cit.*, p. 370.

[26] Frances A. Brown and Alberta J. Frerichs, "A Successful University Shorthand Program," *Business Education Forum* (October, 1959), pp. 7-10.

Tonne, Popham, and Freeman give definite plans for both the first and second semester. One plan, for example, lists the following as a good use of class time during the second semester:

> 5—Oral reading from homework notes. 30-35—Dictation of homework assignment, using the "pyramiding" technique. 2—Chalkboard preview of new-matter, 80-word "take" from Previewed Dictation. 5—Dictation of "take" at 80 words. 2—Preview of new matter, 5-minute 60 wpm take. 5—Dictation of "take" at 60 words.[27]

The psychologist Lawther also advocates "sound mechanics" and the "way to do it."

> The attainment of a high level of skill necessitates the adoption of a form that employs sound mechanics and which is adapted to the structural and functional characteristics of the individual. Form is the "way to do it," the design of performance, the work method. For the individual, it answers his major question after he has a purpose, namely, how to achieve the purpose most effectively.[28]

That's the teacher's job, to show the student how to do it, how he can use his time most effectively. The student most often "gets" this form by imitation; therefore, the teacher should make it easy for the student to imitate.

III-10   Efficient Teaching Requires a Good Classroom Organization

Jennings presents many suggestions on how the student can be brought into the smooth operation of the daily lesson and can help with the planning of the one for tomorrow:

> Must a student give, share, contribute, express, initiate, and evaluate in order to learn? The answer is yes. Regard-

---

[27] Tonne, Popham, and Freeman, *op. cit.*, p. 173.
[28] Charles Skinner, editor, "Learning Motor Skills," *Educational Psychology* (4th ed.; Englewood Cliffs, New Jersey: Prentice-Hall, Inc., 1959), p. 505.

less of the subject to which one is assigned, the teacher should not lose sight of the overall educational objectives, namely, the developing of citizens for a democracy, of personal adequacy by the student and the acquiring of a feeling of personal adequacy, the accomplishing of the ability to sense and to solve problems by thinking scientifically, and the acquiring of knowledge and growth in specific skills.[29]

III-11   The Teacher Must Allow Time So That the Assignment Can Take Its Proper Place in the Lesson's Framework

In good teaching, gone are the days when only a lick and a promise were given to the assignment in the final moments of the class. Clark and Starr suggest the following:

What, then, are the marks of a good assignment? The following list will suggest some criteria for evaluating an assignment:

1. Is it worthwhile?

2. Does it seem worthwhile to the pupil? In other words, does it capitalize on pupil interest or create pupil interest?

3. Is it clear?

4. Is it definite?

5. Does it provide for the differences in pupils—that is, their different aptitudes, abilities, and interests?

6. Is it reasonable as far as length and difficulty are concerned?

7. Does it show the pupil how to go about it? Does it suggest methods and materials which may be used profitably?

8. Does it provide the pupil with the background necessary for completing the assignment satisfactorily, for example, vocabulary? [30]

---

[29] William E. Jennings, "Student Participation in Shorthand Classroom Activities," *Business Education Forum* (October, 1955), pp. 13-15.

[30] Leonard H. Clark and Irving S. Starr, *Secondary School Training Methods* (New York: The Macmillan Co., 1959), p. 76.

The assignment should be made in such a way as to really make the student *want* to do the work. He will want to do it if he sees a reason for doing it and if that ties in with his own personal objective for taking the course. A student must practice with the *intent to improve.*

> Improvement in a skill depends on *practice with intent to improve.* Without the intent to improve, practice establishes a lower level or, what is more frequent, permits gradual retrogression in level of performance. In general, motivation and purpose, and method and equipment establish the level of the skill finally attained. The levels are rarely established by any physiological limit of the individual.[31]

Ausubel adds a different shade of meaning, but the intent to do the job is still dominant:

> It was concluded that intention to remember facilitates retention by enhancing original learning rather than by increasing the stability of existing memory traces.[32]

The following criteria given by Burton for gauging assignments are excellent:

1. The objective, the thing to be done, should be stated in clear, simple language.

2. A provocative and convincing connection should be made between the subject matter of the assignment and the typical activities, interests, and needs of the pupils' current lives.

3. Assignments, while connected with and motivated by pupil need and interest, must also serve desirable social purposes of education, that is, lead to the development of outcomes useful in the organized society of democratic life.

---

[31] Skinner, *op. cit.,* p. 503.
[32] David P. Ausubel, *et al.,* "The Influence of Intention on the Retention of School Materials," *The Journal of Educational Psychology,* XLVII (February, 1957), p. 91.

4. Study guides, questions, and other aids should be included.

5. Assignments must provide for different levels of achievement and for greatly varied learning activities, in accordance with the range of differences in ability, interest, and needs within the group.

6. Assignments should be directed toward study that fulfills pupil and teacher needs, the needs being made apparent either by preliminary discussion or from information about the class which may be secured by the teacher from the cumulative records or other sources.

7. Assignments should initiate and motivate substantial units of work.

8. Assignments should receive all the time necessary for explanations, for answering pupil questions, for developing an adequate plan of action, for arranging subsidiary individual and committee assignments, and for making sure that all know what is to be done.

9. Assignments may be made at any stage of the lesson in such a way as to take advantage of or to develop need or interest and at the same time preserve continuity.

10. Assignments should be such that evidence of progress and achievement can be ascertained each day with reasonable ease.

11. Pupil participation in selecting and developing assignment and methods of procedure is definitely desirable.[33]

III-12   Spelling Aloud Is a Must in Beginning Shorthand

As mentioned in Part I of this chapter, we did not have at our fingertips a valid study proving the importance of spelling aloud in beginning classes, but most authorities seem to be in favor of it. Strony is one of the many who

---

[33] William H. Burton, *The Guidance of Learning Activities* (New York: Appleton-Century-Crofts, Inc., 1952), pp. 344-345.

advocate this technique. In her lesson plan which she presents in this article, she devotes four minutes of the period to the presentation of new material. She insists that this be spelled:

> This spelling lays the groundwork for the new material that will be dictated at some future date—the importance of spelling several times was explained so simply by a young man who was rather slow. He said to the teacher, "You know, it is a good thing we are spelling those things three times because the first time I don't know what's being said; the second, I hear it; and the third time, I say it." [34]

Himstreet agrees with Strony on spelling:

> Spell, spell, spell. These words could be written a thousand more times, as they have been before, without losing their value and meaning for beginning shorthand instruction. Word previews and the introduction of new shorthand principles gain effectiveness when the outlines are spelled according to the sounds involved. Like the use of flash cards in brief form learning, spelling aloud ties the shorthand characters and the sound together. Do not forget that the end result of shorthand instruction is the development of the ability to record the spoken word according to sound! A silent shorthand class is simply too far removed from the end product to be effective. [35]

III-13   In Speed Building, Beginning Stages Particularly, Short Takes Are Better Than Long Ones

There has been an almost universal shift from long periods of intense practice in skill building to shorter ones. In the beginning stages of speed building in shorthand, this is most significant. Strony, for example, says:

> In developing speed, greater progress is made if more time is spent on short takes than on the usual five-minute

---

[34] Strony, *loc. cit.*
[35] Himstreet, *op. cit.*, p. 16.

dictation. One-and-two minute takes at higher and higher speeds (not forgetting control) will make it easier to take a five-minute take at a lower speed. Occasionally, this writer has heard a teacher say, "These students have passed their 100; these, their 80; but these two have not passed their 60 yet, so I am giving them a five-minute, sixty-word test every day in the hope that they will pass one." That is one of the surest ways of killing their chances. They don't need more five-minute takes at 60; they need more one-and-two-minute takes around 80 and 90 with a definite plan of speed building.[36]

In short takes, the student can feel the gist of the whole exercise. This has a settling effect on his speed development. The psychologist Cronbach comments as follows:

> Practice periods would be too short if they did not allow practice of the whole act, preferably several times. As in intellectual learning, a whole-then-part form of practice is best for developing skills.[37]

III-14   Do Not Overemphasize Rules in Connection With the Teaching of Shorthand

We have chosen the following three psychologists to undergird our statement in Part I that rules are relatively unimportant in the learning of shorthand. Thompson, Gardner, and Di Vesta state:

> Understanding and control develop slowly and attempts to give long-winded, involved, detailed explanations or demonstrations, especially at the beginning, are worse than useless. Trials are the chief sources of data for improvements in the pupil's skill. Practice helps to reinforce the more useful behaviors and to eliminate the inappropriate, less efficient ones. The teacher's function is that of directing attention to the essential features of the activity.[38]

---

[36] Strony, *op. cit.*, p. 14.
[37] Cronbach, *op. cit.*, p. 369.
[38] George G. Thompson, *et al.*, *Educational Psychology* (New York: Appleton-Century-Crofts, Inc., 1959), p. 370.

Lawther, using other words, says about the same thing:

> As quickly as the beginner can get the general idea of the act, he should begin his practice trials and revisions. These first individual movements he makes are only partially identified, if at all. They are continually adjusted and changed, anyway, as learning progresses. Only the gross errors need correction at this stage; minor errors are unimportant. The teachers should avoid detailed verbal explanations in the early stages. Word explanations have very little meaning for the beginning learner of a motor skill.[39]

Colville conducted a controlled study in which the following questions were concerned:

1. What is the effect of knowledge of a principle upon immediate learning of a skill to which the principle applies?

2. What is the effect of knowledge of a principle learned in relation to one skill upon subsequent learning of a different and more complicated skill to which the same principle is transferable?

The findings were as follows:

1. There was no evidence that instruction concerning mechanical principles utilized in the performance of a motor skill facilitates the initial learning of the skill to any greater extent than an equivalent amount of time spent in practicing the skill.

2. There was no evidence that such knowledge facilitates subsequent learning as evidenced in the performance of a similar or more complicated skill to which the same principle is applicable.[40]

---

[39] Skinner, *op. cit.*, p. 504.

[40] Frances M. Colville, "The Learning of Motor Skills as Influenced by Knowledge of Mechanical Principles," *The Journal of Educational Psychology*, XLVII (October, 1957), pp. 321-327.

III-15 Evaluation Techniques Should Be Accepted by the Students and Should Be in Line With the Objectives of the Course

In Part II, we outlined five factors we regularly use in making shorthand evaluations. In the following basic principles, Rowe gives us some things to keep in mind in connection with testing. In "The Art of Grading," (*Business Education World*, February, 1960, p. 31), he includes four of our standard five factors—all but "comparison." His broad concept of theory perhaps includes what we check for under comparison. Here are his basic twelve:

1. A major purpose of testing in shorthand is to promote the learning process.
2. The results of a test should reveal the student's relative standing.
3. The techniques and mechanics of the test should be thoroughly understood by the student.
4. Tests should be easy to administer and evaluate.
5. Theory tests should be based upon previous learning experiences. (The mastery of shorthand theory is a maturation and recreation process.)
6. Testing should pave the way for remedial teaching.
7. The results of each test should be given to the student in the shortest possible time.
8. The test score should never be a surprise to the student.
9. All shorthand tests should contain the element of speed and should be timed.
10. A variety of tests should be employed.
11. A knowledge of testing goals and objectives by the teacher is necessary to insure the correct interpretation of this important phase of the teaching act.
12. The end result of all testing in shorthand is the mailable transcript.[41]

---

[41] John L. Rowe, "The Four Arts of Shorthand Teaching, Part 3: The Art of Testing," *Business Education World* (January, 1960), pp. 27-28.

SUMMARY

The chapter may be summed up with an admonition for the teacher to use few word lists, keep material in context, make certain that dictation takes are short and meaningful, check up frequently to see how the students are doing, have them read or take dictation most of the period, see to it that assignments are clear, get plenty of sleep so as to have the extra measure of enthusiasm, show them how it is done, make sure that the slow student also succeeds, try not to be a perfectionist, and enjoy the job of teaching shorthand.

SELECTED BIBLIOGRAPHY

A Handbook for Teachers of Business Education, Twenty-Second Yearbook, Commercial Education Association of the City of New York and Vicinity, 1958.

Anderson, Ruth I. "Analysis and Classification of Research in Shorthand and Transcription," *The National Business Education Quarterly* (December, 1948).

————————, and others. "Helping the Slow Learner in Shorthand and Transcription," *American Business Education* (May, 1954).

Balsley, Irol Whitmore. *Current Transcription Practices in Business Firms,* Monograph 86. Cincinnati: South-Western Publishing Company, 1954.

Blanchard, Clyde Insley. *Twenty Shortcuts to Shorthand Speed.* New York: Gregg Publishing Division, McGraw-Hill Book Company, Inc., 1939.

Business Education Forum, October Issues, Shorthand, 1951-1962.

Douglas, Lloyd V., James T. Blanford, and Ruth I. Anderson. *Teaching Business Subjects.* Englewood Cliffs, New Jersey: Prentice-Hall, Inc., 1958.

Eyster, Elvin S. "Prognosis of Scholastic Success in Stenography," *National Business Education Quarterly,* VII (1938).

Grossman, Jack. "46 Characteristics of Real Office Dictation," *Business Education World* (September, 1950).

Grubbs, Robert L. "Strategy for Second Semester Shorthand," *Business Education Forum* (October, 1955).

Lamb, Marion M. *Your First Year of Teaching Shorthand and Transcription,* Second Edition. Cincinnati: South-Western Publishing Company, 1961.

Leslie, Louis A. *Methods of Teaching Transcription.* New York: Gregg Publishing Division, McGraw-Hill Book Company, Inc., 1949.

——————. *Methods of Teaching Gregg Shorthand.* New York: Gregg Publishing Division, McGraw-Hill Book Company, Inc., 1953.

Lloyd, Alan C. "Practice in Pretranscription Typing," *Business Education World* (December, 1948).

Murphy, Glen E. "An Analysis of the Decisions Made in Transcribing a Letter," *Business Education Forum* (March, 1950).

Reynolds, Helen, and Margaret H. Ely. "Transcription—Early or Late," *Business Education Forum* (October, 1953).

Tonne, Herbert A. "The Need for Office Style Dictation," *The Balance Sheet* (October and November, 1948).

——————. "Letters for Office-Style Dictation," *The Journal of Business Education* (January, 1950, February, 1950, March, 1950).

——————, Estelle L. Popham, and M. Herbert Freeman. *Methods of Teaching Business Subjects,* Second Edition. New York: Gregg Publishing Division, McGraw-Hill Book Company, Inc., 1957.

Whitmore, Irol V., and Samuel J. Wanous. *Effective Transcription Procedures,* Monograph 57. Cincinnati: South-Western Publishing Company, 1942.

Zoubek, Charles. "Different Shorthand Teaching Practices for Different Shorthand Objectives," *Business Education Forum* (October, 1962).

CHAPTER V

TRANSCRIPTION

At one time students with instruction in only basic shorthand went directly into office work. When it became obvious that these graduates were inadequately prepared, schools began to offer arrangements which included practical dictation. From these humble beginnings emerged modern transcription instruction: well-developed terminal programs, experienced teachers to handle them, and a wealth of materials designed to produce the best possible results.*

The present trend is to give more time to transcription and less to basic shorthand. Teachers are competing with one another in their race to teach the basic principles as rapidly as possible. In practice, the time allotted to each is about equal. If there is a two-year course, the first year is devoted to basic shorthand and the second year to advanced shorthand and transcription. In some cases—assuming that the students can type—there is no break at all. Transcription is started the first day that the shorthand class meets.

Although there are some "quickie" systems now on the market that are sold primarily for their personal-use appeal, there is a general agreement that shorthand cannot be justified for personal use. It follows, therefore, that a basic course in shorthand without that vital second part—transcription—cannot be justified. The purpose of devoting so many hours of intensive study to shorthand fundamentals is that the skill may be used in transcription.

---

* Throughout this chapter, "transcription" refers to the process of producing usable typewritten copy from shorthand notes.

Transcription Must Be Taught

Transcription must be taught, not just "timed." The fact that a subject so complicated, demanding such high-level skills, should ever have been left to a trial-and-error process of learning, is difficult to understand. On few points do we find more general agreement than on the concept that transcription needs the full attention of a well-qualified teacher. Merrill, for example, states:

> . . . It is imperative that the teacher *teach* transcription. Transcription is a skill that crowns and unifies the other basic skills of shorthand and typing. While typing is a useful art in itself, shorthand is of practically no value without efficient transcription skill.[1]

Liles and Gratz are equally definite:

> Transcription must be taught; it is not a class to be merely supervised by a teacher who does nothing but correct papers. Therefore, a shorthand class and its corresponding transcription class must be taught by the same teacher.

> Also, many administrators are not aware that the effectiveness of teaching transcription is seriously impaired when, for example, a shorthand class is scheduled in the morning and its corresponding transcription class in the afternoon.[2]

Tonne, Popham, and Freeman state:

> The materials presented are also based on the strong conviction that results being obtained in transcription classes fall far short of the potential that could be achieved if teachers *taught* transcription, utilizing what they know of the nature of skill building. Typewriting instruction has developed tremendously in recent years; shorthand teaching has improved rapidly as we have learned more about the psychology

---

[1] Frances E. Merrill, "Let's *Teach* Transcription," *The Journal of Business Education* (October, 1958), pp. 16-19.

[2] Parker Liles and Jerre Gratz, "Theory and Practice," *The Journal of Business Education* (May, 1955), pp. 365-368.

involved, but little has been done to improve the teaching of transcription. Yet transcription skill is, after all, the basis for stenographic production. *Transcription must be taught, not merely timed.*[3]

Lamb describes teaching transcription as an involved task:

The transcription teacher's task is an involved one. It is her responsibility to see to it that students integrate adequate English, shorthand, and typing skills into acceptable transscribing skill, the skill required to produce acceptable typescripts from shorthand notes with reasonable speed.[4]

Skimin has caught the mental complexity of the combination of skills required for transcription:

The mind is working under greater stress in a transcription situation than it is when the pupil is merely copying from the printed word with the eye following along with less direction of the mind. Writing from shorthand outlines calls for instantaneous decisions in regard to typewritten forms, spelling, the forming of possessives, plurals, syllabication, capitalization, interior and final punctuation. All these things must be decided under pressure, and not with the school standard of 70 per cent, but with the business office standard of 100 per cent. Surely there is more to learning to transcribe than mere dictation of a few letters with instructions to go into the typewriting room and transcribe those letters. . . . Transcription must be taught.[5]

Considerable space has been taken to establish the foregoing point. It is done with the feeling that if the

---

[3] Herbert A. Tonne, Estelle L. Popham, and M. Herbert Freeman, *Methods of Teaching Business Subjects* (2nd ed.; New York: Gregg Publishing Division, McGraw-Hill Book Company, Inc., 1957), p. 184.

[4] Marion M. Lamb, *Your First Year of Teaching Shorthand and Transcription* (2nd ed.; Cincinnati: South-Western Publishing Company, 1961), p. 95.

[5] Eleanor Skimin, "Shorthand Transcription—The Work of the Typewriting Department," *Business Education Forum* (October, 1953), pp. 11-14.

teacher is really aware of the importance of transcription, he will not be so apt to treat it lightly. A student in a methods class once remarked, "Transcription! Why all this fuss? What's there to know about transcription? I dictate, they type it, we check it, and that's it. They go to work anyway before we get half started, so what's the difference?"

Students seldom learn unless they sense a need. (The same goes for teachers.) As stated before, students practice because they *want* to learn; they do not necessarily learn because they practice. Unless the teacher is convinced that he *needs* to know the materials available in transcription, that he *needs* to know some techniques that have proved helpful to others, the material which follows is of little value.

Physical Factors

Transcription must have the physical setup which will enable teachers to do a good job. Having established that transcription needs to be taught, and taught vigorously, the first step would seem to be to set up an atmosphere in which the teacher can do his best work without having to overcome too many physical obstacles.

Ideally, the transcription class should meet for a double period. This class should be held in the typing room, or in a room where enough machines are available to accommodate the class. If transcription is to be taught effectively, the entire process from dictation to the final mailable copy should be in one room and under one teacher. This makes the transcription situation flexible so that remedial teaching can be put into effect immediately when needed.

The above arrangement would eliminate many of the excuses as to why the teacher can't do a good job. "They say we should build up speed in shorthand and typing; improve English, punctuation, and spelling; put into practice good transcription work habits; and still have time to actually transcribe some letters. It's just too much for one period." "I have only fifteen students in transcription, but they are in three different typing classes. How can I do any supervising? These typing teachers consider me a nuisance, always interfering with their typing plans." Complaints such as these could be compiled without end. A transcription teacher must have control of the situation from the beginning to the finished product.

When Should Transcription Be Started?

Except in intensive adult programs, where it usually is not a part of a broad curriculum, shorthand instruction is usually for a period of two years, with transcription taking up at least the last half of the program. There are, of course, many deviations from that pattern. The intensity of the shorthand effort will often determine when transcription is begun. Starting date practices will, therefore, be found from the middle of a two-year program to situations in which transcription is introduced the very first day of the shorthand class, provided the students know how to type. Some would go a step farther—to teach shorthand and typewriting at the same time. These advocates say that students should not be allowed to type from print while they are learning. Typing exercises should be put on the board in shorthand and the students should type them from shorthand the first day of their typewriting class.

The authors have tried introducing shorthand transcription to beginning shorthand students who could type 40 wpm or better, but they are not yet ready to recommend that approach unreservedly. Theoretically this approach is good, but actual practice presents some difficulties—for example, the dropout rate in shorthand is usually high. To some extent this is good, for it weeds out those who probably would not make a success of the advanced part of the course because of deficiencies in English, spelling, punctuation, etc. These students have found out what they wanted to know and have come to the conclusion that shorthand is not for them. Often it is possible to have a room available with enough typewriters for those who have what it takes to make good secretaries or stenographers, but a room with typewriters cannot always be found for all those who might want to try shorthand.

It takes an alert, energetic, forceful teacher to make a success of starting transcription at the beginning of the shorthand course. Unless it is taught well, more harm than good is likely to result.

In a four-semester course in shorthand, transcription may be started at the beginning of the second semester, or when the students have completed the first step of a program designed to lead to mature ability in handling a high-level secretarial position. By this time the students have completed the basic shorthand theory, they know all the brief forms, and they can take dictation fluently on easy, familiar material. They have developed good work habits and can now tackle the new skill involved in transcription with determination and confidence.

During this semester, transcription is introduced gradually in connection with the regular shorthand speed and power-development program. The time devoted to transcription is also increased correspondingly so that at the end of the second semester the class has overcome the introductory hurdles and is ready for solid transcription work involving longer takes and more difficult material.

By delaying transcription a short time, the teacher may be able to get some much-needed help from the English department. There will be plenty of work to be done in the transcription class, but the students will have been exposed to an advanced study of English, spelling, and punctuation. It is often possible for the shorthand teacher to incorporate some of the things the English teacher is doing in the daily transcription exercises. This type of cooperation has proved to be very successful.

In teaching typewriting, teachers like to build basic speed and control together with good work habits as quickly as possible so that the students can use the typewriter for production. It has been proven possible to bring a beginning typing class of junior high students from zero up to 50 to 60 wpm in eight weeks. Likewise, it seems reasonable to bring shorthand classes up to the point where they write fluently at a reasonable speed as soon as possible.

Introduction to Transcription

As mentioned in the previous chapter, a transcription exercise can easily be made difficult enough to discourage an entire class. Transcription needs to be introduced with great care. Every possible block must be taken away so that all that is left in the assignment to puzzle the student is the sheer skill of translating familiar shorthand symbols into equally familiar typewritten words. It often helps to have the teacher compose the first few transcription paragraphs from familiar and interesting incidents that have happened around school. Those teachers using the method advocated in the preceding chapter in beginning shorthand have by this time a whole collection of easy, student-compiled paragraphs, used at that time for speed building, but which can now be used to introduce transcription. If these are not available, paragraphs built around the coming school dance, play, or football game might serve the purpose. The sentence structure of the paragraphs should be simple; the format, full-length line, double spaced. There should be no words that the student cannot spell. The only punctuation mark should be the terminal period. If possible, the student should type this exercise from print several times so that he can "keep the carriage moving" when typing from his shorthand notes. Even so, on the first few trials there will be the typical "mad" for "made" and "gat" for "gate." This type of error is to be expected. It requires no special attention. It will disappear in a day or so without any corrective drill.

Students should transcribe these exercises several times until they get the feel of writing from shorthand notes. If introduced carefully, students will form the opinion that transcription is going to be easy, that it is fun. Each succeeding exercise should be presented in the same careful manner. Exercises should be increased in length and difficulty only as the students develop power to handle them. Rather than pick materials carelessly and then check all the errors made by the students in their initial attempts to transcribe, the teacher should set the stage so that the student will not make many errors. Thus with careful guidance the student passes through the introductory phase of transcription and is ready for transcription proper.

It Takes Time to Learn Transcription

The literature of business education indicates that the teachers are competing with one another to teach basic shorthand in less time. This is a worthy objective, but we should not encourage the teacher or the student to cut short the time for transcription. One executive reports the following incident:

> I hired a girl who could write shorthand well and who could type, but who had not had a formal course in transcription. I temporarily assigned her to other duties until she could complete a standard course in transcription on company time. I was well repaid for the cost involved. When she came back to the office as a stenographer, the difference in her ability to handle this level of office work was amazing. Gone were the days when she constantly interrupted everyone who would listen to her with "How do you spell this? How do you punctuate that? Do you underscore this title?" etc.

It is easy to tell the difference between an entering employee who has mastered a good transcription text, and a person who has just done some transcribing as a part of his shorthand course, using only the basic shorthand text as material.

The number of details and factual, technical, and format information presented in a standard transcription text is enormous. The study of this information should be a part of every secretary's equipment. Therefore, the shorter the time spent on fundamentals, the better—provided we get results.

Importance of Good Transcription Materials

A thorough job of teaching advanced shorthand and transcription requires the necessary tools, the most important of which is the transcription textbook. A good text will take into consideration all the links in the transcription chain, and most texts will automatically consider the techniques now generally recommended in the literature of business education.

Most writers advocate that the teacher should occasionally compare the student's typing speed from print with his speed when typing from shorthand book plates and from his own shorthand. A student who can type 40 wpm from print might be expected to transcribe about 35 wpm from shorthand plates and perhaps 30 wpm from his own shorthand notes. If there is a wide gap in speed attainments, the teacher should try to find the reason and attempt to correct it.

The student's ability to proofread and transcribe can be strengthened by the use of actual rough-draft samples collected by the teacher and students. Balsley and Wanous [6]

---

[6] Irol Whitmore Balsley and S. J. Wanous, *Shorthand Transcription Studies* (3rd ed.; Cincinnati: South-Western Publishing Company, 1958), p. 30.

list several excellent proofreading exercises. Punctuation exercises, word usage materials, spelling, helpful hints on good office procedures, and office-style dictation can be illustrated with the use of proofreading, transcribing, and typing material. One hundred per cent accuracy is imperative.

A teacher who does not insist on a good transcription text with which he is thoroughly familiar is seriously handicapping himself and his students. As a result, he may often be doing a lot of work which has already been done for him by someone else.

In addition to a good textbook, a tape recorder and/or a record player with the necessary tapes and recordings is now considered standard transcription and speed-building equipment. The following items are recommended by Oliverio:

Teacher Reference Library

Methods of Teaching Gregg Shorthand. Leslie. 1953. $5.75. New York: Gregg Publishing Division.

Methods of Teaching Transcription. Leslie. 1949. $4. New York: Gregg Publishing Division.

Magazines in which shorthand teachers will find articles and material related to shorthand include *The Balance Sheet, Business Education Forum* (all issues—featured in October), *Business Education World,* and *The Journal of Business Education.*

Films

The Secretary's Day. 11 min. Color or black and white. Demonstrates the many phases of a secretary's task including the taking of dictation and transcription. Coronet Instructional Films.

The Secretary Takes Dictation. 11 min. Color or black and white. An employer discusses the manner in which an efficient stenographer takes dictation. Coronet Instructional Films.

The Secretary Transcribes. 11 min. Color or black and white. Illustrates many specific devices for efficient transcription. Coronet Instructional Films.

The Secretary: Transcribing. 11 min. Color or black and white. Illustrates efficient transcription from both notes and machines. Coronet Instructional Films.

Tapes

Business Education Library. Five tapes. One office style dictation tape containing all characteristics of office dictation. 60 min. $6.75. Same letters available on *Step by Step Dictation.* 4 tapes. 60 min. each. EMC Recordings Corporation.

Dictation Tapes for Gregg Shorthand. A number of tapes for beginning and advanced dictation. Tapes can be purchased individually or in complete sets. Prices range from $7.75 for one reel to $225 for complete set. See catalogue from Gregg Publishing Division.

The shorthand teacher will find the tape recorder valuable for cutting tapes of additional materials that students can use for practice during their free time in school.

Records

Correlated Dictation and Instruction Records (for beginners). Series of nine 45 rpm recordings correlated with first 54 (Gregg) Simplified lessons. Available individually for 99¢, a complete set of nine records for $8.50. Allied Publishers, Inc.

Dictation Records for Gregg Shorthand. Prices range from $2.40 for each record to $13.50 for set of six, 78 rpm. See Gregg catalogue for complete listings of records available.

Dictation Records. 45 minutes of dictation on each side. 60 to 150 words a minute. Herman Miller Dictation Records.[7]

What Constitutes Mailable Copy?

A college administrator reports the following: "My secretary has higher standards of quality and excellence than I have. Her standard is absolute perfection. If I call a small error to her attention, one which I think can be corrected easily with a little fixing up, crowding, spacing,

---

[7] Mary Ellen Oliverio, "Selected Aids for Shorthand and Transcription," *Business Education Forum* (January, 1958), pp. 29, 31.

ELEMENTS THAT MAKE FOR MAILABILITY
OF LETTERS

I. GENERAL APPEARANCE
1. Good margins.
2. Regular type impressions resulting from good rhythm.
3. Good erasures.
4. No fingerprints, smudges, or other marks on the paper.
5. No strikeovers.

II. SPELLING
A single misspelled word if not corrected will make the finest letter unmailable; therefore, be sure of your spelling.

III. NAMES AND FIGURES
1. Special attention should be given to the inside address. Persons do not like to have their names misspelled.
2. Be sure that you are familiar with names used in the body of the letter. You are justified in asking your employer about names with which you are not familiar.
3. A single error in a figure will make the letter unmailable.

IV. PUNCTUATION
Although a letter is still mailable when the punctuation does not always live up to the best authority, any punctuation that changes or does not make sufficiently clear the intent of the dictator makes the letter unmailable.

V. ENGLISH
The violation of any well-established grammatical principle makes your letter unmailable. The fact that the dictator made a slip when dictating the letter does not permit you to repeat the error.

VI. CONTEXT
Most employers will allow a certain amount of freedom in transcribing dictation. In no event, however, are you justified in changing his meaning.

VII. WORD DIVISION
Any major violation of good rules for word division will render your letter unmailable.

VIII. CAPITALIZATION
The more important and generally accepted rules in regard to capitalization must be observed.

NOTE: It should be kept in mind that many of the errors mentioned above can be corrected easily. If such corrections are made, the letter is often mailable and does not have to be rewritten.

or the like, she insists in doing the letter over." This is unusual. It is frequently the boss who has to put on the pressure for high office standards.

In some offices, the rule is to let the letter go out if the correction does not spoil the appearance of the copy. It saves time and money. This establishes two basic categories in the handling of letters in the school situation: (1) those letters that can be mailed without any correction whatsoever, and (2) those that can be made mailable with a small correction. Many teachers give full credit for all letters in group No. 1, and half credit for those in group No. 2. This system encourages careful proofreading on the part of the student *before* handing the letter in for credit. If the *student* finds the error and makes the correction *before* the "boss" sees it, he gets full credit; if he waits until the teacher points out the error, he receives only half credit.

Transcription Standards

There is no universally accepted standard for mailable transcription copy; in fact, there is no general agreement of what is meant by any given transcription standard. However, there is almost unanimous agreement that mailable copy should be the only ultimate objective. In view of this, the standard given by Leslie should be given thoughtful consideration:

> At the end of four semesters of shorthand and at least two semesters of typewriting, when dictation is given at 80-100 words a minute in a group of letters comprising a total dictation of 800-1,000 words, the learner should transcribe at the rate of 20-25 words a minute with 20 words as the minimum rate acceptable for credit. At least 75 per cent of the letters in any five consecutive daily transcription periods should be mailable.[8]

---

[8] Louis Leslie, *Methods of Teaching Transcription* (New York: Gregg Publishing Division, McGraw-Hill Book Company, Inc., 1949), pp. 51-52.

Some of the items to be considered when setting up standards in transcription are:

1. Speed at which the material is dictated, and how it is dictated.
2. How much coaching is permitted before typing begins.
3. Quality of finished product, and how it shall be rated.
4. Are carbon copies required? If so, how many?
5. If based on letters, what is the average length? Are envelopes required?
6. Difficulty of material used for dictation.

A Suggested Standard[9]

After viewing some of the factors that need to be taken into consideration, the task of attempting to establish a rate of transcription seems hopeless. The following standard is suggested in an effort to provide a beginning from which further refinements can be made.

What shall be the requirements for high school graduation in a four-semester program of shorthand and typewriting, assuming that tests are given near the end of the fourth semester? The following is suggested: six mailable letters an hour, average length—130 words, 600 points. A letter dictated at 100 words a minute is given a credit value of 100 points. Six letters at 100 words would give this required 600 points. A student might do eight or even ten letters but, if only five of the group proved mailable, the total points would still be only 500. A letter dictated at 80 words would equal 80 points. A student would have to transcribe eight letters in order to reach the passing mark. The dictation usually requires about 30 or 40 minutes. Inside address is included in the transcript.

---

[9] For a more complete treatment of this standard, see Harm Harms "A Workable Standard for Transcription," *American Business Education* (May, 1945), p. 174.

The transcribing time is a full 60 minutes. On completion of the dictation the students go immediately to the typewriters. No carbons or envelopes are required. Mailability is determined according to the letter mailability chart given on page 203. If most of the students miss a certain letter because of the same technical difficulty, it is an indication that such an element should not be included in a letter-mailability test at this stage of development. Standard style and factual knowledge elements such as are now included in most typing texts and for which printed tests are available are not to be considered as unusual elements.

The illustration on page 208 is an actual example of one student's progress in transcription, as shown by results of a series of letters-per-hour tests. The dotted line indicates the total number of letters transcribed during the sixty-minute period, the solid line shows the number that were mailable. The figures at the extreme top of the page indicate the speed of dictation. There are two minimum standards—6 mailable letters an hour for material dictated at 100 words a minute, and 8 mailable letters for 80-words-a-minute dictation. This gives recognition to the principle that more errors may be expected as the rate of dictation increases; it encourages students to try for higher levels. In this particular instance Mariwyn first attempted dictation at 100 words a minute. Although she transcribed 8 letters, not a one was mailable. She then changed her technique both in transcription and in dictation. She took the test at 80 words a minute and slowed her typing speed so that she transcribed only 7 letters, of which 2 were mailable. On the third trial she decreased her transcription rate still further, with the result that she had 4 letters mailable. This gave her confidence to try the 100 again; however, she dropped to 2 mailable letters. The next week she took the test once more at 80, transcribed 7 letters,

and had 5 mailable. The following week she transcribed a
total of 8 letters with 7 mailable. Her next trial was at 100;
and although she dropped slightly, she still managed to
transcribe 7 letters with 6 mailable; thus attaining the minimum standard of 600 points. On the final test she trans-
scribed 10 letters, dictated at 100 words a minute, with 9
mailable—a very fine record.

The effectiveness of the above standard cannot be
judged until a large number of schools have experimented
with it. A former president of the National Office Management Association states: "I believe that businessmen in
general will be satisfied if they can depend upon it that the
girls you send them on the beginning vocational level can
turn out an average of six acceptable letters an hour. Such
a fact automatically tells us that these applicants can
spell, punctuate, and type without too many errors. After
office workers are associated with the firm for five or six
months, their efficiency will naturally improve."

Having analyzed the two basic transcription objectives,
mailability and production, the next logical question is, how
can these objectives be achieved?

The "How" in Teaching Transcription

It has been shown in the foregoing discussion that transcription is made up of a complex arrangement of elements.
Osborne comments concerning them as follows:

> Modern practice demands a correlation . . . of at least
> seven major elements: writing shorthand, typing, English,
> punctuation, spelling, word division, and vocabulary build-
> ing.[10]

To this list might well be added the handling of materials,
for it is frequently the handling of materials that accounts

---

[10] Agnes E. Osborne, "The Improvement of Transcription," *The Journal
of Business Education* (February, 1942), p. 19.

LETTERS-PER-HOUR TRANSCRIPTION RATING CHART

Name _Distlehurst, Mariwyn_   Semester __2__ 19___-19___

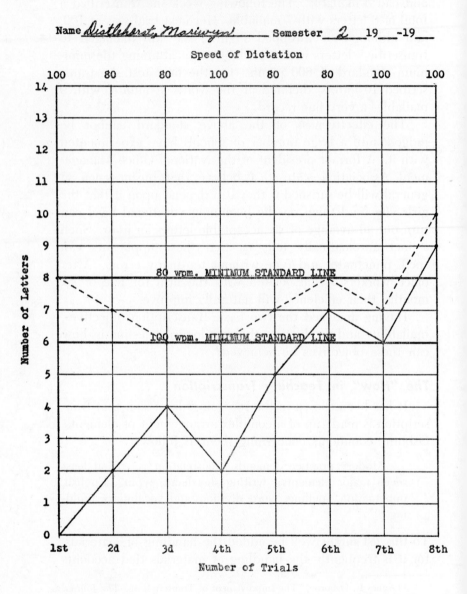

Speed of Dictation

for the great difference in speed when students go from straight copy to a series of letters. *How* to improve transcription will therefore involve a discussion of each of the links in this chain, the strength of which is frequently determined by its weakest unit. Before entering upon a detailed analysis of the above elements, the importance of a proper beginning or introduction to the transcription process should be stressed.

Introductory Techniques for the First Few Weeks of Transcription

Some educators make no special effort to make initial learning stages easy. "It's good for them; shows their mettle," is indicative of a philosophy that sees trait-development possibilities in having students overcome obstacles. In skill development a different method should be used. The initial stages must be as simple as possible so as to inspire confidence and daring. In typewriting it has been suggested that all unnecessary elements be omitted the first day so the students can concentrate on the proper technique of rapid stroking. In shorthand the size of characters and other small technicalities could well be overlooked in order to obtain fluency. In bookkeeping a simple but complete cycle is introduced the first day. From this cycle, other refinements are made.

In transcription, too, the teacher needs to set the stage in such a fashion as to enable full concentration on the isolated transcription factor. Obviously an ordinary letter with a hundred possible difficulties in spelling, word division, choice of words, punctuation, unusual typing combinations, and placement on the page would constitute an ill-chosen exercise with which to begin transcription training.

In the chapters on shorthand and on typing, attention is called to the fact that these subjects can do much to prepare the ground for transcription daily by placing emphasis on anticipated transcription difficulties. Such a preview is the first essential in getting ready for transcription. Other preparatory factors are as follows:

(1) Considerable dictation to the machine in typewriting classes during the two weeks prior to the opening of transcription.

(2) Typing practice on the vocabulary to be used in the first few letters. The identical letters need not be rehearsed, but the preview should be careful enough to make certain that these words do not constitute typing difficulties.

(3) The shorthand exercise to be transcribed should be read orally several times until it can be interpreted with expression indicating the proper punctuation.

(4) Arrangement on the page should receive but little attention during the first few days; therefore, straight copy is perhaps the best material.

(5) Some teachers have found that transcribing from plates (well-written book shorthand) is helpful as an introduction. The validity of plate typing as an aid to transcription seems to be well documented. Notwithstanding, it is the authors' opinion that this can easily be overdone. Students find it more interesting to type from their own notes. If plates are used, the transition to writing from their own notes should be made as soon as possible. If the best way to learn to take shorthand from dictation is to take shorthand from dictation, then the best way to learn to transcribe your own notes is to transcribe your own notes.

After about two weeks of being thus gradually introduced to the subject, the student will be ready to undertake regular transcription routines and problems. Wanous and Whitmore [11] give an excellent example of the care that

---

[11] S. J. Wanous and Irol V. Whitmore, *Effective Transcription Procedures*, Monograph 57 (Cincinnati: South-Western Publishing Company, 1942).

specialists in the teaching of transcription give to the manner in which students are first introduced to the subject. According to this outline, beginners are led gradually over the many transcription hurdles so that each step builds a foundation for the next until the student is ready for office-style transcription.

Office-Style Dictation

An attempt at office-style dictation in classrooms where the rudimentary elements of transcription have not yet been mastered results in utter confusion and a waste of time. Simply to throw learning blocks haphazardly in the student's path is of no purpose and only slows the learning process. On the other hand, if ample time has been allotted to transcription, if the class has advanced to the stage where the students are producing mailable copy regularly, if there is a feeling of confidence that comes from a knowledge of inner power, then the teacher should attempt office-style dictation and use it regularly in the classroom.

The teacher should simulate ordinary office conditions whenever possible so that students might be better prepared for dictation on their first jobs. The teacher should provide helpful hints on what to expect in office dictation and how to cope with minor problems that arise when taking dictation. For example, many beginning stenographers are confused by the informal manner in which their employers might dictate or perhaps the fact that dictators do not say, "Now I am going to dictate." It might be well, therefore, as a sample of office-style dictation, to have the students sit near the desk and have the teacher dictate in a calm, quiet tone—the way an executive must dictate if he is going to keep it up for long periods of time. It is as difficult for the executive to produce good material when dictating as it is for the stenographer to record and transcribe it. It requires mental alertness for both to function well as individuals and as a team.

More and more executives are doing their revisions while the material they have dictated is still in the shorthand stage. This type of efficient teamwork might well be used in all but the most complicated dictation, such as contracts, reports, and involved statistical letters. It is necessary for the stenographer to read back the dictation fluently and with proper expression so that the dictator can actually hear the punctuation that the stenographer plans to use. It means, too, that her notes should not be crowded on the page; she must make allowance for editing. Experience will soon tell her how far she needs to go in making provision for this type of dictation.

It takes a great deal of practice for students to develop this "fix-it-up-while-it-is-in-the-shorthand-stage" skill. As a beginning, the teacher might want to go back now and then and change a word or so. Later, a complete sentence can be slightly reworded, or a paragraph which is in the present tense can be changed so that it will be in the past, etc. At first it is agonizingly slow for students to catch on. After several months the teacher can make a slip, correct, and go right on without hesitation.

Whenever possible the teacher should include in each day's transcription dictation one letter that is actually going to be put in the mail. Students often ask, "Is this for real?" If the teacher says "It sure is," they get nervous and excited. The fact that it is the "real McCoy" seems to do something to them until they get used to it. But when the best letter is selected by popular vote, with the first carbon placed in the department file and the second, with proper recognition, in the student's file, there is a sense of satisfaction of having done something of actual value, of having entered for a brief moment into the lifestream of business.

It is most aggravating to have a secretary who never becomes a part of the job, who won't know tomorrow what happens today, who forgets everything that occurs (except coffee break and paycheck) as fast as it happens—just as though she were some detached entity, hired to go through certain motions until saved by the bell at the end of the day.

Transcription students need to take a series of letters having to do with a certain situation in which they are expected to know and remember what is going on. The alert students will quickly catch small mistakes in dates, figures, names, and the like, because they are familiar with the situation; others will need some time to get into the groove. One teacher set up a small office in the classroom in an effort to develop this *belongingness*.

In the average office there are usually a good many directives that go along with the day's dictation. The ability to follow directions is a skill that can be developed. Drill in following directions is good office-style dictation. The National Business Entrance Tests include check-ups on the candidate's ability to follow directions. One member of the National Secretaries Association keeps a red pencil handy to make memos when her boss gives directions. "Before I start to transcribe," she says, "I take care of the 'red letter' items first." This, or something similar, is a good technique to include in office-style dictation.

The foregoing examples are perhaps enough to give a general idea of what should be stressed in office-style dictation.

A Navy consultant who gives in-service training courses in letter writing, where the classes are made up of supervisory personnel who have recently been promoted and are now expected to dictate, quotes one of his students: "They gave me a private office and a secretary. I have never had a secretary before. I have to dictate letters. I am scared to death. What shall I do?" In such cases, this consultant acts as the secretary and has the class dictate to him while he writes their letters on the board in shorthand. Their first attempts usually leave much to be desired, but after going over the material as a class, they usually wind up with something suitable for mailing. It takes almost as long to train a good dictator as it does a stenographer. This fact might console the young stenographer who is just setting out to earn her spurs.

The Transcription Chain

A station wagon skidded off the road near Clinton, Iowa. The temperature was five below zero. The members of a small group of homeward-bound Christmas relatives shielded their faces from the driving snow. A tow chain was fastened to the front bumper of the stalled car and a huge semi-trailer truck was about to bring the vehicle back on the road. The car moved a few feet, taking a mountain of snow with it; then all eyes shifted their focus to a single link near the middle of the chain. Slowly this link separated at the weld, opened up, widened, and with a clang that rang through the frozen air, the chain broke and the car rolled back down the grade. This chain failed because of one weak link. Had all the other links been ten times as strong, the chain still would have been useless. So it is with transcription. A person's ability to transcribe is only as good as the weakest link in his transcription training.

Pictured below are the six links of the transcription chain. Let us now consider each in turn.

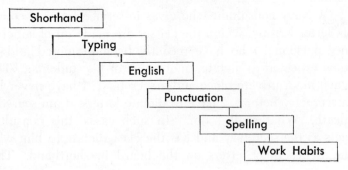

The Transcription Chain—Shorthand

It is quite possible for both shorthand and typing proficiency to deteriorate during transcription unless a regular program of growth in these areas is maintained. When we talk about transcription proper, we assume that the student has completed one semester (or the equivalent) each of beginning and advanced shorthand. The student now needs weekly practice for the building of higher speeds on familiar material and should maintain the speed he now has while moving on to more difficult and longer takes. It is easy for teachers to lull themselves into a sense of false security by taking too seriously the articles stating that "employers do not dictate more than 80 wpm, so we should not worry about higher speeds in our shorthand and transcription classes."

Some time ago, a public relations officer had to report on a symphony concert. He dictated a report—the best he had ever written. It was something like the man seated at the organ and finding the "lost chord." He was proud of himself as he dictated it. Never before had he made such a fine choice of words. He was already looking forward to seeing it in print. When he asked his secretary to read it back, she hesitated, turned red, and then let him have it: "It was a fine concert," she read. She explained that she had been unable to keep up, so she just took down the "gist of it." His masterpiece of literary prose was, like the lost chord, gone forever.

A plan for building speed in beginning shorthand has already been given. In advanced shorthand and transcription, teachers can rely almost entirely on dictation tapes and recordings to do the job. One teacher writes each tape on the board in shorthand as the students take it for the first time. Students then check their notes to make certain they are writing the material correctly. In like manner, they work through the entire tape or recording. The five-minute take at the end of the tape is used as a test. This is transcribed. Students who make a satisfactory transcript are eligible to go on with the next tape. The tapes used for speed building and those used for transcribing are often far apart in speed. Students may be working on the 120-wpm tape when ability to read back from their notes is all that is required, while they are still on the 80-wpm tape for transcription. The recordings are introduced in class and then placed in the libarary for the students to check out and work on at home. Where listening booths are available, students can do much of their shorthand speed-building homework there. If such a program is handled energetically, the teacher has little to worry about when it comes to speed. There are, of course, the usual "book letters" and "live, for-the-mail" letters that form a part of the daily routine.

The Transcription Chain—Typing

Except in regions where English is an abnormal problem, many teachers believe that the lack of proper typing is the basic reason for poor transcription achievement. Just as the idea of a fair day's work for a fair day's pay seems to be old fashioned in some areas of our economy, so the notion of calmly sitting down at the typewriter and being able to type a page of copy without error at fair rate of speed seems to be outmoded. If a student can't type a page with control under ideal conditions—from print—how will he master this feat while typing from shorthand notes? If typing speed and power are good when transcription is begun, proficiency should be maintained; if they do not come up to standard, pressure should be applied to build them up. How this can be done has been described at length in the chapter on typewriting. Usually, transcription books give short paragraphs designed to build higher speeds while typing from shorthand. These same paragraphs can

also be used to build typing speed. The shorthand version
of the carriage throw drills can serve a similar purpose.

The Transcription Chain—English

Persons working with students doing research work
report that even at the graduate level the English leaves
much to be desired. In one instance, after several sessions
in which very little progress was made, the student con-
fessed that never in her life had she written a theme or
term paper of more than five pages in length and that she
had never used footnotes.

A young man employed as a secretary was so good at
English that he specialized in typing papers for English
teachers doing graduate work. They left all the English
problems up to him. Their English was not what one would
expect. Those persons knew all the rules, but they themselves did not apply them.

Many large business firms have given up in their hunt
for office employees who know how to handle our medium
of communication and have organized remedial English
classes of their own on company time.

Some blame the lack of English ability on the "new-
fangled" type of education. We are getting soft, they say;
we need to quit coddling our students, etc. But an examination of papers from "the good old days" shows that, even
with the select group with which they had to work, the
results were not much better than now. The college blames
the high school; the high school, the grades; and the grades,
the parents.

There is just one thing to do—accept English deficiencies
as a problem that will always be with us. We must wrestle
with it the best we can. It takes the cooperative effort of
all teachers in the school system—formal English classes
cannot do the job alone. Often there is little carryover
from formal English instruction to practical-use situations.

But if the two work together, the English teacher setting the stage while the rest of us put the actors through their paces, the correct lines will eventually be ready for the office production.

The Transcription Chain—Punctuation

At Capital University a study was made of all punctuation errors over a year's time. From this study it was found that over 90 per cent of all punctuation used during that year followed definitely established rules. Only in a very small per cent of the situations did punctuation fall in the "it depends" category. Teachers would do well, therefore, to concentrate on the punctuation that follows definite rules and leave the few "it depends" cases to be learned on the job. Punctuation is an art as well as a science. Students need to know that there is something definite and solid about it.

Assuming the usual background training, abnormal difficulty with punctuation is a symptom that something else of a serious nature is wrong. It usually indicates a lack of an elementary understanding of the structure of the English language. A careful study of punctuation will do much to give meaning to the English involved, and vice versa. A functional understanding of English is half the battle in punctuation.

A good transcription book will have in it an abundant amount of material for drill in punctuation. In addition to this, the teacher might want to use alternating sentences to be typed at the student's maximum speed. The first sentence contains the marks in a problem situation properly used; the following sentence is similar in structure but is without punctuation marks. From the tip given in the preceding sentence, the student is urged to fill in the necessary marks without slowing down his typing speed.

In the introductory phases of transcription, some teachers have students place little red check marks above their shorthand where a punctuation mark of some kind is necessary, but the actual marks are not inserted. The punctuation required is then taken up in class, and the reasons are discussed. Later the exercise is transcribed, and the students then insert the correct marks.

The Transcription Chain—Spelling

If spelling were considered solely as an aid to communication, little time would be required for the study of it. However, spelling has acquired a significance with social overtones far beyond a standard required for simple communication.

The fact that a large number of "spelling demon" lists have been published would indicate that persons do not misspell a large number of words; they misspell a certain group over and over again. And people seem to agree on the words they choose to spell incorrectly.

It would seem, therefore, that the first step in improving spelling would be to let the individual find out the words that bother him and then master those words. Some teachers recommend the "little black book" method. It requires a small note pad on which he can write spelling errors made from day to day. When a person is absolutely sure that a word no longer bothers him, he takes that word off the list. The job is never done, for as old words are removed, new ones take their place—but it does improve spelling.

There are, of course, many devices that help in the learning of spelling. Spelling books give certain rules, but most of them have so many exceptions that they are of little value. The "i-before-e-except-after-c" is an example. The exceptions to that rule can be remembered by this simple sentence: "Neither financier seized either species of weird leisure." All the words in the sentence are exceptions to the rule. Not only does this trick help students spell the words in this particular sentence, but it puts the whole "i-e" rule in motion.

For years NOMA has been conducting a campaign to improve spelling. They have a list of 600 words that is excellent. Students study this list, then take a test on words selected from it. If they spell them all correctly, NOMA awards them a prized certificate. Over five million of these lists have been distributed.* One teacher makes it a point to have the students in her transcription class master this list during the first few weeks of the term. "At one stroke," he says, "it does away with half of my spelling difficulties. It makes a big increase in the number of mailable letters my students turn out."

Some years ago, one of the authors, in cooperation with NOMA, conducted a study in which students in their last year of business training were compared with office workers on the job. Four thousand persons were tested, and a large majority misspelled the same words.

The ten most frequently misspelled words in this study were: kimonos, naphtha, picnicking, sacrilegious, paraffin, battalion, supersede, rarefy, liquefy, and tranquillity. On the above list, if not tipped off, college professors usually score about 60 per cent and high school students, 30 per cent. It is not unusual to have a person miss them all.

As in the case of striving for improvement in English, there is no magic formula that can be recommended for improvement in spelling. It simply takes constant effort and attention. Remedial techniques are numerous. The following are a few:

1. Master the NOMA list, using whatever method seems appropriate.

---

* For information write National Office Management Association, Willow Grove, Pennsylvania.

2. Make a list of words missed the day before. Put this list on the board, point out the spelling difficulties involved, put the words in short sentences, and dictate them to the students at their typewriters.
3. Have an old-fashioned spelling bee.
4. Instead of the usual Christmas card, the teacher might give each student a little notebook: "Compliments of your teacher, to help you with your spelling."
5. Pronounce words carefully, indicating syllables. Many spelling difficulties disappear when the words are pronounced properly.
6. By one technique or another, create a determined *desire* on the part of the student to improve his spelling.
7. Put a little check mark before each word in your own private dictionary, words that you have had to look up. If you look up a word and find that it already has a check, that word should be put on a "special attention" list.

The Transcription Chain—Work Habits

Each business day provides ample opportunity to observe both good and bad work habits. Good work habits are characterized by neatness, confidence, and an atmosphere of efficiency that is unmistakable. A part of the transcription teacher's job is to help her students to organize their work so that they can perform their duties with efficiency and dispatch. They need training in working with carbons, in handling enclosures, in addressing envelopes, in consulting reference books, in finding data in the files, and in supplying routine information which the employer did not bother to dictate.

SUMMARY

Man is the sum total of all his experiences. What a person believes to be good transcription teaching procedure is the result of his years in the classroom and of the impact upon his thinking made by his many colleagues who have written on the subject. In listing the following, the authors would like to give credit where it is due, but that is clearly impossible. The ideas presented represent the thinking of many authorities on the subject of transcription.

1. Transcription must be taught vigorously by a teacher who knows how to do it. The know-how is available and can be obtained by attending methods courses, reading the literature of business education, consulting the references at the end of the chapter on shorthand.

2. Transcription should be introduced as soon as the student has mastered the basic principles of shorthand and can read and write fluently when dealing with easy, familiar material. This introduction in many cases would be at the beginning of the second semester.

3. Whereas the time required for learning the basic shorthand principles can often be shortened without harmful effects, ample time should be allowed for the final and most important phase of the shorthand course—transcription.

4. Since transcription is a very complicated skill, it should be introduced carefully by using well-established introductory techniques. In going ahead to new and more difficult material, students should not be forced beyond their power to operate effectively.

5. Transcription should be taught in a double-period arrangement where one teacher has complete responsibility for the entire training operation.

6. Transcription should be taught in the typing room or in a smaller room where typewriters are available.

7. Slow down when dictating for transcription—make sure that students get it; put on the pressure when striving for higher shorthand speeds.

8. Increase transcription difficulties gradually. Always remain within newly developed power limits. This means careful previewing, particularly in the early stages.

9. Recognize two levels of mailable copy: copy that can be used as is and that which can be *made* mailable with one or two minor corrections. The ability to make such letters usable and still stay within good office quality standards will save valuable rewrite time. It is a skill that needs to be developed.

10. Hold off on office-style dictation until the student has the power to handle it; then choose techniques carefully.

11. Build speed in transcription by using a variety of short speed-building exercises.

12. Use short spurts of dictation to the typewriter to nail down some point in punctuation, English, or spelling.

13. The first few minutes of a class period might well be used to transcribe from shorthand plate exercises in an effort to get the greatest number of perfect lines before the tardy bell rings.

14. When starting to work on mailable copy, make the first letters or exercises so simple that most of the students will be sure to get them right. Let the students experience the thrill of actually getting a letter ready for the mail early in the transcription course.

15. Maintain high (but efficient) standards of format quality. Don't be too much impressed by rumors that Mr. Businessman doesn't worry about the quality of his letters.

16. Without going overboard on the subject of office-style dictation, gradually introduce actual office customs, short cuts, techniques, and procedures.

17. Develop a working relationship with the English teachers. Try to capitalize on what they are doing that will help your students' transcription.

18. Students should have a dictionary within reach—it is as necessary as the textbook.

19. Spend enough time on troublesome areas for overlearning to take place.

20. Except in the very beginning, mailable copy should be the standard of achievement.

21. As more and more businessmen revise their work while it is still in the shorthand stage, the necessity for the stenographer to read back fluently with expression becomes more and more important.

22. Six mailable letters per hour is a good terminal transcription standard. These letters should be of average difficulty (if there is such a thing), between 125 and 150 words in length, and the material should be dictated between 80 and 100 wpm. One uncorrected carbon copy should be adequate.

23. Good use should be made of the teaching aids available to the transcription teacher, especially dictation tapes, recordings, and films having to do with office techniques and procedures.

24. Everything possible should be done to make the student feel that he has a part in the show, that *belonging* is something that is expected of the office worker. In the office the secretary is always an important member of a team. It's invariably "we" and seldom "they."

25. The position of a stenographer or secretary is a thrilling one. It's exciting to be working where important wheels are set in motion, where big decisions are made. Training for such responsibility should not be cut short. It is worth all the time it takes. Don't rush it.

SELECTED BIBLIOGRAPHY

The references given in the footnotes in this chapter, the bibliography for Chapter IV, and the *Business Education Index* will provide the reader with an abundance of material for further study.

CHAPTER VI

OFFICE PRACTICE—PART I

FUNDAMENTAL FACTORS IN TEACHING OFFICE PRACTICE

A study of what high schools are offering in office practice indicates three basic areas: (1) secretarial office practice, (2) clerical office practice, and (3) business machines. In some cases, where a double period is possible, stenographic improvement takes up one period; and the clerical skills inherent to any office job form the content of the second period.

Regardless of the particular emphasis, this course is a terminal vocational business course, one in which job competencies should be polished for subsequent employment after graduation. Since office-level work in shorthand and transcription has already been discussed, the bulk of this chapter will be devoted to the clerical and related job performance aspects.

The growing importance of office work and hence the need for basically skilled workers is indicated by various statistical sources. Douglas, Blanford, and Anderson cite the following reference:

> Between 1940 and 1950 the number of persons employed in clerical work increased from 4,300,000 to 6,780,000, an increase of 55 per cent. Between 1940 and 1954, clerical workers in business increased 64 per cent.[1]

---

[1] Lloyd V. Douglas, James T. Blanford, and Ruth I. Anderson, *Teaching Business Subjects* (Englewood Cliffs, New Jersey: Prentice-Hall, Inc., 1958), p. 266.

The *Statistical Abstract*,[2] in a breakdown of labor force
figures, shows that there were 9,539,000 clerical workers in
the United States in 1960. This represents 15 per cent of
the total 1960 labor force of 64,267,000 workers, and shows
an increase of 99 per cent since 1940. This increase cannot
be attributed to any one factor or cause; it comes about
because of the expansion of many areas of the United States
business economy.

Because we recognize the tremendous pressures, economical and psychological, placed on young people to go
to work after graduation from high school or from the junior
college, we have an obligation to provide them with at
least basic employment skills. These "basic" skills and
knowledges are delineated in the following statement:

> The twelve imperatives for persons seeking initial office
> positions, a base on which all other skill should be built, are
> familiarity with the office, desire to please, ability to follow
> directions, desire and ability to use democratic procedures,
> skill in use of fundamentals, neatness and good grooming,
> genuine understanding of value of accuracy, ability to type
> 40-50 words per minute, knowledge of business forms, ability
> to take dictation at 80 words per minute (for stenographers
> only), knowledge of the alphabet, and familiarity with com-
> mon office machines. The prime requirements for students
> seeking office positions (skill and personality competencies
> assumed) continue to be general over-all familiarity with
> office atmosphere, customs, and procedures.[3]

This is fertile ground for sowing seeds in our present
high school classes. How well we meet the challenge will
depend in great measure on the concept we hold of overall
office work. How many of us still concern ourselves with

---

[2] U. S. Department of Commerce, *Statistical Abstract of the United
States* (Washington, D. C., 1960), p. 216.
[3] Harm Harms, "Standards for the Office of the Next Decade," *The
Business Education Program in the Expanding Secondary School*, from *The
Bulletin of the National Association of Secondary-School Principals* (Janu-
ary, 1957), p. 72.

only the mundane textbook exercises in our teaching! Pointing to the future, Harms indicates the direction that our teaching of potential office workers must take:

> The office of 1965 will be a production-line office. Because of the additional services it has assumed, the office costs have risen more rapidly than factory cost; therefore the office manager is under fire. It can be expected that production-line techniques in offices will be enlarged. Every possible opportunity for efficiency will be investigated.
>
> The office of 1965 will have a different atmosphere. The accomplishments that office managers now brag about will then be routine. Of course, the lighting will be according to standard specifications. Air conditioning? Naturally! The five-day work week will be the rule. Coffee breaks, vacations, posture chairs, punch button files—yes, all of these and many more.
>
> Office managers have found that girls who play on the volleyball team and boys who take dancing lessons and persons who are enrolled in education classes stay longer with the firm than those who do not do these things. Therefore, it is expected that the whole social program will eventually become a standard procedure in most large offices. Teachers need to bring to the attention of their students this broad opportunity for social, cultural, and physical growth that is now part of some modern offices.[4]

Any definition of office practice should be one that arises out of the need which originally brought this subject into the curriculum; namely, the urge to establish a connecting link between school and business—to bring about a closer association between office managers and teachers of business; to lessen the in-service training period of beginning workers; to answer the criticism of business—that applicants possess so little "business sense." Office practice has for one

---

[4] *Ibid.*, p. 75.

of its purposes the development of new skills and the integration of skills already learned. Office practice is the connecting link between school and business by means of which the student is initiated into business practices and procedures. The more effective this initiation process, the more like actual business the schoolroom becomes; the more fundamental knowledges of business practices and procedures the student absorbs, the better will be the course in office practice.

This, then, is the task of the office practice instructor. For the new teacher, or one who has not taught the course, there is the necessity of know-how, the need for method. In the pages that follow, a number of fundamental factors are outlined, all based on sound psychology of learning. These basic considerations are necessary to the successful attainment of the general aims of the office practice course.

I-1   Adequate Advance Planning is the Nucleus of Successful Teaching in Office Practice

Being "ready" for the office practice course implies that the teacher has given careful consideration to several aspects of good planning: (1) course objectives, (2) routines and procedures, and (3) physical facilities.

Objectives. The present needs of business together with what we can reasonably expect them to be in the near future determine in a large measure the objectives of the office practice course. Today's graduates are finding employment in a variety of job situations—generally in one of two major classes: specialized office routines of the large office, or general office duties of the small-business office. Regardless of the situation, the general objectives of a good office practice course might well be stated as follows:

1. To help potential workers become familiar with the atmosphere of an office and with the world of business.

2. To help them develop certain personal traits that make for success in office employment.

3. To help them develop an ability to perform efficiently the responsibilities and duties generally assigned to office workers, particularly beginning office workers.

4. To help them develop and apply skill in such fundamental tools as arithmetic, written English, and punctuation.

5. To help them develop an operational proficiency with a number of the most commonly used office machines and a general familiarity with others less commonly used, but nevertheless a part of the general office picture.

6. To help potential stenographic workers develop a "finished" skill in typewriting and in shorthand and transcription.

7. To help potential workers see the picture of office employment more clearly by many pre-employment contacts with businessmen and women through cooperative relations with community resources.

8. To help them understand the significance of clerical competency and its important contribution to economic and industrial efficiency.

Several significant sources relating to statements of objectives will be cited in Part III of this chapter.

Routines and Procedures. The office practice teacher must be ready the first day of classes to plunge headlong into a three-ring circus of varied activities. Selection of material may prove to be a problem because there is so much of it. The preplanning covers a wide area of possible ideas. When actually meeting the class for the first time, however, certain cuts may have to be made or new items added. The application of routines to the selected content material to produce the desired outcomes is then dependent upon the approach that is most useful: the rotation plan, the battery plan, the integrated plan, or the cooperative plan. The selection of the approach will be determined somewhat by the job to be done, the number of students enrolled, the physical equipment and space available, and the philosophy of the teacher.

Physical Facilities. Physical facilities is the key to planning an office practice course. Planning for the first session of such a class is a unique experience. One teacher comments as follows: "I didn't get to bed until 2 a.m. As soon as registration was over, I went to see how many I had enrolled in the class. 'An even thirty,' they told me. I knew I would have to fit these students into the facilities available and team them up in such a fashion as to make the maximum use of each machine and to give every student the optimum practical, 'I-can-use-this-on-the-job' type of experience. This involved setting up a rotation schedule with actual names—a schedule that would have to go into effect the minute the bell rang in the morning and keep going until the end of the term. Every step had to be planned in advance. We had 'rotation within rotation,' a battery system for filing, and a set-up where we made an attempt at integration. Everyone who has had experience with this type of thing will agree with me, I am sure, that this is no job for a novice. It's a difficult piece of engineering. I was glad for one thing—I had a large room all my own, to use as I pleased. This gave me the necessary elbow room so imperative for maximum efficiency in office practice."

There is, of course, a certain amount of administrative resistance against "special purpose" rooms because they cannot be used for other classes. However, the office practice room is generally in use the entire day because of practice periods and the varied activities going on in the class.

In a short time the teacher's planning will begin to pay dividends—the class will be a smoothly functioning operation. Office practice is a unique type of teaching situation and does not permit the minute-to-minute, or day-to-day, planning that is sometimes used by teachers. Flexibility, however, should be an important part of the original pre-planning.

I-2   Pupils Learn By Doing

The "learning by doing" concept is well documented in the literature of education. It applies with double force to office practice. An office practice course must include a great deal of activity. What was stated earlier in connection with teaching typewriting and shorthand can be underscored in office practice instruction. That is, when the pupils leave the class the first day, there should be an air of general enthusiasm about them. This air of "get-up-and-go" is not generated by the teacher lecturing on the "history of the computer," worthy as the subject may be. Most students who enter the office practice room for the first time come with a feeling of eager expectation. Let's not kill this spirit by an extended lecture. *This is a class for doing.* Principle I indicates that doing can be accomplished the first day if properly planned for.

The idea of "doing" extends through the entire course. This doesn't mean that there is no place for discussion or demonstration. In fact, demonstration (Principle I-4) is most significant as a part of the program. Student participation in planning the conduct of the course is a part of "doing" and should be taken into consideration in the preliminary planning.

I-3   Not Every Student Will Have the Same Homework

Teaching office practice is different from the teaching of other courses and requires unique techniques. This is particularly true in relation to assignments. Nowhere in the hurly-burly rush through the teaching day is the need for preparation to handle the variety of student materials so great as it is in office practice. The business teacher who exclaims, "With all these different papers coming in, how can I keep up with my grading?" is in a tight spot; but he doesn't *have* to be. Assignments designed to meet the varying needs and levels of skill of from fifteen to thirty or more pupils can be handily developed. This assumes (1) a frame of mind to accept the condition, and (2) readiness through systematic routine.

The important fact is that there *must* be considerable variance of assignments because of the very nature of the course itself. Individual differences have to be met. There may be times when some students have no out-of-class assignments because of the nature of their immediate task, such as running stencils or spirit duplicator masters. At other times, as in the study of general office theory or filing, considerable headway can be made through homework.

One method that has appeared to work quite successfully is in the use of job instruction sheets. A description of a number of instructional devices is given in Part II.

I-4   Know the Machines

It has been said that a good teacher is one who shows the pupil how to do something and then lets the pupil do it. This system was recognized long before the day of the modern "progressive" education. A demonstration of an office machine is worth a thousand words of explanation. Some words *do* need to be used in carrying out the demonstration, but these words are underscored by the visual impact of the concrete illustration. The effectiveness of the learning situation is enhanced through the student's ability to see the "whole" of the operation rather than to struggle through a series of isolated steps, never quite being able to tie them together.

An interest-building advantage in teaching office practice lies in the reality of the activities. Sometimes teachers are embarrassed because they cannot operate the machines called for in the rotation schedule. Although we read mildly amusing anecdotes about Sergeant Marty Maher, long-time favorite man-of-all-skills at the United States Military Academy, remembered by graduates of the Academy as the non-swimming swimming coach, few teachers can teach skills in this manner. One way a teacher can remedy such a situation is to get a run-of-the-mill office job during the summer before commencing to teach the office practice course; he can brush up on office machines and business practices.

Another approach is to have the teacher obtain private instruction from the representatives of machines companies, and, if necessary, have a representative on hand when the machine in question is officially introduced.

I-5 A System of Repair of Office Machines Keeps the Course Moving

The ideal learning atmosphere has a minimum of confusion. One source of confusion in office practice arises when the room is filled to capacity, everything is humming, then a student calls for help as her calculator runs wild. The teacher is in danger of losing control of his group unless such an occurrence has been anticipated. Most of us would like to have at least one reserve machine on tap for emergency use. This may prove to be impractical or too expensive in terms of machine utilization. If reserve machines cannot be provided for, then planning in advance (see I-1) should include some supplementary nonmachine exercises for such emergencies. This extra work can be in the form of a duplicating job where extra students can be easily absorbed.

Office practice teachers are not expected to be equipment repairmen, but a knowledge of "what to do till the doctor comes" can save much time. A tenet of procedure is to observe preventive measures rather than rely on repair. To keep repairs at a minimum, we offer the following suggestions: do not permit pupils to operate machines until they have received preliminary instructions; work out a system of regular repair service with the agency dealer; instruct students in preventive measures, such as what to do when a machine jams; disconnect electric machines when not in use; keep the machines covered when not in use.

There is no general agreement on whether or not schools should have a standard contract with dealers for maintenance of equipment. In some instances, dealers are willing to work out a minimal repair service at no extra cost to the school.

I-6 *Students Learn Best By Doing REAL Jobs*

Nowhere in the business curriculum is the need to produce a vocational atmosphere so imperative as in office practice. This is not an exploratory course; it is fashioned as a "finishing" course. One teacher has called it the "frosting on the cake" in reference to the business curriculum.

By the time students start a course in office practice, they have developed a variety of basic skills. Now is the time to crystallize them for production competency. There are many kinds of work, real work, readily available for excellent laboratory experiences: assistants for the school office; a service bureau for the school for typing and duplicating materials; cooperative assistants to teachers in which dictation and other skills can be sharpened under the direction of nonbusiness classroom conditions; cooperative experiences under the direction of businessmen in the community, or a well-organized standard cooperative program.

The cooperative work-experience program is not a new idea. It is a method that permits business students to find

out what a day's work really means. The students may
have to work hard, but they experience the satisfaction of
accomplishment and are convinced by the feel and taste of
the job that "this is for them" and that what they learn
in related courses in school makes easier the tasks in the
business office.

Methods of selection for cooperative training vary. In
most high schools, however, placement comes near the end
of the time in school, usually in Grade 12, and is the cap-
stone of the vocational curriculum. A brief description of
the cooperative program and its relation to office practice
experiences will be given in Part II.

I-7 Efficient Learning Can Take Place In Mixed-Level Groups

Living in a world without individual differences, such as
is often pictured in the space age, would be a drab existence. As yet we have not reached this stage. Instead, we
tend to emphasize individual differences. In our classes we
must be prepared to work with students who have a wide
and varying range of abilities and experience backgrounds.

The many jobs of business call for persons with different
abilities. Just as industry provides jobs to meet these varying
capabilities to produce, so the classroom teacher must arrange educational work experience for all levels. This is a
difficult task, but it *can* be done. Archer, for example, states:

> Fortunately, the flexibility and latitude that the office-
> practice course permits the teacher should make it possible
> for her to strike some responsive chord in almost every
> student. Remember, the businessman isn't setting his sights
> too high these days; so, if the teacher can do only a little, it
> may still be sufficient for achieving employability in some
> appropriate threshold job.[5]

---

[5] Fred C. Archer, "Time for a Seasonal Checkup," *Business Teacher*
(November, 1960), p. 15.

I-8   *Learning Takes Place In An Office Atmosphere*

The work in the office practice "laboratory" is a simulation of the real thing. Duties that are performed will not be of the same type as those in smooth, "in-concert" typewriting classes. For example, office employees are quite often given handwritten copy with which to work. Practice of this sort, especially if the handwriting is not particularly good, is typical of the office situation and will provide excellent exercises for the students. The authors have used this technique and know what to expect the first time: a siege of questions, such as "What's this word?" "What does he mean in this sentence?" and "Shall I follow this style the way it's given in the rough draft?" All of these questions are reasonable. However, it behooves the office practice teacher to let students get this kind of practice in school rather than get caught "cold" on the job.

One relatively standard procedure to help create an office atmosphere is to develop a "model" office setup. Certain students can act in the roles of office managers, assistants, clerks, and receptionists. Each student who in turn serves his post as a group director tends to gain a sense of appreciation (and sympathy) for the employer or manager in his task of keeping office routines moving. Especially is this valuable in bringing home the implications of absenteeism—how absence and tardiness cut down the efficiency of the whole operation.

The office practice course also can introduce the student to the slogan of "first things first" that prevails in the office. Newcomers to office employment are quite frequently frustrated by the necessity of putting aside a half-completed job in order to complete a "rush-rush" job. Frustrating? Yes! True to life? Yes! With the experience approach, office practice students can enjoy the feel and spirit of the real office and thus develop a higher level of job intelligence and job sense.

I-9   Machines Alone Do Not Motivate

Machines alone do not motivate the pupil to learn. Of course, the potential is there, especially in office practice. This naturally-generated enthusiasm to learn, however, can be stifled if: (1) the teacher does not know the vocational aspects of the machines and equipment being used; (2) he sets unreasonable standards or unrealistic and nonpractical goals; (3) he does not use good judgment in admitting students to the class.

After a few weeks of instruction, it may be well for the teacher to carefully reconsider what has happened. Are the students still eager and responsive? Are there those who approached the course somewhat dubiously and are now its greatest boosters? Do the students appear to be working toward acceptable goals? These are flags that indicate good motivation.

I-10   Manipulative Skill Is Not the Only Factor In Job Success

At the same time that instruction is being provided for various units in skill development, consideration must be given to additional learnings that include effective work habits, getting along with fellow workers, and responsibility to the employer.

One of the primary reasons for lack of job success, as numerous studies have pointed out, comes about because of an apparent inability of new office employees to get along with fellow workers on the job. The office practice course is not complete if it fails to emphasize the necessity of being considerate, courteous, and tactful with fellow employees. Opportunity to practice these subjective qualities must be provided.

Most office practice texts call attention to and give suggestions for conditioning the student to:

1. Be on time.
2. Observe office routines meticulously.
3. Keep office secrets.
4. Be loyal to boss and organization.
5. Take initiative in going beyond bare minimums.
6. Plan work for tomorrow if today's job is done.
7. Be prepared for "rush" jobs, for peak loads.

Throughout this text, because of space limitations, the authors have constantly emphasized "the most significant factors." It might be well, however, to devote a page or so to the little things of office life. The following little things make a big difference for students who plan to be secretaries or general office workers.

1. *Find out what the boss wants and when he wants it.* He may be thinking to himself "That Miller letter has got to go out today," but forget to say anything about it. All your fine work will get little praise if the important items do not meet the deadline.

2. *Show an interest in what is going on.* If the firm is struggling with some difficult problem, be concerned about it. Before you come to work, run over in your mind what happened yesterday and last week. If you do, you will soon get a reputation for being bright and alert, when in reality you have only done your homework. Don't let the boss catch you "cold."

3. *Give him his coffee.* Find out when the boss likes his coffee and see that he gets it. If he has guests, perhaps they would like some.

4. *Be on the lookout for things that irritate the boss.* Don't spend too much time on the telephone talking to husband or boy friend. Don't look glum when the boss doesn't accept one of your suggestions—better luck next time. Don't allow yourself to get to the place where the boss has to "sell" you on *his* ideas. When the boss asks you to come

in, come promptly. Don't let him wait while you finish
something that you think is more important. His time is
worth more than yours—so the payroll clerk says.

5. *That's not my job!* Don't be a "that's not my job"
girl. Help the boss in his efforts to get an important piece
of work out on schedule.

6. *Be there every day on time.* The human organism,
especially the American organism, is noted for its ability to
work on schedule. The director of a famous choir has not
missed an appointment in 25 years. A university professor,
retiring after 40 years of service, apologized for using *five*
days of sick leave during those 40 years. To be there every
day and on time is the expected thing in American business.
If, because of an emergency, you do have to be late or
absent, call the boss and let him know you are concerned
about it.

7. *Do it with a smile.* When the boss asks you to do
something (even if it means working overtime), respond
with a cheerful "Yes, sir!" Then, if you wish, you can
go into the matter and give him the facts of life—"It will
take three extra girls. Can you dig them up for me?"

8. *Help make the work station of the boss attractive.*
Most executives are poor housekeepers. Give your boss a
hand. The janitor will do the rough work, but you can help
with the finishing touches. One girl took a course in
Japanese flower arrangement and put a touch of beauty to
the office. If you see that the boss is getting "buried,"
perhaps you can help him in getting the papers organized
and out of sight.

I-11   Practice Is Essential

"Practice makes perfect" if the practice procedures are
psychologically sound. Because there is such a wide range
of activities in the office practice class, from filing to the

building of personality, development of a sound pattern of drill is essential. Psychologically sound techniques involve the following factors:

1. It is important that the skill be practiced correctly the first time it is attempted by the learner. The first practice determines to a large extent the manner in which the work will be performed in succeeding attempts.

2. The sooner the pupil can practice the skill after he has seen it demonstrated, the easier it will be for him to perform it correctly.

3. The more often the practice of skill is repeated by the learner, the more fixed the habit will become.

4. The first impression which the learner receives of the skill is the most lasting. This means that the teacher's first demonstration of the skill must be clear and accurate.

5. The learner must know why he is doing a specific drill and at the same time have a short-range objective for that drill.

Because of the tendency to move away from double-period classes in skill development, some arrangement must be made to provide access to the office practice room in periods when it is not being used for regular classes. Individual differences in the class will necessitate additional drill sessions for a number of pupils.

I-12 Continuous Evaluation Is a Guiding Light for Students

Office practice work must be evaluated in terms of acceptability under the standards of business employment. To say that work can be graded under degrees of acceptability, such as "A," "B," "C," or "D" work, is not being realistic. Most of us grew up with a rating system of some sort, but one of the hardest "facts of office life" we found is that in business there is only one real system: acceptable work or unacceptable work. To make the office practice course meaningful, the teacher should consider these aspects of evaluation:

1. Evaluation of skills should be as nearly like real office standards and methods as possible. One procedure suggested by a number of prominent authorities is to invite businessmen in occasionally to evaluate work being completed. In many instances, Civil Service Commission tests can be used for practice.

2. Evaluate at the completion of a specific unit. This means that students will be taking tests on machines or on other aspects of their work continually throughout the term.

Ideally, no grades would be given as such in the course. Since there is no justification for the acquisition of knowledge for its own sake in this area of learning, the only purpose of the instruction is to develop acceptable business behavior and vocational use of skills. Yet the school administration, and also the pupils, to meet their psychological needs, require a measurement of achievement in order to show progress.

Whether this evaluation process is fair and accurate will depend upon the extent to which the teacher is familiar with evaluation techniques and procedures. The final judgment should reflect more than the acquiring of business facts. It should also be a reflection of the pupil's probable readiness to take his place as a competent person in a business office. The more valid the evaluation, the more difficult it is to make.

I-13 Work From the Whole To the Part—The "Why" of Instruction

"Here is your instruction book and there is your machine. Go to it." This is a common direction from the harried office practice teacher to a student just beginning a new unit of work. With a number of varied activities going on, it is easy to fall into the trap of forgetting the fundamental psychological fact that pupils learn best when they can get a glimpse into the "inner sanctum" of understanding what it is all about. Learning is more meaningful and more economical if it can be closely linked with its application. This only emphasizes the fact that the student learns more rapidly an activity for which he sees the need. When the size of the unit is not too large, it may be advisable to practice the whole while keeping in mind various parts that need special attention. Determining the proper whole is one of the arts of teaching. For example, Jack may see mimeograph operation as a whole, while Pete may have to have his "bite" of the entire process limited to feeding the paper through the machine.

I-14   Build a File of Source Materials

"Here I am about to teach a class in office practice! What can I use to enrich the course, aside from the textbook?" This is a common thought that occurs to many beginning teachers in this area of business education. The variety of units to be taught makes it necessary to cast about for many different types of teaching materials. Bulletin boards constitute an excellent teaching aid in office practice. The bulletin board is not a room decoration; it, too, must make its contribution to the learning experience. Although teachers may share with students the responsibility for the bulletin board, the teacher should have materials to start each project. This is true also of other types of displays. A series of special suggestions on source materials is presented in Chapter X.

OFFICE PRACTICE—PART II

METHODS IN TEACHING OFFICE PRACTICE

The preceding part of this chapter has been set up in the form of principles—abbreviated guides for teachers of office practice. Perhaps these principles can be one means of encouraging teachers to teach better than *they* were taught.

This part of the chapter is directed toward the same goal—specific analyses which we hope will be of assistance in office practice. It is hoped that this material will aid the teacher to plan, present, demonstrate, individualize, use sensory aids, evaluate, and develop an understanding of the various teaching procedures. Providing job-simulated work experience may help the student to make a realistic bridge from the classroom to the office.

The first of the *Ten Imperative Needs of Youth* of the Educational Policies Commission best expresses the direction of the office practice course in the high school and in post-high school institutions:

> All youth need to develop salable skills and those understandings and attitudes that make the worker an intelligent and productive participant in economic life. To this end, most youth need supervised work experiences as well as education in the skills and knowledge of their occupations.[6]

Many beginning teachers have expressed the desire to have at hand a "list" of procedures which they might use as guide lines in the teaching of office practice. The procedures that follow have been selected *because they work.* They do not represent everything that has been written about office practice methods.

---

[6] National Association of Secondary-School Principals, *Planning for American Youth* (Washington, D. C.: The Association, 1944), p. 43.

II-1   *Planning Is of Primary Importance in the Teaching of Office Practice*

Office practice is the connecting link between school and business. It is by means of this link that the student is initiated into business practices and procedures. The more effective the teacher makes this initiation process, the more knowledge of business office policies the student absorbs and the better will be the course in office practice.

The following elements have a direct bearing on successful planning in this area:

1. *How to make the most of school facilities and how to meet the requirements of business.* No blanket statement about a course can be made without first examining conditions in the school and community. Each type of school mentioned below will need to make different arrangements for office practice.

A. Size of school

    (1) Small, rural, consolidated school where business education must definitely meet rural needs.

    (2) Small high school—only commercial subject is a course in typewriting.

    (3) Small town high school, perhaps only one teacher in the business department.

    (4) Average- or medium-sized school with several teachers in the business department.

    (5) Large city institution with program of departmentalized business education.

B. Type of school

    (1) Business department as a part of the regular high school organization.

(2) Commercial high school—entire plant devoted to business training.

(3) The private business school.

(4) The junior college.

(5) Regular four-year college with a degree in
secretarial training.

(6) Teacher-training institution where secretarial
training is part of the program in the department of education.

C. Purpose of the school

(1) Trains graduates chiefly for college.

(2) Emphasizes the vocational—few go to college.

A number of studies have been made over the years of
what the businessman expects of his new employees. Reference will be made to some of these in Part III. Such demands are not always consistent, for communities differ on
what they think the businessman needs. The most practical suggestion that can be made to the beginning teacher of
office practice is that before actually teaching the course, he
should spend a period of time examining the needs of the
community.

There are, moreover, specific reasons for knowing something about area demands, particularly when the purchase
of relatively expensive equipment, such as fully-automatic
rotary calculators and bookkeeping machines, is under consideration. A demonstrated need should exist before equipment purchases of this kind are made. The results of a
community survey give the teacher excellent ammunition
when presenting his case for equipment acquisition to the
school board or the budget committee.

2. *Planning for classroom procedures.* A course in office
practice may be organized under various plans: The rota-

tion plan, the battery plan, the integrated office plan, the cooperative plan, or some combination of all of these. The two most significant of these are the rotation plan and the battery plan.

Rotation Plan. The students may work individually or in small groups. Under this plan the student operates a certain machine for a given length of time and then shifts to another. The group plan and the individual plan are feasible, depending on the number of machines and equipment available. Before the course is completed, each student will have had some time at every machine or work station. The time schedule should be arranged so that those who show special aptitude at any machine may be given additional practice in its operation. Under the rotation plan students are not expected to acquire occupational competency in the operation of these machines. If occupational competency is the objective, an intensive course using the battery plan is more desirable. For example, some high schools have an entire room of bookkeeping machines, and instruction is given much as in a course in typing.

In getting ready to handle a class by the rotation plan, the teacher first takes an inventory of machines and equipment available or that will be purchased for the department. The next step is to ascertain the number of students in the class. The machines are then arranged in groups, and students are assigned to these machines. For administration of the plan, a rotation schedule is made. This is a *control sheet* for the handling of the class. It assures each student a chance to work on all machines at some time during the term. The rotation plan on page 248 is a sample of such a sheet. Other examples are given in Part III of this chapter.

Battery Plan. In the battery plan, all students work on the same subject matter at the same time. The rotation sheet on page 248 includes a battery element in the teaching of filing. The key to the battery plan is equipment. There must be enough units—for example, rotary calculators—to enable a group to be taught as a class. For many schools with limited facilities, this constitutes a handicap. Therefore, some use a plan which is a combination of rotation and battery. Teaching under the battery plan lends itself to filing units, arithmetic review, and clerical typing.

Integrated Office Plan. The integrated office plan endeavors to duplicate an actual office setup. Usually a model office is arranged with appropriate duties for each member of the class. Students learn as they see the flow of business papers in simulated business situations. In some instances it requires quite a stretch of the imagination to feel the "office atmosphere," while in others the staging is quite complete with telephones, individual departments, special work areas, and so on. One of the best models of this approach is reviewed in full in Part III for the benefit of teachers who have the facilities to plan in this direction.

Other Factors In Planning. Regardless of the choice of plans, student supervisors or assistants are an important part of effective procedure. They are of tremendous value to the teacher in seeing that basic, routine features of the instruction are carried out. Class supervisors, or managers, can assist in the following responsibilities:

1. Obtain work assignments from teacher and distribute them to class.

2. Check student performance.

3. Assist members of the class in following rotation schedule, including the supervisory techniques.

4. Make certain that all students work the full period.

5. Check finished work and see that it is properly filed.

6. See that supplies are available and that they are used economically.

OFFICE PRACTICE ROTATION CHART

1st 6 weeks	2d 6 weeks	3d 6 weeks
FILING Group A	FILING Group B	FILING Group C

The filing group is taught as a class (battery).
Each student has a set of filing practice materials.

DUPLICATING Group B	DUPLICATING Group C	DUPLICATING Group A

Each student must do a standard list of jobs;
additional work warrants extra merit points.

MACHINES Group C	MACHINES Group A	MACHINES Group B

See chart below for rotation of
students within the machine group.

STUDENTS IN
Group A
1. Meyer
2. Harris
3. Jones
4. Pitzenbarger
5. Dean
6. Massey

Group B
1. Little
2. Barber
3. Kohler
4. Snyder
5. Douglass
6. Henderson

Group C
1. James
2. Donovan
3. Smith
4. Lytell
5. Mason
6. Anderson

ROTATION SCHEDULE FOR
MACHINE GROUP

	Students 1, 2, and 3			Students 4, 5, and 6		
	1st wk.	2d wk.	3d wk.	4th wk.	5th wk.	6th wk.
Comptometers.......						
Monroe calculator...	4	6	5	1	3	2
Underwood Sundstrand	5	4	6	2	1	3
Billing machine.....	6	5	4	3	2	1

EQUIPMENT

Filing practice materials
1 mimeograph and supplies
3 comptometers
1 Monroe calculator
1 Underwood Sundstrand adding machine
1 billing machine

7. See that all materials are put away promptly and that machines are left in an orderly condition.

Most textbooks and their workbooks are quite clear; however, they are not written for the individualized approach of the rotation plan. Job sheets specifically developed for the particular class are necessary to make the rotation plan work successfully. They do not take the place of the teacher, but they do enable work to go ahead while the teacher is circulating from group to group. Job sheets also provide practice in the type of office instruction often given by the busy employer. One of the best sources of samples of job sheets is the Bureau of Business and Distributive Education, the University of the State of New York, Albany, New York. Because of the adaptability of these job sheets for the individualized rotation plan, a copy is reproduced on pages 250 and 251.[7]

3. *Miscellaneous suggestions in planning office practice areas and units.*

Types of stencil duplicating jobs with which students should be familiar.

Job No. 1: Any assignment that has to do with straight typing, such as the average letter, examination questions, and job-sheet directions.

Job No. 2: Any assignment involving the use of the mimeoscope—lines, simple rulings, and other straight-line work in connection with typewritten copy. Samples of this type are invoices, billheads, and error charts.

Job No. 3: Advanced statistical reports, such as payrolls, financial statements, inventories, and various other jobs where breakdowns from original totals are required.

---

[7] *Job Instruction Sheets—Machines* (*Adding and Calculating*), *Office Practice* (Albany, New York: The University of the State of New York, Bureau of Business and Distributive Education), pp. 49-50.

OFFICE PRACTICE I
(Acquaintanceship Level)

Job Instruction Sheet No. M (A & C)-2

(Ten-Key Adding-Listing Machine)

ADDING AND SUBTRACTING ON THE TEN-KEY ADDING AND LISTING MACHINE

Pupil's name_____ Evaluation_____

Period____Date started_____ Date finished_____

Approved_____   :_____
              (Instructor)   (Person for whom work was done)

EQUIPMENT: Ten-key adding and listing machine, desk, chair.

MATERIALS: Textbook or manual, pencil, answer sheet.

DIRECTIONS:

Adding larger amounts or amounts with a varying number of digits (4.54, 54.76, .89) on the ten-key adding and listing machine is done in the same way as the simple addition performed in Job Instruction Sheet No. 1. However, in adding long columns of items the operator sometimes desires to know the total of items listed up to a certain point without clearing the machine. In this case he takes a sub-total. In your textbook or manual on p. _____ find out how to take a sub-total on your machine and how the sub-total is indicated.

Locate on your machine the minus (-) key or subtract lever. These parts will be used in subtraction problems. Review these terms minuend (top number); subtrahend (number to be subtracted); remainder (answer).

Steps	Key Points
1 Position machine and materials correctly. Assume good posture.	1 Machine should be at right and at a slight angle; materials in writing position.
2 Adjust tape and clear machine.	2 Clear symbol must precede each new problem.
3 To add: 6.83 45.52 .37 (sub-total) 7.51 6.02 123.10 (total) Add the first 3 items into machine. Take a sub-total. (Refer to your manual or textbook for directions on your machine.) Sub-total should be 52.72 S.	3 For fingering method, refer to Job Instruction Sheet No. 1.
4 Continue to list remaining items in the usual manner. Take a total. Total should be 189.35.	4 Symbols following the sub-total and total amounts should differ.

5 On p. _____ of your textbook or
   manual do _____ addition problems.
   Record both sub-total and total on
   your answer sheet indicating by an
   S the sub-total amount.
   (Example: 52.72 S)c
                189.35)

6 To subtract 869 (minuend)
               -371 (subtrahend)
                498 (remainder)
   Clear the machine. Add in the
   minuend in the usual manner.

7 Depress the keys for the subtrahend (371). In your textbook or
   manual p. _____ find out how the
   subtracting operation is completed.

8 Take a total in the usual way.

9 On p. _____ of your manual or textbook do _____ subtraction problems.
   Record your answers.

10 Subtraction is also used when an
   item is listed in error. For example: 417 is listed for 471.
   To correct this: Add 417 into
   your machine. Subtract the same
   amount (417). Add the correct
   amount into machine (471). Take
   a total. The correct amount, 471,
   will appear.

11 Do all addition and subtraction
   problems again. Time yourself.
   Compare your tapes. Compare items
   where answers disagree and recheck incorrect problems on the
   machine.

5 Indicating on the tape, in pencil, the number of the problem
   will aid you in recording the
   answer.

9 Clear machine before each new
   problem. Number problems on
   tape.

10 An amount may be cancelled by
   a subtraction of the same a-
   mount. Use this method when
   an error in listing occurs in
   your adding of a column.

11 You should be able to do all
   problems in Step 11 in _____
   minutes. Use checkmark to
   indicate correct answers.
   Use X to indicate an incorrect
   answer.

QUESTIONS:

1 On your machine how is the sub-total amount indicated?   the total
   amount?
2 Why does one take a sub-total?
3 On your machine how is subtraction done?

NOTE:

   Attach your answer paper and folded tapes to this Job Instruction
   Sheet and submit to instructor as directed.

Job No. 4: Advanced mimeoscope work. A sheet involving drawings to illustrate a given idea. Weekly sales sheets of neighborhood grocery stores furnish excellent material for elaboration.

Job No. 5: Programs. This includes jobs of various kinds that require folding, such as programs for recitals, banquets, and church suppers.

Job No. 6: Post card assignment. This involves changing from a letter setup to the adjustment necessary for a card job. On some machines it means hand feeding and protection against offsetting by some form of slip-sheeting.

Job No. 7: Color Assignment. Although color jobs are not ordinarily required in the average office, students should at least be familiar with the principles involved in doing a color job.

A Class Project Useful in Introducing Stencil Duplicating. Office practice students in some instances have had experience with stencil duplicators in connection with advanced typing. If such is the case, assignment of a project and help as needed is all that is necessary. Where no previous instruction in duplicating has been available, the following procedure is suggested.

A class of twenty, for example, may be divided into units of five students each. A stencil is given each section with instructions such as are found under stencil typing in the usual typing text. Each student writes a paragraph of straight-copy material and types his name beneath. Each group, with the aid of the teacher, puts the stencil on the machine, and enough copies are run off for the class. These are assembled into booklets, one for each member of the class. Sometimes the teacher writes a paragraph on each stencil. The booklet is then criticized in class. After a session of this kind, one fundamental point is usually established; namely, that good typing is basic to good stencil duplicating. The following are common errors of beginning students.

1. The touch used is too light.

2. Poor rhythm, some letters struck too hard, others not hard enough.

3. Too heavy a touch, machine cuts out the "o's." Since all students used the same machine, the fault must be with the operator.

4. Punctuation marks driven through—"pull your punches."

5. Faulty use of shift key. Take your time on capitals.

6. Capital letters not legible. Go over capitals twice, or strike them slowly and deliberately the first time.

7. Failure to disengage the ribbon.

8. Strikeovers are taboo when typing stencils; only rarely can this device be used to make a correction.

The Duplicating Workshop. If space is available, a separate room might well be set aside for duplicating work. This room should have a workshop atmosphere. Work tables, tables for mimeoscopes, and all tools should be placed so that they can be used most efficiently. An empty cardboard box with rows of holes will make a neat arrangement for styluses. Rulers, guides, celluloid designs, and similar items should all be within easy reach. Paper should be neatly arranged on proper shelves. The machines and the necessary supplies should likewise be efficiently organized. The duplicating room may breathe an air of efficient, pleasant activity, or it can easily become the most untidy room in the building.

Filing Stencils. Standard racks for filing stencils are on the market. Stencils may also be filed in the original stencil boxes, properly labeled and organized for ready reference. The following is a simple method of preparing a stencil for filing. A supply of newspapers should be available on the work table. The wet stencil is laid on this paper and blotted with another paper. The process is repeated until the stencil is dry. A copy of the mimeographed material is clipped to the stencil and the unit is ready for filing. Special folders for filing stencils are now available. These make stencil filing a simple procedure. The folder is automatically labeled by running it through the machine. After the used stencil is placed in the folder, it may be filed immediately.

The Offset Duplicator. Stencil duplicators represent the most common form of duplicating. In recent years several other processes have come to the fore. One of them is the offset process, quite extensively used in business offices. The copy is typed directly on a paper or metal (zinc) master, a special sheet from which hundreds of copies can be made. It reproduces anything that can be photographed; it is used to make copies of maps and diagrams and the like.

The Liquid Duplicator. One of the chief circumstances that has caused a decided growth in the use of the liquid duplicator is the large increase in government business. Government orders require a large number of duplicate copies. One firm recently reported that it needed from 20 to 30 copies of each invoice. "We use the liquid duplicator for this work and find it very satisfactory." One manager says, "We used to complain about four copies; when the required number reached ten, we were about at our wits' end. Now we have done away with carbons and use the liquid duplicator; though it is more expensive, it has many advantages."

Filing. A functional filing course might well be built around the following units.

Alphabetizing. Alphabetizing is a skill required of all those who would do filing. Such a unit might well serve as an introduction to the filing course. Most filing textbooks give exercises of this kind. Names may be typed in correct filing order (transposed or not, as the rule indicates) on new or used 5 x 3 cards. They can then be alphabetized in one complete list. These can be checked in class to determine difficulties. After all points in question have been cleared up, the teacher may wish to assign another exercise to provide additional practice and to assure that all principles are now understood. The class is now ready to proceed with the actual business of filing.

Field Trip No. 1. In spite of miniature filing equipment now available for classroom use, students often get queer notions about filing as it is done in the business office. In order to bridge the gap, a field trip should be taken early in the course. The purpose of this trip is to give a general overview so the students may see batteries of filing cabinets, drawers, folders, tabs, guides, and sorting trays as they function in business. Such an experience gives the teacher an opportunity during the days that follow to use such expressions as "This is much like the way they did it at the Bennett Company, remember?"

Basic Techniques. A full-sized three- or four-drawer demonstration file is exceedingly helpful in connection with the unit on basic techniques. Students then may see the various positions, the two types of folders—the individual and miscellaneous—and how correspondence is placed in each type. A good policy is to have available a stack of correspondence for this file and to have students go through the various processes of opening the mail, coding, sorting, and placing it in the file. Filing is one activity that the student must actually see and do in order to understand.

Practice Sets. A number of good practice sets and other practice materials are now on the market. The teacher should consult the various publishers to see which type is best for his particular needs.

Miscellaneous. In addition to the standard topics presented above, the teacher may wish to introduce methods of handling mailing lists, charge and follow-up methods, transfer methods, special types of filing equipment, and the like. This material is usually well covered and illustrated in the better filing texts.

Testing and Grading. The testing exercises used for grading should be as practical as possible. The mere reciting of rules and procedures does not always indicate vocational competency in filing. Here again the publishers and equipment manufacturers can be of assistance in helping the teacher to assemble materials for testing purposes.

Field Trip No. II. After the students have completed their course in filing, another field trip should be arranged. Careful preparation should be made for this trip. Several firms should be visited. Students should know exactly the things they are going to look for at each place. Now they can intelligently appraise the different systems they will see in use.

Filing an Important Skill

A good motivating device for filing is to help students to realize the importance of it in modern business. The importance of filing in the business office is indicated by the following table taken from a study made by Potter.[8]

---

[8] Thelma Potter, "An Analysis of the Work of General Clerical Employees," *Contribution to Education No. 903* (New York: Bureau of Publications, Teachers College, Columbia University, 1944), p. 26.

How Office Employees Spend Their Time

Typewriting and preparation for duplication 24.8%
Nonspecialized clerical work 24.7
Filing 18.1
Adding-calculating machine operation 17.8
Miscellaneous machines 14.6
                                            _____
                                            100.0%

Potter, in her conclusion, emphasizes the importance of filing. A thorough knowledge of filing and the ability to do production work in the typing of office forms will be exceedingly helpful in securing that first position or in gaining a promotion.

Machine Transcription

The most common method of instruction in mechanical transcription is to secure a set of practice materials and the accompanying textbook from the voice-writing companies and have the student transcribe these materials using the textbook as a key. The following suggestions supplement this method of instruction:

1. If a choice is possible, the members of the office practice class who rank best in typing should take their machine transcription work first. This will allow the others further opportunity to improve their typing.

2. Preview material is given in connection with each disc or belt in the transcription text. This can be used in the regular typing class.

3. Teachers should drill students on machine transcription speed techniques. Students should do an easy disc or belt over and over again, each time trying to overlay just a little further until they are able to type almost constantly while listening. The techniques for increasing efficiency in shorthand transcription and machine transcription are

quite similar. In *Shorthand Transcription Studies* by Balsley and Wanous,[9] there is a short letter of 83 words on page 72. Students are asked to transcribe this over and over again until the entire class can write it in two minutes or less, from the book shorthand and then from their own notes. This same technique can be used in machine transcription to speed up the transcription process. In this case, the stimulus comes through the ear instead of the eye. This procedure should be followed by a letters-per-hour test.

4. Students should have access to several different types of practice materials so that they may get used to different machines and dictators.

5. After they have become proficient in transcription, students should transcribe material to be actually mailed. It is necessary, therefore, that in addition to the regular quota of transcribing machines, the school should also have a dictating unit or a combination machine. This unit may be placed in the school office in order that school administrators and teachers may supply the office practice shop with a continual flow of material for transcription.

6. A better insight into the skills required to produce good dictated material may be obtained by having students team up in pairs and each dictate a job for the other to transcribe. If the student who is transcribing cannot understand the dictator, the dictator is asked to produce additional dictated material.

7. Care should be taken to have the transcribing unit properly adjusted. Students should be urged not to have the volume any louder than necessary. Likewise, a high pitch is often responsible for the headaches about which machine operators sometimes complain.

---

[9] Irol Whitmore Balsley and S. J. Wanous, *Shorthand Transcription Studies* (3rd ed.; Cincinnati: South-Western Publishing Company, Inc., 1958), p. 72.

Computing Machines

These may be divided into two categories:

1. Nonlisting machines
   a. Key-driven calculators
   b. Rotary calculators

2. Listing Machines
   a. Full-keyboard machines
   b. Ten-key machines

It requires only a few hours' training for basic operations on most of these. The key-driven calculator is an exception; some schools offer a two-semester course in order to have the student obtain occupational competency. Standards and further details are given in the pages that follow.

Bookkeeping Machines

The bookkeeping and billing machine may be learned in a relatively short time. Interesting sets of invoices and sales slips are available from most companies that sell bookkeeping machines. One teacher reports a technique wherein the students first perform the posting with pen and ink to a bound ledger and then do the same operation on the bookkeeping machine to the loose-leaf ledger. There is a bookkeeping machine for almost any type of work that needs to be done in the field of record keeping. Electronic equipment is frequently used where the volume is large enough to warrant its installation.

Private Branch Exchange, or the PBX

Even though it is impractical in most teaching situations, some schools nevertheless handle this part of the course through demonstrations at the school PBX unit. One school has an arrangement in which the class is divided into four groups. These groups meet evenings and during the lunch hour at which time they take turns as operator, supervisor, executive, and outer office clerk. Thus practice is obtained in actual opration, which is probably superior in value to some equipment now in use in the classroom.

In the above plan each student, after preliminary tests have been covered, is required to work officially at the school switchboard for a minimum of five hours. Some do as much as a week or more.

After the class is familiar with PBX technique, a field trip should follow. Several offices may be visited on one trip, perhaps the telephone company, a large office with several boards, and the average small office with the combination telephone operator, receptionist, file clerk, typist, etc.

Physical Layout and Equipment

The challenge to plan a room arrangement and layout from blueprint comes but seldom. At the College of Guam, the authors had this once-in-a-lifetime opportunity to develop an ideal office practice setup; the one-room pattern on page 261 was the result. Although it may not be possible for everyone to follow this arrangement, it nevertheless presents possibilities for adaptation.

The plan provides for five definite work areas—sufficient room for a beehive of activity: (1) duplicating area; (2) filing instruction area; (3) office machines area; (4) shorthand-transcription area; and (5) reception and "management" area. The facilities are not unusual except perhaps for the size of the room. We all know the story of the bellhop and the first-time traveler. "What's the average tip for that service?" The bellhop replied, "One dollar, sir."

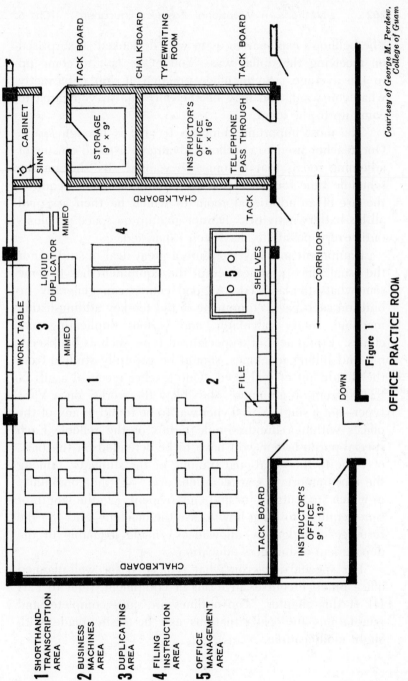

OFFICE PRACTICE ROOM

Figure 1

Courtesy of George M. Perdew,
College of Guam

1 SHORTHAND-
TRANSCRIPTION
AREA

2 BUSINESS
MACHINES
AREA

3 DUPLICATING
AREA

4 FILING
INSTRUCTION
AREA

5 OFFICE
MANAGEMENT
AREA

The bellhop's explanation as to why he looked so surprised on receiving the dollar was, "You're the first to come up to the average." So in office practice, if you get exactly what you want, you may be the only one in your area to come up to the ideal.

The most important thing to try for is enough space. One teacher used to excellent advantage a small cluster of adjoining rooms that no one else wanted. By shifting the schedule time for office practice, another teacher acquired the use of an additional room to which he then assigned all his battery activities. Do not give up on space problems until every possibility has been exhausted.

Equipment purchases require a great deal of study. For the usual office practice setup, the equipment has become somewhat standardized. A good course can generally be built on such basic equipment as the ten-key adding-listing machine, rotary calculator, and various duplicating machines. Equipment of a specialized type, such as bookkeeping and billing machines, should be carefully studied from the standpoint of real need. One teacher received a gift of $2,000 from an alumnus. She "blew the works" on a Varityper—not a single Vari-Typer was to be found in any of the offices within a hundred-mile radius of the school. Each special-purpose item will have to be defended on the basis of value to the vocational training of the students. Among the most important considerations are: (1) the community in which students are to find employment, (2) the length of time required to learn how to use the machine, and (3) the resources (budgetary allowances) made available to the department of business education.

For specific ideas on what is needed for well-planned office practice courses in terms of equipment, refer to Part III of this chapter. The outlines are quite complete, and adaptations to local situations can be easily made with slight modifications.

II-2 Pupil Participation in Office Practice Is Essential

Offices practice is a "doing" situation and should be treated as such. Students participate in planning and enter actively into the class routine. The office practice course may become involved and frustrating for the teacher unless full use is made of the potential leadership that can be developed in the students. Studies in psychology show that students are motivated when they have a part in setting up goals and routines. That is, if students have a definite part in initiating an activity through their own planning, they become extremely interested in seeing it through to completion.

In the office practice class, there are some routines that are performed daily, such as checking over the machines, seeing that supplies are available, checking attendance, checking in assignments, checking out machines manuals. All of this could occupy more time than a teacher ought to spend. Developing routines in which students have a part in planning has two values: (1) it develops initiative, and (2) the cooperative planning and work routines contribute to the necessary on-the-job traits, including the ability to work with others.

There are numerous activities in which the students can do more than "just listen." Among the most valuable projects that the office practice teacher can initiate is the production of "real" materials: a form for the school office, direct-mail sales letter projects, materials needed for charity fund drives, and so forth.

The atmosphere created is no longer one of "Is this good enough for a grade?" but one of "Will it meet the standards of the main office?" The matter of economy of time is also made more realistic. They know that *this* job has to be completed today.

The school office will appreciate the help of the office practice class members in preparation of routine jobs. This type of work should be considered not a nuisance but a splendid opportunity for student participation in important work *that will be used.* Good judgment is necessary, of course, to see that these outside jobs fit into the objectives of the total course. The office practice program involves more than operating a school print shop. Every job must be justified on the basis of learning experience. The office practice teacher who is skilled in the basic techniques of guidance enjoys the unique opportunity of helping his pupils explore their own problems concerning office employment.

II-3   Office Practice Assignments Deal With a Large Variety of Materials

Success in any course depends in part on the ability of the teacher to develop meaningful assignments, to check those assignments, and to make the results available to the students. Worthwhile jobs, successfully completed, are a strong motivational force that should not be overlooked.

Assignments in office practice work are varied. One of the most productive ways of handling these materials is to use the "folder" system. Students place samples of their mimeograph and other duplicated work in one section of the folder, sheets on which answers to adding and calculating machine problems have been recorded in another, and miscellaneous reports and materials in another. Students then file the folder in a file cabinet provided for special use of the class. The Remington-Rand Classifile folder with its multiple divisions is excellent for this purpose. Assignments, or jobs, are checked off on a control sheet fastened in the folder. These folders are inspected frequently by the teacher with a notation of "Audited." Student assistants can perform a valuable service in making sure that the class members file materials properly.

Uniform sheets on which answers to computing machine problems are recorded by students simplify the work of checking accuracy of performance. These sheets may be duplicated and are particularly useful if the business department owns the problem manuals and does not permit answers to be entered in the books themselves. The uniformity of these sheets does away with the problem of trying to check accuracy of solutions turned in on a variety of kinds of paper. Illustrated below is a sample of a sheet that can be adapted to use with most machines problem manuals.

II-4 Demonstration Removes the Vagueness of Verbal Explanation

Demonstration is one of the most effective teaching methods available to the office practice teacher. It clarifies

---

UNIFORM ANSWER SHEET

NAME _Ellen Lou Campbell_
MACHINE _10-Key Underwood_
JOB NUMBER _#1_
DATE _April 10, 19—_

P. 11	P. 15	P. 17
1. 1210	54. 340.31	70. 27.93
2. 1239	55. 315.36	71. 33.62
3. 1567	56. 345.14	72. 27.30
4. 1520	57. 577.47	73. 31.95
5. 1522	58. 421.54	74. 34.57
6. 9983	59. 419.75	75. 34.30
7. 14023		76. 22.18
8. 17103		
9. 11277		
10. 13473		

the purpose of drills, it shows correct motions, and it serves to motivate the student, assuming, of course, that *the teacher himself is proficient.* The tempo, or speed, of the demonstration depends on the class situation. At times speed is not essential; for example, the demonstration of the bookkeeping-posting machine. At other times the pace should be increased to high-level touch performance, as in the use of the 10-key adding-listing machine.

A distinguishing feature of demonstration in the office practice classroom, as opposed to the typewriting class, is that the demonstration will be completely individualized or used for very small groups. In instances of whole-class demonstrations, good use can be made of equipment salesmen for demonstrating their products.

Demonstration teaching is most effective when students see the procedure and hear the explanation. Today, with a variety of visual aids available, especially films, the teacher's effort can be reinforced by such films and by filmstrips showing important factors in the machine and its use. In addition, the overhead projector, with its "big screen" and ease of preparation of transparencies, can play an important role in visualization. Diagrams and drawings can be transparentized and flashed on a screen 6 x 6 feet or larger and are helpful when reviewing certain processes for the whole class.

Although individual instruction is perhaps the best single approach for machines operation, the visual aids available for demonstration-discussion teaching are invaluable for such phases as filing, office procedures, or any unit in which the battery plan is used. In planning visual aids the teacher might well ask himself the following questions:

1. Does the device enable the students to participate in the activity?

2. Does the device produce desired changes in student attitudes and interest?

3. Does the device provide for individual differences?

4. Does the device enable the students to realize success?

5. Can the device be prepared in the normal preparation time available to the teacher?

II-5 A System of Repair and Maintenance Must Be Developed

Other departments may have their problems, but those problems seem insignificant when compared with the time-consuming task of the office practice teacher who attempts to keep his equipment in working condition. This is a constant, daily pressure. For example, Archer relates this very common example of a classroom "situation":

> "My machine is jammed, teacher, and ink is leaking all over the place." If she responds to the call for help, how much time can she afford to spend there? If the difficulty can be solved in a minute or two, there is no problem, but suppose it will be a 15- or 20-minute repair job? [10]

In order to avoid the harassment of being detained at one work station for an undue amount of time, or having certain machines out of order for days, the teacher must work out a maintenance and repair system. Two of the patterns that have proved to be successful are:

1. Service equipment periodically.

2. Repair breakdowns promptly.

Many teachers, particularly those with relatively small office machines inventory, find it impossible to simply tag a machine, put it on a shelf, and wait for the visit of the repairman. The machine is needed *right now*. Of course, emergency work can be planned for the student, but this is useful for a short time only.

---

[10] Fred C. Archer, "Conserve Time—Save Yourself—and the Course," *Business Teacher* (November, 1959), p. 15.

II-6   Work Experience Is An Important Aid In Making Class Work "Real"

Earlier in this chapter emphasis was placed on the fact that office practice ought to bridge the gap between business and the classroom. Assigning the student to actual work experience in offices while he is going to school is one important factor in bridging the gap successfully.

Work experience in education is frequently referred to as cooperative education. When compared with other phases of business education, the cooperative idea is relatively new. In 1919 the Federal Board for Vocational Education recommended cooperative part-time instruction in connection with business courses in public high schools. Logically then, when office practice was introduced into the curriculum—its chief purpose being to furnish a link between school and business—various methods of cooperative endeavor were organized, frequently in connection with office practice courses but often as a department or school program.

Many of the articles that appear in the literature of business education describe cooperative office practice plans which are phases of work experience and not a part of a comprehensive cooperative office practice plan. In general, these experiences amount to doing work in the school office, taking over the switchboard to relieve the regular operator, taking dictation, grading papers for instructors, and occasionally helping out on a special job in a downtown office. These plans are frequently loosely organized and function as opportunities for work occur. Such practices might well be labeled "work experience" but could hardly be considered on a level with the carefully worked out cooperative part-time education programs.

Cooperative education curricula are firmly established in the field of distributive occupations, partly through the impetus of federal aid, by means of which schools with carefully articulated programs may apply for federal aid, and partly through the means of progressive educators in the field of vocational education who early saw the need for this type of learning experience.

It has been found, too, that if a community presents a plan that is well organized and has within it the makings of a successful contribution to business and to education, funds can be obtained for office practice programs of a cooperative nature. Several such programs are in effective operation. Many state plans and federally aided vocational education make it possible to organize office practice programs of a cooperative nature.

Forms of Cooperative Occupational Experience. A cooperative work experience program may take various forms. For example:

(1) Two students work as a pair, changing about; one works while the other, his partner, is in school.

(2) Two students work as a pair, half a day in school and half a day on the job.

(3) A single student works part time regularly.

(4) Student works catch-as-catch-can on holidays or after school.

(5) Student works full time for short periods, such as Christmas vacations.

(6) School operates a demonstration store.

(7) Student receives experience through an integrated office practice plan such as was described earlier in this chapter.

(8) Student works in the school office during free periods.

(9) Student works for faculty on a special project.

(10) School does work for business firms on a class production basis.

Organizing a Cooperative Office Practice Program.
Some cooperative plans have failed because an over-
enthusiastic business teacher attempted to put the plan
into operation without first orienting the community for
such a project. The business teacher should keep in mind
that there are a great many factors which have a bearing
on the situation: other teachers in the school, the parents,
the school administration, the merchants, the general make-
up of the community. The community may be such that its
very nature makes it improbable for a cooperative office
practice plan to succeed. If the town is made up of small
offices, where each employee usually serves a long period
of induction, a cooperative plan on a large scale has a small
chance of success.

Since more and more emphasis is being laid on the community throughout all education, some cooperative office
practice arrangement might be one way of getting business
and school together. A joint meeting of the teachers and
school officials with the usual business leaders, such as the
Lions, the Rotarians, the Kiwanians, the members of the
Chamber of Commerce, and others, might afford a good
opportunity to discuss plans of cooperative endeavor.
Mimeographed copies of successful plans in cities of similar
size might also be helpful. The important element in the
entire situation (assuming the community is the right type
for a cooperative) is a willingness on the part of all to give
the experiment a fair trial. This may take some salesmanship on the part of the organizing committee. The above
comments are not intended to discourage the business
teachers but to warn them not to attempt the program
alone.

Work experience of this kind combines practice with
theory, a tenet that is rapidly becoming a part of the accepted philosophy of modern education. Such programs
offer experience extremely difficult to obtain in school. They

develop certain insights that lead to business intelligence. Students learn how to work, a skill that some feel is rapidly becoming extinct, and they learn how to get along with people. Part-time education offers the student an opportunity to satisfy his curiosity for work and enables him to earn part of his way through school.

The employer often benefits, too, in that he comes in contact with a constant stream of hand-picked potential personnel from whom he can choose when the time comes.

There are, of course, some weaknesses that may creep into a cooperative program. The work may be of such a nature that it ceases to have educational value. The employer may take advantage of the students. The jobs to which students are assigned may not be representative of good business practice.

II-7 *Initial Motivation Must Be Supplemented*

Teachers sometimes make the error of assuming that the office practice course will carry itself along because machines "interest" people. This is true, *for a few days*. Studies of the interests of people, particularly of youth, tell us to expect rapid changes in the interest span. A semester is a long time to attempt to hold someone's interest based simply on mechanical factors. What may appear to be real interest may be only innovation.

Motivation has been described as *extrinsic* and *intrinsic*. Intrinsic motivation, stated as simply as possible, means that the factors involved are directly and functionally related to the activity itself; extrinsic motivation factors are artificial. Specific examples of each in business teaching are: (1) *intrinsic*: the inherent challenges with the subject itself, recognition of the student as an individual, realistic problem material, desires of the student, and (2) *extrinsic*: class competition, progress charts, bulletin boards, and recognition—awards and rewards of various kinds.

Office practice students are usually highly motivated when they enter the course. The teacher must capitalize on initial interest by being ready to provide additional experiences the very first day and in the days that follow in order to keep the enthusiasm alive. Just as we find it true in other business subjects, short-term goals are better than long ones; goals closely associated with the task at hand are better than a dissertation on "how worthwhile this skill will be when the student is on the job."

The authors have stated that success is crucial in learning shorthand. This factor of learning is equally applicable to all other skill areas. If careful attention has been paid to Principle I in this chapter, provision will be made in the preplanning stage for the student to leave the class with a feeling of accomplishment—"I did something today."

The teacher must find *something* he can sincerely praise each period, even if this "something" is not of world-shaking importance. All indications point to the fact that students do well whatever they find they *can* do well, particularly if "doing well" is recognized by the teacher.

II-8 The Intangible Factors of Nonskill Concepts Are Perhaps As Important As the Skills

Charm is an attribute of personality which cannot be turned on or off as we desire. It is that part of one's self which radiates graciousness and all the finest quality of living. It is the quality the bearer exemplifies when he becomes interested in *you* as a person, an individual, a human being. Charm is hardly that big smile and handshake you give the boss when you are trying to pull yourself out of the mire by the bootstraps. It is most likely that inner glow you feel after having done a good deed, which very likely will be known only to the recipient, yourself, and your God.[11]

---

[11] J. Russell Coffey, "Charm," *The Physical Educator* (May, 1959), p. 47.

This comment on one of the attributes of personality is of particular significance in the modern-day office employment picture. More persons obtain positions and promotions because of personality factors than for any other reason. More people lose their jobs because they lack these traits than for almost all other reasons combined. Many personnel managers are so concerned about personality that they prefer the interview method as their basic tool of selection, using other testing techniques only incidentally. It stands to reason, therefore, that teachers should be seriously concerned with personality development not only in business education but also in all areas of education. The office practice course provides the opportunity to give special attention to personality.

Personality Defined. Dame, Brinkman, and Weaver define personality as,

> . . . that group of qualities and characteristics that makes of one an individual, that sets him off from other individuals. In short, it is the sum total of abilities, talents, skills, interests, and physical and mental characteristics that he possesses, or better still, the combination of all these. Defined thus, it comprises everything that an individual has inherited from his forebears, with necessary training added.[12]

Of the many traits that may be listed as desirable, the following classification, according to the above authors, includes those requisite for business success and efficiency:

1. Physical Traits	2. Social Traits
a. Appearance	a. Manners
b. Dress	b. Courtesy and tact
c. Health	c. Cooperation
d. Endurance	d. Poise

---

[12] J. Frank Dame, Albert R. Brinkman, and Wilbur E. Weaver, *Prognosis, Guidance, and Placement in Business Education* (Cincinnati: South-Western Publishing Company, 1944), p. 127.

3. Mental Traits
   a. Memory
   b. Judgment
   c. Concentration

4. Emotional Traits
   a. Self-confidence
   b. Ambition
   c. Initiative
   d. Will power

5. Character Traits
   a. Honesty
   b. Loyalty
   c. Punctuality
   d. Morality

6. Technical Traits
   a. Skill
   b. Speed
   c. Accuracy [13]

One of the encouraging findings to come out of psychological research is the certainty that the human organism has been shaped to a large extent by the buffeting of the forces of its environment. John B. Watson, leader of the behaviorist school of psychology, made the following statement based on his many years in the field:

> Give me a dozen healthy infants, well-formed, and my own specified world to bring them up in, and I'll guarantee to take any one at random and train him to become any type of specialist I might select—doctor, lawyer, artist, merchant-chief and yes, even beggarman and thief—regardless of his talents, penchants, tendencies, abilities, vocations, and race of his ancestors.[14]

Sargent, in his compilation of the best basic knowledge that has been recorded in the field of psychology, also states that:

> Heredity provides the raw material from which a person is made. What he becomes, how the material is molded, depends chiefly on environment. Good materials placed in good hands result in a fine finished product.[15]

This is good news, particularly for the individual in need of personality improvement. It means that by artificially

---

[13] *Ibid.*, p. 128.
[14] Quoted in S. Stansfeld Sargent, *Basic Teachings of the Great Psychologists* (New York: Barnes and Noble, Inc., 1958), p. 79.
[15] *Ibid.*, p. 80.

utilizing desirable forces, desirable personality traits *can* be developed. If this is true, then one would expect personality development as a natural by-product of a well-conducted business education laboratory or a good model office. Here, in school but under occupational conditions, the student is free to express himself, and the teacher has an opportunity to guide this exercise in the right direction.

In response to his letter to a young high school graduate, urging her to thoroughly prepare herself before she went job hunting, a college professor received this reply: "Job hunting! Why, I've had three offers already and I can't even type." It is true that at the moment even the marginal office worker is finding employment. But it may not always continue to be so. There are signs that a change is approaching, a change that will once again call for good job-getting techniques.

In addition to a knowledge about jobs and a careful inventory of one's own offerings in the way of skill, knowledges, and personality characteristics, there still remains the technique of job-getting. This consists chiefly of the following: (1) the application letter or its equivalent, (2) filling in the application form upon arrival at the office, (3) the oral interview, and (4) the taking of some sort of a test. A significant amount of the total time for the course should be allotted to a study of actual job-getting know-how.

II-9 Grading and Evaluation Should Be Geared To Realistic Vocational Standards

Although in certain courses we have dual objectives— vocational and personal use—the consensus of business educators is that office practice ought to be treated as a vocational course, designed to prepare the student to meet the requirements of his first job. The chief characteristic of the classroom work should be purposeful activity in skill building, discussion of factors that will enable students to become acquainted with the essential facts of office employment, and the development of attitudes conducive to successful job performance.

Granting that the primary aim is vocational preparation, then the big job for teachers is to work with students to prepare them to meet employment standards. But it is not that simple. Except for speed in shorthand and typing, there appears to be little agreement among businessmen on tangible standards. In the periphery skills there seems to be much that is vague. We do have a few sources of general standards, however, that can be adapted and used with relative success. These are given in detail in Part III of this chapter. In addition, the Office Practice Section of the National Business Entrance Tests [16] is of value in rating students in terms of general business demands. The NBET testing program is a joint effort of the National Business Education Association and the National Office Management Association. It represents one of the best attempts at teacher understanding of the needs of business. Though these test results do not tell the whole story, they are valuable to the office practice teacher in providing comparative criteria valuable for student, teacher, and course evaluation.

For grading purposes, it becomes necessary to develop functional standards based on community needs to verify the teacher's judgment. These should be checked against other schools' standards. Volume VII of the American Education Yearbook [17] can be of help to the office practice teacher in his evaluation problems. The "folder" system described on page 264 provides the teacher with a checking and evaluating method that can be used readily for the purpose of assigning grades.

---

[16] *National Business Entrance Tests*, National Business Education Association, Joint Committee on Tests, Washington, D. C.

[17] *Evaluating Competence for Business Occupations*, American Business Education Yearbook, Vol. VII (New York: New York University Bookstore, 1950).

OFFICE PRACTICE—PART III

WHAT OTHERS HAVE TO SAY ABOUT TEACHING OFFICE PRACTICE

In Parts I and II we attempted to provide the beginning teacher with some rather specific ideas and techniques that can readily be adapted to any classroom situation.

It remains for leaders in the field and other classroom teachers to verify and augment the suggestions already presented. In the pages that follow, certain proven concepts are presented by well-known teachers in business education, particularly those who have spent a great deal of time in the area of office practice. Consistent with the pattern already established, comments, ideas, and outlines that appear to be of most immediate value to the beginning teacher in office practice are presented in the following sections.

III-1 Planning Pays Dividends

The comment has already been made that successful planning in office practice encompasses three specific areas: (1) objectives, (2) routines and procedures, and (3) physical facilities. One of the best statements of objectives that has been made in recent years, one that recognizes up-to-date desired outcomes for office practice is contained in Bulletin 274, the office practice syllabus of the Commonwealth of Pennsylvania:

1. To contribute to the development of appreciations, ideals, and socially desirable attitudes and work habits which are necessary for success in an office situation.
2. To maintain and further develop knowledges and skills that have already been learned.
3. To help bridge the gap between formal instruction offered in school and the responsibilities of an initial job in the business world.

4. To offer experience in as practical a situation as possible in the performance of routine office jobs.

5. To develop the ability of judging the marketability of one's own work and to make the necessary adjustments or corrections.

6. To build both speed and accuracy in work performed in the business office.

7. To set forth desirable standards of office performance.

8. To develop proper attitudes toward promotional possibilities, as well as the realization of additional responsibilities.

9. To give pupils experience in applying for a position.

10. To acquire additional competencies such as knowing how to operate the more commonly used office machines.

11. To learn to take care of equipment and supplies.[18]

Office practice is a terminal course in skills and knowledges and the development of personal traits and work habits. Green develops an extensive outline having to do with the aims of office practice; the major considerations of which are as follows:

1. The ability to attack problems successfully.

Among the many component parts of whatever it is that goes into the ability to attack problems successfully, there are five elements which the clerical office practice teacher can definitely help to develop:

a. A confident attitude.
b. Proper orientation to the problem situation.
c. Mastery of skills necessary for satisfactory completion of the problem.
d. Logical approach to the problem.
e. Ability to work as a member of a team.

---

[18] *Office Practice for Business Education Departments in Pennsylvania's Public Schools,* Bulletin 274 (Harrisburg, Pennsylvania: Department of Public Instruction, 1959), p. 43.

2. Ability to handle directions.

Chief among the reasons why students *can't* or *won't* follow directions is the fact that we as teachers have not stressed this ability enough, have not insisted upon their doing it enough, have not provided sufficient opportunity in its exercise, varied our routine enough, or taught them the importance and necessity for following directions. Here are some things you can do:

a. Insist that each student have a notebook for writing down assignments. See that he writes them down in the beginning until the habit has begun to jell.

b. Vary the type of directions. Sometimes give written directions, sometimes oral, sometimes a combination of both.

c. Give partial or skeletal directions at times. This does not mean indefiniteness. But as students advance in ability to follow directions, sometimes purposely omit giving explicit directions for some necessary or obvious step.

d. Fit the directions to the level of performance and understanding.

e. Demonstrate as well as write or tell.

f. Teach students to triple check directions before beginning a task.

g. Teach students to recheck directions against the completed work before handing the work in.

h. Give some definite recognition in your grading scale to "following directions to the letter."

i. Learn to state directions clearly, concisely, and in logical sequence with proper subordination of procedure and ideas.

j. Weed out ambiguities and indefinite statements in giving directions.

k. Develop situations in which students must exercise discernment, judgment, and creative ability in carrying out directions.

3. Ability to utilize time and materials efficiently.

   a. Making students aware of what are considered to be acceptable production standards for beginning workers on various types of clerical work and of comparing their own production rates with an eye toward improvement.

   b. Utilizing more "production" units of work.

   c. Demonstrating time-saving short-cuts and techniques of efficient handling of papers.

   d. Teaching students to utilize free time.

   e. Setting an excellent example in the effective and efficient use of both time and materials.

4. The ability to work under pressure of time.

   We are familiar with the worker who, under pressure, gets so angry that his anger interferes with both his efficiency and his relations with his fellow workers. As clerical office practice teachers, we have a responsibility to help our students develop the ability to work efficiently under *pressure of time*. Here are some of the things we can do to help them develop this ability:

   a. Make students aware of the fact that most jobs in today's world have periods of stress—that there will be many times when pressure of time is of utmost importance.

   b. Increase students' understandings of why there are deadlines in business and of what happens if these deadlines are not met.

   c. Give much training in production jobs in all clerical areas covered in the course. Make time required to do a job an integral part of the grading scale.

5. Concern for detail and accuracy.

   a. The use of student-work appraisal sheets completed by individual students or by committees of students.

   b. Work and assignments completed or performed are actual exercises, not just textbook or classroom work.

   c. Proofreading or checking a partner's work. Two heads are really often better than one, especially in the matter of spotting inaccuracies in another's work.

6. Wholesome attitude toward work.

If there is any one facet of the whole area of building an employable personality and developing desirable work habits in which the *caught* rather than the *taught* element is stronger, it would probably be in this attitude toward work area. Some of the most significant techniques for helping develop a wholesome attitude toward work are these:

a. Talks by employers, talks by former students, films, and articles on the subject.
b. Student-teacher planning concerning just what classroom duties students can take over.
c. Part-time employment of cooperative work experience.
d. Simulating whenever possible model office conditions.

7. Poise and self-assurance.

Poise and self-assurance on the part of our students are both rooted in confidence. Such confidence stems both from the knowledge on the part of the student that he has the skills and personal qualities sufficient for getting and holding a job and from a degree of familiarity with what business is like. Some suggestions for helping our students acquire poise and self-assurance include:

a. Providing opportunity for self-evaluation.
b. Providing opportunity to become more familiar with business and specific types of jobs through carefully planned field trips.
c. Providing opportunity to practice social graces.
d. Giving consideration to grooming and dress.
e. Providing opportunities for practice in employment interviews.[19]

Every teacher will have his own particular problems in getting started in the office practice course. However, ex-

---

[19] Helen H. Green, "Development of Personal Traits and Work Habits through Clerical Office Practice," *Business Education Forum* (February, 1958), pp. 17-20.

periences of others in the field can be of valuable assistance in overall planning. Hicks offers one of the better broad outlines:

1. Make preliminary plans. The secret of organizing is to make preliminary plans. Items such as the following should be taken care of before the first day of class:

   Selection of text materials.

   Checking on kind and condition of your equipment and supplies.

   Checking on the condition of the room itself—lighting, bulletin boards, chalkboards, arrangement, etc.

   Finding out, if possible, how many students will be in the class.

   Preparation of whatever supplementary materials you need.

2. Make a schedule for each day. Set up a day-by-day schedule for the entire semester. You will probably have to work with three sets of instructional materials—for machines, filing, and background (procedures and human relations).

3. Orient students carefully. It is wise to devote the first week to orientation—introduce the students to the course and give demonstrations on each machine.

4. Make assignments well in advance. If class discussion is for each Monday, for example, the students have ample time to ready their materials for the Wednesday typing laboratory and for the discussion to be held the following Monday.

5. Use a workable rotation plan.

6. Include a comprehensive review.[20]

---

[20] Charles B. Hicks, "How to Organize the Subject Matter of Your Secretarial Practice Course," *Business Education World* (February, 1954), pp. 14-15.

Regardless of how much planning is done or how carefully it is considered, the success to be derived from this planning must be compatible with the best of what we know regarding the psychological principles underlying the learning process. Much of the work in the office practice class has to do with skills. An occasional review of such basic principles as outlined by Price are a necessary element of planning:

These things help learning:

A. Good classroom conditions and atmosphere.

B. Students knowing whether they are progressing, and why, and what helps or retards their program.

C. Students knowing the purpose of each moment's effort—what to do, and why, and precisely how.

D. Success. It accelerates effort and achievement.

E. Students knowing how a skill is used on the job and practicing it exactly the way it will be used.

F. Providing for individual differences by:

   1. Using a variety of teaching methods and procedures, and

   2. Judging success by flexible standards and as much by extent of progress as by actual achievement.

G. Purposeful practice for specific improvement.

H. Guiding students in doing things the right way and avoiding wasteful trial-and-error experiences.

I. Using short, not long periods of intensive practice; and spreading practice over several days.

J. Imitation of good performance. Teacher shows how.

K. Emphasis on the positive, not negative, approach.

L. Learning in context, not in isolation—for retention is better when learning is related.[21]

---

[21] Wilmoth C. Price, "A Practical Review of Skill Psychology," *Business Education World* (September, 1954), p. 38.

In Part II, many approaches to the teaching of office practice were given. The experience of hundreds of teachers emphasizes the need for reality in the classroom situation. The plan that follows is presented in its entirety because it appears to be one of the most feasible and workable ideas published in recent years. This plan not only keeps the routine learning moving, but it also provides opportunities for the participants to learn how to organize and conduct meetings and how to get departmental staff into action:

Business is dynamic and practical—so must be the business teacher's technique in preparing the student to meet its demands. A functional plan which has proved successful in aiding the student to make this all-important adjustment is the model office layout. This effect may be achieved by deviating from the traditional row-by-row arrangement of tables and typewriters and by sectioning off the room into departments. By skillfully shifting the tables around, the teacher will be amazed with the amount of space remaining after the room has been sectioned off. In St. Joseph High School (Shawnee, Kansas), where this plan is functioning, the classroom is divided into four main departments: typing, transcription, filing, and publications. These particular departments were chosen because of the type of equipment on hand and the nature of work usually performed in the typing room. Each department is labeled with signs lettered in India ink and covered with celluloid. The filing department is separated from the others by a right-angle railing. Behind it are two filing units on wheels. Next to this department is the transcribing department with five dictation machines and typewriter. The typing department occupies the entire other half of the room. No office would be complete without a receptionist's desk. On the desk is a "receptionist" placard and telephone. Here the students take turns being caller and receptionist.

The appointment of an office manager and department heads will stimulate and increase enthusiasm and a sense of responsibility. The teacher appoints the office manager for a period of two weeks, and he is chosen because of the conscientious, efficient manner in which he has discharged his duties as department head. The manager in turn chooses the department heads.

They (department heads) may be responsible for collecting assignments, checking daily attendance, distributing workbooks, and posting bulletin board displays, while the latter (office manager) may supervise the work as it is being performed in the various departments and inspect the office at the close of the period to see that it is in order, and if it is not, to inform the person in charge of the particular department concerned.

The chief duty of the office manager, however, is to plan an agenda for a meeting of the department heads which can be easily scheduled during the class period. A meeting is called toward the beginning of his first week to formulate plans and another at the end of the second week to see if these plans were carried out successfully. Interoffice memorandums stating the time, place, and subject to be discussed are issued. Ideas for these discussions may be encouraged by placing a suggestion box in a convenient spot in the office where any student can deposit his contribution. During the meeting, the office manager appoints someone to record the minutes, which are later organized, read aloud to the class, discussed, and finally posted on the bulletin board.[22]

The "model office" procedure offers unmatched possibilities for realism and purposefulness in developing vocational attitudes and skills. Archer and Roughsedge endorse this pattern of procedure:

> The model office plan of classroom operation affords an opportunity to achieve the goals because the classwork is based upon a flow of common office procedures.
>
> In almost any office, for example, the clerical work involved in processing a customer's order begins with the job

---

[22] Sister M. Pauline, "The Model Office in Teaching Business," *Catholic School Journal* (March, 1958), pp. 43-44.

of opening and sorting the mail. Then, the orders are read and interpreted. Prices are determined from catalogs and the cost of the order is computed. In the next operation the invoice is prepared with several carbon copies. The original is sent to the buyer. The copies, in turn, become the basis for such clerical operations as posting to the customer's account, adjusting stock records, analyzing sales, and computing sales commissions. In the model office, students are assigned to work stations along the paper production line to learn the different kinds of office jobs by actual "doing." They rotate from one job to another to get a well-rounded experience.[23]

The State of New York syllabus for teaching office practice in Grades 11 and 12 offers excellent suggestions for various possibilities in teaching machines on a rotation basis:

> Several charts are given which illustrate different types of class organization based upon the rotation plan. The time basis used is 180 days. Using 180 days as the time basis for office practice permits additional time that can be used for preliminary class organization, pretesting, special holidays, unexpected disruptions, field trips for the entire class and the like. The charts are based upon the following time schedules for the six basic units.[24]

Suggested number of periods to be devoted to different training levels

Basic units	Title	Acquaintance-ship level	Practical use level	Vocational competency level
I	Typewriting	30	75	255
II	Machine transcription	15	60	180
III	Duplicating	15	60	180
IV	Machines (adding and calculating)	30	75	255
V	Filing	30	75	120
VI	Office practice and procedures	15	60	180
	Total time for six basic units	135 periods		

---

[23] M. Gertrude Roughsedge and Fred C. Archer, "How Does the Principal Evaluate the Effectiveness of the Teaching of Clerical Practice?" *Bulletin of the National Association of Secondary-School Principals* (January, 1957), p. 151.

[24] *Syllabus and Teaching Suggestions for a Course in Office Practice, Grades 11 and 12* (Albany, New York: The University of the State of New York, 1958), pp. 25-30.

Charts showing different rotation plans for single-period courses (180 periods)

PLAN 1

NOTE: Each block represents 15 periods.

Pupils	First semester						Second semester					
5	I	I	II	III	IV	IV	V	V	VI			
5	IV	IV	I	I	II	III	VI	V	V			
5	V	V	III	II	I	I	IV	IV	VI			
5	I	I	IV	IV	III	II	VI		V	V		

This chart indicates a rotation plan for four groups of five pupils each, based on minimum equipment requirements. Each block represents 15 periods. Numbers in the blocks represent six basic units. Forty-five periods are available for training beyond the acquaintanceship level.

PLAN 2

Pupils	First semester						Second semester					
4	I	I	V	V	III	II	VI		IV	IV		
4	VI	I	I	III	IV	IV	V	V	II			
4	IV	IV	I	I	V	V	III	II	VI			
4	II	III	VI	I	I		IV	IV	V	V		
4	V	V	IV	IV	I	I	II	III	VI			

This plan is prepared for five groups of four pupils each. All other conditions are the same as in Plan 1.

NOTE: These blocks indicate free time, not specifically designated for any particular unit under the 180-day period. The time is not necessarily available as a block of time that falls near the end of the school year, but will be used up during the term for examinations, school holidays, field trips, and the like, or may be used for instruction beyond the acquaintanceship level in the various units.

Charts showing possible rotation plans for single-period courses (180 periods)

PLAN 3

Note: Each block represents 15 periods.

Pupils	First semester						Second semester					
4	I	I	V	V	II	III	VI		IV	IV		
4	I	I	V	V	III	II	IV	IV	VI			
4	V	V	I	I	IV	IV	II	III	VI			
4	IV	IV	I	I	V	V	III	VI	II			
4	V	V	IV	IV	I	I	VI	II	III			

This chart covers the same conditions as in Plan 2. The units are arranged differently.

PLAN 4

Pupils	First semester						Second semester					
5	I	I	IV	IV	II	V	V	III	VI			
5	I	I	V	V	IV	IV	III	II	VI			
5	I	I	II	V	V	III	IV	IV	VI			
5	I	I	III	II	V	V	VI		IV	IV		

This chart indicates a battery plan for the typewriting unit (where a typewriting room is free) and a rotation plan for all other units. Provision is made for four groups of five pupils each. Forty-five periods are available for training beyond the acquaintanceship level.

An example of a rotation plan is illustrated on the next page. It is most important that the teacher develop a plan similar to the one described on the next page before the opening of school.

ROTATION PLAN

24 pupils divided into six groups	Six three-week periods on rotation plan					
	1st period Sep... Oct...	2nd period	3rd period	4th period	5th period	6th period
Group A (Names of 4 pupils)	M	D	A	T	K	R
Group B	R	M	D	A	T	K
Group C	K	R	M	D	A	T
Group D	T	K	R	M	D	A
Group E	A	T	K	R	M	D
Group F	D	A	T	K	R	M

M—Manual Typewriters   T—Transcribing Machines
R—Rotary Calculators   A—Adding-Listing Machines
K—Key-Driven Calculators   D—Duplicating Equipment

Much has been written about the selection of the equipment necessary for an adequate office machines course. Basic to the purchase of *any* equipment or development of special facilities is the philosophy regarding the outcomes desired. Walker points out this fundamental factor:

> Sound planning for equipment should begin with the established objectives of the school and more particularly with the purposes of the business department. The curriculum is essentially a written expression of the educational objectives. Physical facilities—room space arrangements, furniture, machines, and appliances—are the tools necessary for the implementation of the courses of study. Criteria for the purchase of instructional equipment will be twofold: the department must (1) meet the urgent need to obtain equipment to facilitate the mastery of such basic skills as typewriting, shorthand, filing, arithmetic, and keyboard manipulation, and (2) provide certain desirable machines and appliances on which operational skills must be developed as an independent tool.[25]

Occasionally, a teacher is not only faced with the job of making his very first office practice teaching plan, but he is also asked to make suggestions for outfitting the room. Office equipment is expensive; the business department must justify each item of equipment. This requires careful study before encumbering funds. Meehan calls attention to some specific vocational guides:

> Regardless of how a survey is conducted, the following information concerning office equipment being used by the graduates of the business department in the employment area should be secured:
>
> 1. The machines used, the makes and models.
>
> 2. The degree of skill required to get a job on the machine and progress attained after employment.
>
> 3. The types of work performed on the machine.

---

[25] Arthur L. Walker, "Planning and Budgeting for the Equipment You Need—1. In the Smaller School," *Business Education World* (April, 1960), pp. 8-11.

4. The in-service training, if any, given within the company and required before the worker is assigned to
such a machine.

5. The age and experience required of workers on the
machine.

6. The turnover of labor in the job requiring the use of
that machine.[26]

Bulletin 274, the office practice syllabus of the Department of Education, Commonwealth of Pennsylvania, offers
a basic listing for the minimal course, as shown below and
on page 292.[27]

EQUIPMENT FOR THE OFFICE PRACTICE ROOM

General Equipment   *Estimated Cost*

16 individual tables, varying in height from 27 to
  30 inches (table top: 18 by 24 inches) ...... $ 320
16 straight-back chairs 160
12 individual tables (for adding-listing machines
  and calculators) of varying heights 28 to 30
  inches (table top: 18 by 32 inches) 264
6 individual desks or tables (for one long-carriage
  electric typewriter, one standard electric typewriter, and four standard typewriters) equipped
  with means of adjusting height, or of varying
  heights from 27 to 30 inches (desk or table top:
  20 by 36 inches)* 168
6 copyholders 6
4 drop-head single pedestal typewriting desks (for
  four standard electric typewriters and four
  transcribing machines) with drawers on the
  right side (desk top: 32 by 42 inches) 440
22 posture chairs (to be placed at the tables and
  desks where the machines are located) 550

---

[26] James R. Meehan, "Obtaining Adequate Facilities and Equipment,"
Improvement of Business Education Practices, *American Business Education
Yearbook*, Volume VIII (New York: New York University Bookstore,
1951), p. 282.
[27] *Office Practice for Business Education Departments in Pennsylvania's
Public Schools, op. cit.*, p. 29.
* Desks or tables which are adjustable cost approximately twice as
much as those that are not adjustable.

2 tables, 30 inches in height (table top: 30 by 50
    inches)°°   85
4 standard typewriters   640
1 long-carriage electric typewriter (to be used in
    conjunction with the duplicating equipment)..   355
1 stencil duplicator and cabinet   280
1 fluid duplicator and cabinet   250
1 drawing board including lettering guides, screen
    plates, and styli   150
2 full-bank adding-listing machines   350
2 electric ten-key adding-listing machines   580
4 rotary calculators   1,200
4 key-driven calculators   1,060
4 transcribing machines   1,360
5 standard electric typewriters (one to be used in
    conjunction with the duplicating equipment
    and four to be used in conjunction with the
    transcribing machines)   1,475
1 bookcase or open bookshelves (10 by 36 inches)   50
2 filing cabinets (18 by 36 inches)   200
1 teacher's desk (desk top: 32 by 54 inches) and
    accompanying chair   150
                               ————— $10,093

Miscellaneous Equipment

1 paper cutter $25
1 paper punch   2
1 pencil sharpener   3
1 stapler   4
1 wastebasket   5
2 wooden desk trays   6

                               ————— 45

    TOTAL $10,138

Robert D. Balthaser, supervisor of business education of
Ohio, suggests consideration of the table below in the study
of types and cost of equipment. This information was
derived from a study of Ohio public schools, not including
vocational schools: [28]

°° These tables should not be placed in an office practice room which is
less than 990 square feet in size.

[28] R. D. Balthaser, "Administering the High School Clerical Program,"
National Business Education Quarterly (Winter, 1959), p. 43.

TABLE 2.—Suggested office machines requirement for a business
EDUCATION DEPARTMENT WITH OFFICE PRACTICE PROGRAMS OR
COOPERATIVE OFFICE EDUCATION PROGRAMS

School Size:	Smallest Plan		Next Step		Ultimate Goal	
(Electric)	Number	Cost	Number	Cost	Number	Cost
Rotary	1	$ 475	2	$ 950	3	$1,475
Key-driven	1	535	1	535	2	1,070
Full-key	1	153	2	306	3	459
10-key	1	230	2	460	4	1,100[a]
Voice Transcriber[b]	1	357	2	658	4	1,260
Stencil Duplicator	1	660	1	660	1	660
Scope and Supplies		100		100		100
Fluid Duplicator	1	450	1	450	1	450
File Units	5	25	10	50	10	50
Typewriters:						
Manual	20	3,600	28	5,040	38	6,840
Electric	1	295	4	1,180	12	3,540
Student Stations						
Desks & Chairs @ $80	33	2,640	53	4,240	76	6,080
Total New Cost[c]		$9,520		$ 14,629		$ 23,084
Increase		....		$ 5,109		$ 8,455

[a] One calculator
[b] One master in each plan
[c] Does not include teacher's desk and equipment, bookcases, and built-ins

III-2   Student Participation In Class Planning Is Essential

Purposeful pupil activity is the foundation for every part
of the classroom program. The accepted *modus operandi*
of the elementary school (participation) is also the norm
for office practice classes. The idea that learning is enhanced
through active participation and that the learner is something more than a passive recipient of knowledge is not new;
this type of activity was part of the teaching procedure of
Froebel and Pestalozzi in early European education. When
classroom work is cooperatively planned by pupils and
teacher, there is opportunity for self-expression, creativity,
and the freedom to exercise imagination and initiative.

Recognition of this fact is emphasized by Steele in this
statement regarding planning:

The office practice class should meet and fulfill the needs
of students of various levels of ability and achievement. Since
each student will enter the class at a different level of learn-

ing and with varying degrees of unknown skills, the class should be organized for several purposes: to give general information to students as a class; to provide discussion periods that clarify understanding; to give individual instruction to students in any phase of work where help is needed to improve their skills; and to develop at least one marketable skill. The office practice class should be considered by the students as a place where they can receive advice, counsel, and assistance in any area that will help make them efficient employees.[29]

The importance of recognizing the "skill" of creative thinking through cooperative teaching-learning situations is pointed out by the chief psychologist for an important lumber firm in the United States:

> We recognize that an employee is often slow or even "suspicious" in accepting guidance and direction. Give him a part in planning, prescribing and, executing.[30]

III-3   Individual Differences Must Be Recognized

Hicks points out that there are many ways to recognize and handle the different levels of accomplishments found in the usual office practice class. He sets up the following outline for consideration:

1. Self-analysis and improvement.
2. Varying unit introductions.
3. Individualized project work.
4. Committee selection.
5. Special objective.
6. Student work kits.
7. Class standards.
8. Individual teaching.[31]

---

[29] Helen L. Steele, "Adapting a Clerical Office Practice Course to Students' Needs," *Business Education Forum* (October, 1958), p. 24.

[30] W. A. Eggert, "Individual Differences in Business," *American Business Education* (October, 1955), p. 13.

[31] Charles B. Hicks, "How to Meet Individual Differences in Your Secretarial-Practice Course," *Business Education World* (May, 1954), p. 16.

To take one of these in detail, the following description illustrates the meaning of these methods:

> *Committee Selection.* The secretarial-practice class offers many opportunities for committee work—in projects, in taking care of classroom routines, in duplicating units, in filing units, in a number of office procedure activities. The wise teacher will see that each committee will include both a "good" and a "slow" student and will emphasize that the *entire* group must do the work and must reach the same minimum-achievement objective. Thus, the better student is encouraged to help the slower students; ordinarily, too, he will be able to contribute much more than the teacher could find time to give.[32]

The need to recognize all of the factors of individual differences that will probably be present in the office practice class is emphasized by Goodman:

> Individual abilities can vary considerably in a machines class because of such factors as these: (1) student's age; (2) recency of exposure to business arithmetic and degree of command of arithmetic functions; (3) intellectual capacity; (4) skill in reading, understanding, and following written instructions; and (5) personal motivation in learning machine functions and application.[33]

III-4 Good Demonstration Is Accomplished Through Knowledge of Machines and Procedures

The demonstration is a commonly used method in teaching typewriting and shorthand. It must also be a part of the teacher's performance in the office practice classroom. The demonstration may be provided by the teacher or by resource persons—for example, equipment company representatives. The demonstration provides a visual foundational experience for whatever verbal explanation may follow.

---

[32] *Ibid.*
[33] David G. Goodman, "We Stopped Teaching Machines by the Rotation Plan," *Business Education World* (September, 1959), p. 31.

The office practice teacher has the particularly challenging job of demonstrating a variety of totally different machines. With a comprehensive major in business education, the business teacher is generally well qualified for this task. If not, he must spend some exacting hours in preparation before the course begins. This preparation the teacher owes the student who is in the class solely to get ready for a vocation. Bauernfiend emphasizes this point:

> From the standpoint of specific training and development as related to the teaching and operation of the various office machines, we should consider the importance of the instructor as a competent operator. In order to have occupational competence, it is necessary for the instructor to learn all phases of operation of the machines. Combined with this training, it is necessary for the instructor to build a skill which compares with standards of production which are demanded in the business office. A competent office machines instructor can demonstrate all operations, as well as check the operational ability of the students.[34]

Agnew verifies this phase of instructor preparation:

> Young teachers frequently find it difficult to know all about the subject matter of office practice—particularly the operation of all machines. It behooves every teacher to know his work. Read the textbook that has been selected for use in the course and find time to practice on the machines before or after class, especially models that are different from the ones you learned on in your teacher training school. Students quickly lose confidence in teachers who do not know their work and who cannot efficiently operate the machines. If you do get stuck, however, do not fake it; simply sit down with the student and the instruction book and suggest to the student that you work it out together. But do not let it happen too often.[35]

---

[34] Harry B. Bauernfeind, "Office Machine Instructors—Their Professional Development," *American Business Education* (March, 1954), p. 180.

[35] Peter L. Agnew, "Teaching Office Practice," *American Business Education* (May, 1956), p. 254.

The demonstration *is* important. Reinforced by good background preparation, the office practice teacher will find that to demonstrate is to be able to develop skill concepts quickly and efficiently. Franques makes this comment on the demonstration:

> Small group demonstrations within the class are an effective device used by teachers in teaching the steps in problem solving and in machine operation. In such demonstrations, the teacher explains the steps thoroughly, shows the operation, and then presents a quick review of the points made. Effective teacher demonstrations help to reduce the learning time on the part of students.[36]

III-5 "Real" Jobs Are Necessary for "Real" Learning

Not too long ago this statement was made before the Toledo, Ohio, chapter of the National Office Management Association:

> Vocational education is for all who must provide a livelihood for themselves and their families. In this country, with its characteristic attention to financial success, it is natural that the 66 million men and women who are its workers should have a deep and abiding realization that vocational training is an inescapable part of preparation for life. We must help our students to learn how to earn their living and encourage them to work hard in that direction.[37]

It is relatively easy for the school to establish valid objectives for its office practice course. It is not easy, however, for a teacher to fulfill these objectives. Connelly delineates this broad area of teacher responsibility:

> A high school teacher, charged with the responsibility of training skilled machine operators, realizes that with the

---

[36] Marie Louise Franques, "Some Problems and Trends in the Teaching of Office Machines and Appliances," *Business Education Forum* (March, 1955), p. 28.

[37] Wilbert E. Scheer, "Are We Helping Our Students Face Reality?" *Business Education World* (March, 1958), p. 24.

widespread use of semi- and fully-automatic machines her students must be able to bring a basic skill and arithmetic knowledge to the initial job. What machines are being used in your community? What processes of arithmetic are needed by the clerical office worker? What skill demands are being made on the beginning office worker? Are your students being denied the opportunity to work on modern equipment because you have not kept up to date as a clerical-practice teacher? How does the teacher know whether or not her course of study is adequate to prepare the student for employment in his own community, and does the student have the skill needed to adjust to on-the-job requirements? How can the teacher know the answers to these questions? [38]

In addition to the in-school classroom work, there are a number of realistic job-type activities such as community service projects, part-time employee service to other teachers, and duplicating and typing service for the school office. A down-to-earth employment experience can be provided through a cooperative work-experience program. This has value for both the student and the teacher in improving instruction, as Connelly points out:

> The clerical-practice students will have a better knowledge of office requirements if they have had an opportunity to participate in a cooperative work-experience program. This type of program may be organized in many ways. Such a plan brings the teacher in close contact with business and the demands being made on clerical workers. The teacher finds out very effectively what units of work she needs to include in her school program. [39]

A description of principles and procedures for developing work-experience programs was given in Part II of this chapter.

---

[38] Mary E. Connelly, "The Business Community as a Laboratory," *American Business Education* (May, 1957), p. 232.
[39] *Ibid.*, p. 234.

III-6   To Be Realistic the Classroom Must Resemble the Office

The activities in the office practice classroom have at times been compared with a three-ring circus. In further developing this analogy, it is well to realize that the activities in the three rings of a circus do not conflict with one another; it is a free-flowing, on-going show. The efficient office is one in which a number of different activities are performed without clashing. More and more, large concerns are using the "open office" situation, in which walls are removed entirely, leaving a huge space completely integrated into one activity.

The office practice course should prepare students for this modern concept of the office. Connelly emphasizes this point in her statement:

> The clerical practice course is not a reading course but an action course. Real business situations or experiences should be presented in the classroom that will help the students to feel the office atmosphere. Our clerical practice classes should be taught in an office laboratory, just as we teach science in a science laboratory. One room in the high school should be converted into a model office, and this room should be used by business preparatory students only. There should be enough equipment so that the student can get the "feel" of an office and participate in the clerical processes.[40]

Free flow of work is a desirable business office procedure. It is necessary that the office practice teacher be able to illustrate business efficiency in the classroom situation. In an attempt to help develop this concept in the teacher, Archer makes these suggestions:

> Teachers who complain that they do not have enough hands to do everything that they would like to do in the office practice class are overlooking the fact that there are lots of

---

[40] Mary E. Connelly, "Successful Unit Planning in Clerical Practice," *Business Education Forum* (February, 1952), p. 7.

"extra hands" available for the asking. Why should the teacher permit herself to become buried in routine paper work when she might use student assistants on a rotation basis? Why should the teacher tax herself to handle supplies issuance when additional student assistants might be designated? Why should she be the one who dashes around to show the students where the outlets are or where the machine adjustments devices are located when a student trouble-shooter could do just as well? [41]

Allee and Seufer further clinch the necessity of the "work" atmosphere in this statement:

> The sooner the student understands that he is working in an office (rather than the classroom), that he is a beginning clerical worker (rather than a student), and that he is responsible to his supervisor (rather than his teacher), the quicker he will become accustomed to the real office atmosphere essential to an easy transition from classroom to office. The teacher has the responsibility to "set the stage" for this type of classroom atmosphere, which is characterized by work-station arrangement of like equipment, a freedom of student movement in the classroom where necessary for performance of duties, realistic job assignments, the teaching of co-operation in working with fellow students and with the teacher, and a personal responsibility for the job done by acceptable office standards. [42]

III-7 The Business Machines Aspect of Office Practice Should Not Be Overemphasized

In the volumes of materials that have been written about office practice, clerical practice, or whatever title is assigned to the course, the reader is sometimes led to believe that machine manipulation is the "be all" and "end all" of the course. Don't be misled. There is an article entitled "Teach-

---

[41] Fred C. Archer, "Conserve Time—Save Yourself—and the Course," *Business Teacher* (November, 1959), p. 15.

[42] W. A. Allee and Elizabeth Seufer, "How to Teach Clerical Practice," *National Business Education Quarterly* (Winter, 1959), p. 37.

ing What Ain't in the Book," in which the author makes this opening comment:

> We need to re-examine our office practice courses, excluding unessentials and emphasizing more the myriad of little things which can cause real problems in the office.[43]

She relates several instances of conversations with former students that point up the necessity for looking further than mere proficiency:

> Couldn't we put into that course practical, down-to-earth things, and the almost intangible things that haven't been learned in any books, that don't lend themselves to book learning, but that must be learned somehow, some way—by doing. The little vitals that the beginning office worker wishes she knew because it's this little thing or that little thing that made her seem so stupid today when asked to do it; or that made her seem unwilling because it didn't occur to her that she should have done it. What are these little things?
>
> "They're all the little things that you don't think are important until you come on the job and then you find that they count more than all the things you worked so hard to learn in school. Like anticipating what your boss might want— such simple little things, I suppose, as remembering to bring in your notebook when he asks you to come into the office. Like going in to him the first thing in the morning to ask him what things he would like cleared up." [44]

Where but in the office practice course do business teachers have that last opportunity to get at the heart of the intangible factor called "personality," an intangible that becomes very real on the job, as studies of job failures show. It is perhaps true that we cannot see the immediate results of our efforts, but try we must. The responsibility of the office practice teacher is outlined by Van Derveer in this comment:

---

[43] Roberta C. MacDonald, "Teaching What Ain't in the Book," *American Business Education* (March, 1954), p. 168.

[44] *Ibid.*, pp. 168-169.

Subject matter is important, but the growth of the ability of each pupil to meet irritating situations, to work under pressure, to react in a responsible manner, to be trustworthy are concommitant learnings as important or more important than any subject matter.

To bring about desired personality development and correction there must be an interest on the part of the teacher and a desire on the part of the pupil to make a change. The pupil must accept, first of all, that a "desirable" personality is a personal asset; second, that personality development is a never-ending process; and third, that it is possible to change or improve personality characteristics.[45]

A number of writers have attempted to show the integration of these aspects into the regular skill training. Others pay particular attention to special objectives, as indicated by the following "guides" for beginning office workers:

1. How to acknowledge the introduction to the office staff.
2. How and when to accept or decline the invitation to go to lunch when invited to join others.
3. How to keep business secrets without giving offense to others.
4. How to receive instructions.
5. How to react to supervision and correction.
6. How to enter the "closed-door" employer's office.
7. What to do in case of absence or tardiness.

We are not advocating one phase of training over the other; we simply admonish the office practice teacher to use a well-balanced approach in developing the "complete" office employee. One of the most authoritative "business-man" statements on requirements for beginning office employees is that of the Columbus, Ohio, chapter of NOMA: [46]

---

[45] Elizabeth T. Van Derveer, "Developing the Character and Personality of Pupils," Improvement of Business Education Practices, *American Business Education Yearbook*, Volume III (New York: New York University Bookstore, 1951), p. 84.

[46] Harm Harms, "Imperatives for Persons Seeking Initial Office Positions," *Bulletin of the National Association for Secondary-School Principals* (November, 1949), p. 88.

IMPERATIVES FOR PERSONS SEEKING INITIAL OFFICE POSITIONS

A beginning office employee should have:	RATING SCALE			
	Excellent	Good	Average	Poor
1 A general over-all familiarity with office layout				
Customs				
Regulations				
Basic procedures				
2 Desirable business attitudes such as				
A desire to please				
Ability to accept criticism graciously				
A desire to do a fair day's work				
3 Ability to read with comprehension				
Simple directives				
Written directions when clearly stated				
Routine written communications ...				
4 Ability to follow oral instructions				
When clearly stated				
When given over the telephone				
5 Ability and desire to use democratic procedures				
In everyday living				
In getting along with others				
In "fitting in" the office				
6 Acquired desirable habits of				
Neatness and good grooming				
Willingness to contribute his share or more				
Making the office a desirable place to work				
7 Reasonable degree of skill in fundamentals				
Simple arithmetic				
Legible handwriting				
Spelling				
Punctuation				
8. A real understanding of the value of accuracy				
9 Ability to type from 40 to 50 WPM with an acceptable degree of accuracy				
10 Knowledge of most frequently used business forms and experience and skill in filling them in				
By hand				
Using the typewriter				
11 Stenographic skills, if interested in a stenographic position, at these levels				
Take dictation at about 80 WPM ..				
Read back fluently when called upon				
Transcribe from five to six usable letters of average length in an hour				
12 Filing knowledges and skills as follows				
Ability to alphabetize				
Fundamentals of filing procedure ..				
Knowledge of common filing systems				

III-8 *Practice Sessions Require Careful Development*

The psychological principles underlying the practice of a motor skill have already been developed. It is not in recognizing that practice is essential that the beginning office practice teacher may err, but in *how* this practice is best used. We know from studies that, personality problems aside, lack of accuracy or poor attitudes toward the necessity of accuracy are primary problems in office employment.

In the development of practice sessions in the skill-building phase of the office practice course, these principles of practice, stressing accuracy, are outlined by Ashby:

> In the teaching of office appliances the following principles should be kept in mind:
>
> 1. Prevention of errors is better than correction of errors.
>
> 2. Emphasis should be given to the correct operational procedures.
>
> 3. Accuracy is the result of good speed-building techniques.
>
> 4. Students should understand the objectives of the instruction.
>
> 5. Practice activity cannot be evaluated merely in terms of time.
>
> 6. "Does the answer look reasonable?" is perhaps the most important check in any problem having to do with figures. One girl blithely put down $5,000 as the cost of a single textbook—that's what her machine said!

The second problem combines knowledge of operation and manual skill with emphasis on speed of manipulation of the operative parts of the appliance. This is the area that receives the most attention in terms of time and effort in the classroom. The practice of repetitive motions until they are overlearned or until they become automatic is the objective of this instruction. Often this goal is difficult if the student is not aware of the necessity of hours of practice. Indifference toward practice on the part of the student is a source of improper operational technique that may result in many types of errors.[47]

III-9 Evaluation Should Be Continuous and Realistic and In Terms of Today's Demands On the Worker

Evaluation in any business course, whether office practice or any of the basic business subjects, should be in accordance with the program objectives. Evaluation should ascertain whether or to what extent the objectives have been realized and what changes or improvements are necessary. Evaluation should be based on the actual needs of the students in terms of actual employment requirements in the potential area in which the youth will work.

We are not always sure of what business does want; however, it is not realistic to go our own way disregarding what the employer feels is a reasonable standard. Wilsing reviews this picture for us as follows:

> What businessmen say, or think, or feel is undoubtedly the most important measure of the success of high school business education in terms of meeting employers' needs and desires, regardless of any "objective" evidence to the contrary.[48]

Difficulty arises in finding out just what standards ought to be. One approach is to attempt to find out what has definitely been written about standards. In office machines and general office tasks, one of the most authoritative compilations is that of Collins, a portion of which is reproduced below: [49]

---

[47] Wilson T. Ashby, "Concept of Accuracy for Clerical Practice," *Business Education Forum* (April, 1957), p. 25.

[48] Weston C. Wilsing, *Is Business Education in the Public High Schools Meeting the Needs and Desires of Businessmen?*, Monograph 99 (Cincinnati: South-Western Publishing Company, 1960), p. 23.

[49] Marian Josephine Collins, *Handbook for Office Practice Teachers*, Monograph 91 (Cincinnati: South-Western Publishing Company, 1954), pp. 11-14.

Table I

PERFORMANCE STANDARDS

Operation	Measurement Unit	Rate	Additional Details	Source
Alphabetizing 5 x 3 cards	cards per hour	150	with approx. one guide for each 30 cards	NOMA 50
Alphabetizing 8½ x 11 sheets	sheets per hour	100	with approx. 24 guides per drawer	NOMA 50
Filing (all operations) 8½ x 11 sheets	pieces per 8-hour day	600–833	coding, marking, sorting, filing, lookups and chargeouts; alphabetic systems	Odell and Strong 51
Filing 5 x 3 cards	cards per minute	1.9–5.16	cards previously sorted and arranged in alphabetic sequences	Odell and Strong 51
Sorting and arranging 5 x 3 cards	cards per hour	268	using table top	Odell and Strong 51
Typing gummed labels	labels per hour	85	for use on file folder	Odell and Strong 51
Pasting gummed labels	labels per hour	60	on file folder	Odell and Strong 51
Inspect, sort, and file	pieces per day	200	alphabetically	NORS 52
Find correspondence	pieces per hour	22	in an alphabetic file	NORS 52
Search for particular piece of information	pieces per hour	6–8	in several possible places in the file	NORS 52
Make preliminary sort of correspondence	pieces per hour	250	into specified dimensions	NORS 52
Sort in distributor; remove; re-sort in main file	pieces per hour	275	alphabetic	NORS 52
Look up references	pieces per hour	50	in alphabetic file	NORS 52
File 8½ x 11 letters	pieces per hour	300	in alphabetic file	NORS 52
File account cards	pieces per hour	225	in alphabetic file	NORS 52
Mark 8½ x 11 letters and rough sort	pieces per hour	250	alphabetic filing	NORS 53
Machine transcription	cylinders per hour	¾	cylinders with 10–12 letters of 2–3 paragraphs each	NOMA 54

---

50 National Office Management Association, "Survey Summary No. 10," as cited in *Curriculum Construction and Schedule Planning for Continuation Schools,* Florida State Department of Education, Tallahassee, 1950, pp. 4-5.

51 Margaret K. Odell and Earl P. Strong, *Management and Filing Operations* (New York: McGraw-Hill Book Company, Inc., 1947), pp. 301-306.

52 *National Office Ratio Survey,* as cited by Margaret K. Odell and Earl P. Strong, *ibid.,* p. 306.

53 *National Office Ratio Survey, loc. cit.*

54 *National Office Management Association, loc. cit.*

Table I (continued)

PERFORMANCE STANDARDS

Operation	Measurement Unit	Rate	Additional Details	Source
Machine transcription	letters on 40-minute test	8 (142 lines) 6 (106 lines) 5 (88 lines)	Excellent Good Passing	Ediphone 55
Machine transcription	net 60-stroke lines per hour on a 30-minute test	125	minimum at end of 50–60 hour course; mailable; unfamiliar material	Dictaphone 56
		200	attained by good students	
Machine transcription	lines per hour	100–200	under work conditions	Neuner-Haynes 57
Typing — straight copy	words per minute	45	for ten minutes with 5 errors or less	NOMA 54
Typing — straight copy	words per minute	40–60	for ten minutes with not over 1 error a minute	NYSS 58
Typing letters	letters per day	65	15-line letters	Maze 59
Typing statements	statements per day	4	11" x 17" 10-column	Maze 59
Typing statements	statements per day	24	8½" x 11" 3-column	Maze 59
Typing addresses on labels	addresses per hour	125–159	from typewritten copy	Maze 59
Typing fill-ins	fill-ins per hour	100–150	four-line	NYSS 58
Typing form letters	letters per hour	10	average length	NYSS 58
Typing ledger sheets	sheets per hour	98–125	——	Maze 59
Typing tabulations	tabulations per hour	3–5	Simple	NYSS 58
Typing masters	masters per hour	5–7	for gelatin or fluid type; average 200 words	NYSS 58
Taking dictation	words per minute	80	Beginners; unfamiliar material	NOMA 54
Transcription	words per minute	30	from notes; unfamiliar material of mailable quality for 10 minutes	NOMA 54

55 Thomas A. Edison Co. standards, as reported in *Tentative Syllabus and Teaching Suggestions for a Course in Office Practice, Grades 11 and 12,* New York State University, Albany, 1951, p. 43.

56 Report of educational representative of the Dictaphone Corporation, January, 1952.

57 John J. W. Neuner and Benjamin R. Haynes, *Office Management and Practices* (Cincinnati: South-Western Publishing Company, 1947), pp. 528, 531.

58 *Tentative Syllabus and Teaching Suggestions for a Course in Office Practice, Grades 11 and 12, op. cit.,* pp. 43-44.

59 Coleman Maze, *Office Management* (New York: The Ronald Press Company, 1947), pp. 783-809.

Table I (concluded)

PERFORMANCE STANDARDS

Operation	Measurement Unit	Rate	Additional Details	Source
Affixing stamps manually	stamps per hour	1,116	———	Maze 60
Sealing envelopes manually	envelopes per hour	1,170	———	Maze 60
Addressing envelopes by hand	envelopes per hour	98–124	from handwritten copy	Maze 60
Addressing envelopes by hand	addresses per hour	118–150	from ledger books	Maze 60
Labeling envelopes	addresses per hour	1,620–2,057	———	Maze 60
Collating 8½ x 11 sheets	sheets per hour	3,000	3 sheets to the set	Maze 60
Folding of mail manually	sheets per hour	723	mostly 2-fold	Maze 60
Inserting folded mail into envelopes manually	pieces per hour	395	———	Maze 60
Typing — cutting stencils	lines per hour	200	under work conditions	Neuner-Haynes 61
Typing — cutting stencils	stencils per hour	4–6	averaging 200 words	NYSS 62
Emboss Addressograph plates with name and address	plates per hour	54–69	Range	Maze 60
Tab Addressograph plates	plates per hour	600–762	Range	Maze 60
Prepare Addressograph stencils	stencils per hour	125	under work conditions	Neuner-Haynes 61
Post accounts on bookkeeping machine	accounts per hour	214–271	Range	Maze 60
Operate Moon-Hopkins or Burroughs Calculating Billing Machine	strokes per hour	5,000	———	Neuner-Haynes 61
Feed envelopes through postage meter	envelopes per hour	7,100–9,017	Range	Maze 60
Prepare envelopes for feeding through postage meter	envelopes per hour	4,950–6,287	Range	Maze 60

---

60 *Ibid.*
61 Neuner and Haynes, *loc. cit.*
62 National Office Management Association, *loc. cit.*

Once the teacher is able to determine what can be accepted as realistic business standards, the task becomes one of fitting these proficiency goals to the particular teaching situation. Frisch has this to say on evaluation in relation to classroom teaching:

> Although school standards and business standards do not have to be the same, some basic standards have been sufficiently well established that they can be used as guideposts for setting school standards.[63]

The administration of standards in relation to classroom grading must be considered in the light of a well-conceived philosophy, such as that set forth by Kallaus:

1. Install the standards officially with proper explanation of the program and the students' part in it.

2. Assign substantial credit to passing the standards. As a general rule, the student will tend to work harder and get more accomplished if he has something to work for and gets some tangible reward for his efforts.

3. Provide sufficient opportunity for practice prior to testing time.

4. Allow several attempts at passing the qualifying standards.

5. Give the tests near the end of a unit so that the student has a maximum period of time to prepare himself for it.[64]

Complete, valid, and reliable standards to be used in connection with objective grading are difficult to find. In many instances, the published standards are not reliable because they are not related to the particular situation. With the basic knowledge that is generally accepted as a beginning, it may be necessary for the office practice teacher to

---

[63] Vern Frisch, "Let's Be Realistic about Standards," *Business Education Forum* (November, 1957), p. 28.

[64] Norman F. Kallaus, "Building Proficiency Standards for Computing Machines," *Business Education Forum* (February, 1961), p .9.

develop standards for grading, keeping in mind the particular characteristics of the business community in which the school is located.

III-10   Resource Materials Should Form the Backdrop for Building Office Practice Concepts

Research in principles of learning invariably point out that teaching can be made more effective through the use of a variety of teaching aids. For the office practice class the possibilities are limited only by the imagination of the teacher and the students. In Chapter X a comprehensive listing of sources of materials is given. An example of this material is the large "life-size" chart usually furnished free by office machines companies. These charts are valuable in making demonstrations to small groups. After such demonstrations, students can generally go ahead on their own.

SUMMARY

Office practice is a necessary part of the preparation of young men and women for the office occupations. It is an important part of the business education curriculum. Studies show that more and more attention is being given by businessmen to proficient use of an array of skills and knowledges not always completely developed in a class in shorthand, typewriting, or bookkeeping. These skills and knowledges are the content of the office practice course.

There is no magic formula for teaching these important concepts. What is needed is the teacher who can richly supplement the vocational skill training by setting up conditions in the classroom through which students learn to make decisions, carry responsibility, become self-reliant and adaptable, practice leadership and cooperation, and develop their personalities. These tools of success in business employment are sometimes complex and require realistic practice conditions.

The most common types of classroom methods by which office practice can be taught successfully have been outlined in detail in many instances in this chapter. Suggestions have been made that can well serve as models for beginning teachers.

SELECTED BIBLIOGRAPHY

A Guide to Sound Teaching Practices in Business Education, Twenty-Fourth Yearbook. New York: Commercial Education Association of the City of New York and Vicinity, 1962.

The Clerical Program in Business Education. American Business Education Yearbook, Volume XVI, New York: New York University Bookstore, 1959.

Collins, Marian Josephine. "Handbook for Office Practice Teachers," *Monograph 91,* Cincinnati: South-Western Publishing Company, 1954.

Cook, Fred S. "A General Clerical Course for Seniors," *Business Education Forum* (February, 1962), 7-9.

Douglas, Lloyd V., James T. Blanford, and Ruth I. Anderson. *Teaching Business Subjects.* Englewood Cliffs, New Jersey: Prentice-Hall, Inc., 1958.

Evaluating Competence for Business Occupations. American Business Education Yearbook, Volume VII, New York: New York University Bookstore, 1950.

Evaluation of Pupil Progress in Business Education. American Business Education Yearbook, Volume XVII, New York: New York University Bookstore, 1960.

Frisch, Vern. "Let's Be Realistic About Standards," *Business Education Forum* (November, 1957), 28.

Green, Helen H. "Development of Personal Traits and Work Habits Through Clerical Office Practice," *Business Education Forum* (February, 1958), 17-20.

Harms, Harm. "Standards for the Office of the Next Decade," *The Business Education Program in the Expanding Secondary School.* The Bulletin of the National Association of Secondary-School Principals (January, 1957).

Hicks, Charles B. "How to Organize the Subject Matter of Your Secretarial Practice Course," *Business Education World* (February, 1954), 14-15.

Job Instruction Sheets—Machines (Adding and Calculating), *Office Practice*. Bureau of Business and Distributive Education, Albany, New York: University of New York, 1955.

Laird, Donald A., and Eleanor C. Laird. *Practical Business Psychology*, Second Edition. New York: Gregg Publishing Division, McGraw-Hill Book Company, Inc., 1956.

Lawrence, Nelda R. *Secretary's Business Review: A Professional Handbook*. Englewood Cliffs, New Jersey: Prentice-Hall, Inc., 1959.

Neuner, John J. W. *Office Management and Practices*, Fourth Edition. Cincinnati: South-Western Publishing Company, 1959.

Potter, Thelma. "An Analysis of the Work of General Clerical Employees," Contribution to Education, No. 903, Bureau of Publications, New York: Teachers College, Columbia University, 1944.

Roughsedge, Gertrude, and Fred C. Archer. "How Does the Principal Evaluate the Effectiveness of the Teaching of Clerical Practice?" *Bulletin of the National Association of Secondary-School Principals* (January, 1957).

Tonne, Herbert A., Estelle Popham, and M. Herbert Freeman. *Methods of Teaching Business Subjects*, Second Edition. New York: Gregg Publishing Division, McGraw-Hill Book Company, Inc., 1957.

Van Derveer, Elizabeth T. "Developing the Character and Personality of Pupils," *Improvement of Business Education Practices*. American Business Education Yearbook, Volume VIII, New York: New York University Bookstore, 1951.

Walker, Arthur L. "Planning and Budgeting for the Equipment You Need—1. In the Smaller School," *Business Education World* (April, 1960), 8-11.

White, Jane F., and Thadys J. Dewar. *Successful Devices in Teaching Clerical Practice*. Portland, Maine; J. Weston Walch, 1959.

FILMS AND FILMSTRIPS
Films

Do I Want To Be A Secretary? Business Education Films, 4607 16 Avenue, Brooklyn 4, New York.

Eight Parts of a Business Letter, Business Education Films, 4607 16 Avenue, Brooklyn 4, New York.

Filing Procedures in Business, Business Education Films, 4607 16 Avenue, Brooklyn 4, New York.

Improve Your Personality, Coronet Instructional Films, Coronet Building, Chicago 1, Illinois.

Improve Your Spelling, Coronet Instructional Films, Coronet Building, Chicago 1, Illinois.

Mimeographing Techniques, Bailey Films, Inc., 6509 Delongpre Avenue, Hollywood 48, California.

Office Courtesy, Business Education Films, 4607 16 Avenue, Brooklyn 4, New York.

Office Etiquette, Business Education Films, 4607 16 Avenue, Brooklyn 4, New York.

Office Teamwork, Business Education Films, 4607 16 Avenue, Brooklyn 4, New York.

What's An Office Anyway? Audio-Visual Center, The City College, School of Business and Public Administration, 17 Lexington Avenue, New York 10, New York.

Work Simplification, Audio-Visual Center, The City College, School of Business and Public Administration, 17 Lexington Avenue, New York 10, New York.

Writing Better Business Letters, Coronet Instructional Films, Coronet Building, Chicago 1, Illinois.

Filmstrips

Duties of a Secretary, Underwood Corporation, One Park Avenue, New York 16, New York.

Tagline for Success, Bristol-Myers Company, Education Service Department, 45 Rockefeller Plaza, New York 20, New York.

CHAPTER VII

BOOKKEEPING—PART I

PRINCIPLES OF LEARNING APPLIED TO BOOKKEEPING

The twentieth century has been notable for its trend toward the utilization of systematic planning and programming of ideas. Bookkeeping and accounting are accepted systematic procedures for maintaining records and analyzing records of financial transactions. Increased use of machines has not diminished the need for accounting knowledge because the use of financial records has increased manifold over the past quarter-century.

One of the main reasons for the use of such extensive records is that they are kept for both business and tax purposes. Many small businesses would not keep careful records if it were not for the purpose of having information available for government reports. Businesses, of course, also make standard use of records for determining profit and loss, cost analysis, and internal control. Musselman and Hanna underscore this increased need for financial recording when they state:

> The value of bookkeeping knowledge to business executives, operators, and managers is becoming increasingly recognized. At one time, only those business records desired by management were kept. Many businesses kept no records; others kept records which, by present-day standards, would be considered entirely inadequate. Federal and state laws, however, now require that both businesses and individuals keep financial records.

The Income Tax Laws, the Federal Insurance Contributions (Social Security) Act, the State Unemployment Insurance Act, the Fair Labor Standards Act, and the Wage and Hour Laws are but a few of the many federal and state laws regulating business and prescribing the types of records that shall be maintained.[1]

It would be difficult in the limited space available to attempt to describe bookkeeping as it exists in business today. Certainly it is characterized by standardized forms, many of them loose-leaf so that they can be adapted readily to the bookkeeping and computing machines that now form an integral part of many bookkeeping processes. Another characteristic is the extent to which division of labor is being used. Seldom in any large office does a bookkeeper have an opportunity to work with the entire bookkeeping cycle, and fortunate is the office worker who is able to see through the interrelated mechanisms and devices that go to make up the entire picture. A number of persons work with sales tickets; some type invoices for use on duplicating machines; others write checks on bookkeeping machines; a department head visits all machines at a specified hour and obtains balances for the controlling account sheet (card); special clerks watch the IBM equipment compile summaries and statements, stock controls, and inventories. This list could be extended almost indefinitely. Such is the picture of bookkeeping in a large modern office.

In the small office, clerks perform clerical routines, depending upon the nature of the business and the equipment available, while accountants balance the books and make tax reports and statements. In some cities portable bookkeeping offices go from store to store during the evening hours and do the necessary bookkeeping in a very short

---

[1] Vernon A. Musselman and J Marshall Hanna, *Teaching Bookkeeping and Accounting* (New York: Gregg Publishing Division, McGraw-Hill Book Company, Inc., 1960), pp. 4-5.

time through the use of standardized forms and machinery designed for the job. In the small shop and on the farm a simple multi-column combination cash book and journal is frequently adequate to meet the owner's needs.

This emphasis on record keeping is indicative of a trend in American society. For the schools this means an increased attention to bookkeeping instruction. Conditions in business impose a responsibility on business education—particularly on instruction in bookkeeping and accounting—for the best possible kind of program, a program that is realistically planned and that employs teaching and supervisory services of the highest order.

A clear appreciation of the job of the teacher in the classroom as a part of the school is a first essential of good teaching. Since the content of this book is directed toward the improvement of teaching as well as for the introduction of the newcomer to the classroom, this chapter is centered on principles of teaching that can provide success in this endeavor.

In the classroom and in other organized or informal learning situations, the teacher seeks to influence the behavior of the pupils. The *direction* in which he seeks to influence their behavior depends on what the teacher accepts as the goals of education. The *effectiveness* with which he influences behavior depends on the methods he selects. Not all teachers will choose the same methods when working with youth in the schools. Teachers use many different methods of instruction. In the selection of a method, the teacher has made a choice. He has rejected certain ways of teaching skills and knowledges and has accepted others; he has made decisions with respect to organizing the class for learning and with respect to organizing subject matter. This is a challenging task. Whether there are ten students or forty students, they all need intensive attention and direction as *individuals*. Some choices of method we make are on-the-spot decisions, such as, "Shall I include the section on payroll taxes this term, or include it as a part of the work of next term?" Some are long-range decisions which involve a great deal of thought.

Methods, to a large extent, determine the effectiveness of the teacher. It is assumed that the teacher is enthusiastic about his own method. The important thing is to be consistent. It is our purpose to provide some assistance in making intelligent decisions concerning the selection of methods. Certain time-tested approaches to the teaching of bookkeeping will be presented. Other parts of this chapter contain specific research by leaders in bookkeeping instruction.

The twenty principles of learning that follow are not new in themselves, nor are they necessarily restricted to bookkeeping instruction. They have been around for years, but we have not always used them. In fact, there are times when it seems that we are deliberately going out of our way to violate them.

I-1 Teach Thoroughly

"A little knowledge is a dangerous thing: Drink deep or taste not the Pierian Spring." So wrote the poet Alexander Pope. The principle is apropos when applied to the teaching of bookkeeping and accounting. How often do we leave students with just enough knowledge to get them into really deep water! At times a teacher finds that his students have completed a work sheet in an apparently masterful fashion, yet a "quickie quiz" on *understanding* shows complete ignorance of the application of the principle. A standard procedure in bookkeeping classes when introducing the work sheet can be as follows: As soon as it is completed and presented by students, ask the question "So what?" Everyone in the class will know what to expect: specific questions on the *use* of the work sheet.

The discussion continues until everyone thoroughly understands. Learning bits and pieces of a process leads to *mis*-understanding rather than understanding.

I-2 *Organize for Learning*

Whether experienced or just out of college, a teacher will find that his work can be exciting and invigorating if he uses a systematic approach to classroom management. Established routines that involve student participation will result in much timesaving. For example, the "accounting office" system in practice set work (see II-7) means that there is no standing around, waiting to be "told." Members of the class know exactly what to do when they enter the room because of specific routines they themselves helped to formulate. This, of course, does not just happen. It is planned for. The teacher operates under the assumption that students *are* capable of doing some of the planning that results in a cooperative spirit throughout the period and the school year. Not only do they realize that there is an order of things, but they assist one another in getting set. To expedite this "settling-down" process, the teacher must observe good principles of classroom management:

1. Select suitable teaching materials and equipment necessary to hold the attention of the class.

2. Make only a few rules for classroom conduct, but always carry them out.

3. Keep records so that students are aware of their progress.

4. Prepare work in advance.

5. Keep the room in an orderly condition.

6. Seat students so that individual needs are met.

7. Plan carefully so that classes are dismissed on time.

The success of any management system is the acceptance of the system by those expected to use it. This is accomplished through employee participation in business and industry; in the classroom, acceptance of a system is accomplished through student participation. Of course, there are always a few cases in which the teacher may find it necessary to be dogmatic in order to get action.

I-3   Demonstration—A "Must" in Teaching Bookkeeping

The development of visual and audio-visual education has been based on a cliche, but one that is nevertheless valid: a picture is worth a thousand words. Students learn from what they see. For the bookkeeping teacher, showing and demonstrating is a necessary part of the instruction. If students can't learn from concrete illustrations, how can we possibly expect them to learn from abstract presentations? Nowhere in the business curriculum does the use of visual aids have such possibilities, and nowhere else is it as necessary as in bookkeeping.

Included in the teacher's planning should be materials and procedures for maximum use of visual and audio-visual aids. The more skill a teacher can develop in handling them, the better will be his teaching job. Demonstration devices are not the easy way out, but the average bookkeeping teacher can be quite successful if a few basic principles are observed. For the development of some techniques, see II-2 of this chapter and refer to Chapter X for some good sources of materials.

I-4   If There Are Several Approaches To a Problem, Pick One and Teach It Well

A great deal of confusion sometimes comes about in bookkeeping because a teacher introduces a "pet" theory that conflicts with accepted practice. Students may find it difficult to follow through in the textbook. One should avoid introducing too many alternative explanations of a process—building too many "grooves" at the same time. We all want our bookkeeping students to develop maneuverability in record keeping and accounting; but in our eagerness we may move in too many directions at once, all to the confusion and frustration of our students.

I-5   The Urge To Learn—Motivation

Effective teaching is that which *motivates*, not merely for the present but for future exploration of any particular field of study. Teaching that provides negative motivation writes *finis* to further exploration and development.

A story is told of the biology teacher who was able to get more work out of his students than any other teacher in the school. His students absorbed great amounts of information. They classified, they sorted, they analyzed ontogenetically and phylogenetically. Momentarily these students were all "pepped" up because of this biological "shot in the arm." However, at the end of the term they put aside their science books and said, "Thank goodness, that's over." They probably never opened another biology book again. Some conscientious students stay with us throughout the course only that they may "save face" and maintain their previous grade point average. But they make sure they will not get in this position again, at least not with us.

In addition to training for a vocation, bookkeeping instruction must motivate the students to be eager to fill a significant place in the business world and to continue to grow in the field. While watching a commencement rehearsal, one of the school's professors overheard this remark, "If I ever get out of this place, you won't catch me opening a book as long as I live!" If we create such attitudes, we have not succeeded in attaining one of our most important objectives. Somewhere we have failed in our motivation. Failure to motivate brings sporadic attendance, discipline problems, and excessive dropouts.

I-6   Get Attention—Maintain Interest

"You can lead a horse to water, but you can't make him drink." From actual experience, however, we find that if a horse is fed considerable salt with his food, he will soon be physically in a condition to want to drink. The bookkeeping teacher may be unable to *make* the students learn, but he can feed him the "salt" of interest in a variety of different ways. For example:

1. Visit local firms for a look at real accounting systems.

2. Have local accountants and businessmen talk to students in the classroom.

3. Turn the classroom into a laboratory, not a lecture room.

4. Work out a system of cooperative work experience for students.

Learning is interesting when pupils feel they are getting something worthwhile from the instruction. Therefore, bookkeeping instruction should contain realistic and interesting projects.

I-7   Bookkeeping Is a Real, Vital, Living, Functional Experience and Should Be Taught As Such

Bookkeeping is a real occupation; accounting is a real profession. Our primary consideration in the teaching of bookkeeping should be to show students how it is *actually* done on the job. In bookkeeping classes the usual procedure is to assign problems, exercises, and practice sets and to use some audio-visual aids occasionally to drive home the textbook lessons. After all this, however, the basic concepts may still be vague or "bookish." The teacher should provide opportunities for the students to see bookkeeping in action under the best conditions. This is made possible through field trips, actual accounting materials, and other activities mentioned above in Principle I-6.

The room can become an "office" too. Particularly is this possible where some periods are set aside as "laboratory" periods. Most schools now have flexible furniture that can be moved to simulate office conditions and provide the much-desired "office" atmosphere.

I-8 Accept the Student For What He Is and Go On From There

All students do not learn at the same rate, they do not start at the same point, and they do not have the same external (out-of-class) problems. Only if the teacher recognizes this fact can learning proceed effectively. Grambs and Iverson summarize these possible differences in terms of four categories:

1. Differences in growth and maturational patterns.
2. Differences in background experiences.
3. Differences in needs, interests, and abilities.
4. Differences in school level.[2]

In bookkeeping classes in particular we find that students differ in their reasons for taking the course almost as much as in their ability to master the subject. Often they take the course because they feel that bookkeeping has less of an "academic" flavor than other subjects. Regardless of the student's limitations, it is necessary for the teacher to provide tasks appropriate to his ability (for example, see II-6, II-7, and II-8). This requires an approach different from the lecture or lecture-demonstration, in which everyone is expected to move along together.

I-9 Discipline Is No Problem

Satlow[3] states in a review of good bookkeeping methods: "Keep them busy, or they'll keep you busy." Many

---

[2] Jean D. Grambs and William J. Iverson, *Modern Methods in Secondary Education* (New York: The Dryden Press, 1952), Chapter 1.
[3] I. David Satlow, "20 Maxims for Teaching Bookkeeping," *Business Education Forum* (April, 1955), p. 30.

beginning teachers dread the first day of *real* teaching. They have all heard of the "blackboard jungle" and of the obstreperous youth in the high school classroom. Let's be realistic. Even a good, experienced teacher needs to do careful planning to control a group of 30 youngsters.

In teaching bookkeeping we like to feel that we are "blessed" with a course that has instantaneous motivational power. Nothing can be further from the truth. Bookkeeping can be the same dry drudgery for students that other courses may be. Uninteresting assignments and lessons that are either too hard or too easy contribute to unrest. Students will *do something*. If the teacher is not able to provide the needed direction, students will fend for themselves. If work is planned (see II-1), materials ready, and procedures well organized, the class will soon take on a business-like atmosphere.

I-10 Know Your Subject

Most states require six semester hours or more of college accounting for certification as a bookkeeping teacher. If a teacher does not come up to this standard, he himself is the first to notice the deficiency.

If knowledge of bookkeeping fundamentals is shaky, extra effort will be necessary before actually facing the class. Summer is a good time to brush up, either in school or by taking a temporary job in an office. Summer job experience will give the teacher something tangible to which he can refer in the next bookkeeping assignment. In order that a teacher may see pupil reaction to problem situations, he must know his subject well enough to be independent of the textbook.

I-11 Idea Assignments Are the Most Challenging

Experience in bookkeeping instruction has indicated that most pupils are eager to do their assignments, at least at the outset of the course. The teacher must work to maintain enthusiasm throughout the course.

The crux of the assignment problem lies not in the work itself, but in the degree of understanding by both the teacher and pupil of the true goal to be served by solving problems. Unless a pupil knows *what* he is doing and *why* he is doing the assignments, the only outcome for the majority of students is a painstaking filling out of work sheets and other accounting papers with an attitude of "what's the use, anyway." Even if the sheets come back beautifully written out, subsequent tests often cast doubt on the value of such homework.

Whatever the circumstance, proper mind-set is important. A bookkeeping teacher who is prone to divide the textbook into "so many pages a day" will find that while the reading has been done, *it is already forgotten.* If, in planning for the next period, attention is given to making the assignment important for the pupils, they will leave the class fairly itching to get into the problem. Teachers need to set the stage so that students will be in a proper frame of mind to energize the newly kindled interest. Instead of simply assigning Problem No. 14, for example, the teacher should take time to comment on some phase of the exercise. A simple introduction is enough, such as "I'm going to ask you to work the next problem outside the class. Poor Mr. Miller! He worked so hard and yet didn't make a profit." This followed by a story about a certain lumber dealer, much like Mr. Miller, who undersold everybody in the community. To his friends he was known as a go-getter; to the home office, as the dealer with the lowest net profit in the state. His margin was too small. His gross profit wasn't large enough to take care of his legitimate expenses no matter how he pared them down. Before the class leaves the room, they are irresistibly impelled to do something about Mr. Miller. Some general suggestions on assignments and how to handle them are given in II-4.

I-12   The "Plus" Factor—Elimination of Learning Blocks

Pupils are, in most cases, eager to learn. The successful teacher of bookkeeping is one who is an "engineer," not a mere "mechanic" of skill building. He is a teacher who realizes that there is more interaction going on in a classroom than mere performance of skills or recitation of information. In many instances pupils come to class with a "hangover" of outside influences—poor home conditions, quarrels with boy friends, failure to succeed in other classes, and so on. The clever teacher recognizes these inner disturbances and skillfully helps the student to take his mind from his troubles to a healthful class participation. There is an atmosphere of calm understanding that fits teacher methods to student needs and is referred to as the "plus" factor:

> What is it that has stood the test of twenty years or more? Seldom does it have to with the square of the hypotenuse or the dates of the French Revolution or the declension of a certain verb, but generally with the experiences in the area of human relations—the time teacher bolstered up Bill's ego by appointing him chairman of the open-house program, or the time away back in the grades when he told about his pet gopher the teacher asked him to bring to school and show to the class.
>
> If one were to make an exhaustive study of such cases, it would indeed be difficult to find an all-encompassing phrase to fit these experiences. For want of a better term, let's call them *plus factors*.[4]

Learning blocks take many forms—fear, frustration, inability to concentrate. The writers refer to another form, perhaps more "real" than those mentioned above—inability to read.

---

[4] Harm Harms, "The Plus Factor in Teaching," *American Business Education* (March, 1956), p. 182.

Bookkeeping should not be a memory subject. It calls for the use of simple logic, a meaningful vocabulary, and much common sense. A great deal of the material in bookkeeping textbooks is too difficult. Students cannot comprehend it and therefore resort to memory. The entire concept, let's say, of making an adjustment for unused supplies at the end of a fiscal period, if not thoroughly understood, is often memorized as a last resort. If his memory fails, the student is lost. As long as he is depending on his memory to tell him how to make certain entries, he has not yet grasped the fundamentals of bookkeeping. A completely different approach must be found or he may go through the entire course and perhaps through life without ever actually seeing the point.

Leading bookkeeping teachers have recognized this reading block. Satlow comments on the reading problem as a significant factor in the learning of bookkeeping concepts:

> Bookkeeping has a language of its own. For true effectiveness, the language of bookkeeping must be taught and used many times functionally. Memorization of definitions is not of much value. In planning lessons, teachers should pick out new words and make certain their meaning is taught as part of the lesson. Pupils should not be given reading exercises until the teacher is certain that they will understand the language used in the assignment. Poor readers do poorly in bookkeeping because they cannot read textbooks, or transactions in exercises, and know what they mean.[5]

I-13 The Bookkeeping Teacher Is a Teacher of Arithmetic

In every bookkeeping class there will be a number of students who are not able to do the necessary arithmetic

---

[5] I. David Satlow, "The Fundamental Processes in Bookkeeping," *American Business Education Yearbook,* Volume XII (New York: New York University Bookstore), 1955, p. 234.

computations. Where this skill is deficient, it is the book-keeping teacher's job to do something about it. How he does it will depend on circumstances. Some authors have included drill problems in texts or supplementary materials. Others prefer to wait until a student experiences the need for arithmetic when attempting to do a problem. Satlow points out this approach in a summary statement stressing the need for arithmetic teaching in the bookkeeping class:

> Very often, bookkeeping furnishes an inner drive or moti-vation for the pupil's learning of arithmetic. Many teachers have found that some pupils see no need for arithmetic until they get into the bookkeeping class. If a pupil evinces an interest in a topic such as his income tax return and sees the need for arithmetic skill, of course, nothing should be done to prevent his learning arithmetic. As a matter of fact, class activities and homework assignments should be directed to this end.[6]

We have ample evidence that genuine learning takes place only when students are motivated to learn. Effective learning of the needed arithmetic skills can be developed through meaningful relationships developed by the book-keeping teacher, with an avoidance of rules, formulas, or memorization of processes.

I-14   Machines Have Not Eliminated the Need for Neat Handwriting

In this machine age the value of handwriting is under-estimated by most of us. In spite of all our elaborate elec-tronic developments, in the majority of cases it is still necessary to convert thoughts into symbols in order to com-municate. For this, handwriting remains our principal tool. How important it can be to bookkeeping and record keeping is indicated by this case-history statement of a national handwriting consulting service:

---

[6] *Ibid.*

In many large department stores a Charga-Plate system is used. This insures legible names and addresses provided, of course, that the Charga-Plate is undamaged and that carbons are carefully placed between the order sheets. This, however, does not provide for the legible writing or lettering of items of merchandise and the numbers indicating the cost of same. Many costly errors are due to illegible number information. It is estimated that the average cost in time alone to correct a single error is one dollar. Large stores may have from 50 to 100,000 transactions a year that find their way into the adjustment department. Legible handwriting is, therefore, one of the very important items in error control in a department store.[7]

Neatness in handwriting is transferable. If the bookkeeping teacher can foster this habit in his classes, the general overall standing of the pupil will improve. We, as teachers, can encourage or discourage neatness in students' handwriting. Hastily scrawled T accounts with hardly legible entries on the chalkboard is not an encouragement to the students to be neat in their own work.

I-15   Evaluation Is a Means To An End

The 1960 *American Business Education Yearbook* is devoted to an appraisal of student progress in business classes. In this volume Garrison points out the real challenge:

> Evaluation in bookkeeping, accounting, and business arithmetic is a continuous and inseparable part of good teaching. Teachers who consider evaluation a minor aspect of teaching involving only the giving of an occasional test and perhaps making a few casual observations are shortchanging their students. The principal value of evaluation lies in the contribution that it makes toward more effective and efficient student learning.[8]

---

[7] William L. Rinehart, "The Case for Handwriting," *American Business Education* (March, 1959), p. 162.

[8] Lloyd L. Garrison, "Bookkeeping, Accounting, and Business Arithmetic," *American Business Education Yearbook*, Volume XVII (New York: New York University Bookstore), 1960, p. 239.

The good teacher is one who so organizes his work that the process of evaluation is continuous (II-9).

All problems that are assigned should be checked, but this does not mean that the teacher must necessarily spend hours doing the work himself (II-4). Valuable learning results come about when students correct their own problems. One explanation given on the spot, in context with the subject, is more valuable than a dozen "red marks" the next day.

The volume of paper work is indisputable. Hanna reports that a teacher with one bookkeeping class of 35 students would handle about 20,000 papers a year.[9] The teacher must be prepared to deal with this situation.

There must be a significant purpose behind the testing that is done in the bookkeeping class. In general, tests serve two functions: (1) the test serves as a basis for remedial instructional work, and (2) the test furnishes information on which to partially determine a grade. Whether the teacher uses printed tests furnished by the publisher of the textbook or by other agencies or makes his own, certain considerations of good testing procedure must be kept in mind:

1. Tests given must be related to the teaching being done.

2. Testing may hinder the progress of education just as easily as it may help.

3. A test may be objective in terms of scoring, but leave certain personal factors such as attitudes unchecked.

Evaluation serves as the method to detect the quality or lack of quality of instruction. If there are an overwhelming number of low grades, it may be an indication that the teacher needs to review his teaching materials and methods.

---

[9] J Marshall Hanna, "Bookkeeping," *Business Teacher* (April, 1954), p. 28.

I-16   Help Bookkeeping Students To See the "Whole"

Bookkeeping teachers should at various times check to see if the pupils in the class can visualize the entire process they have been studying. Results of such an evaluation are sometimes enough to throw the teacher into the "Slough of Despond" described by Bunyan in *Pilgrim's Progress*. After all, says the teacher, the students have been doing *something* all this time! Papers have been submitted, theory tests given, practice sets completed—all these seem to indicate that pupils know what is going on. However, given an examination of a type that covers the "complete cycle" relationships, the result may be dismal.

Gestalt psychology has influenced much modern teaching. The "whole" approach is perhaps the missing link between the mechanical learning and real understanding. One way to help students visualize the bookkeeping cycle is the "Complete Cycle" approach described in detail in Part II of this chapter (II-8). In using the complete-cycle, the standard bookkeeping cycle is developed quickly—the whole of it during one class session—as simply as possible the first time through; that is, without adjusting entries and with only simple journals and ledgers. Each time the student works through the basic problem again, he adds basic information. On some trips around the cycle, the student adds merchandise adjustments; on other trips, he adds returns of merchandise, and so on. An important part of this approach for "whole" understanding, is to construct the problem so that everything needed is on a single sheet of paper. The student not only goes through the steps of the bookkeeping cycle, but he also can literally see it develop in a unified, purposeful whole.

I-17   Teach Analysis of Simple Transactions Without Involved Vocabulary

Just as anyone who learned to write longhand can also learn to write shorthand, so anyone who can do average work in the usual school subjects can also learn bookkeeping. If students fail to learn, the chances are that the fault lies with the teacher. Perhaps his students are not comprehending the "bookkeeping lingo." Thus, the leader seems to be setting up a barrier to learning.

We *do* have an obligation to teach the language of bookkeeping. Fundamentally, double-entry bookkeeping is built on the Paciolian foundation of *debitori* and *creditori*. It is necessary to understand how this principle functions. Some teachers have found their greatest success, at least for students at a certain level, in having the class memorize "left side for debit; right side for credit." However, rote learning is not lasting and certainly is not explanatory. The words "debit" and "credit" themselves are a source of confusion to many students. Winnett, for example, points out common misconceptions placed on the words "debit" and "credit" and shows where this can lead in immature or illogical reasoning:

> You will have to use all of the intelligence, knowledge, and ingenuity at your command to search for ways to relate daily experiences of students to the work of the bookkeeping class. "Credit" in the mind of students represents something good. Therefore, since "debit" is opposite to "credit," "debit" must be bad. But, the mind of the student reasons, additions to cash are said to be "debits," and that of course is good. How confusing this vocabulary is to students.[10]

By approaching this fundamental principle from a student point of view, omitting technical terms for the time being, the teacher will give his pupils an opportunity to develop *what* is being taught in their thinking in relation to *how* and *why* with a minimum of memorization of terms or rules.

---

[10] William L. Winnett, "Debits and Credits at the Blackboard," *National Business Education Quarterly* (Winter, 1958), p. 29.

I-18   Adjusting Entries Need Not Be a Stumbling Block

Moss refers to a teaching pattern from which we might all benefit in our bookkeeping classes:

> Obstacles (to basic understanding) are encountered at every turn. This can be eliminated, or at least smoothed considerably, by a step-by-step presentation of the material, with accompanying illustrations. One teaching technique is to (1) lead the student through the brambles, then (2) tell him *where* he has been, and (3) still later, tell him *why* he has made the trip.[11]

To get lost "in the brambles" of adjusting entries is not uncommon. Adjusting entry difficulties are not limited to weak students; they also trouble those who seem to have a fair grasp of bookkeeping concepts. It is at this point that the teacher needs every technique at his command. Even with excellent textbooks and supplementary materials, students can benefit a great deal from clear explanation, illustration, and practice on adjusting entries. Demonstration techniques described in II-2 and in III-3 are possible avenues to teaching success in this area of instruction.

I-19   Credit Is "Big Business"

Consumer debt in the United States in 1961 was at a new high of over $50 billion. This is over $6 billion more than the previous two-year period; the trend is ever upward. The ordinary citizen will be called upon to do more and more bookkeeping in his personal affairs.

Bookkeeping teachers may dislike teaching interest and discount, but the need for handling such matters both for personal use and in business is daily becoming more pronounced. The role of the bookkeeping teacher is again one of analyzing transactions. To have students read about the

---

[11] Kermit C. Moss, "Paper Grading—An Accounting Instructor's Dilemma," *The Accounting Review* (January, 1957), p. 125.

process of accounting for notes and interest helps them but little. The teacher must actively develop usable materials to impress this concept on students.

I-20   Effective Use of Practice Sets Is Essential

One of the important principles of learning mentioned earlier in this chapter set forth the tenet of *learning by doing* (I-6). Nowhere in the teaching of bookkeeping can this be done as easily as in the use of practice sets. It is in the use of this supplementary material that pupils are given an opportunity to "try their wings" in applying the principles studied during the preceding weeks.

The practice set, as it is generally used, has been handled by teachers in almost every possible way in order to obtain its maximum potential. This means sets completed in class under the direct supervision of the teacher, sets completed at the leisure of the pupils, sets completed partly in class and partly outside the class. No conclusive evidence has been presented that one method is more favorable than the other. However, certain approaches show that excellent possibilities exist for success (II-7, III-12).

Students learn by doing. One primary principle that should apply to the use of practice sets, regardless of the particular approach used, is to make sure that every student, whether talented or slow, has success in the application of a phase of the work. One way in which to assure that all students can achieve some success is through the "accounting office" system: organization of the work into job segments, such as journal bookkeeper, ledger bookkeeper, and supervisor, with provisions made for rotation of jobs. This pattern, which deviates from traditional methods of "filling in" the set, stimulates the students to supervise work on the sets. High-ability students are given the opportunity to act as directors of activities, in which they can exercise their leadership abilities.

BOOKKEEPING—PART II
THE "HOW" OF THE BOOKKEEPING TEACHING SITUATION

Part I of this chapter has been devoted to a description of sound principles of learning applied to the teaching of bookkeeping. Many of these call for discrimination and good judgment on the part of the teacher, and the method used will depend largely on the circumstances of a given situation. The pages that follow contain a number of practical ideas applicable to these principles. These suggestions have to do with areas that teachers find most troublesome, for example, the efficient use of practice sets. Many teachers, in small communities, do not have access to libraries of reference materials. Perhaps some of the methods outlined here will make it possible for them to teach first-year bookkeeping with some measure of accomplishment.

II-1 Organizing and Planning Are Crucial Factors In Teaching Bookkeeping

Being properly prepared for the first day's class gives poise to the teacher and confidence to the student. Confidence in one's self is a necessary element in successful teaching and learning. The beginning teacher will do well to use written outline forms of the type that follow to plot the scope and sequence of the course, both from an overall point of view and for day-to-day activities.

Planning and Organizing (General). Preplanning consists of selecting and listing materials that are to be used—textbook, supplementary readings, audio-visual materials, etc.—in a comprehensible manner for the entire course. A duplicated form like the one on the next page serves as a useful aid for this purpose.

Good planning means that every minute of the class period is used to the best possible advantage. Every class period should be based on an established lesson plan, the

GENERAL COURSE OUTLINE

SUBJECT: _____

OBJECTIVES: _____
_____
_____
_____
_____
_____
_____

COURSE MATERIALS:

1. Textbook: _____
_____
_____

2. Supplementary reading material: _____
_____

3. Supplies: _____
_____
_____

4. Films: _____
_____
_____
_____
_____

   Filmstrips: _____
_____
_____
_____
_____

   Other audio-visual material: _____
_____
_____
_____
_____

COURSE CALENDAR

Meeting Dates	Course Material	Assignments

(Continued)

335

detail of which will depend on the background and experience of the teacher. In a good lesson plan one usually finds the following:

Review: (Elements of recording transactions in the cash receipts journal, for example.)

Assignment Check: (Through the use of the chalkboard, charts or overhead projector, a "quickie" review or a self-audit of the previous day's assignment.)

Presentation (New Material): (Take the students through the new elements of the day's material.)

Discussion (or Drill): (Question and discussion of the new concepts, followed by a short practice period.)

Summary: (A drawing together of the new concepts presented.)

Assignment: (A brief but thorough review of the instructions and special materials to be used in the assignment.)

A well-developed, more detailed description of the lesson plan is illustrated by Boynton,[12] part of which is presented on pages 337 and 338.

---

[12] Lewis D. Boynton, *Methods of Teaching Bookkeeping* (Cincinnati: South-Western Publishing Company, 1955), pp. 106-107.

COMMON STEPS IN THE OUTLINE OF A FORMAL DAILY
LESSON PLAN, WITH EXPLANATORY REASONS
FOR EACH DIVISION OR STEP IN THE PLAN *

Step or Division	*Purpose*
1. Title of Lesson (Topic)	For reference or filing purposes.
2. Aim of Lesson (Objective) (Goal) (Purpose)	To require teacher to state in simple, concise sentences what is to be accomplished this day. Helps keep teacher on track in the planning that follows, and can help him during lesson presentation from straying or letting students wander too far from the day's objective.
3. Preclass Preparation (Materials Needed)	To be sure that necessary materials are on hand before the lesson starts. Student interest and attention can be lost and class time wasted if the teacher must stop during the lesson to hunt for illustrative material, paper, books, or other materials and supplies that he or his students need.
4. Preparation (Motivation) (Connection with previous learning) (Introduction) (Review)	To arouse student interest and get student attention. Such opening remarks, questions, or classroom activity must have a relationship and lead into the presentation that follows.
5. Presentation	To present the new knowledges or skills to be learned. This is the heart of the lesson. All remarks, all questions, all activity should be outlined or planned so that this aim is completed.

---

* Alternate names for steps or divisions are given in parentheses.

Step or Division		Purpose
6. Application or 7. Drill	T e s t i n g	To help reinforce or fix the new learnings that were taught in the presentation. To enable the teacher to find out (test informally) whether the students understand and can apply what was taught. Drill is application, but application is not always drill. Application could accompany presentation.
8. Summary		To organize and clinch the teaching. This could be a brief oral summary by the teacher, or, in order to test understanding and application, the students could do the summarizing.
9. Assignment		Usually to give the students opportunity for further application of what was learned or further drill on the skill involved in the new learnings. Students should realize that such is the case, and the teacher should find time to point this out for each assignment. Assignments should not, however, always follow the same pattern. Some assignments should require students to delve into new material before the teacher presents it in class. A teacher who *always* introduces new learnings in class before giving students a chance to study new material on their own is cheating some students of a way of learning at which they may be best, or which will have to be acquired later for college use.
10. Teacher's Remarks		For immediate reference as to shortcomings or omissions in today's presentation that should be corrected or covered tomorrow. For future reference when this lesson is again presented. Such remarks should include the strong and the weak points of the plan as used and should be written down immediately after the lesson plan has been used.

One of the most significant teaching aids in planning and organizing is the duplicating equipment now readily available to practically all classroom teachers. Much time can be conserved for class instruction if standard information is prepared and duplicated for use in advance of the first day. The filing cabinet of the teacher can have one section of each drawer set up for folders containing introductory material for each course. A folder, for example, might be made up of first-day activities—projects to do while the class is in the process of settling down to business. Lengthy expositions should be held to a minimum—the students are eager to "bookkeep," so the sooner we get them going on a problem of some kind, the better.

Visual and audio-visual aids are an important part of the general planning. For a list of useful films, see the selected references at the end of this chapter and the listing in Chapter X.

Planning and Organizing (Specific). In addition to the course-planning sheets and outlines illustrated, the teacher should take a look at what he plans to do in the first week in bookkeeping. The alert teacher will have on hand certain very specific projects that will help him to capitalize on the initial eagerness of the students and ease the strain on himself. This specific planning should become a continuing practice. A teacher had an accident coming to school on a Monday morning. From the hospital he sent word, "Look in the upper right-hand desk drawer." There the principal found plans for the week in such detail that a substitute could follow them without difficulty. Sometimes unexpected calls for community service make last-minute preparation impossible. The teacher who leads a hand-to-mouth existence in planning is often in for trouble.

Some specific first-week suggestions for the beginning teacher are given on the following pages.

1. *Make detailed memo-plans, especially for the first few weeks.* Study the first chapter of the text carefully and *know* every detail of the concepts involved. A *detailed* outline is best for the beginning teacher, who is apt to wander off on a tangent. The standard lesson plan outline has been stated above. In addition, for use with the "presentation" phase of the lesson plan, the beginning teacher will be wise to work out step by step the exact material he intends to present. The three sample lessons on pages 341-343 constitute examples of such skeleton notations that will help the teacher to maintain his poise in presenting new material.

2. *Keep assignments within a reasonable length.* A weakness of the inexperienced teacher, especially in the first few class meetings, is that he is apt to "pile it on" in an effort to make sure that all students are kept busy. One way to gauge the amount of homework is for the teacher himself to work the textbook problem or exercise. The American Accounting Association suggests a 4:1 working ratio (teacher time to do problem times four equals student time) for test problems. This standard can also be applied to homework assignments. Some authors give an estimated minimum-maximum working time for their problems. However, this estimate is based on the time required to do the entire problem and is not of great value to the teacher who wishes to use only part of an exercise or to modify it in some way to meet the needs of the particular class.

3. *Defer testing for the first week or so,* or give tests on which there is no undue emphasis on the grading.

4. *Make directions definite.* If the teacher is vague in stating what he expects of the class, he can expect the results to be equally vague. Some might call giving careful directions and explanations "coddling" the student. It would seem that the teacher should be more than a person

Textbook Materials: Chapter 1

Assignment: Q. 1, 2, 3, 6,--Chapter 1

I. Property and Property Ownership

Property--those things of value which are subject to the ex-
clusive control and enjoyment by an individual or
group of individuals. (Assets)

Property Ownership--the right to possess, use, and to transfer the property.

A. Proprietorship--secondary claim. The equity of the
owner of the property. Also: net worth; capital.
B. Liabilities--the rights of creditors in the assets.
Primary claim.

Measure of value--the monetary unit: The dollar.

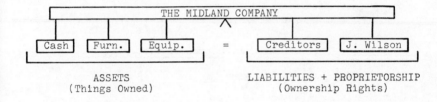

ASSETS
(Things Owned)

LIABILITIES + PROPRIETORSHIP
(Ownership Rights)

II. The Accounting Equation

Assets = Property Rights

Assets = Liabilities + Proprietorship

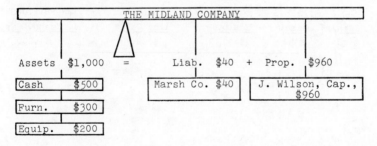

LESSON _2_

Textbook Materials: Chapter 1

Assignment: Problem 2-1

I.   (Restate illustration of previous lesson.)

II. Changes in proprietorship. (Use outline from previous lesson.)

    A. Transactions:
       1. Purchased additional equipment, $100
       2. Paid on account, $30
       3. Purchased merchandise for cash, $100
       4. Sold merchandise for cash, $100, for which cash, $75, had been paid
       5. Expenses paid in cash, $10

III. (Use illustrative problem from textbook, pp. 5-8.)

IV. Accounting Statements

    A. Income Statement--picture of the past

    B. Balance Sheet--picture of the present

    C. Budget--picture of the future

LESSON _3_

Textbook Materials: Chapter 2

Assignment: Problem 2-A

I. Balance Sheet

    Purpose: Summary of assets, liabilities, and proprietorship; to supply information to show the financial condition of the business.

ASSETS			=	LIABILITIES	+	PROPRIETORSHIP
Cash +	Mdse. +	Equip.		Acme Co.		J. Mason, Capital
$500	$300	$400		$200		$1,000

(Continued)

Simple Balance Sheet

J. Mason
Balance Sheet
January 31, 19__

ASSETS		LIABILITIES	
Cash . . . .$	500	Accounts Payable . . . . .$	200
Merchandise . . .	300	(Acme Co.)	
Equipment	400	PROPRIETORSHIP	
	$1,200	J. Mason, Capital	1,000
			$1,200

Classified Balance Sheet

J. Mason
Balance Sheet
January 31, 19__

ASSETS		LIABILITIES	
Current Assets:		Current Liabilities:	
Cash . . . $500		Accounts Payable $200	
Mdse. . . 300		(Acme Co.)	
Total C. A. $ 800		Total C. L. 200	
Fixed Assets:		PROPRIETORSHIP	
Equipment . . . 400		J. Mason, Cap., Jan. 1 $700	
		Net Profit for	
		Month . . .$600	
		Less With-	
		drawals . . 300	
		Increase in Cap. . . . 300	
		J. Mason, Cap., Jan. 31 . 1,000	
Total Assets $1,200		Total Liab. & Prop. . . . $1,200	

II.   Classification of Balance Sheet Items

    A.   Current Assets

    B.   Fixed Assets

    C.   Current Liabilities   Define classifications

    D.   Fixed Liabilities

    E.   Proprietorship

III.   Special Emphasis

    A.   Heading of Statement

    B.   Classification indentions

    C.   Rule for total on same level

    D.   Double rule for completion on same level

who merely "dishes out" the material. One method that
has been used to good success is to hand out an outline
during the first week. An example is given below. The
student can fasten this sheet in his book, where it will serve
two purposes: (1) a general study guide, and (2) an
assignment record. Dates are omitted from the duplicated
copy and are inserted as the lessons and assignments are
developed. Allowances are made on this sheet, as in the
teacher's own outline, for interruptions for field trips, school
holidays, and the like.

ACCOUNTING ASSIGNMENT RECORD

Due Date		Textbook Material	Problem Number	Extra Credit Problem(s)
Sept.	27	Chapter 3	3 - A	3 - B
	30	Chapter 3	3 - 2	3 - 3
Oct.	1	Chapter 4	4 - 1	—
	3	Chapter 4	4 - 2	4 - A
	5	Chapter 4	4 - 3	
	7	Test (Chapters 3-4)	—	—

II-2 Good Demonstration Inspires Confidence

Seeing, understanding, and participating are three important factors in demonstration. The T account, for example, must be seen to be understood. One student thought
the teacher had been talking about a "key" account before
he *saw* it on the board. Work sheet and payroll problems
can best be presented through demonstration. Students can
fill in the forms without supervision, but directed instruction is more productive.

How can we get these materials on the board when
there is so little time available between classes? For a
number of years the writers used a canvas sheet, painted
on one side with chalkboard paint. This made an excellent

"chalkboard" surface. The work sheet, or any problem involving a great deal of writing, was filled out on the canvas sheet before class. Then the "board" was hung on hooks provided for it on the regular chalkboard. A lot of work? Certainly! But the satisfaction that is gained when students are thus able to grasp an entire process in a minimum of time is well worth the extra effort. A variety of visual aids of all kinds are now available.

The overhead projector (Vu-Graph, Visual-Cast, and other makes) provides valuable assistance in demonstrating difficult concepts. Whole problems can be filled in either before class or along with the class in good form with a minimum of last-minute physical arrangements. While the teacher is writing on the transparent slide, he is facing the class and can answer questions or explain points without losing the attention of the class. The advantages claimed for the overhead projector have not been exaggerated:

1. The instructor operates the machine from the front of the room and faces the class. This facilitates group discussion while the instructor remains at the machine.

2. The instructor alone operates the machine, which requires no handling beyond the flick of a switch and the mere laying of the material to be projected on the glass plate before him. The projected materials face the instructor for easy reading and for pointing with a pencil (which reflects upon the screen.) The various materials to be projected may be placed and replaced upon the machine virtually without time consumption. Machine operation is noiseless.

3. The transparencies may be made up easily and used repeatedly. Blank plastic rolls, which may be attached to the machine, are available for the build-up of data in the classroom for temporary purposes.[13]

---

[13] American Accounting Association, *Accounting Teachers Guide* (Cincinnati: South-Western Publishing Company, 1953), p. 150.

For professional-looking transparencies it takes only a supply of inexpensive 10″ by 10″ cellophane, Vu-Graph carbon paper, and a regular or Ampli-type typewriter. Professional, permanent-type transparencies can be easily made with diazo acetate sheets or with Clear-Positive film.

On these finished transparencies as much material can be filled in as the teacher desires and the significant points left blank for classroom completion. For extended problems that cannot be completed in one period, such as some work sheet or payroll problems, the transparencies can simply be put aside for the next day's work—no more "do not erase" notes for the teacher to fret about.

The best demonstration device universally available to the bookkeeping teacher is the chalkboard. The teacher should use every possible opportunity to practice and develop his skill in the use of the chalkboard.

One need not be an artist to do good work on the chalkboard. A little practice on a uniform lettering or writing style will do the job for the bookkeeping instructor. In general, we try to teach too much too quickly in a demonstration, and often the writing becomes hard to read. The teacher should be prepared to illustrate good style in bookkeeping forms, rather than talk about them. Because most rooms are used by a number of other instructors, the bookkeeping teacher should have his own basic equipment. This consists of good quality chalk, in various colors for emphasizing points in discussion, and a good straight-edge instrument. Experienced teachers like to use a ruler such as that illustrated and described by Musselman and Hanna:

1. Use an extra-wide yardstick. A T square from which the end-piece has been removed makes an excellent stick.

2. Attach a hand grip to the stick. This permits you to hold the stick firmly in place with one hand and rule with the other. A window-sash lift makes a convenient grip. It can be fastened to a small block, which in turn may be fastened to the stick.

3. Place the hand grip on one side of the stick so that it can be held without interfering with the ruling along the other side.[14]

If the chalkboard is not in immediate demand by other teachers, semi-permanent forms for ledgers, journals, and other books of record can be lined on the board by first wetting the board and then drawing the lines on the wet surface. These lines will last for at least two weeks of fairly heavy use and can be easily removed for new material by washing the board; or they can be renewed by wetting and relining. Perhaps the bookkeeping teacher should carefully examine the room schedule before drawing these long-lasting forms on the board. One non-bookkeeping teacher remarked not long ago when attempting to erase the board for his English class, "That fellow has put some kind of arithmetic problems on the board so that I can't erase them. What *sort* of chalk does he use anyway?" Chalkboard space is a critical factor.

Finding time to get the materials on the board is also a problem. It is in this respect that a student assistant, or "chairman," can be of great value to the teacher in helping him organize class materials. A part of the effectiveness of the demonstration is lost if the teacher has to spend an inordinate amount of class time getting ready.

II-3   One "New" Thing at a Time

Students come to class each day with enthusiasm when they have something "new" to look forward to. One thing at a time does not mean that the subject matter is separated

---

[14] Musselman and Hanna, *op cit.*, p. 84.

into small bits, to allocate one each day. Rather, the opposite is true. This "one thing" is well illustrated in the complete-cycle approach (Principle II-8). First, Mrs. Miller's business, together with her recordkeeping system, is presented as a whole; the "new thing" of the next day is the opening of a set of books. The "one new thing" of the third class meeting is the sales-purchases concept; that of the fourth day, special journals. Each new problem is taught as a whole, simple complete unit, without branching off into various allied understandings. The complete cycle problem is a valuable instruction device in that every student does a whole operation each day, and he also does something different and challenging each day.

An example of "what not to do" for the sake of avoiding confusion, is to attempt to teach, all in one period or even in adjacent periods, the alternative methods of handling the adjusting entries. The "reversing" and "nonreversing" methods are commonly placed together for convenience in the textbook. One method, preferably the simpler nonreversing method, should be taught thoroughly before moving into the alternative pattern.

The matter of timing is important. The success of the approach depends in part on getting the "one idea" of the bookkeeping process across in a single period. The problem may be worked through twice, with time to spare for questions and to tie up loose ends. If the concept involved can't be presented in one period, then it becomes necessary to rethink the process so that a *complete* concept can emerge.

II-4 *Assignment Planning Should Be Carefully Done*

Educational data and studies on the principles of assigning lessons and problem materials will be cited in Part III of this chapter. The following outline, handed to students in duplicated form and carefully explained, has proved to be valuable as a "road map" of what to do next:

ACCOUNTING CLASSES *

Assignment Instructions

I. All papers submitted must include the following information in the upper right-hand corner:

1. Name.

2. Problem number: that is, Problem 1, Chapter 10.

II. Problems are due on the class meeting one week from the date of the assignment; that is, assigned Wednesday, due on the following Wednesday.

III. Assignments are due at the beginning of class on the due date. Penalties for late assignments:

1. Later than the beginning of class on the due date, but within one week after the due date—marked as "late" for final evaluation purposes.

2. Later than one week after due date—no credit allowed.

IV. Neatness is very important. It is assumed that no premium will be given for neat papers, but penalties will be assessed for deficiencies. Neatness includes the following:

1. Handwriting that is legible.

2. Figures that are clear and readable—important in pencil foots.

3. Rulings and style that conform to the text or to good accounting procedure.

4. Erasures that are neat—not difficult since work is in pencil.

5. Papers that are fastened together with clips—"dog-eared" papers are not acceptable.

Papers which are correct in computation but unacceptable because of noncompliance with the principles of neatness will be returned to the student and may be resubmitted for "late" credit at the following class meeting. Papers returned to the student, but then not resubmitted, will not receive credit.

V. A minimum of 70 per cent of the assignments must be completed in order for the student to receive a passing grade.

---

* Some parts of this outline have been adapted from the *Accounting Teachers Guide* (Cincinnati: South-Western Publishing Company, 1953), pp. 87-88.

The method of estimating a reasonable length for the homework assignment was discussed briefly in Principle I and can be used as a general guide.

Checking assigned homework can be handled in a variety of ways. One practical method of handling assignments and one that is economical of class time, but *does* take some of the teacher's out-of-class time, is placing problem solutions on large sheets of ordinary wrapping paper with a Flo-Master pen. These sheets can be attached to the chalkboard surface with scotch tape. Students can then check their homework quickly. Another method, if an overhead projector is part of the instructional equipment, is to prepare the solution on 10″ x 10″ transparencies. This can be done with the typewriter, by drawing, or by direct-photo copy.

The important thing is to review the solution of the assignment *quickly* and *thoroughly*. Students like to know where they stand. They like to check their own work. Corrections are made by the students in red pencil for future guidance. These papers are then filed by the students in special personal folders that are left in the room but may be checked out for review purposes. This process of filing also enables the teacher to review the work of the students periodically for appraisal of progress.

Because "degree grading," that is, "A," "B," "C," is not particularly useful on the daily assignments, only one mark is placed on the paper by the teacher—a rubber-stamped date that indicates the paper was submitted on a certain date and on time. Of course, occasional comments on the excellence of the work or on ideas for improvement can be written on the papers by the teacher in his frequent checkup of the folders.

The method of handling assignments described does not relieve the teacher of the necessity of checking some of the papers himself. It can be done quite easily, however, by reviewing the file folders on given days.

Student checking of papers must be well organized so that it does not take too long, in order to leave time for adequate treatment of weak points and the presentation of new materials. Too much "checking time" may encourage the student to copy instead of to actually do the homework.

II-5 Learning Blocks Need To Be Eliminated

Any device that increases tension, disappointment, fear, or distrust should be eliminated. Careful thought must be given to the approach that will create the best atmosphere for learning.

Fear of failure is perhaps the most persistent block to learning. One way to eliminate or to reduce this fear is to present a lesson the first day that enables every student to successfully do the problem and to understand it. Boynton provides an excellent outline of the development of such a class situation that can serve as a model for the beginning teacher. Part of such a plan is given on pages 352-354.

Confidence in his own ability helps the student to overcome learning blocks. New concepts should be presented slowly and carefully. For example, in teaching how to journalize, the teacher might read the transactions along with the students, analyze the transactions *with* them, and cooperatively work out the journalizing along with them. Thus working together, all students get a chance to recite, to complete their work, and to feel a sense of accomplishment.

Students can sometimes do better working together in small groups than they do by themselves in one large group under the immediate direction of the teacher. Modern bookkeeping room furniture makes it easy to change the class from a one-unit plan to a multigroup setting.

If outside assignments are kept reasonably short, even though comprehensive, students are likely to have the work ready on schedule. Nothing is more frustrating than never quite finishing a problem during the time available.

LESSON PLAN [15]

Introducing Students to Bookkeeping

II

Topic:	Motivating Students for Bookkeeping Study—or— The Need for Records in Determining Financial Worth.
Aims:	To bring students to an understanding of (a) the meaning of financial worth, (b) how financial worth is determined, (c) the need for records (bookkeeping) in determining the financial worth of an individual or a business.
Supplies Needed:	Plain paper and textbook, workbook, or mimeographed problems to be worked in class and for homework.

MOTIVATION

TEACHER

First suggestion for motivation—if homework assignment indicated in Lesson I was given to students.

"Yesterday we examined and discussed many reasons why people study bookkeeping. Will you give me a few of the reasons?"

Student:

1. *To help in a business I want to run; to meet requirements of secretarial course; because guidance counsellor recommended it, etc.*

"At the close of the period yesterday, I asked you to try to find out why people think that bookkeeping is so important. Let us see what you found."

Remarks:

This will connect the start of today's lesson with what was done yesterday and help reinforce learning.

Teacher calls upon individual class members to tell whom they interviewed and what replies were received to the question, "*In what way has bookkeeping been important to you?*"

Teacher writes this question on blackboard and summarizes students' findings under it.

Student:

(Common answers to be expected.)

1. *Helps me keep within my budget.*
2. *So I know how much I can spend.*
3. *So I know what income tax to pay.*
4. *So I know where I stand.*
5. *So I know what I own.*
6. *So I know how much I am worth.*
7. *etc.*

---

[15] Boynton, *op. cit.*, pp. 249-252.

Remarks:

Students who do a homework assignment usually possess a psychological set or anticipation for reporting on this first. Teachers who ignore such assignments or frequently postpone reference to them usually are failing to derive maximum motivational help and learning from such assignments.

TEACHER

Teacher then refers to response dealing with, "So I know how much I am worth," and points up what is to come in the presentation with the following story:

Second suggestion for motivation—
Teachers who might prefer to apply this plan as their initial plan for introducing bookkeeping to students could *start* their lesson and motivation with the following story:

"Recently, when I was riding on a bus, two men sitting on the seat directly behind me started to discuss, in voices which I couldn't help overhearing, a third man whom both knew.

"One asked the other, 'Do you know Johnny Bucker who lives over in Plainville?' His friend replied, 'Sure! Johnny is worth a barrel of money,' and for emphasis added, 'A big barrel of money.' The other denied this loudly and exclaimed, 'Johnny isn't worth any barrel of money. Johnny isn't worth a cent.'"

Teacher asks class, "On the basis of these remarks, what do you think Johnny Bucker is worth?"

"What is 'a barrel of money'?"

"Is it possible for a person to be worth 'not a cent'?"

Remarks:

Story telling, if brief and to the point, can be an excellent device for getting attention and interest. If well done, it takes the students out of the class, out of themselves, and gets them thinking. It gives the teacher the opportunity to move easily and naturally to the presentation rather than introduce it with the deadening remark, "Today we are going to learn about—." Daily motivation or interest-getting need not, in fact should not, always be through the technique of connection with the previous day's learning. Teachers should feel that they have "poetic license" to concoct a good story or illustration. This is an important phase in the creativeness of teaching—in lesson planning.

Student:
"A great deal of money."

"Thousands of dollars, maybe."
"Hard to tell."

"No. You're always worth something."

Remarks:

The questions here are suggestive for the teacher in leading and controlling the discussion on a person's worth. The individual teacher, naturally, may choose to use different questions.

PRESENTATION

TEACHER

"How do we determine what a person is worth?"

"How would you determine which people in our community are the most valuable, the most worthwhile to the community?"

"If we were to prepare a list of the ten people worth most to our community, would they also be the richest people in dollars and cents?"

Student:

"By what he does or what he has."

"Find out the people who have done things that benefit other people in the community rather than just themselves."

"Not necessarily."

Remarks:

The purpose of the discussion is to guide students to see for themselves that there is a difference between financial worth and social or moral worth. This extends their knowledge of the term *worth* and gives a sharper and discriminatory meaning to the bookkeeping term *financial worth*. Learning in this manner is more effective than if the teacher simply tells students the difference. Telling does not always stimulate thought.

"Let us jot down on a sheet of paper three people you know about who have contributed the most to improve the community."

Student:

Students write names.

Remarks:

This activity also gives some clue to the student's knowledge of the community in which he lives and indicates to the bookkeeping teacher whether there is some need for a study of or reaching out into the community.

II-6 Individual Differences—Let's Do Something About Them

Individual differences in students, except in physical appearance, will not be evident to the bookkeeping teacher on the first day. These differences show up as soon as assignments begin to come in. Students in college accounting classes often come with a wide variety of pre-college bookkeeping experience, a circumstance that cannot be readily ascertained at registration time. One method used in post-high-school institutions to uncover some of these differences is to give a preliminary test to determine the extent of bookkeeping knowledge. Students are then assigned to class sections that best fit their needs.

Regardless of attempts made to get "uniform" classes, there will continue to be a wide range of ability levels in the same classroom. The teacher should recognize this spread and immediately build a class organization that will take care of each individual's needs. Classification of these differences by teachers will vary. Musselman and Hanna [16] refer to them as problems in reading, arithmetic, handwriting, good work habits, and attitudes.

What to do about these differences is an important problem for any teacher. A number of possibilities are available:

1. *Emphasize group participation for certain types of bookkeeping study.* Studies in education have attempted to determine the efficiency of group learning. One such study is that of Shaw who sought to determine whether individuals or groups were able to solve arithmetic problems more accurately and more efficiently.[17] The outcome showed that groups seemed assured of a much larger per-

---

[16] Musselman and Hanna, *op. cit.*, Chapter 2.

[17] Marjorie E. Shaw, "A Comparison of Individuals and Small Groups in the Rational Solution of Complex Problems," *Readings in Social Psychology*, T. M. Newcomb and E. L. Hartley, editors (New York: Henry Holt and Company, 1947), pp. 314-315.

centage of correct answers since the members were able to reject incorrect answers and check errors. Groups did not make as many errors as the average individual. Other studies show that although the quantity of group work is not so great, the quality of the work is superior to other types. Perhaps the greatest value of small groups is that differences are reconciled, each student finding his own niche in the unit. This approach of handling individual differences is developed in detail in the description of practice set procedures (Principle 7-1).

2. *Use extra-credit assignment plans.* Students frequently respond to the "extra-pay" plan in which superior students earn points for additional work. These extra points give the student prestige.

3. *Establish positions of leadership in the class organization.* Superior students can become class leaders and assistants, thus getting additional experience in developing leadership. Less able students also have "extra-special" duties, such as getting the projection equipment ready, writing materials on the board, etc.

4. *Give special attention to skill needs—arithmetic, handwriting, reading.* Deficiencies in these areas of learning are quite evident to many business teachers. A portion of each class can be devoted to rapid-fire arithmetic drill in the commonly used bookkeeping tools of addition, subtraction, multiplication, and division. Special reading quizzes, showing understanding or lack of it, can be devised to help the reading problem. In solving the handwriting problem, the teacher himself can provide an impetus in the right direction by presenting neat, well-written demonstrations. In order to present usable papers, Boynton [18] suggests lettering as a means of helping students whose script is "hopeless."

---

[18] Boynton, *op. cit.*, p. 232.

5. *Use the potential of cooperative work-experience programs.* Experimentation has indicated that some of our "hopeless" students perform quite well in routine, on-the-job activities. Superior students, too, can use this opportunity to develop unawakened potentials. A complete description of this type of program was outlined in Chapter VI.

6. *Community projects.* Projects involving community service can be used to challenge superior students. Not long ago, for example, the authors were asked to help organize a bookkeeping system for a rehabilitation program. This offered an excellent opportunity to make use of the talents of our more advanced students in the elementary accounting class.

7. *Field trips—Reports.* A field trip with its summarizing report makes use of student interest and ability at all levels.

8. *Use of a variety of learning materials.* Differences in abilities, levels of accomplishment, and academic background can in some measure be reconciled through a variety of learning materials. Where the bookkeeping teacher may obtain these materials is pointed out in Chapter X.

II-7 Make the Most Efficient Use Of Practice Sets

Most bookkeeping teachers will agree that the practice set is an essential part of their teaching materials. Sets *do* take time to complete, time that some teachers may feel is not too productively used. This latter viewpoint is not too unusual if the set is not *taught* but is simply used as a summarizing device. If correctly used, the practice set plays a vital part in the total bookkeeping learning process.

A workable practice set procedure, even for the beginning bookkeeping teacher, is a method sometimes called the *accounting office* system. Although this is only one of several relatively standard methods, this approach stimulates interest and helps in two specific ways: (1) it helps the extremely fast student who completes the set in a very short time, and (2) the extremely slow student who never gets quite finished. The *accounting office* approach provides for both types of students:

> The following plan has been used successfully: When the class is ready to begin the first practice set, it is divided into work groups of three or four students to each group. The work groups are so divided that bright and rapid workers are teamed with an average student and a slow student. The team works as a group on one practice set. One member of the team keeps the cashbook, another member keeps the general journal and the sales and purchases journal, and another member keeps the ledger. The members of the team rotate every ten or twenty transactions so that each student gets the experience of keeping the other books. The teams are given a set time in which the transactions are to be completed. When the end of the fiscal period is reached, they work together in taking a trial balance, with each member of the team making a trial balance. They again work together in making the adjusting entries, in making the profit and loss statement, and in making the balance sheet. Each student prepares a copy for himself. The closing entries are completed by the group and are posted, and a final trial balance is taken. Before proceeding to the transactions for the next fiscal period, this team takes another practice set and again goes through the recording of the transactions in exactly the same manner. If student "A" began with the cashbook the first time through, he would begin with the journals, and the other members of the team would rotate in like manner. Each team keeps an accurate record of the number of minutes necessary to make all the transactions, and during the second time through the set they are required to do the work in one half the time required for the first time through. They again take a trial balance to insure the accuracy of the work and go through the other phases of the end of the fiscal period. When this set is completed, the team of three students again goes

through the same practice set attempting again to cut the
time in half. When the set has been completed the third
time, the students proceed with the next fiscal period in the
same manner.

Experience has shown that three students, working cooperatively as they would in an office, can go through three
practice sets and complete the work of the fiscal periods in
the time usually required for the average student to go
through the set once. The great advantage of the team
method of work on the practice set is that it actually gives the
student *practice* and *repetition* under timed pressure to the
extent that he attains a vocational skill for which business
will be willing to pay.*

The following suggestions will help the newcomer to
this system to put it into use. By the time the practice set
work comes up, a number of students have demonstrated
capabilities for record keeping. These students form the
nucleus for the staff of the accounting office. A limited
number of these top-level students are appointed to "supervisory" positions. There may be two or three other students
under the direction of a supervisor. The preliminary organizational work of the group involves selection of the journal
bookkeepers, general ledger bookkeeper, filing clerk; other
divisions of labor may be needed. As soon as the group
organization is complete, work commences on the set.

The teacher plays an important part in the accounting
office system, or in any other method used for practice set
work, both in preliminary planning and in periodic and final
evaluations. In order to save time and to get the set started
without extraneous explanation, an instruction sheet is distributed to each student. See a sample on page 360.

Evaluation of work is important to both students and
teacher. For student use, an "audit" outline has proved
helpful. A sample is shown on page 361.

---

* Authors' note: For a complete description of this treatment of practice set work, see: Hamden L. Forkner, "The Practice Set in Modern Bookkeeping," *The Balance Sheet* (December, 1943), pp. 148-150.

ELEMENTARY ACCOUNTING

Practice Set Instructions

I. Materials: Practice Set I

Ink pen

Ruler

II. Procedure

A. Beginning activity
    1. Open Envelope 1.
    2. Count forms in envelopes as instructed.
    3. Follow instructions for Envelope 1.

B. Corrections
    1. Follow procedures in Chapters 4 and 9 for corrections.
    2. Follow special instructions given by the teacher.

C. Evaluation
    1. Completion score--based on Practice Set Audit Sheet. The work of the student will be rated according to a numerical score of 100, based on the Practice Set Audit Sheet criteria. Look this sheet over carefully before proceeding. It will serve as a primary basis for the evaluation of the practice set work.
    2. Practice set test.

III. General

A. Successful work depends on both neatness and accuracy. For example, a carelessly kept set of records is of no real value to the users of these papers because illegible figures cannot be interpreted.

B. Conferences with the instructor may be necessary at given intervals before proceeding too far in error.

C. Use your textbook to the fullest extent as a guide. Very little if any detail is presented in the practice set that is not illustrated or explained in detail in the textbook.

Completion Deadline No. 1 _____

Completion Deadline No. 2 _____

NAME		SCORE

ITEM	EXPLANATION
APPEARANCE	
Failure to use ruler in ruling or correcting	
"Written-over" numerals	
Different colors of ink used	
General neat appearance of books	
FORM	
Omission of dates	
Accounts incorrectly ruled	
Journal footings omitted	
Column totals incorrectly forwarded	
Ledger footings omitted	
Ledger folio numbers omitted or incorrect	
Omission of key letters on working papers	
Incomplete explanation of ledger corrections	
Failure to record and post adjusting and closing entries	
ACCURACY	
Incorrect journal column totals	
Incorrect after-closing ledger balances	
INCOME STATEMENT	
Net Sales	
Cost of Goods Sold	
Gross Profit	
Selling Expenses	
General Expenses	
Net Operating Income	
Other Additions or Subtractions	
Net Income	
BALANCE SHEET	
Asset Items	
Liability Items	
Equity Items	
MISCELLANEOUS	
Incomplete Schedules	

REMARKS

Has the student learned anything from the practice set experience? A checkup test will give both student and teacher the answer. An excerpt from a practice set test is shown below. The following "short check-up test" will give both student and teacher the answer:

PRACTICE SET TEST

<u>James Wholesale Shoes</u>

<u>Directions</u>: Write the proper answer in the space provided at the left.

1. _____ What was the proper amount of cash received during the month?

2. _____ What is the net increase in capital for the month?

3. _____ How much cash was paid out during October on accounts payable?

4. _____ What is the amount of James' long-term liabilities at the end of the month?

5. _____ How much were the cash purchases during the month?

II-8 The Complete-Cycle Approach Promotes "Whole" Understanding

As an approach to bookkeeping, the complete-cycle method means that (first-day stage-setting procedures excepted) the teacher faces the class with the challenge of presenting the entire story of bookkeeping in one sitting: journalizing, posting, pencil footing, trial balance, balance sheet, the check with the original capital to find the profit for the period, the income statement, and again, the net profit check. The complete-cycle method is also an excellent review device which can be used to good advantage before introducing the practice set. Complete-cycle problems may be used as remedial exercises for students who are confused and who fail to see the significance of the various steps in the cycle.

No attempt is made to introduce the cycle on the first class day. There are too many adjustments that need to be made before teacher and pupil can work together effectively. However, much can be accomplished during the first meeting of the class that will help to make the first day of the cycle more successful. The story of Mrs. Miller (proprietor in the problems) and how she came to go into business can be told. Foundations established in general business courses can be enlarged. A few basic terms such as assets, liabilities, and net worth can be clarified.

One of the important factors of complete-cycle problems is to have the entire exercise on one page—all writing to be done directly on this page. The technique is simple. The sheets are passed out to the students, and the teacher and students work the exercise together in class. Explanations as to "why" are held to a minimum. Experience in the use of this method with high school classes has shown that not every member of the class will understand the process. This is to be expected. A duplicate sheet is given each student at the end of the period when homework is the rule. With the sheet worked in class as a guide, the students again do Problem No. 1. The next day the entire class repeats the exercise; the good students help those who have not yet grasped all phases of the problem.

During the first few days of the course and in the week following, if desired, a new complete-cycle problem is given each day. Problem 2 would introduce the old inventory and sales on account; Problem 3, purchases and sales returns; Problem 4, the special journals. The illustrations of Problems 1 and 4 on pages 366 and 367 show how the statement of the problem and the necessary forms—general ledger, accounts, trial balance, income statement, and the balance sheet—are provided on a single page.

In the use of the complete-cycle method, the cycle is developed quickly—during the space of one class period—

and usually without adjusting entries or other complicating features. Each time the student works through the cycle he adds to his basic understanding of the activities required in double-entry bookkeeping.

After the complete-cycle problems have given the student a mental toe hold on the subject of bookkeeping, the regular text can be used to complete the job, or the students can proceed to the regular practice set work. As in any Gestaltist picture, the details can now be filled in. However, instead of listing a few more assets here and some more sales returns there, as is so often the case, the growth will now be from within—an internal integration and development of a student. The student sees the steps that are necessary in order that the final objective—profit or loss for the owner—may be ascertained and recorded properly. It should be kept in mind, however, that tasks of the bookkeeper do not always include a complete cycle.

The following factors apply to the bookkeeping cycle:

1. Sometimes the bookkeeper does only part of a complete cycle.

2. At times the bookkeeper will move into an activity not directly cyclical, such as checking the accounts receivable ledger against the controlling account. After completing this check, he will return to the basic cycle of activities.

3. The basic cycle activities can be performed at any time rather than just at the end of a fiscal period.

Complete-Cycle Teaching Suggestions. The following precautions should be observed in presenting and working with students on complete-cycle exercises:

1. Omit explanations under journal entries.

2. Omit posting references; use check mark in journal, none in ledger.

3. Give students mimeographed form with all the necessary rulings for the complete cycle.

4. Type in the account headings—the words "assets" and "liabilities" in the balance sheet, and the income statement terms.

5. Omit all references to supply inventories and like items that need adjusting.

6. Do not require books to be closed in the first day's presentation. This can be done at the end of the week.

7. Use extremely simple figures and in round numbers—no cents.

8. Give sales totals to save time and to eliminate chances of error in figuring amounts.

9. Avoid any discussion having to do with the why of things. "We are planning to take that point up in detail in a day or two," will generally rest the matter.

10. Do not introduce new elements until this basic cycle problem is mastered.

11. Use simple and meaningful language.

12. Do not feel that it is necessary to mention the words "debit" and "credit" on the first day. Later these terms can be introduced in such a manner as to leave the correct meaning—simply a matter of left and right rather than some other meanings that the student may have associated with these terms before coming to class.

Advantages of Complete-Cycle Approach. Advantages accruing to the bookkeeping teacher through the use of the complete-cycle approach may be summarized as:

1. The student has a complete cycle before him at all times, on a single sheet of paper.

2. No blank spaces are left in the cycle to be filled in later as the student studies additional steps. Neither does he receive a description of all the steps and then have to wait several weeks to find out what the steps actually mean.

3. As special journals and ledgers are introduced, they are considered as refinements of the basic cycle.

COMPLETE-CYCLE PROBLEM No. 1

Mrs. Miller has received permission to place her ice box in a corner of the ice cream store in which she is working as a cashier. She plans to sell flowers as a little business of her own. She is to pay $5 a month rent. She begins business Sept. 1 by bringing the ice box, value $300, and by investing cash, $50. She continues to transact business as follows: Sept. 2, purchases flowers wholesale, $15; Sept. 3, sold flowers for cash, $7; Sept. 4, sold large bouquet for cash, $10; Sept. 5, miscellaneous small sales, $5; Sept. 6, purchases flowers wholesale, $25; Sept. 7, sold flowers, $12; Sept. 8, cash sales for today, $6; Sept. 9, paid expenses: wages, $3; rent, $5; Sept. 10, Mrs. Miller is eager to know whether she has made a profit, so she counts all roses on hand and finds she has a total wholesale value of $19. This is known as the new inventory, or the inventory of Sept. 10.

GENERAL JOURNAL											

CASH

OLD INVENTORY

NEW INVENTORY

EQUIPMENT

RENT

MILLER, CAPITAL

WAGES

PURCHASES

PROFIT AND LOSS

SALES

TRIAL BALANCE

BALANCE SHEET

Assets			Liab. & Prop.	

INCOME STATEMENT

Sales . . . . $
Purchases . . . . $
Less Sept. 10 inv. . . . $
Cost of Goods Sold . . . . . $
Gross Profit . . . . $

Expenses

Rent . . . . $
Wages . . . . $ $
        NET PROFIT $

COMPLETE-CYCLE PROBLEM No. 4 (SPECIAL JOURNALS)

On Oct. 1 Mrs. Miller decides to change to special journals. The ledger of last month will be continued. Accounts given below show totals. Oct. 2, purchased from Ames Co., $10; sold to Capital University, $5; to Harmony Haven, $8; Oct. 3, purchased from the Best Co., $15; cash sales, $12; received cash from Capital University, $15, from Harmony Haven, $10; Oct. 4, cash sales, $20, sold to Harmony Haven, $11, purchased from Ames Co., $15; from Best Co., $10; Oct. 5, paid wages, $3, rent, $5, cash sales, $15; paid Ames Co., $33, paid Best Co., $15. Goods on hand, $25.

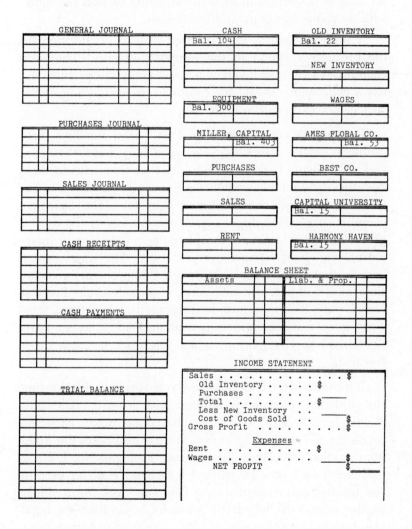

367

4. This method can be used in the development of understanding of bookkeeping principles regardless of the textbook being used. In addition, it does not displace well-accepted principles of bookkeeping and accounting; it simply acts as a method to help the students to "see the light" without weeks of agony and frustration.

A service business may be used instead of the mercantile business outlined in the sample problems. The merchandising situation involves a more complete picture and has a little more "meat" for complete understanding of the various activities in the cycle.

Complete-Cycle Check-Up Test. After the first three problems of the complete-cycle series have been presented and all students have demonstrated that they can do them fluently, it might be well to have a quick check-up to see what the students have learned thus far. The Spielman exercise (page 369) might serve for such a test. To do this problem, either standard complete-cycle forms or ordinary journal and ledger paper may be used. The usual experience is that students "sail" through this problem in record time and without any difficulty. Complete-cycle Problem No. 4, page 367, may now be presented at any time; however, most teachers prefer to wait and use it as an introduction to special journals when this work is taken up in the text.

The One-Month Complete-Cycle Review. By this time the student is thoroughly familiar with what it takes to do a complete-cycle problem. He has done three, each one involving ten days of business. He has also done the Spielman problem as a check-up exercise. Problems No. 1, No. 2, and No. 3 may now be worked as a unit. For this exercise the teacher may design a new complete-cycle form similar to the ones with which the student is familiar—on legal-size paper—to allow room for a month's transactions.

COMPLETE-CYCLE REVIEW PROBLEM

Mildred Spielman has just received $1,000 from her uncle in Europe. She has, therefore, decided to open up a hat shop on Drexel Avenue. The first thing Mildred does to start the wheels turning is to deposit her $1,000 in the Ohio National Bank. She arranges with the Drexel Beauty Shop for one-half of the shop at a rental of $25 a month. Since today is March 1, she will pay her rent.

March 2   Mildred buys 5 red hats from the New York Hat Company on account, at $1 each.

Buys 10 blue hats from the Philadelphia Hat Company at $2 each.

March 4   Hires Miss Ellen Locsos to work in the store during noon hours and sometimes after school. (Pay to be determined later.)

March 6   Buys some furniture and other equipment for $100 cash.

March 7   Sells one of the red hats for $2 each.

March 8   Sells to Miss Wright, on account, one blue hat at $5.

March 9   Buys from the Chicago Hat Company 5 green hats at $5 each.

March 10   Sells to Miss Rutherford one green hat at $10, on account.

March 11   Mildred is called out of town on business for a week. When returning on March 18, she finds that Miss Locsos has sold the following merchandise for cash:

2 red hats at $2 each
5 blue hats at $5 each
1 green hat at $10

Pays Miss Locsos $5 for her services up to that time.

Remaining Inventory, $25.

Required:

1. Mildred wants to know whether or not she has made any profit and how much, so she is asking you to make journal entries for all transactions and to list them on the day on which they occur.

2. Post these to ledger accounts.

3. After posting to the ledger, make a trial balance, a balance sheet, and an income statement.

The teacher may, of course, use standard journal and ledger paper. The use of legal-size paper enables the student to see the whole of bookkeeping on one sheet. Attention should be called to the fact that the profit for the month now equals the sum of the profits obtained on the three ten-day problems.

II-9 Evaluation Is More Than Testing

In Chapter II reference was made to the necessity of helping the student receive a daily answer to his question "How am I doing?" Every bookkeeping teacher faces the problem of evaluation. Since the classroom teacher must in most cases assign a final grade to the pupil, it behooves him to do so only after he has carefully considered how this grade, together with how it was determined, fits into the framework of the course objectives. Whether or not this grade is accurate will depend upon the extent to which the teacher has used the various evaluation techniques and procedures which are available to him.

The final grade is often based on too narrow a foundation—printed test scores plus a few quizzes. The bookkeeping teacher need not limit himself to this narrow concept; there are other choices available, some of which lend themselves to a good overall analysis of student progress and effort. It seems reasonable that the following criteria could well be applied in most cases:

1. Written problem assignments.
2. Participation in classroom discussion.
3. Regular announced tests and quizzes.
4. Practice set work.
5. Attitudes displayed in the classroom, including attendance and punctuality.
6. Mid-term and final examinations.

Written Problem Assignments. The handling of assignments has already been described in Principle II-4 of this chapter. A major problem for most beginning teachers is how to score and grade the volume of papers. The "quick-review check" system described earlier is of significance. A mark is placed on the papers by the teacher in a quick check of the problems in the folder: $+1$ (for high quality excellence), O.K. (for work that has most of the elements necessary for clarity), and -1 (for those papers that fall short of useful application of principles). This marking system, used together with the self-check by the students, helps the students keep themselves informed as to their progress in problem work.

Practice Set Work. The analysis of the practice set was described in Principle II-7, illustrating the "audit" sheet and "quick review" test. For grade purposes, a numerical weight is given to each element on the audit sheet, the total score representing 100. A useful approach is to assign an audit score to each part of the usual two-part practice set and to the "quickie" test. The two audit scores will then have a weight factor of $\frac{2}{3}$ of the total score and the test score, $\frac{1}{3}$.

Regularly Announced Tests. Testing can be either problem-point or based on objective-type tests, such as true-false, multiple-choice, and completion, or even essay. The best approach seems to combine problem testing with objective-type theory tests. The philosophy of the teacher concerning the evaluation approach will determine whether he is more interested in problem application or in verbal definition and classification. Students should be given the chance to demonstrate their abilities to analyze as well as perform problem routines. A two-part test with one part devoted to "theory" and one part containing a problem that can be completed within the time limits of the period seems to work best. It is assumed, of course, that the teacher will check with the publisher of his textbook to make certain that he has the testing materials that are designed to accompany the text.

Other Elements. This title indicates that there are other considerations beside numerical scores that should be considered—the intangible yet insignificant factors businessmen rate highly: neatness, accuracy, cooperation with fellow workers, ability to cope with unusual situations, and the whole perplexing array of "nonmeasurable" attributes that make for job success.

Lack of space does not permit a full treatment of the formalities of testing, including the standard mathematical procedures. However, two sources of information for the beginning teacher in terms of this problem are imperative:

American Accounting Association, *Accounting Teachers Guide,* Cincinnati: South-Western Publishing Company, 1953.

Hardaway and Maier, *Tests and Measurements in Business Education,* Cincinnati: South-Western Publishing Company, 1952.

In summarizing the evaluative criteria, each of the most objective elements might well be weighted as follows:

Written problem assignments	— ¼
Test and quizzes	— ¼
Practice set	— ⅛
Other elements	— ⅛
Final and mid-term exams	— ¼

The weights applied will depend on the importance of the element to the objectives of the course. The important thing is that the teacher give consideration to a *number* of factors in determining the final grade for the course.

BOOKKEEPING—PART III

WHAT OTHERS HAVE TO SAY ABOUT TEACHING BOOKKEEPING

A vast array of books and magazine articles on teaching bookkeeping are now available. The majority of these are useful, if used intelligently and adapted to the particular situation. For inexperienced teachers of bookkeeping, this great volume of "advice" may be confusing by its very size; therefore, in this chapter we have tried to select a workable set of principles, some specific methods, and some comments by accepted leaders in business education. To start our summary of valuable ideas from experts, we have chosen a list of 19 questions developed by Satlow:

1. To what extent do you avail yourself of information on file concerning your pupils?

2. To what extent are your pupils properly selected for bookkeeping?

3. To what extent do you avail yourself of the flexibility offered by the bookkeeping syllabus?

4. To what extent do your pupils see "meaning" in bookkeeping knowledges and skills taken up?

5. To what extent does your teaching reflect current business practice and procedures?

6. To what extent do you avoid confusion in pupils' minds by eliminating arithmetical difficulties?

7. To what extent do your pupils read the language of bookkeeping properly?

8. To what extent do you succeed in getting legible work from your bookkeeping pupils?

9. To what extent do you teach your bookkeeping pupils to think?

10. To what extent do you guide proper growth in personality, attitudes, and work habits in bookkeeping?

11. To what extent do you afford your pupils proper drill in bookkeeping?

12. To what extent is the bookkeeping that you teach articulated with the work of other departments and levels of the school system?

13. To what extent are you contributing to the evaluation of the core program?

14. To what extent do you employ proper evaluating procedures?

15. To what extent do you make use of the results of a testing program in your bookkeeping instruction?

16. To what extent do you practice sound principles of mental hygiene in the classroom?

17. To what extent do you inject variety into your work?

18. To what extent do you utilize your class time economically?

19. To what extent have you developed an inquiring attitude toward your teaching procedures? [19]

Some years ago Forkner outlined the characteristics of a good bookkeeping teacher. These twenty-two suggestions summarize much of what has been written in the modern day about bookkeeping instruction:

1. The successful bookkeeping teacher knows enough about the subject of bookkeeping to be able to converse easily and intelligently with his students about actual workings of bookkeeping systems in business firms in his community. . . .

2. The successful bookkeeping teacher is a source of information and counsel to firms or individuals in the

---

[19] Satlow, "The Fundamental Processes in Bookkeeping," *op. cit.*, pp. 222-246.

community who are in need of advice regarding the organization of simple bookkeeping systems or concerning problems of interpreting bookkeeping records. . . .

3. The successful teacher knows what will be expected of his students on their initial jobs as office workers. . . .

4. The successful teacher will, either through actual employment at intervals or through frequent contacts with a few offices, keep informed about business practices and systems of records so that he can base his teaching on actual knowledge rather than on theoretical knowledge. . . .

5. The successful teacher will belong not only to one of the major professional organizations in the field of business education, but he will also be associated as actively as his location will permit with the professional field of accounting through membership in such organizations as the American Institute of Certified Public Accountants (if he is eligible), the National Office Management Association, or other comparable groups. . . .

6. The classroom of the successful bookkeeping teacher will have the appearance of a business laboratory or an office. . . .

7. The student-teacher relationship is similar to the supervisory or employer-personnel relationship in a well-managed and a well-organized business office in which human relationships are at a high level. . . .

8. The teacher in a successfully operated bookkeeping class is not a teacher in the usual sense, but a supervisor of a working situation. . . .

9. The successful class is one in which every student is working to his fullest capacity. . . .

10. The teacher makes certain to check on the fundamental arithmetic skills of each student so that no one leaves the course without a thorough competency in the simple arithmetic processes. . . .

11. The fundamental skill of handwriting receives special attention on the part of the good bookkeeping teacher. . . .

12. The successful teacher starts his instruction in bookkeeping with simple, understandable ideas which are as near to the common experiences of his students as possible. . . .

13. The successful teacher makes use of all the teacher and student aids available to him by the authors and publishers of his bookkeeping textbook. . . .

14. The successful teacher makes use of every opportunity available around the school to bring actual bookkeeping situations into the classroom to provide actual work experience for as many of the students as possible. . . .

15. The successful teacher arranges with business firms or with farmers or tradesmen in the community to have his students gain real work experience for pay while carrying their school program. . . .

16. In the successfully conducted classroom there is no lost time in beginning the class period and in getting the class under way, nor is there a loss of time at the end of the period by having students begin to get ready to leave the classroom several minutes before the period is over. . . .

17. The work of a good teacher goes on uninterrupted regardless of whether he is present in the classroom during every minute of the period. . . .

18. The successful teacher does not depend upon the "key" to help him solve the students' problems or to locate their errors. . . .

19. The successful teacher uses bookkeeping situations to teach students about problems of the consumer, of the taxpayer, of the owner of a business, of the ethics of business, of the relationships between the worker and his employer, of the relationships between the employee and his fellow employees. . . .

20. The successful teacher can stress the importance of accuracy and the dependence upon accuracy which bookkeeping records require. . . .

21. The successful teacher knows that the students learn best by doing while the teacher demonstrates the way to do. . . .

22. Every student knows why he is taking bookkeeping and what the subject aims to prepare him for, whether it be for a job, for personal use, for economic understanding, or for all three purposes.[20]

III-1 Organize For Learning—Lesson Planning

How much planning is necessary before going into the classroom or beginning the school term? Of what value is this planning? Green lists excellent criteria for planning:

1. Aid the teacher in thinking through a problem.

2. Assist in securing adequate and definite preparation for the lesson.

3. Give the teacher a feeling of self-assurance, security, and poise.

4. Provide her with opportunity to develop initiative and resourcefulness in using instructional materials.

5. Assist her in harmonizing her teaching with the best in philosophy and theory.

6. Aid in adjusting the class work to the ability and interests of pupils.

7. Help in evaluating subject matter, methods, processes, material.

8. Aid in selection of what shall be taught out of all that is available.

9. Help to make the best use of time.

10. Help the teacher to see the relation of each unit to the whole of the work.

11. Aid in gaining freedom from slavish adherence to the textbook.[21]

---

[20] Hamden L. Forkner, "The Characteristics of Good Bookkeeping Teaching Practices," *The Balance Sheet* (January, 1944), pp. 206-209.

[21] Helen H. Green, "Lesson Plans," *Business Education World* (February, 1955), pp. 14-19.

Turille underscores this general outline for procedure in his summary statement on lesson planning:

> To teach effectively, the subject-matter must be well organized and the materials accessible and fully utilized. The written daily lesson plan will contain (1) the breakdown of the unit to be studied with advance planning as to the form of procedures to be employed according to the organization of the units, (2) course objectives—general and specific, (3) teacher aim, (4) pupil aim, (5) materials—student and teacher, (6) class activities connected with the presentation of the subject matter, (7) summary of the presentation with measurement of the outcomes of learning, and (8) assignment.[22]

What students feel and say about the bookkeeping course can be gauged to some extent by the reaction to the first few days. This is a critical time. Boynton points out the very real need for planning and getting a good start:

> The importance of a good start by both pupils and teacher at the beginning of any course cannot be overestimated. During the opening day of the course and the first week all-important impressions, student opinions, and student reactions are formed. Unfavorable reactions that take a few brief minutes or classroom periods to form may not be corrected or eradicated the rest of the year. With a good beginning, students inwardly say, "I like the teacher," "This course makes sense," "This is not going to be as tough as I thought," "I'm glad I signed up for bookkeeping," "I'm going to learn something in this course." Without forethought to develop a good beginning, such reactions as, "What's it all about?" "I don't like the teacher," "This is going to be too tough for me," can become the modus operandi for the student during his tenure in class.[23]

---

[22] Stephen J. Turille, *Principles and Methods in Business Education* (2nd ed.; Staunton, Virginia: McClure Printing Company, 1958), pp. 49-50.
[23] Boynton, *op. cit.*, p. 239.

III-2 *Appeal To the Five Senses—Demonstrate*

Students learn from seeing and observing. Showing and demonstrating bring into use more than just the ears of the students; they can also *see* what is going on. How many senses we can activate in the bookkeeping class is touched upon by Huffman:

> Strumming the ear-drums with our voices alone will not teach all the students bookkeeping principles.
>
> The ear-minded student needs more than the teacher's voice, however pleasing and instructive. Questions, answers, class discussions, sound pictures, and visitors stimulate learning via the ear.
>
> The eye-minded student readily learns through visual presentations of bookkeeping principles. Charts, tackboards, chalkboards, posters, and pictures stimulate his learning in different ways.
>
> The touch-minded student learns from handling actual or simulated business forms; practice sets with business papers; and journals and ledgers and registers bound separately.
>
> The muscle-minded student learns from writing things out—even rote copying of information. His memory work is best done repeating the lessons aloud—exercising the vocal chords and muscles.
>
> The more senses we use in our teaching of bookkeeping principles, the better we reach students of differing sense perception.[24]

III-3 *Teach for Understanding*

In our teachers' conventions and in local gatherings a great deal of conversation takes place concerning the primary objectives of teaching bookkeeping and accounting.

---

[24] Harry Huffman, "Supervision of Bookkeeping Instruction Through Stress on Learning Aids," *Business Education Forum* (December, 1954), p. 4.

Hall comments on the need for *real* understanding of the subject in its relationship to use value:

> The financial records of a business are kept with a central purpose in mind—to help guide management in its eternal quest for a profit on its operations. What better time or place is there than during the study of the income statement to develop an understanding of such basic concepts as the following:
>
>> Businesses exist to produce and distribute, in exchange for profit, the goods and services people want.
>>
>> It is the hope of profit that provides the incentive for people to risk savings in the investments needed to maintain and expand production.
>>
>> In business the possibility of loss, as well as profit, is great.[25]

III-4 Bookkeeping In Its Practical Application

Some of the confusion concerning classroom teaching of bookkeeping comes about because students do not grasp the fundamental relationship between what is done in class and what happens on a real job. Triplett points out:

> In learning bookkeeping and accounting, students often become confused, and wonder whether or not textbook writers and their teachers are also confused. They find in their textbooks and in the lectures of their teachers statements that appear to be inconsistent and conflicting. They may exclaim, "We were taught to do this, and now we are told to do something else! Why?"[26]

For a number of years the authors have handed to their bookkeeping and accounting students an essay written a number of years ago on the relationship of bookkeeping as

[25] J. Curtis Hall, "Teach Basic Economic Concepts in the Bookkeeping Class," *Business Education Forum* (December, 1960), p. 7.
[26] Richard J. Triplett, "Why Are Books Kept As They Are?" *The Balance Sheet* (May, 1956), p. 391.

taught to actual practice on the job. Because of its demonstrated usefulness, a major portion of this article by Hoogstraat is included:

As a beginning student in accounting, you will probably not be aware of an apparent discrepancy between accounting principles as taught in the classroom and accounting practice as it is actually followed in business establishments. However, if and when you handle bookkeeping records and attempt to solve accounting problems in actual business operations, you may find yourself asking the question, "Why did they teach us accounting the way they did, when actual accounting practice is so different?"

There is *no* conflict between taught and practiced accounting. There may, however, *appear* to be a conflict, and it is merely this apparent discrepancy that I shall attempt to clear up here.

To make more clear the reasons for the classroom approach to the study of accounting, an analogy to the method of training as an automobile mechanic seems suitable. The principles involved in this case are much the same as they are in the training of accountants.

The general automobile mechanic must be prepared to repair any make or model of automobile, of which there are hundreds of types and varieties. If it is desired to teach an auto mechanic how to repair a 1951 Chevrolet, and nothing more, the training could be successful if it included only the understanding of what wrench and what screwdriver to apply in what way at what place on the automobile when such and such symptoms are present. The mechanic with such a training could probably repair 1951 Chevrolets quite successfully, unless, of course, he ran across a symptom he had not studied in school, or if the prescribed treatment had not brought satisfactory results. Under such a situation, without any training in the fundamentals of the operation of internal combustion engines, transmissions, electrical systems, and so forth, he would be at a complete loss to figure out a solution. An even greater drawback of such a training would, of course, be the fact that he would be completely befuddled if a customer brought a 1938 Plymouth into his shop.

Let us assume, as a second case, that the auto mechanic is given a thorough training in automotive theory. He now understands the principles of operation which apply to *all* automobiles, and if he has had no past experience with a specific model which has been brought into his shop, an application of mechanical theory will soon give him the answer to the particular mechanical trouble. At first, he may not be as rapid a mechanic with a 1951 Chevrolet as the one who had studied no theory, but who knew all the prescribed tool manipulations necessary to cure particular defects on that particular model, but he can operate on *any* automobile. He can do the more uncommon jobs on the 1951 Chevrolet, and with practice he will probably become a faster and a more capable workman on all types of automobiles.

Which automobile would make the better working model if the emphasis in teaching is on theory and general principles—a simple model such as a Model A Ford, or a complex model such as a 1951 Cadillac? It would be possible to use the Cadillac, but the teaching process would probably be longer and the student would, of necessity, have to become familiar with a greater number of nonessential paraphernalia. Essential theory can best be taught with the use of a Model A Ford. It may be older, but the automotive design and operation, and the learning process with the use of the simpler model will be quicker and easier. This situation is roughly analogous to that in teaching accounting, where a simple system is used as the basis for instruction in theory, even though the typical system is more complex.[27]

In order to lend practicality to the classroom situation in bookkeeping, Satlow, Rosettie, and Weiss suggest use of equipment similar to that used in the community:

---

[27] Emerson E. Hoogstraat, "Is Classroom Accounting Practical?" *The Balance Sheet* (December, 1951), pp. 151-152.

"Current business procedures" includes the use of business machines in the keeping of business records. In those communities in which the graduates will be expected to do their bookkeeping computations by machine, classroom instruction should include the use of machines.[28]

To utilize the community as a giant workshop and to bring into being a closer relationship between the local business organizations and the school business department has been a major objective for years. House outlines a number of ways in which bookkeeping classes can work toward achieving this aim:

1. *Visiting local business firms.* Field trips to various business firms provide excellent opportunities for students to observe and analyze bookkeeping as it is practiced in the local community.

2. *Using guest speakers from business.* Guest speakers can be used as another means for providing students with an opportunity of learning how books are kept in local business firms.

3. *Having students interview businessmen.*

4. *Collecting business forms from local firms.* Many business forms can be collected by members of the bookkeeping class from local business firms. Sample forms including sales slips, invoices, checks, purchase orders, notes, journal pages, ledger pages, work sheets, statements, and the like can be obtained.

5. *Participating in service projects.* Needless to say, this type of activity can be projected far beyond its usefulness as a learning activity for a bookkeeping class.

6. *Organizing a work-experience program.*[29]

---

[28] Satlow, "The Fundamental Processes in Bookkeeping," *op. cit.,* p. 232.

[29] F. Wayne House, "Individual and Special Needs of Students in Bookkeeping," *Business Education Forum* (December, 1956), pp. 18-19.

Forkner says this about the realism of practice necessarily being related to classroom practice:

> To do the job right, the teacher will have to draw upon personal experiences of the students. Let's invite various bookkeepers to come to the class and tell the students how they get information for making entries for sales and purchases of all kinds. Another thing, I will have to make certain the textbook is made realistic by showing my students how it follows business practices and bookkeeping practices, but that each business has methods that are peculiar to its type of operations.[30]

III-5   Recognition of Individual Differences

Current educational practices require that we accept all types of students in the high school. This has resulted in a wide variety of ability levels in grade groups. If each student is to progress as far as possible in bookkeeping, some preliminary observation should precede the teaching. Ruth Strang suggests this self-evaluation check list for the teacher:

1. Does every student in my classes have work so suited to his abilities and needs that he can succeed with reasonable effort? Do I help students to learn from their failures?

2. Is my room free from an intensely competitive atmosphere? Do I help students to get recognition for the use of their abilities in class projects?

3. Do my students feel free to express their feelings about school, thus avoiding accumulated tension and a clash of wills that might divert their energy from study?

4. Do I realize that much of the behavior that makes teaching difficult represents students' attempts to find a way out of a difficulty, or to meet their developmental needs?

---

[30] Hamden L. Forkner, "Primary Records and the Bookkeeper," *Business Education Forum* (December, 1955), p. 10.

5. Do I really like the boys and girls in my classes? Do I treat my students with as much courteous consideration as I do my friends and professional associates?

6. Do I respect each individual's personality and have faith in his ability to realize his best potentialities?

7. Do I provide group experiences in which students develop a sense of shared responsibility for enterprises and get satisfaction from the success of the group? Does each student help others to feel that they are accepted by the group?

8. Do I help students to discover and evaluate their own abilities, strengths, and weaknesses and to meet difficulty or criticism in a constructive way?

9. Do I arouse students' interests in my subject and acquaint them with its cultural and vocational values? Are the goals of the class determined by the entire group, including the teacher?

10. Do I cooperate with the students' teacher-counselor, other teachers, the principal, and guidance specialists?

11. Do I avoid labeling a student or making a generalization about him on the basis of a single incident or limited observation?

12. Do I try to understand him rather than judge him? [31]

We *are* concerned with the different levels of abilities in our classes, although there may be a tendency at times to override certain groups in favor of others. Freeman points out that in recent years the average bookkeeping teacher has perhaps been too concerned with the progress of the slow learner, to the neglect of others in the class:

> He (the bookkeeping teacher) has been much too busy and concerned with the many slow learners in his class ever to give much thought to the fast learner. Every once

---

[31] Ruth Strang, *The Role of the Teacher in Personnel Work* (4th ed., Bureau of Publications, Teachers College, Columbia University, 1953), p. 160.

in awhile, however, it is good for us to take a careful look at all the students in our class to see whether we have been overlooking some of their individual needs and abilities. To pause long enough in our daily teaching activities to consider carefully the possibilities of serving better some of the more capable students in our bookkeeping classes.[32]

In considering this existing situation of individual differences, Kahn and Freeman emphasize the necessity of perspective:

> Elementary bookkeeping should be taught in public secondary schools through *class instruction.* We are not justified in a public school giving individual instruction or private tutoring in a subject that can be taught just as successfully to a whole group at the same time.

> In some cases where teachers ask what to do about students who differ in ability, there is the likelihood that the teacher is not using class time most effectively for the benefit of all students. Success in teaching elementary bookkeeping to all students depends on the use of good teaching techniques.[33]

III-6 Homework Should Be Carefully Considered

There are frequent comments by students that bookkeeping homework assignments are too long or take more time than those in other subjects. House points out significant factors in the matter of making assignments:

1. There is a direct connection between a student's success in bookkeeping and his spending enough time on his assignments to complete what he has been assigned.

2. There is a direct connection between a student's lack of success and his belief that his assignments take an unreasonable amount of time.

---

[32] M. Herbert Freeman, "Providing for the Fast Learner in Bookkeeping," *American Business Education* (May, 1958), p. 202.
[33] M. Herbert Freeman and Gilbert Kahn, "Handling Ability Differences in the Bookkeeping Class," *Business Teacher* (March, 1957), p. 5.

3. There is a direct connection between a student's lack of success and his spending more time on assignments in bookkeeping than in assignments in other subjects.

4. There is a direct connection between a student's lack of success and his finding assignments to be difficult. If they're hard for him, so is the whole course.[34]

Satlow comments on the assignment of homework:

> The main purpose of the pupil's attendance in school is to learn something, not to be saddled with onerous assignments. Consequently, class time should be devoted largely to learning and to verification of learning—and not to assigning of homework and elaborate checking of the homework.
>
> The giving of the homework assignment should be administered expeditiously. In a business class particularly, the assignment should be given in a businesslike fashion. Since this phase of the assignment is purely one of classroom mechanics, it can be reduced to routine.
>
> 1. The assignment appears on the board at the beginning of the period.
>
> 2. A special section of the board is reserved for the assignment.
>
> 3. The assignment is written on the board by a pupil.
>
> 4. It is entered into assignment books by pupils upon their arrival to class.
>
> 5. The copying of the assignment is done in ink.
>
> 6. The assignment is read aloud from one pupil's copy book for all to verify.
>
> 7. Recourse to duplicated materials eliminates the need for elaborate dictation or extensive writing on the board.[35]

---

[34] F. Wayne House, "Bookkeeping Students Say Their Assignments Are Too Long, Hard . . . ," *Business Education World* (October, 1954), p. 19.

[35] I. David Satlow, *Helpful Hints in Teaching Bookkeeping and Accounting,* Monograph 96 (Cincinnati: South-Western Publishing Company, 1956), p. 23.

Because of the serious implications in the possibility of losing valuable classroom time in the handling of assignments, we present the following detailed outline by Satlow:

1. Check-up

   a. Homework is checked daily.

   b. The teacher circulates about the room and inspects the homework while the class is occupied at some task.

   c. Homework papers are collected at a set point in the progress of the lesson (or at fixed intervals during the semester).

   d. Papers are collected occasionally at the very beginning of the period. (For example, when the assignment was quite simple.)

   e. A homework record is kept.

   f. The record employs a simple rating scheme, e.g., (1) vg–g–w–wo, (2) A–B–C–F, or (3) 3–2–1–0

   g. Specific deductions are made for each homework that was not submitted.

   h. The homework record enters into consideration when ratings are computed for the semester or marking period.

2. Correction

   a. The lesson plan indicates the specific items that are to be verified in class.

   b. In his inspection of the papers, the teacher looks for the quality of work done, particularly how certain specific items were treated.

   c. During his inspection of the papers, the teacher notes the difficulties that were common to the members of the class.

   d. During his inspection, the teacher selects the students who are to place homework on the boards.

e. During his inspection, the teacher points out to individual students the errors appearing on their papers.

f. The teacher directs to the class oral questions on the more difficult aspects of the assignment.

g. Students are called upon to recite selected portions of their homework.

h. Chalkboards are used for the analysis of difficult entries.

i. Classmates correct errors found in homework that was placed on the boards.

j. Homework items which were included in the day's quiz are not gone into if the quiz had been discussed.

k. Students at seats make pencil corrections on their papers as the homework is gone over.

l. Occasionally, students exchange papers, correct their neighbor's work, sign and return the papers.

m. A set of papers is occasionally returned with personalized comments noted thereon.

3. Time Factor

a. The inspection of homework at the desks by the teacher is done speedily while the class is copying the new assignment or is occupied with some warmup exercise at the beginning of the period.

b. The placing of the homework on the boards is divided up among several students.

c. Student volunteers place their work on the board either at "passing time" or at the beginning of the period.

d. Work is placed on the boards by having selected students asked to arrive early in order to assist with such placement.

e. Only the difficult items are placed on the boards.

    f. The class is busy with some other activity, such as oral review of the previous day's lesson, while the work is being placed on the boards.

    g. Desks are cleared of all other materials while the homework is gone over.

    h. Upon signal by the teacher, the boardwork is checked by inspection, with an opportunity for students to question or challenge any answer.

    i. Questioning and reciting are confined to the difficult phases, all obvious items being ignored.

    j. The work is called to a halt, boards are cleared, credit is entered for those who worked at the boards, and papers are collected speedily and systematically.

4. Work Habits

    a. Students have their name, class, date, assignment number, and "filing number" (row-and-seat number) on each paper they are ready to submit.

    b. Students show a sense of responsibility by handing in their assignments on time.

    c. Work that was missed is to be made up.

    d. Certain assignments may not be submitted beyond the deadline date.

    e. A special record is kept of students who habitually submit uncompleted jobs.

    f. Work that is below standard for legibility, neatness, and form is rejected summarily or returned the following day.

    g. The first time a student submits substandard work, he is required (or permitted) to re-submit it; his next attempt to submit substandard work is penalized by rejection, with no further opportunity for resubmission.

    h. Corrections are made in pencil on the papers as the work is gone over.

    i. Upon completion of the correction of homework, students enter into their notebooks the transactions which they had solved incorrectly together with the correct entries for them.

5. Mental Hygiene

    a. Students are put at ease while the homework is checked and corrected.

    b. The teacher is patient while pupils disclose their difficulties.

    c. Individual criticism of the homework paper is rendered quietly and unobtrusively while the class is at work on something else.

    d. There is private and public commendation for improvement noted.

    e. A perfect paper is praised, but not extolled unduly.

6. Teacher Guidance

    a. A careful analysis of homework papers early in the term helps to locate some of the slow learners and those who were incorrectly programmed.

    b. The inspection of the papers reveals the individual weaknesses of students as the basis for a program of remediation.

    c. The response on the homework highlights the entries that should be retaught to the class.

    d. As a result of the difficulties that came to light in the check-up of the homework, the lesson plan for the preceding lesson is modified in terms of presentation, length of the assignment or its degree of difficulty.[36]

III-7 *Learning Blocks Exist In a Variety of Forms*

Sometimes it is possible to find direct causes of learning blocks. More often, these are hidden under a facade of

---

[36] I. David Satlow, "Attending to the Previous Day's Bookkeeping Assignment," *The Balance Sheet* (September, 1957), pp. 9-10.

attitudes that reveal nothing significant. Bookkeeping instruction is not so different from motor skill learning that we can afford to forget about blocks caused by excessive tensions and their effects on learning. Lamb mentions a number of these distracting influences that affect the efficiency of the learning process:

> What are some of the environmental factors that affect youngsters in school? First, there is the matter of name. The child's name is an identifying label indicating his family and sometimes his race or nationality and religion. Some sensitive youngsters belonging to minority groups are ashamed of their names and are further plagued by feelings of guilt because they are ashamed. Some youngsters have to cope with humorous names that are good collectors' items for teachers but are no laughing matter to their owners. Very few little girls have the fortitude to endure without some resentment names such as "Yetta Weil," and "Henrietta Weiner," for example, yet these are actual names.[37]

It is relatively easy to deal with the obvious learning blocks. But not so easily handled are those similar to the ones mentioned above or those which reflect the state of our society, as described below by Wentzel:

> Unquestionably, there is an ambivalence existing in our American culture. The youth are taught not only to believe in competition, but also in godly virtues. They are taught they must love their neighbor but at the same time excel him. They are taught that they must be kindly and self-sacrificing but also must push their way to the top. They are indoctrinated with a strange mixture of beliefs in the necessity of carving out a position of power and prestige for themselves and at the same time of being considerate of their fellows and dealing democratically with them.[38]

---

[37] Marion M. Lamb, *Your First Year of Teaching* (Cincinnati: South-Western Publishing Company, 1956), p. 117.

[38] Dwight L. Wentzel, "Developing An Atmosphere Conducive to Good Mental Health in a Skill-Building Classroom," *The Balance Sheet* (December, 1954), p. 155.

III-8   If Necessary, Teach Arithmetic, Too

A review of comments and opinions concerning arithmetic in the high school shows that bookkeeping teachers are spending much time reteaching basic arithmetic when they should be concentrating on fundamental bookkeeping concepts. Be that as it may, arithmetic understanding is necessary to successful manipulation of bookkeeping records. This is true not only in record keeping, but in everything that goes on around us. Huffman attempts to point out the significance of the *number* in our daily living:

> We need more mathematics than ever before. Whenever possible, we reduce all information to numbers. The doctor takes our temperature, blood pressure, and blood count, and records them in numbers. Our employers use numbers to rate personality and potential for advancement. The businessman measures production, sales, and profit in numbers. The weatherman tells us about the degree days. Eliminate numbers and arithmetic, and we should soon scamper back into the forests, gathering berries and nuts and sleeping in caves.[39]

Douglas, Blanford, and Anderson ask for a careful review of the need for reteaching of arithmetic processes by the bookkeeping teacher:

> Another problem often confronts bookkeeping teachers: that is weakness on the part of students in the fundamental processes of arithmetic. Oftentimes teachers will find that some students have difficulty in addition, subtraction, division, and multiplication, all of which are so often used in bookkeeping. . . . There is no one solution to this problem. It will be up to the individual teacher to make his own decision on whether to teach arithmetic or not, if the students are having difficulty.[40]

---

[39] Harry Huffman, "A New Arithmetic Course for Your High School," *Business Teacher* (December, 1956), p. 8.

[40] Lloyd V. Douglas, James T. Blanford, and Ruth I. Anderson, *Teaching Business Subjects* (Englewood Cliffs, New Jersey: Prentice-Hall, Inc., 1958), p. 374.

III-9   Include Neatness In Handwriting As a Fundamental Factor

Earlier in this chapter, the tremendous cost of mistakes in business was traced in part to lack of neatness in employee handwriting in recording business transactions. Hardaway and Maier suggest that teachers include neatness and quality of penmanship as a significant part of the student's grade in evaluation:

> While the teacher's evaluation of the quality of a student's penmanship and neatness may not be entirely objective, such a rating should be made known to the students.[41]

Satlow also attempts to call attention to this need for clear handwriting:

> Penmanship sometimes seems to be a lost art. The handwriting of pupils (and of teachers) is frequently far from good. Even those pupils who write legibly cannot be said to have good penmanship—uniform size, slant, spacing—as judged by our standards of previous years. For those whose handwriting is illegible, there should be remedial penmanship classes just as there are remedial arithmetic classes.[42]

III-10   The "Whole" Approach Is Important In Teaching the Cycle

In Part II, a detailed description was given of the "complete-cycle" approach to learning bookkeeping fundamentals. Psychologists were cited in Chapter II, indicating recognition of the importance of the pupil's ability to see the whole picture before proceeding. The pupil must experience a "feel" of heading in the right direction. Bender underscores the need to recognize this fact in his statement:

---

[41] Mathilde Hardaway and Thomas B. Maier, *Tests and Measurements in Business Education* (2nd ed.; Cincinnati: South-Western Publishing Company, 1952), pp. 133-134.

[42] Satlow, "The Fundamental Processes in Bookkeeping," *op. cit.*, p. 235.

All bookkeeping teachers will agree that there is more to teaching bookkeeping than having the student record narrative information in the proper columns of a journal, ledger account, or report. The best teaching method develops understanding. Teach the whole rather than unrelated parts. The cyclical method must be obvious, especially to the beginner.[43]

III-11   Recording of Transactions Should Be Learned

All of us, at one time or another, have felt a degree of frustration when we examined the amount of learning that should have taken place in the fundamental phases of the bookkeeping course. In some classes, bookkeeping teachers can get almost 100 per cent accuracy when asking students what to debit and what to credit. This is usually because the teaching has "made sense" to the students. In other classes this may not be the result.

One of the most informative sources in recent years for the bookkeeping teacher is the *Business Education World* series on "Teaching the Fundamental Elements of Bookkeeping." Since journalizing is the first in the series of steps leading to a full cycle of bookkeeping activity, how the teacher teaches this concept is important. Freeman, Hanna, and Kahn, the authors of the series, give the following statement about the *presentation* of the journalizing concept:

> Journalizing is, in itself, a simple mechanical process. Teaching how to journalize is, therefore, a relatively easy matter. However, the analysis of the business transaction that precedes the making of the journal entry is the most important part of the whole procedure. Before the bookkeeping teacher can teach the student the simple mechanical process of journalizing, he must realize what it is necessary for the student to know.[44]

---

[43] Robert F. Bender, "Bookkeeping Can't Be Taught Sitting Down," *Business Education Forum* (December, 1955), p. 19.

[44] M. Herbert Freeman, J Marshall Hanna, and Gilbert Kahn, "Teaching the Fundamental Elements of Bookkeeping—2. How to Teach Journalizing," *Business Education World* (November, 1958), p. 34.

Musselman and Hanna emphasize the need for a careful build-up of the knowledge of the student to this point:

> Some teachers report that their students make very satisfactory progress in bookkeeping until they come to the unit on journalizing and then, as one teacher puts it, "The class just falls apart at the seams." If this should be the situation —and unfortunately all too often it is—the trouble is not with the unit on journalizing but with what has gone before. Quite contrary to the teacher's opinion, trouble with journalizing is an indication of *unsatisfactory* progress on previous units. Journalizing is merely a technique, a procedure. It is the "thinking" process preceding the actual recording in the journal that causes students difficulty; that is, the analysis of transactions to determine what accounts are affected and the proper debit and credit elements.[45]

High on the list in difficulty of learning is the process of adjustment for deferred and accrued items. Together with a well-outlined description, which does not permit inclusion here, Freeman, Hanna, and Kahn refer to *readiness* as an important factor in the learning of this process:

> These adjustments are not complicated concepts or theoretical abstractions. They are simple and logical steps in determining the correct profit or loss earned during a fiscal period. Why are they so difficult to master? The answer is simple. Most first-year bookkeeping and accounting students are exposed to deferred and accrued income and expense items before they feel the need for these adjustments. Eventually they may learn *how* to make these entries, but they do not really understand *why* they are making them.
>
> This obviously suggests that the teaching of deferred and accrued items should be put off as long as possible. After the student has acquired a thorough understanding of typical business practices and procedures, he will sense the need for accurate reports. If he is then taught why and how

---

[45] Musselman and Hanna, *op. cit.*, p. 134.

these entries are made, in a careful step-by-step presentation, the feeling of confusion and despair will never develop.

Deferrals and accruals are easy to teach and easy to learn, but they must be *taught*. The average student cannot be expected to master this unit by reading about it in the textbook.[46]

III-12   Effective Use of the Practice Set Clinches Ideas Previously Taught

Bookkeeping cannot be learned by talking about it—students must learn by doing. The practice set with its many variations and forms, with and without business papers, has given the bookkeeping teacher an effective device to clinch the principles that have been illustrated in previous instruction. For the purpose of defining the direction of practice set work, Musselman and Hanna propose a pattern which, if followed, should provide for outcomes worthy of the time spent:

1. The teacher should work the practice set before using it in class.

2. The set should be related to the community.

3. The practice set should be taught.

4. The business forms, journals, and ledgers used in the set should be carefully explained.

5. Recording of opening entries should be carefully supervised.

6. Difficult transactions should be previewed.

7. Diversified teaching aids should be used.

8. Daily guideposts should be established.

9. Regular evaluation must be planned.[47]

---

[46] M. Herbert Freeman, J Marshall Hanna, and Gilbert Kahn, "Teaching the Fundamental Elements of Bookkeeping—8. How to Teach Deferred and Accrued Items," *Business Education World* (December, 1960), p. 25.

[47] Musselman and Hanna, *op. cit.*, pp. 294-296.

SUMMARY

It has been said that almost any plan of teaching book-keeping can bring satisfactory results if used by an energetic, alert teacher who observes the fundamental principles of learning. In the preceding pages some suggestions have been offered to serve as guidelines to help make the teaching successful regardless of the particular textbook or plan used.

Planning is a significant part of teaching success. Perhaps we don't do enough of it. The planning should fit the objectives of the school, the teacher, and the student. Time should be taken to perfect a classroom organizational pattern that will make it easy for the teacher to hold his job, save the teacher and student time, and provide for the differences found in these students.

SELECTED BIBLIOGRAPHY

American Accounting Association, *Accounting Teachers Guide,* Cincinnati: South-Western Publishing Company, 1953.

Boynton, Lewis D. "Bookkeeping," *American Business Education Yearbook,* Volume XVIII, New York: New York University Bookstore, 1961.

Boynton, Lewis D. *Methods of Teaching Bookkeeping.* Cincinnati, South-Western Publishing Company, 1955.

Business Education Forum, Special Bookkeeping Issues (December Issues).

Douglas, Lloyd V., James T. Blanford, and Ruth I. Anderson. *Teaching Business Subjects.* Englewood Cliffs, New Jersey: Prentice-Hall, Inc., 1958.

Freeman, M. Herbert, J Marshall Hanna, and Gilbert Kahn. "Teaching Fundamental Elements of Bookkeeping" Series, *Business Education World,* January, February, March, May, June, September, October, November, December, 1960; January, 1961.

Grambs, Jean D., and William J. Iverson. *Modern Methods in Secondary Education.* New York: The Dryden Press, 1952.

Hardaway, Mathilde, and Thomas B. Maier. *Tests and Measurements in Business Education,* Second Edition. Cincinnati: South-Western Publishing Company, 1952.

House, F. Wayne. *Factors Affecting Student Achievement in Beginning Bookkeeping in the High School.* Unpublished Ph.D. Dissertation, Ohio State University, 1951.

Kessel, Robert M. "Realizing Bookkeeping Objectives," *Business Education Forum* (April, 1961), pp. 31-32.

Musselman, Vernon A., and J Marshall Hanna. *Teaching Bookkeeping and Accounting.* New York: Gregg Publishing Division, McGraw-Hill Book Company, Inc., 1960.

The Psychology and the Instructional Pattern of Teaching Bookkeeping. Monograph C569, Cincinnati: South-Western Publishing Company.

Satlow, I. David. "The Fundamental Processes in Bookkeeping," *American Business Education Yearbook,* Volume XII, New York: New York University Bookstore, 1955.

——————. "Bookkeeping Classroom Management" Series, *Business Education World,* September, October, November, December, 1956; January, 1957.

Sister Mary Xavier. "An Office Procedure Method of Working Bookkeeping Practice Sets," *The Balance Sheet* (January, 1958), pp. 212-214.

Tonne, Herbert A., Estelle L. Popham, and M. Herbert Freeman. *Methods of Teaching Business Subjects,* Second Edition. New York: Gregg Publishing Division, McGraw-Hill Book Company, Inc., 1957.

Turille, Stephen J. *Principles and Methods in Business Education,* Second Edition. Staunton, Virginia: McClure Printing Company, 1958.

FILMS AND FILMSTRIPS
Films
Bookkeeping and You, Coronet Instructional Films, 65 South Water Street, Chicago, Illinois.

The Accounting Cycle, Business Education Visual Aids, 104 West 61 Street, New York 23, New York.

The Language of Business Accounting, American Institute of Certified Public Accountants, 270 Madison Avenue, New York 16, New York.

Filmstrips
Bookkeeping Cycle Series, Society for Visual Education, Inc., 1345 West Diversey Parkway, Chicago 14, Illinois:

> *Bookkeeping Cycle, Part I—*Recording and Posting
> *Bookkeeping Cycle, Part II—*Journal Entries and Trial Balance
> *Bookkeeping Cycle, Part III—*Work sheet, closing activities

Bookkeeping Film Strips, Teaching Aids Exchange, P. O. Box 1127, Modesto, California:

> *Bookkeeping Equation and the Balance Sheet*
> *Use of Accounts and Analysis of Transactions*
> *Journalizing and Posting*
> *Preparing the Trial Balance*
> *Preparation of the Work Sheet and Financial Statements*
> *Closing Entries*
> *Introduction to Accounting*
> *Direct Ledger Entry—Routine*
> *Direct Ledger Entry—Year-End*
> *How to Balance Accounts*
> *The Journal—First Lesson*
> *Posting—One Journal, One Ledger*
> *Controlling Accounts*
> *Petty Cash Systems*
> *6%, 60-day Interest Method, Part One*
> *6%, 60-day Interest Method, Part Two*
> *Errors, How to Locate, Correct, and Avoid Them*

CHAPTER VIII

TEACHING THE NONSKILL SUBJECTS

The Evolution of a Nonskill Teacher

Introduction

Several experienced business educators were discussing the question "What makes a good nonskill teacher?" The majority of those present began their classroom careers by teaching the skill subjects of shorthand, typewriting, and bookkeeping. Each one told how under pressure he first agreed to teach something in the nonskill area. Most of them were of the opinion that they now preferred the nonskills. One member of the group drove home the fact that the techniques required for teaching typewriting, for example, are entirely different from those needed in the basic business subjects. "In fact," said he, "it is difficult to imagine anything more unlike. What is good in the skills—time clocks, speed pressures, repetition, production—has very little place in the teaching of the nonskills. That is why many teachers fail in their first attempt. They usually try to adapt their skill-teaching methods to general business, when what they need is an entirely different approach."

It is like trying to learn a foreign language. As long as one is still translating from English to French, he hasn't arrived as a French student. It is only when one begins to *think* in French that he finds himself making progress in the language. So it is with the teaching of the nonskill subjects. One has to think in terms of nonskill techniques—not in the techniques used for shorthand, typewriting, or bookkeeping.

This is not easy. In a study made by Gress,[1] junior business training heads the list of those subjects for which beginning teachers felt they were inadequately trained. The changeover often takes a long time. The transition for the average teacher is a progressive experience. One might call it the *metamorphosis* of a nonskill subject teacher. In this chapter, therefore, are presented a series of guiding principles for teaching the nonskill business subjects. The principles are tied in with illustrations to make them as meaningful as possible. In Chapter IX, techniques are presented by means of which these principles can be put into action.

The Metamorphosis

What are the first signs of an awakening interest in the nonskills They differ with the individual. In some cases the teacher is "warned" that next year he will have to teach one or more classes in the nonskill area. This teacher then goes to summer school and takes a graduate-level course in the methods of teaching the nonskill subjects. He will read and write as much as possible in the special subject area that has been assigned to him. He will make use of the opportunity to build up a strong resource unit in each of the subjects in his fall schedule. Thus he will become a nonskill teacher. For those not so fortunate, the induction process may have to be more gradual.

"In my own case," said a former skills teacher, "I think the first step in developing an enthusiasm for the nonskills came when I realized one day that it was fun not to do all of the talking—that I could capitalize on student discussion. I realized that direction of discussion requires a great deal of skill and that there is satisfaction in the results. I resolved to find out more about this technique."

---

[1] John J. Gress, *Teaching Difficulties of Beginning Business Teachers*, Monograph 78 (Cincinnati: South-Western Publishing Company, 1952), p. 10.

The chart on page 404, based on an idea of H. G. Enterline, shows the steps by which a skills teacher may progress when endeavoring to increase his professional usefulness through development of competence in the nonskill area.

Physical Factors Influencing the Effectiveness of the Nonskill Teacher

What are the essential physical factors that make possible a setting in which discussion can thrive?

1. Room Size. The room should be just large enough. The group should not feel crowded, hemmed in; neither should it occupy but a corner of a room that is much too large.

2. Room Furniture. It is not by accident that we speak of King Arthur's Round Table or that we see the members of the President's Cabinet seated around an oval table— that's the way they do their best work. The furniture in a nonskill classroom, or a classroom that is occasionally used for nonskill purposes, should be movable. Tables should not be too heavy to be arranged in a large rectangle or in small groups as circumstances demand. Comfortable but sturdy lightweight chairs are a part of the setting. A tour of elementary school classrooms indicates that their furniture is usually much better adapted to intimate discussion than that found in many high schools and colleges.

3. Freedom from Noise. Many put freedom from noise high on the list as a necessity for a good discussion group. Not all persons have perfect hearing. Even those who have no difficulty with average conversation have trouble when the hearing organism has to sift out or disregard many distracting noises. Some people become nervous and irritable in the presence of conflicting sounds. It is for this reason that discussion leaders stress freedom from noise.

THE STEP-BY-STEP DEVELOPMENT OF A NONSKILL TEACHER

STEP No. 1 —	Teacher does most of the talking. Students "recite." Learning the textbook is the goal. Much rote memory work, much drill. Teacher resents being "stuck with this class"; is looking forward to next term and a change in the schedule.
STEP No. 2 —	Teacher introduces workbook. Students do all the exercises, whether they are apropos or not. Teacher makes some use of material at the end of the chapter—if answers are in the teacher's manual or key.
STEP No. 3 —	Teacher brings in some supplementary material, makes bulletin board display and ties it in with the lesson for the day. Is proud of his display. Shows a film—no discussion, no follow-up. Students, nevertheless, have brief interchange of ideas. Teacher does not interrupt discussion to "bring class back to order."
STEP No. 4 —	A student spontaneously makes a report on something interesting that he has read. Students talk about it. Teacher begins to see value in the process. Teacher checks library for interesting things in connection with the next chapter. Encourages outside reading. Outlines definite reading program. Enthusiasm is growing. He no longer says, "I got stuck with this course."
STEP No. 5 —	Teacher has been reading in methods of the nonskill subjects. Makes careful plans for each unit. Talks unit over with some of the better students. The unit is broken down into suitable study sections. Committees are appointed. Students are encouraged to bring in their own material, make their own bulletin board displays, handle their own classroom organization.
STEP No. 6 —	Teacher helps class select or slant problem to tie in with something of general school interest. Plans all class sessions carefully. Attempts to use good group-discussion techniques. Is rapidly gaining power in this type of work. Is familiar with techniques listed in Chapter IX and makes frequent use of them.
STEP No. 7 —	Student associates what he is doing with real-life situations. Self-evaluation techniques have been established. Students are more and more handling their own affairs by democratic and scientific methods learned in class. They use these concepts to interpret and analyze other life situations. Teacher is happy in work.

4. Freedom from Other Distractions. The intercommunications system has been a great boon to the central office, but it has wreaked havoc with many a class. In some schools, the faculty has taken the initiative to establish policies which keep class interruptions to a minimum. The managers of theaters and concert halls feel that freedom from distraction is so important that doors are often locked after the performance begins, and latecomers are admitted only at certain intervals. Teachers might strive with the same diligence to eliminate objectionable factors of distraction.

5. Last-Minute Preparations. If at all possible, the discussion leader should personally check to see that everything is in order. One small detail can often mar the effectiveness of a meeting. At an audio-visual aids conference, the light bulb in a major piece of equipment burned out during the first five minutes of the demonstration, and no replacement was immediately available. In another case, the chalkboard had been delivered, but there was no chalk. On still another occasion, there were charts to be hung, but no provision had been made for hanging them. At a speech conference, the screen was so far away from the speaker that it was difficult for him to get any unity into the discussion. The constant shifting of their eyes from screen to speaker became very annoying to the participants.

We all, of course, can remember many conferences where every detail was arranged beforehand. It is only when something is missing or when equipment does not function that we become aware of the significance of careful planning and preparation.

Organizational Factors—Planning

It is safe to say that when discussion-type nonskill classes fail even though the physical conditions are satisfactory, the reason generally lies in poor organization and planning. Most professional golfers run over in their minds before the tournament starts the entire rounds they are about to play. They map out strategy for each hole in relation to the competition they will have to face. A good discussion leader or a nonskills teacher will plan his lesson well in advance. He may select one or more of the devices mentioned at the end of this chapter in order to achieve his objective, or he may plan various steps within the discussion itself.

He may want to take another look at the problem for discussion. Is it one in which the entire group is interested? Have those present had actual experience with it? Is it so stated that the average person will immediately catch its meaning and significance? Is there a solution to the problem? Can it be solved by discussion?

If the discussion leader arrives at a satisfactory answer to the above questions, he might look to see if it is possible to get the necessary facts for arriving at a solution. How are these facts going to be obtained? How are they going to be validated? What technique is he going to use to determine which facts are related to the problem?

If in his planning the leader has scored a hit on both a significant question and the method of arriving at a solution, then he must consider the next and most important aspect of all, the evaluation and formulation of a workable conclusion. The leader needs to have a definite plan as to how he is going to proceed at this stage of the discussion. How can he help the group to evaluate what has been done? How can he help them formulate in effective, straightforward English a statement of the decisions of the group? What technique is he going to use to check on the workability of these conclusions? To what extent will these conclusions have the support of the group concerned? Are these solutions in line with basic established company policy? If not, what should be done to change either the conclusions or the company policy so that they will harmonize?

The Honorable Peyton Smith, a famous discussion leader in New England, once made the statement that it is often far easier to plan and give a major address than it is to prepare and lead an important discussion. A study of the points mentioned above does not make it difficult to accept such an assertion.

Some teachers like to have a complete set of officers for each class: president, secretary, etc. This is good if it contributes to the smooth operation of the group. If, however, there is danger of becoming bogged down in a parliamentary procedure, the less of such organization, the better. A good person to have in the class is an observer. Technically a disinterested person who sits on the sidelines, he gives his opinion of the functioning of the class as a discussion group. Since it would be difficult to find someone outside the class, a student is usually selected. The position is rotated so that all members will have at least one such opportunity during the term. Reports from observers are often most interesting and to the point. They frequently go something like this: "Joe's question got us off the track. Took us a long time to get back." "Everybody seemed to have an opinion; no one produced any facts." "No material from the reading list was presented."

Participation

Many of the well-known techniques listed at the end of this chapter and discussed in detail in Chapter IX are particularly useful in getting full class participation: the group project, the field trip, the film, the debate, and so on; but it is not always easy to get full participation in a straight discussion class.

The direct question is often advocated as a technique to "draw into" the discussion those who are not taking part. As we shall see when we discuss questioning, that technique is being frowned upon today by those who have made an intensive study of the art of questioning. The danger of using the direct question technique to get someone to take part in the discussion was brought out recently in a faculty meeting. The professor—let's call him Jones—was the only member present representing his department. The chairman turned to him and said, "Dr. Jones, what do *you* think about it?" Dr. Jones seemed startled at the question. Later he protested such questioning procedure, saying that he had been embarrassed. Thus, we may need to look for other methods to get full group participation.

There are many ways in which this can be done. The problem itself should, of course, be of vital interest to the entire group; the physical setup should be conducive to full participation, etc. One of the most effective participation-getting devices that has recently come to our attention is one observed when visiting a class taught by Dr. Cameron W. Meredith at Northwestern University. Dr. Meredith told us that some of his students were talking too much, while others were not talking at all. He said he was going to do something about it—and this he did. His technique was a simple one. He invited us to come in and see how it worked. He gave a liquid duplicator master to one of his student helpers. On this master was the seating arrangement of the class. The teacher asked his helper to make lines indicating the flow of the conversation during the entire period. If the teacher spoke to a person in seat No. 6, a line was drawn from the teacher's desk on the chart to No. 6. If Nos. 6 and 10 interchanged ideas, lines were made to indicate that fact.

When the class was over, Dr. Meredith duplicated enough copies for the class. The illustration on page 409 shows the result of that day's discussion. It points out plainly that most of the activity had involved the teacher and No. 7, No. 18, and No. 15. Fourteen members of the class had not made a single contribution during the course of the period.

CLASS PARTICIPATION CHART

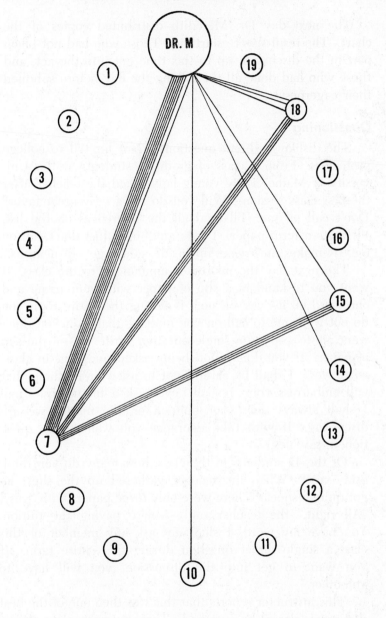

The next day Dr. Meredith distributed copies of the chart. The results were startling. Those who had not taken part in the discussion up to this time got into the act, and those who had done all the talking the day before subdued their eagerness.

Questioning

The dislike of direct questions is not limited to college professors. From a class of graduate students at the University of Maine, a shy young lady asked the teacher after the first class session, "Will you do me a very great favor? Don't call on me. I'll read all the references on the list. I'll write a term paper. I'll do anything. Just don't call on me. It makes me freeze up inside, and I get all nervous."

The next day the instructor announced to the class, "I want you to hand in a slip of paper with your name and one word on it—'yes' or 'no.' If during the entire term you do not want me to call on you in class, that is, if you don't want me to ask you a single question, write 'no' on the slip of paper. If you don't mind being asked questions in class, write 'yes.' I shall be careful not to ask you anything that will embarrass you. I shall never ask a factual question. I shall always seek your opinion on the matter we are discussing. If with that assurance you want to be questioned, say 'yes.'"

Of the 42 students in the class, how many do you think said "yes"? When the teacher gathered up the slips, he got quite a shock. There were only *three* papers with "yes"! "All right," the teacher said, "you're paying the tuition. You have my word, I shall not ask any member of this class a single direct question during this entire term. If you want to get into the discussion, you will have to volunteer."

This instructor reports that this was then one of the best discussion classes he ever had. There was complete relaxation and freedom from fear. The experience caused a complete about-face in his style of teaching. He discontinued the use of the direct question altogether, even as a device for getting nonparticipating members to join in the discussion.

Of course, the adoption of such a rule makes it harder on the teacher. One can no longer use the old-fashioned question for which there is a single, definite answer—the yes-or-no-type, the dead-end interrogative. What is needed is the chain-reaction question, but it is not always easy to construct.

Among the more pleasant memories in connection with the senior author's graduate work is a class with Dr. Boyd Bode, an artist in the use of the chain-reaction question. The writer thought it must be wonderful to have such a gift—to be able, during the course of a discussion, to find just the right way to phrase a question so the discussion would gain momentum.

One night Dr. Bode invited a class of five to dinner at his home. As the group left to go to the campus for class with him, Dr. Bode gathered up five sheets of paper and added a few more words to the pages he had already written. The material consisted solely of questions. Dr. Bode explained, "I always like to have plenty of ammunition." Here was a man whose ability was much envied loaded with five pages of handwritten questions for his class—one single class! Many student teachers (and some others) think they have done well if they read over before class the suggested questions given by an author at the end of a chapter!

Emotional Factors

Astronomers tell us that if we look beyond our universe of sun, moon, and stars, we shall find other universes something like ours. In a nonskill class, each individual represents a universe in which there are no limitations of time and space—the body may be in class, but the mind is apt to be in Australia, or in the moonlight with a friend, or back in the preceding class where things didn't go well. Just as we need a transitional sentence in order that the reader may go smoothly from paragraph to paragraph, so there needs to be a transition from class to class, from activity to activity.

If the students in a certain class are all pepped up about a school dance, it might be well to have them get it out of their systems by a brief discussion about it; then by some clever device, make the transition to the subject of the day.

In one form or another, to a greater or lesser degree, all students come to our classes with mental involvements that are difficult to synchronize with what we as teachers are attempting to do. There are times when the majority of the members of the class are excited about something. Students may be unhappy about a surprise test given during the preceding period. The class could be allowed to talk for a few minutes about whether there should be tests of this kind and about testing in general. From that, the teacher could go to some evaluation problems in his own class and then to the topic of the day. The transition will work, and a fine class discussion will result because everything is again calm, all emotions under control.

If there has been a recent emotional "blow-up" in class, this is a good time to discuss what psychologists have to say about controlling one's feelings. A nonskill class where the discussion is apt to become pretty heated at times is a good place to practice this type of mental adjustment. Every victory won here will help to condition the person for the office job after graduation. Exhibitions of temperament and gross deviations from the norm are not tolerated in office employment. A survey of the chief causes for dismissal will bear out that fact.

The teacher of a discussion class should be quick to discover an emotional situation before it builds up. He should do something about it before the explosion takes place. The teacher might interrupt with a "We probably need more information about this particular phase; in the meantime, why don't we see what we can do about Mike's suggestion?"

The treatment of mental illness requires more hospital space than physical ailments; and since health heads the list of educational objectives, it is the duty of all teachers—particularly those in the nonskills—to devote some time, as occasion gives the opportunity, to do something about mental health. The following list of suggestions might serve as a beginning. Some of these are taken from a compilation by Dr. Robert V. Seliger, Baltimore psychiatrist:

Tips for Sound Emotional Health

1. Avoid worry. Everybody worries, but don't let worries upset you. Problems are a great source of concern. Life is made up of problems. Business executives hire assistants because of problems. If it were not for problems, many of us would not have jobs.

2. Avoid hurry. Take it easy. Most scientists feel that hurry does not make for speed and is the result of lack of foresight. A half hour of planning well in advance will often save hours of time later on.

3. Avoid kicking against the annoyances of life. No one is exempt from daily irks or irritations both at home and at work.

4. Avoid self-pity. A good antidote is honesty combined with a sense of humor. Also try to take yourself less seriously.

5. Avoid looking for motives in people. Stop spending all your time trying to find out what meanings people have behind what they say and do.

6. Avoid exalted standards. When our personal standards for success are too exalted for our abilities, we block our way to self-esteem.

7. Avoid the conscience bogey. Conscience can bedevil the best of us out of self-respect if we permit it to become a bogey. Condemning ourselves for past mistakes won't rectify them. No individual is perfect. We all have our faults.

8. Avoid being shy and sensitive. The shy, over-sensitive person builds a wall about himself. He should understand that hypersensitivity is a form of hostility, a chip-on-the-shoulder manner of reacting to people.

9. Avoid running away from or fighting your emotions. Learn to live with your emotions by controlling them through will power. Don't be an adult baby.

10. Avoid continually analyzing yourself and thoughts. Don't always try to figure out why you do everything. Stop looking for motives inside yourself.

11. Avoid lack of self-confidence. This is really a dissatisfaction with our performance in life. Self-confidence can be fostered by interests that have nothing to do with our daily work—golf, for example.

12. Avoid poor and improper diet. Jitters, shakes, fatigue, and emotional swings may be due to a poorly balanced diet. Find out what you should weigh; then maintain that weight. Establish a sensible calorie intake and a mode of eating and living that will give your best weight.

13. Avoid insomnia. Sufficient sound sleep is needed for happiness, emotional health, and a vigorous body.

14. It is generally best to believe the best. Nine-tenths of the things we fear never really develop anyway. Therefore, until you positively know otherwise, believe the best.

15. Stop thinking that certain persons "have it in for you." If the person who seems to give you that feeling has enough time to fuss with such things, his opinion is of small consequence, and you need not worry about it. If the one who seems to have it in for you is really an important person, the chances are that he is too busy to even consider such a thing.

16. Make it a habit to think and talk about the pleasant things of life. Fill your memory storehouse with beautiful fragments of literature, music, art, and gems of social experiences. Get rid of the unpleasant, surplus junk as quickly as possible.

17. Find happiness in your work. If you are not happy in what you are doing, make a change. Remember Solomon, who, after much investigation, came to the conclusion that in good, productive labor lies man's greatest chance of happiness.

18. Don't apologize for the hours you spend on recreation. The time to catch those tensions is before you get them.

19. If you find a depressing mood has overtaken you, check quickly to see what caused it. Do something about it, and forget it.

20. Make decisions promptly. Nothing dissipates mental energy more quickly than constant vacillating between decisions. Thousands of doctoral dissertations are unfinished because the candidate just couldn't make that one final decision. Get the facts. If you feel there will be no new facts tomorrow, make the decision *now*.

21. Periodically get a thorough medical check-up; then quit looking under the hood.

22. Learn to love people. Don't hate anybody—it isn't worth it. Don't bear a grudge. Look for the good in every person with whom you have contact.

23. Control your temper. Don't allow yourself to enjoy the luxury of getting mad. Remember, any person can give

himself a No. 1 headache just by pretending he is angry at something or with somebody. Let your emotions work *for* you, not against you.

24. Expect a certain degree of adversity. Why should anyone of us in particular be exempt? When adversity comes, meet it head on.

Fire Power

During World War II, the circumstance of the well-known phrase "too little, too late" was responsible for our losing some of the early encounters. A class discussion, likewise, will be weak and uninteresting if there is no real fire power in the group. When his father was in his nineties, the senior author really enjoyed visiting with him. His dad's perspective of almost a century was fascinating. One day when he asked, "Dad, why don't you go down to the post office any more to talk with your cronies?" the reply was, "There hasn't been a new idea in that group in the last six months."

A class that has to rely on the individual experiences of its members will soon run dry. They need reinforcement. They need to supplement their "fire power." This power is acquired through reading. It is the nonskill teacher's business to carefully select the reading material and make it readily available. Here, as was mentioned in the skills, the teacher needs to prime the pump by introducing the class to the material. It helps to actually show them the books, pamphlets, and magazines from which the readings are taken. It helps to read interesting excerpts from these references. It helps to ask for volunteers to report on certain specialized readings.

In our nonskill classes, we get used to frequent requests from discussion leaders wanting to know something about the fire power in the group. Out of these requests grew the "reading control sheet" (see page 417). On the reading

READING CONTROL SHEET

NAME_____	TOPIC_____
	(In support of which
	this reading has been
COURSE_____	done.)

The purpose of this sheet is to give the discussion
leader some idea of the fire power of the group. In
the spaces below, please give the references you have
read recently which you think have a bearing on the
above topic. Please add a few remarks of your own
in connection with each title.

AUTHOR	TITLE	PUBLICATION

REMARKS:

AUTHOR	TITLE	PUBLICATION

REMARKS:

control sheet, each student reports briefly what he has read
on the subject and adds a few comments about the readings.
These sheets serve two purposes. (1) They encourage wider
reading. (Reading usually doubles or triples after the introduction of these sheets.) (2) It gives the discussion leader
an idea of the kind and amount of idea-ammunition in the
class.

The Resource Unit

A resource unit is a body of ideas, teaching suggestions, and techniques, questions, discussion topics, visual aids, and materials of all kinds that will help a teacher to teach a given unit or course. A powerful resource unit can turn a dull class into one that is a pleasure for the student and a joy to the teacher. An excellent example of one such resource unit is presented in Chapter IX.

Just as we speak of the necessity for students to have abundant fire power in order to contribute to the class discussion, so the teacher needs some good resource units to give him additional ammunition for his nonskill classes.

Duties of the Discussion Leader

How much should the teacher or discussion leader talk? How can he know when he is talking too much or too little? How much of himself should he give? That, of course, depends upon circumstances. In the usual course evaluation at the end of the term, if the majority of the students say, "You had so much to offer but gave us so little; we can hear these students prattle any day," then perhaps you did not talk enough. If they say, "We had some important people in the class; they had a wealth of experience, but we did not get to hear from them," then the chances are you talked too much. If the ratio is about 50-50, that is, 50 per cent say you talked too much and the other 50 per cent maintain that you should have talked more, then the chances are that your balance was about right. It is probably safe to say that the teacher who gives freely of himself—not only of that which lies in the narrow confines of the immediate subject matter but also of such other things as his philosophy of life, his aesthetic experiences, sports and recreational interests, opinion on world events—will provide greater take-home values of intellectual and lasting quality.

Lest we give the idea that the ideal discussion leader has little to do, here is a list of responsibilities of a conference leader as given by W. M. Baker: [2]

Responsibilities of Conference Leader

1. Arrange room for the conference.
2. Make plans.
3. State problem clearly.
4. Start discussion.
5. Bring out all phases of the problem.
6. Keep discussion on topic.
7. Encourage free discussion.
8. Give sufficient time for members to think.
9. Be impartial in the discussion.
10. Record statements.
11. Rephrase some statements.
12. Cite cases and personal illustrations.
13. Practice good methods of conference leadership.
14. Act naturally, but with confidence.
15. Respect confidence of group.
16. Make each session interesting and profitable.
17. Summarize the discussion.
18. Keep notes and prepare final report (optional).

Duties of Conference Members

1. Contribute their ideas and experiences.
2. Do not make a speech to "show off."
3. Keep personal prejudices out of discussion.
4. Give individual attention to discussion.
5. Confine discussion to problem being analyzed.
6. Do not engage in long, drawn-out arguments.
7. Do not come to conference with mind-set.
8. Assist leader in formulating statements to be recorded.
9. Cooperate with leader in summarizing the discussion and reaching a conclusion.
10. Be in attendance at each meeting.

---

[2] W. M. Baker, *How to Lead a Business Conference*, Bulletin No. 3141 (Washington, D. C.: Federal Security Agency).

Making the Generalization—Coming to a Conclusion

Not long ago the writers were invited to visit an Armed Forces class in management. After the meeting, the teacher was very enthusiastic. "That was a fine discussion we had today, don't you think? We really got them stirred up, eh?" Before we could answer, one of the supervisors from the group came up and confirmed the teacher's opinion: "We had a wonderful time today, Dr. Dixon. Brother! Did Harry show that guy up!"

Fortunately, no one pressed us for a comment, for our verdict would have been that the session was a complete failure. The problem under consideration had to do with a recent ruling. The group was trying to decide what to do about it. True, there had been much discussion—some of it pretty heated—but there was no attempt to get all the facts on the table in an orderly fashion; no effort made to cut off the fruitless arguing in order to leave time to look at the facts that were available; no effort made to seek a possible solution, even though tentative; no effort made to try a dry run with a tentative solution; and, finally, there was no effort made to arrive at a workable solution. In our opinion the meeting was a complete failure.

Just as a salesman's efforts will, for the most part, be in vain unless he gets the signature on the dotted line, so the loudest and most vigorous discussion is not much more than idle talk unless the teacher or discussion leader succeeds in getting something on the dotted line—some conclusion or workable solution which will add to the smooth operation of the organization.

Efficient learning is based upon insight. The outcome of a well-directed discussion brought to a significant conclusion should be greater insight into that particular problem, the frame of reference in which the problem is found, and other problems of a similar nature. Problem solving is not the result of reinforcement of correct responses by success over many trials unless reinforcement and success are both thought of in terms of greater insight.

A skillful arbitrator has found the following diagrams helpful in leading a group from a deadlock to a working agreement:

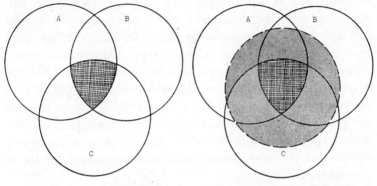

Groups A, B, and C in deadlock   A, B, and C in a working agreement

The three circles represent three groups with conflicting interests. They are in a peacemaking session, hoping to reach an agreement. The small black area in the middle represents the few points on which they all agree. It seems impossible ever to reach a solution acceptable to all.

Patiently, the discussion leader seeks for areas of compromise where only two disagree. He succeeds in getting a concession here and a little less opposition there until he has reached an area of agreement large enough for the company to operate effectively. The initial stage of the discussion is pictured at the left; the final solution at the right.

The area of agreement, even though not at all what each one originally had in mind, represents an arrangement where dignity has been maintained, and the profit margin is still such that the work can continue successfully. The slogan is: Keep your eye on the spot in the center, the area of agreement.

The Follow-up

Just as a letter that is actually to be put in the mail adds zest to a transcription class, so will decisions that lead to action stimulate a discussion group. No one likes to engage in make-believe activities when the real McCoy is available.

Likewise, in our high school nonskill classes, we can select problems the solution of which will benefit the school and the business community. One teacher coming back from a NOMA meeting where irregularities in observing coffee breaks were discussed took the matter up in his office practice class. It served as a springboard for a general consideration of office etiquette. To condition themselves for the coffee break which was soon to become a part of their daily experience, this double-period office practice group introduced its own coffee break and formulated rules to govern its control.

Business classes can tie their solutions of economics problems, for example, to the national scene and check them with decisions made by Congress. The "so what?" of the modern generation needs to be answered. In a nonskill class this can be done by using problems that are meaningful and by following up the solutions.

Evaluation

Those who speak about evaluation in connection with the nonskill subjects usually talk about two things: (1) the evaluation of the teacher or discussion leader, and (2) the evaluation of the class in terms of the objectives set for the course. Let us consider the evaluation of the teacher first.

1. Evaluation of Teacher Effort. Teachers, like students, must know how they are doing in order to be happy in their work. The self-rating chart on page 423 might serve as a beginning for teachers, discussion leaders, and committee chairmen.

CHECKLIST OF PERFORMANCE OF CONFERENCE LEADERS

The Conference Leader	Excellent	Fair	Unsatisfactory
1. Stated problem clearly			
2. Stimulated free discussion			
3. Made good use of blackboard			
4. Made use of cases to bring out facts			
5. Used good questions to stimulate discussion			
6. Knew where he was going and held discussion to the point			
7. Refrained from answering questions but referred them to group			
8. Maintained an easy, helpful manner			
9. Made advance preparation for conference			
10. Summarized conference discussion			
Other comments:			

A nonskill teacher should ask himself the following questions; then he should decide upon the philosophy under which he wishes to operate: *

---

* Based on a lecture by Dr. Cameron Meredith, Northwestern University.

What Style of Leadership Do I Prefer to Provide as a Teacher? One in Which I:

Dominate	Offer choice situations	Observe
Decide all issues	Ask for contributions	No formal decisions reached
Supply all information	Utilize resources from group	Answer questions only if asked
Keep aloof from participation	Participate as a member; maintain *fluid* participation	Maintain complete non-participation
Personally accept criticism	Objectively accept criticism	Have no interest in project
Allow little group initiative	Encourage group initiative	Allow complete member-freedom
Keep responsibility	Delegate responsibility	Make no attempt to regulate or orient
Allow little humor or fun	Encourage humor and fun	———
Regard discipline as obedience to authority	Regard discipline as growth from dependence to independence	Maintain no order
Make and enforce rules	Encourage group to formulate guides to conduct and to discuss suggestions for improvement	Make or enforce no rules—chaos
Think in terms of *I* and *My*	Think in terms of *We* and *Our*	Think in terms of *You* and *Their*
Provide many *failure* situations	Attempt to provide many *successes*	———
Encourage competition among members	Encourage cooperation among members	———
Determine marks	Meet with student and parent for evaluation	Make little attempt to evaluate
Demand respect from members	Encourage mutual respect for each other	Encourage little mutual respect
Rely upon extrinsic motivation—rewards and punishments	Rely upon intrinsic motivation	Have inconsistent motivation
Have little experimentation	Encourage experimentation	Have aimless activity

Autocratic		Democratic		Laissez-faire
	Leader-Centered		Group-Centered	

To what degree am I, a nonskill teacher, democratic in my classroom procedures? As we work toward a more desirable style of leadership, it is the *direction* which is *significant progress* rather than the style of leadership at any one time. An efficient, cooperative, and happy climate is the result of hard work:

Leader-Centered	Group-Centered
Members are permitted freedom and rights, but they flow from the leaders.	Members have freedom and rights in their own hands. Permission of leader is not required. Leadership often rotates.
Leader takes responsibility for good discussion and adequate summary. Takes responsibility for not fulfilling his role.	Discussion is a group responsibility. Leader reluctant to keep things going and to summarize. Often assumes role as a member.
Leader presents several alternate goals, activities, etc., and lets group select.	Leader gets group's suggestions for goals, activities, etc., and then the group selects.
Time allocation and way in which group proceeds is in hands of leader. He may delegate.	Time allocation and way in which group proceeds is gradually relinquished. Group becomes independent of leader as *leader*.
Leader takes responsibility for group troubles. Leader may ask for suggestions, but usually gives suggestions and allows group to choose.	Leader tries to get group to diagnose group troubles by getting group suggestions first. It is made primarily a group responsibility.
Leader uses methods of evaluation, but does not discuss them unless asked.	Techniques of evaluation and group evaluation is a topic of discussion.
Leader assumes role of resource person concerning matters of information. He controls selection, order, and presentation level of content. He may delegate, but control remains in his hands.	Leader gradually relinquishes control of content. Members decide what is to be discussed, order, and presentation level. He exploits group for information rather than promptly giving his own.
Leader is the source of support, rewards, and punishments.	Group is source of support, rewards, and punishments (not malicious punishment).
Leader makes no particular attempt to aid identification or perception of interdependence among members.	Leader tries to develop identification and perception of interdependence among members.
Leader will phrase situations more often in terms of *I* and *You.*	Leader will phrase situations in terms of *We.*

A summer school class at the University of Maine, under the co-chairmanship of Clara Swan and Mildred Bradford of Husson College constructed a nonskill teacher evaluation chart as its project for the term. The following instrument, with some modifications by the authors is the result of their study:

NONSKILL TEACHER EVALUATION CHART

(10 points is a perfect score for each part; 100 points for perfect score on all parts.)

THE TEACHER .... (   )
Does he seem to know his subject? Is his speech such that it can be heard in the rear of the room? Poise? Appearance? Sincerity? Does he like to teach? Eye contact? General adequacy?

THE STUDENT .... (   )
Is the student an important part of the picture? Is the class interested in what is being done? Do the students seem to *want* to learn? Are there factors which seem to disturb the growing interest of the class?

OBJECTIVES .... (   )
Are they clearly stated? Illustrated on blackboard or otherwise? Is an effort being made to have students underwrite them? Are they worthwhile? Needed? Attainable? Needed now?

ATMOSPHERE .... (   )
Has a mood or mind-set been created for the lesson? Is the general atmosphere of the classroom conducive to efficient learning? Light? Ventilation? Noise? Size? Moveable furniture?

EFFICIENCY .... (   )
Has the lesson been well planned? Is the teacher getting the most out of the period? Is the tempo too slow? Too fast? Is there evidence of marking time? Materials at hand well organized? Getting things done?

INTERACTION AND PARTICIPATION .... (   )
Is there active participation on part of *all* members of the class? Are individual differences being met? Is the teacher making use of one or more of the basic non-skill teaching techniques (See Chapter IX)?

MOTIVATION .... (   )
Are the simple psychological rules for good motivation being observed? Knowledge of progress? Is problem meaningful? Need solution? Student level? Praise? Success? Are devices pertinent? Aspiration set at attainable levels?

VISUAL AIDS AND WORKING MATERIALS .... (   )

Is efficient use being made of the chalkboards? Of the bulletin boards? Other forms of visual aid? Does he have at hand the routine materials? Reference books? Other texts? Methods books?

MEANINGS .... (   )

Are the students actually getting something out of the lesson? Does it mean something to them, really? Can they use this particular knowledge in business? In later school work? Is the student now a different person?

EVALUATION .... (   )

Is some effort made to check up before the end of the period to see what has been accomplished? Do students take an active part in the evaluation? Is it realistic? Does it serve as a learning device?

The following factors cannot be rated at every individual lesson—they pertain generally to the unit. Use judgment and answer as occasion warrants.

Classroom organization———— Committee activity———— Use of Community resources———— Unit teaching———— Resource unit available———— Use of the library———— Is democracy in action?———— Contribution to health———— Better living————

2. **Evaluation of Student Effort.** The ability to properly evaluate student effort is a power that one develops with experience. As the teacher gains confidence in handling the nonskill subjects, as objectives become more meaningful, he will also acquire insight into how one should evaluate outcomes in terms of course objectives. This growth in the power to evaluate usually develops along the following pattern. Beginning teachers frequently use only *Stage No. 1.*

Stage No. 1: Term grade is based mostly on the final examination, with some value given to the mid-term examination, if there is one. In order to make a high score, the student must learn and remember a great many facts. Company-published, textbook-correlated, printed tests are frequently the only method used in ranking students. The teacher, of course, does everything. Objectives of the course are generally not clearly stated, and the final examination often has little in common with these objectives.

Stage No. 2: Stage No. 2 is similar to No. 1, except that an effort is made to enlarge the base used to determine the final grade. Projects like term papers, reports, and class tests are considered in the final score. Teacher uses "home-made" tests to supplement printed tests. Teacher still assumes full responsibility and does all the work.

Stage No. 3: After the term is underway, and the class is functioning nicely as an efficient body of learners, teacher and students review the objectives of the term. They then discuss techniques whereby they can best evaluate themselves; they seek to find how the actual outcomes at the end of the term compare with the anticipated outcomes established in the beginning. Teacher and students work together to determine mark for the term. A "grading committee" representing the students often works with the teacher.

Stage No. 4: Students grade themselves. Teacher remains in the background as group leader, helps in establishing valid criteria.

3. **The Evaluation Control Sheet.** The specific method of evaluation used in any class will, of course, depend upon the subject and the objectives set for the course. Regardless of the system used, the base should be a broad one—broader than that encompassed by a printed textbook test.

In the preceding chapters, when discussing the skill subjects, the authors presented various "evaluation control sheets." In the nonskill subjects, we likewise recommend the use of a control sheet. The control sheet serves much the same purpose as the worksheet in accounting: it enables the teacher to get on one sheet all facts that should be taken into consideration in order to arrive at a valid mark for the term. These factors can be weighted to correspond with the importance that has been placed on the various units or discussion areas covered during the semester. The authors have used the following control sheet, modified as needed for any given class, with good success:

EVALUATION CONTROL SHEET
(For Nonskill Subjects)

TEACHER'S ESTIMATE (100 points) . . . . . . _____
REPORTS, TERM PAPERS, ETC. (100 points) . . _____
MID-TERM EXAMINATION (100 points) . . . . . _____
MAJOR TERM PROJECT (100 points) . . . . . . _____
FINAL EXAMINATION (100 points) . . . . . . _____
                     TOTAL SCORE . . . . . . _____

It is suggested that the teacher make an evaluation blank for each student and that he begin to make entries on this sheet early in the term. The official roll book will, of course, be kept as usual, but from time to time the teacher might wish to make notations on the student control sheet. For example, on the first item, "Teacher's Estimate," he might want to enter in pencil a beginning score of 75 points. Then at each time during the term when a student goes up in the teacher's estimation because of some unusual contribution, the teacher might want to raise the score; or, if because of absenteeism, tardiness, or lack of cooperation the teacher's rating of a student goes down, the teacher might wish to lower the score. If nothing significant happens one way or the other, it might be an indication that the final score of "Teacher's Estimate" should be not more than the original 75 points. The other blanks can be filled in as tests are given or as term papers and reports are turned in.

At the end of the term, when all facts are in and all items have been entered, the teacher totals the control sheet. A perfect score would be 500 points. This, divided by five, puts the score sheet on a percentage basis—a perfect score of 100 per cent. To arrive at the usual "A," "B," or "C," marks, the following scale might be adopted: 90 to 100 percent equals "A"; 80 to 89, "B"; 70 to 79, "C"; 60 to 69, "D," and below 60, an "F." The teacher may wish to grade the class on the curve of normal distribution or on a combination of the fixed scores and the curve.

At various times parents may protest a mark made by a son or daughter. If the teacher has something on the order of a control sheet to show the protesting parent, the teacher can usually establish that the mark awarded was fair and reasonable. When the teacher has only a single mark in his grade book to justify the student's grade for the term, explanations are difficult.

An Experiment in Self-Evaluation

An experiment in student self-evaluation was conducted by one of the authors at a university a few years ago. The students were told that they would be allowed to grade themselves for the term. It soon became evident that in order to grade themselves they would need criteria on which to base their judgments. Two days were spent developing these criteria. On the basis of its findings, the class developed a scale. The instructor acted only as the discussion leader, with the students organizing the standards for letter grades. The class listed the following factors as necessary for a grade of "A":

1. *Opinion of the class.* It must be the spontaneous judgment of the class that this person deserves an "A."

2. *Teacher judgment.* The teacher, without doing any figuring or averaging of any kind, should have this student pegged as an "A"-calibre student.

3. *Outside reading.* An "A" student on his own initiative goes far beyond the line of duty in his reading.

4. *Contribution to the class.* An "A" student is the one who always brings something new and interesting to class. He soon becomes known for his fine contributions. He is

thus an outstanding and valuable member of the group. Even the teacher often learns something from what this student has read or observed.

5. *Logical organization of knowledge and experiences.* The "A" student is the one who welcomes the opportunity to bring to the group in organized and well-written form the outcomes of the term as he sees them. The entire class benefits from the fine presentation of his term paper or report.

6. *Leadership.* The "A" student eagerly assumes leadership responsibilities. It is the "A" student who volunteers to be chairman of class committees. It is through these committees that the term problem is broken down into its component parts, each committee working intensively in its own particular area. The results of all are then put together for the total outcome of the entire term.

After these criteria had been established, scales were also worked out for "B" and "C" grades. A few of the factors that characterize the "C" are as follows: student should be there every day; he must do the minimum reading; he must participate in committee work when asked to do so; he must make contributions to class discussion if and when inclined to help; he must be familiar with the basic understandings and knowledges that form a part of the outcome of the course. Space does not permit a full outline of the "B" characteristics, but they lie somewhere between the "A" and the "C."

While the class was working on the criteria, some of the author's colleagues thought he was in for trouble. "They'll all want 'A's.'" However, when a poll was taken in the class, only three out of a group of 36 wanted an "A."

Here, then, was a class with the basic fear removed—the fear of not passing the course or of being embarrassed by a low grade.

Techniques Useful in Conducting Nonskill Classes

We have discussed, thus far, general principles under-lying group dynamics as a whole, principles that apply to almost any specific technique the teacher may want to use. The principles listed in this chapter lose some of their effectiveness unless they are applied in connection with specific nonskill instruments or teaching procedures. The following is a list of 21 techniques that teachers in the non-skill subjects have found useful. These devices will be de-scribed in detail in Chapter IX:

1. The straight lecture
2. The lecture—augmented with chalkboard illustrations
3. Question-answer method
4. Problem solving
5. The demonstration
6. Guest speakers—community resource persons
7. The panel discussion
8. The case problem method
9. Brainstorming
10. The buzz group
11. Role-playing—dramatic skits
12. The class report
13. Scrapbooks—notebooks
14. Motion picture films
15. The project—individual and group
16. Field trips—educational tours
17. The stunt
18. Bulletin boards—display boards
19. The tape recorder
20. Television
21. Miscellaneous techniques—debate, term papers, "an-alytical approach," team teaching

SELECTED BIBLIOGRAPHY

Cogan, Morris L. "Theory and Design of a Study of Teacher-Pupil Interaction," *Harvard Educational Review* (Fall, 1956), 315-342.

Enterline, Herman G. "Using Discussion Techniques in Teaching General Business," *The Balance Sheet* (October, 1955).

Getzels, Jacob W., and Herbert A. Thelen. "The Classroom Group as a Unique Social System," *The Dynamics of Instructional Groups*, The Fifty-Ninth Yearbook of the National Society for the Study of Education, Part II. Chicago: The University of Chicago Press, 1950.

Gilbreth, Harold, and Gladys Bahr. "How Does the Principal Evaluate the Effectiveness of the Teaching of Basic Business?" *The Business Education Program in the Expanding Secondary School*. Washington, D. C.: The National Association of Secondary-School Principals (NEA), 1957, Chapter XXIII.

Grambs, Jean D., William J. Iverson, and Franklin K. Patterson. *Modern Methods in Secondary Education*, Revised Edition. New York: The Dryden Press, 1959.

Hoffman, W., and Robert Plutchik. *Small Group Discussion in Orientation and Teaching*. New York: G. P. Putnam's Sons, 1959.

How to Use Group Discussion. No. 6, How to Do It Series. Washington, D. C.: The National Council for the Social Studies, 1952.

Lewis, Lanora Giessler. "Using the Case Method in Basic Business Subjects," *Business Education Forum* (May, 1961), 34.

MacKeachie, M. J. "Student-Centered Vs. Instructor-Centered Instruction," *Journal of Educational Psychology* (March, 1954), 143-150.

Smith, L. N. *Group Processes in Elementary and Secondary Education* (*What Research Says to the Teacher*). Washington, D. C: National Education Association, 1959.

You and Your Students, Third Edition. Cambridge: Office of Publications, Massachusetts Institute of Technology, 1959.

CHAPTER IX

NONSKILL TECHNIQUES AND DEVICES

Introduction

The area of nonskill business education, or basic business, is one that has as a major aim the development of general understanding and knowledge necessary for successful business employment and everyday living. This area is without question one of the most challenging in which a business teacher can work. There is frequently an understandable feeling of insecurity on the part of the teacher who was "pushed" into teaching the nonskill courses. At almost every gathering of business teachers a lack of confidence in "how to teach" these subjects is revealed; knowledge of subject matter is seldom a problem.

Even some of the leaders in the business education field feel that "business teachers have oversold the specialized skill phases of education for business at the expense of the nonspecialized skill area of general or basic business education." [1] This rationalization that the skill areas are all-important has in many instances led to the "general and unfortunate idea that any teacher can take over a basic business class—'You know, anyone can go in there, talk about common business information, and keep the students too busy for mischief.' " [2]

It is incumbent on the business teacher, whatever his special preference in subject matter, to develop teaching

---

[1] M. Herbert Freeman, "General Business Education in the Small High School Program," *The National Business Education Quarterly* (Summer, 1954), p. 18.

[2] M. Herbert Freeman, *Basic Business Education for Everyday Living,* Monograph 74 (Cincinnati: South-Western Publishing Company, 1951), p. 27.

techniques that will enable him to do a high-level job of teaching and to create conditions under which students will learn. Kincaid refers to this development of the art of teaching as a "teaching plus"—"that something extra that enables the teacher to practice his art with more satisfaction to himself and with more enduring values in the lives of his students." [3] Harms also refers to this "extra" in the illustration of the following diagram: [4]

(OPFB diagram)	The plus teacher does all the work of the ordinary teacher, hence the "0."	In addition he helps his students to realize their maximum personality potentials, hence the "P."
	He helps his students with fundamentals, hence the "F."	He gives freely from a rich background of subject matter and experience, hence the "B."

Porter points out the importance of the well-informed teacher in the business education program when he says:

> Probably in no phase of education have more rapid strides forward been taken in recent years than in business education. Instructional materials have been greatly improved, audio-visual aids have been developed, and the equipment utilized in instruction has been modernized. Fine new physical facilities are being provided today in new school buildings or in buildings which have been renovated and remodeled. Yet, surrounded by new facilities, excellent equipment and the best of instructional materials, the teacher remains the key factor in any program of education for business. [5]

If the "plus" teacher will search diligently, he can uncover ways and means to generate life in basic business courses such as economic geography, business law, con-

---

[3] James K. Kincaid, "Teaching Pluses," *American Business Education* (December, 1955), p. 107.

[4] Harm Harms, "The Plus Factor in Teaching," *American Business Education* (March, 1956), p. 183.

[5] Gerald A. Porter, "Evaluating the Competency of a Business Teacher," *The National Business Education Quarterly* (Summer, 1956), p. 16.

sumer economics, general business, and others. Musselman attempts to point out the possibilities available for this "interest-getting" element:

> We know that students learn best when they are interested. How, then, do we interest them in a new topic in general business? There are many handles that fit this tool—variety, visual aids, demonstrations, dramatizations, pupil participation, utilization of community resources. Aids for introducing new unit topics include:
>
> 1. Films or filmstrips.
> 2. Bulletin board exhibits or the flannel board.
> 3. Dramatic skits.
> 4. Newspaper accounts of some happening in the local community.
> 5. Student or teacher demonstrations.
> 6. Well-illustrated supplementary materials.
> 7. Oral reports that were assigned a few days earlier.
> 8. A case history of one of your own experiences or one you have observed.
> 9. A visiting speaker from the local community.
> 10. A pretest—include in it unusual and interest-stimulating items.
> 11. An overview of the unit.[6]

It is not difficult to determine from the foregoing list that teachers should recognize the importance of variety in their methods. The following partial list from Shorling also shows the range of possible devices "if one wishes to avoid the very bad habit of restricting his work to a few procedures": [7]

1. A pupil makes an oral report.
2. A committee demonstrates.

---

[6] Vernon A. Musselman, "Helping General Business Students to See, Hear, and Think," *The National Business Education Quarterly* (Winter, 1958), p. 34.

[7] Raleigh Shorling, *Student Teaching* (New York: McGraw-Hill Book Company, Inc., 1949), p. 196.

3. A film is presented with comments.
4. A talk illustrated with slides is given.
5. The teacher reports on common errors found in test papers.
6. Pupils and teacher discuss a basic question.
7. A teacher lectures.
8. Pupils engage in a debate.
9. A dramatization is presented.
10. A class engages in a rapid oral review.
11. A pupil demonstrates.
12. A teacher demonstrates.
13. The class discusses supplementary reference material.
14. The class considers the written report of a class excursion.
15. Pupils discuss an assignment and anticipate difficulties and plan reports of source materials.[8]

Crank points out an attribute of a "plus" teacher:

> The level of understanding will depend greatly on how thoroughly the teacher explores the possible insights, relationships, conclusions, and generalizations. One of the most common mistakes made by teachers is failure to "nail down" the understanding. This "nailing down" procedure probably is best accomplished by asking students to verbalize the understanding. Students need help in seeing relationships and drawing conclusions.[9]

A teacher will either "teach as he was taught to teach," or "teach as he was taught." Because teaching the basic-business subjects poses a challenge of greater proportions than the skill subjects for many beginning teachers, the patterns that follow will be of some help in selection of the method to be used under given circumstances.

---

[8] *Ibid.*, pp. 197-198. (The entire list of 35 excellent devices is given in the cited work.)

[9] Floyd L. Crank, "Improved Methodology in Basic Business Education," *Business Education Forum* (March, 1960), p. 7.

The Straight Lecture

The straight lecture, in some areas of education and at some levels, is still the most frequently used method of instruction. The weaknesses of the lecture method, particularly in high school classes, have been pointed out forcefully on many occasions. One might draw the conclusion that it does not have a place in the classroom. This is far from true. The lecture method seems to be the best method when the following conditions are present:

1. When a nationally known authority possesses a large body of information and experiences not shared by his listeners, and when these listeners are eager to have this information.

2. When the subject matter dealt with is factual in nature and there is very little opportunity for differences of opinion or for problem solving.

3. When time is limited—speaker will be available only for a day or so.

4. When the straight lecture is later reinforced by other techniques. A recent observation of lectures given to classes of two hundred or more showed the following pattern: No questions were permitted during the first hour; there was no discussion. During the following period, the class broke up into sections of fifteen students where the points presented during the lecture were taken up in detail and discussed. (The decisions were later reported to the assembly as a whole by a single person representing his particular group.)

The lecture as a teaching method is more generally associated with college and university teaching than at the level of the secondary school. This is consistent with what is known about the learning abilities of young people and adults and of abstraction compared with concrete or sensory experiences. The lecture, when used at all, should be supplemented by demonstration, discussion, and practice. Brooks and Pierson feel this is true even at the university level:

> It is extremely doubtful that students in a survey lecture course are going to have much opportunity to apply newly acquired knowledge to problem solving. There would be no time for discussion in class, a fact which leaves the students with the task of memorizing meaningless data. They learn least from having an instructor prescribe a solution without giving them any opportunity to question or criticize; most from their own efforts to deal with a situation. They should be participants rather than members of an audience.[10]

It has been said that too much of secondary school business education consists of a maximum of lecture and a minimum of discussion, demonstration, and student participation. This condition is changing rapidly as more and more high school teachers are availing themselves of the newer techniques and procedures presented in nonskill methods courses.

In deference to its time-honored place in teaching method, the lecture, when used effectively, requires a great deal of preparation and a well-refined manner of presentation. The occasional use of the illustrated lecture procedure brings verbal description within the learning limits of the students. It provides an opportunity to talk with students, to exchange questions and answers with them, to explain and to demonstrate for them.

The Lecture—Augmented With Chalkboard Illustrations

Probably the most common variation of the straight lecture is one in which the chalkboard is used to clarify

---

[10] Wayne A. Brooks and A. P. Pierson, "Case Vs. Lecture Method for the First Course in Business Law," *Collegiate News and Views* (May, 1960), p. 29.

abstract concepts. A professor of oriental history provided the authors with an excellent method of procedure. His lectures were very formal. They were packed with content. The vocabulary—names and places—in these courses were totally unfamiliar to the students. These names would have had very little meaning had not he used two sets of chalkboards and a set of maps to augment his lectures. He made elaborate preparations for each lecture. He brought in two portable chalkboards so that he could outline his material before class and be sure it would not be disturbed. In the front of the room was his array of maps—including blowups of small areas to give details. To the right was a portable chalkboard on which he had hand lettered all the names and places in the order in which he planned to take them up in class. To the left was his outline for the entire lecture. He would first go over this outline quickly with his class, showing them what he was going to cover during the period. On his desk were numerous reference books from which he would occasionally read interesting anecdotes having to do with kings, rulers, generals, and statesmen that were to pass in review. What a contrast between these classes and those in which an instructor "drones" through an hour's lecture using nothing more than his lecture notes!

Question-Answer Method

Use of the question-answer method is as common in business education as it is in other areas. It is frequently used as an oral quiz technique, and it can be effectively used to stimulate discussion by posturing controversial questions.

Question-answer procedure may be used to advantage in uncovering student attitudes, needs, interests, and problems; in probing for understanding; and in guiding discussion. The wise selection and timely use of questions, and the observation of good questioning techniques, may revitalize student interest in the nonskill subject under study. Login gives the following review of the questioning technique, a matter of concern because of the frequent use of the method: [11]

1. Before you call upon a particular student, are your questions:
   a. Directed to the entire class?
   b. Digested by the class?
   c. Directed to the pupils in irregular order?
   d. Directed to the pupil who is inattentive?
   e. Distributed among all pupils?
   f. Of difficulty directed to brighter pupils? Of factual recall directed to slower pupils?
   g. Varied in tone and phrasing to avoid a monotonous manner?
   h. Returned to the pupil who failed to answer a similar question?

2. Do you avoid the following form of questions?
   a. Multiple
   b. Ambiguous
   c. Tugging
   d. Echo
   e. Categorical
   f. Concert or chorus
   g. Leading
   h. Guessing
   i. Pumping
   j. Repeat

The greatest value of direct questioning lies in the amount of forethought that has been given to the possible questions that can be used to fully develop an idea or concept under discussion.

---

[11] Abraham Login, "Questioning," *A Handbook for Teachers of Business Education,* Twenty-Second Yearbook of the Commercial Education Association of the City of New York and Vicinity, 1958, pp. 23-24.

Problem Solving

Problem solving as a method of teaching the nonskills is consistent with the idea that business education experiences should serve needs of students and assist them in managing their personal affairs. It has the added possibility of using hypothetical situations for the purpose of centering attention, creating interest, and stimulating pupil activity. This method is demanding on the teacher because it places a premium upon the wise selection of course content, sources outside of the textbook, timely use of selected materials, and guided study of individual progress.

The initial task of the teacher and the students is the determination of what constitutes problem solving. The following is a standard listing of the steps:

1. Definition of the problem.
2. Analysis of the problem.
3. Division of labor for different class members.
4. Procurement of source materials.
5. Finding, analyzing, and interpreting the information needed.
6. Determination of a conclusion.
7. Consideration of other solutions.

Lebeda gives an excellent illustration of this method in a basic concept found in a number of nonskill courses—"Putting Money to Work." In brief, her approach to the problem follows this pattern:

1. Broad areas are subdivided into kinds of stocks, advantages and disadvantages of ownership of stock, who invests in stocks, how to read a financial page, how to know a good stock, and many others.

2. The next task is to determine where and how to find the necessary information. For this purpose, the class may be divided into committees, or individual class members may work by themselves. Some of the information will

be in the textbook, and students can learn to use the book as a source of information rather than as a means of reading and studying a certain number of assigned pages each day.

3. The teacher should also have available materials from educational bureaus and institutes, business magazines, and financial sections from local newspapers. Students may contribute some materials from their homes.

Films may furnish information, and either the teacher or a committee of students may invite a local businessman to speak on some phase of investments.

4. After the students have gathered information about their particular questions or problems, analysis through class discussion can be made.[12]

The Demonstration

Whether provided by the teacher, by resource persons, or by the students themselves, the demonstration provides visual experience which quite frequently transcends verbal explanation. Most demonstrations in the business subjects do not require extensive equipment or laboratory techniques and are well within the capacity of any teacher. This fact makes possible the use of the demonstration in almost any classroom. It is less time consuming than some individual procedures, and it emphasizes essential points which might otherwise be minimized.

While demonstrations are most used in the skill areas of business education, they are of particular importance in the verbalized nonskill areas. A symposium of leading business educators recently gave these examples of the use of the demonstration in consumer economics:

One teacher, through the cooperation of the science department, arranged for students to put on a demonstration

---

[12] Agnes Lebeda, "Problem Solving in Basic Business," *Business Education Forum* (February, 1958), p. 29.

of testing refrigerators. Another teacher, through the cooperation of the home economics department, arranged for a demonstration which identified qualities and values of foods. Another teacher used successfully the technique of having the better students lead a group in putting on a statistical demonstration of the current cost of living.[13]

Heimerl makes this comment on the use of the demonstration:

> Demonstrations are valuable in consumer education: burn tests on cloths and fabrics; weight tests; what questions to ask a salesclerk; how to analyze advertisements—these and other demonstrations do more than teach how; they also teach the importance of understanding, of knowledge, of wariness and confidence, and so on, and these are the fundamentals of consumer training.[14]

Musselman advocates the use of pupil-demonstration to drive home points in the basic business courses:

> Have you tried initiating your class study of Shipping Services by having a pupil demonstrate the correct way to wrap a package in contrast to an incorrect method? It's a good way to hold attention. One way to launch a unit on Communication would be to have a committee of students demonstrate the various ways of sending a message—semaphore, blinker light, flags, Morse code, telephone, telegraph, etc.[15]

It is important that complete and detailed preparations be made for the demonstration. The most important pre-demonstration considerations are:

1. Be aware of the specific purpose of the demonstration before presenting it.

---

[13] W. Harmon Wilson, *et al.*, "Providing for the Fast Learner in Consumer Economics," *American Business Education* (May, 1958), p. 223.

[14] Ramon P. Heimerl, "Ten Basic Social-Study Techniques Applicable to a Consumer Class," *Business Education World* (June, 1954), p. 17.

[15] Vernon A. Musselman, "20 Ways to Launch a General Business Unit," *Business Education World* (December, 1954), p. 28.

2. Be sure to know the demonstration procedure through rehearsal before class.

3. Have all materials and equipment.

4. Examine the room situation beforehand to make sure that everyone can see.

5. Make use of the "whole" method so that even if parts are presented, they can be tied in with the whole activity or process.

6. Try to anticipate the steps which are most difficult for students to grasp and be prepared to clarify these points.

7. Arrange to have all but the most pertinent questions asked after the demonstration is completed.

8. Direct the pupils' observation and attention by words and gesture—avoid talking too much.

Guest Speakers—Community Resource Persons

The use of guest speakers in the nonskill business classes brings to the classroom the varied skills and experiences of many persons who, by virtue of specialized training or experience, have a contribution to make to business education. These persons can discuss matters of immediate concern to the young people in the classroom. They can provide information, give demonstrations, use unique illustrations to stimulate interest, and provide motivation in ways not generally used by the teacher. The supply of these persons is usually greater than the demand for their services.

Careful planning for the use of speakers is essential. Just any time won't do. The hour chosen should be the period of greatest student interest in a particular business problem. The visitor should be advised as to the grade level of the group and their interest in and knowledge of the problem. The speaker should be told what will be expected of him. He should be informed as to the exact class meeting time and be asked whether or not he will be available to answer questions or grant personal and group interviews after the talk. The invitation to appear may be issued by the teacher or it may be a committee project of the class.

The teacher needs to recognize that it is possible to overdo the number of visits in a given semester or year; that quality rather than quantity is desired; that the purpose is to enrich the general business education experiences of the class members. The business program will profit most from the use of guest speakers when instruction is developed around the needs, problems, and interests of the class rather than around arbitrarily fixed business textbook content.

In order to ascertain class reaction to the use of guest speakers, a device of some sort is needed. Lewis suggests the questionnaire that follows on page 447, [16] with the hope of reconciling the possible negative reactions from the class members:

1. How will the students react to an outsider?
2. What adult would care to spend part of his busy day addressing high school students in addition to the time he must give to preparing his remarks?
3. Can the businessman adapt the material for his talk to the understanding of the secondary school freshman?
4. Are not we who have had years of training better qualified to present the same material to our students without exerting ourselves to arrange for what may be unwilling guests? [17]

Just as the field trip has excellent value when thoughtfully planned and executed, visits of speakers and resource persons from the community require careful thought. There should be a pattern of mechanics by which to ensure that all value possible will be derived from the visit. Callan presents an excellent checklist that should cover most of these contingencies:

---

[16] Harry Lewis, "Do We Want Guest Speakers?" *Business Education World* (December, 1954), p. 10.
[17] *Ibid.*, p. 9.

STUDENT QUESTIONNAIRE

Through the following questions, we are trying to determine your reaction to the lesson you had on Social Security last Thursday. Your answers will be of great value to us in planning this unit's work for future classes.

Place a check mark in the space provided before the answer that most closely approximates your attitude.

1. You found the film to be:
   _____ Very interesting
   _____ Interesting
   _____ Dull

2. You feel that the speakers from the Social Security Agency were:
   _____ Very interesting
   _____ Interesting
   _____ Dull

3. You think the speakers dealt with you as:
   _____ Adults·
   _____ Children

4. You believe that this lesson:
   _____ Should be given as the first lesson on Social Security
   _____ Should be given as the last lesson on Social Security
   _____ Should not be given at all

5. You found that the program:
   _____ Cleared your mind and answered all questions
   _____ Didn't answer all questions completely
   _____ Wasn't of any help
   _____ Raised new questions that need answers

6. It would be of greater value if this talk were given to you as seniors rather than as part of the Business Arithmetic course:
   _____ Yes
   _____ No

7. You would advise that this lesson be given to Business Arithmetic classes in the future:
   _____ Yes
   _____ No

If there is anything further you would care to add, we should greatly appreciate it. Please use the reverse side of this paper for these comments.

1. Have all factors concerning the location for use of the resource person been considered?

2. Have the students been prepared for the speaker or demonstrator?

3. Do the students know who the resource person is, the company he represents, and what they might expect to learn from him?

4. Has the class formulated questions to ask the resource person? Have these questions been forwarded to the resource person?

5. Do the students understand the importance of courteous conduct and attention?

6. Has the resource person been given complete information concerning the group to be addressed?

7. Has a time limit for the resource person been set? Is he aware of the time limit?

8. Has the resource person been told the important points that the teacher wants stressed?

9. Has a follow-up plan been given consideration so that the students will be able to relate the resource person to the classroom work? [18]

The follow-up has been singled out as a point of primary significance by Giffin and is referred to as "recognition" of the visitor:

In the interest of good public relations it is wise to give the visitor the recognition he deserves for the time and effort he has given the class. This may be done by the class in the following ways:

1. Send the speaker a "thank you" letter after his appearance.

2. If the speaker is an employee, send his employer a letter of appreciation.

3. Write a news article about the speaker for publication in the community newspaper and the school news.

4. Prepare an account of the visit for a regularly scheduled news broadcast if you have a local radio station.[19]

[18] John Henry Callan, *Community Resources Handbook in Business Education,* Monograph 87 (Cincinnati: South-Western Publishing Company, 1954), pp. 16-17.
[19] James F. Giffin, "A Community Resource: The Guest Speaker," *Business Education Forum* (January, 1956), p. 9.

This is not the easy way out; the teacher must accept the facts of using the method. *It takes time.* Belt summarizes the method with this comment:

> Many instructors who read this will probably comment that a tight teaching schedule does not leave time for special lectures, trips, etc. Granted, time is limited. . . . There is hardly time to present even a portion of the material included in a textbook. It then becomes a question of weights and balances. . . . Do not be a slave to the textbook and do remember that the businessman can be a valuable assistant to the business instructor.[20]

The Panel Discussion

The panel discussion is another way of using class participation to get a job done, a concept taught. The panel serves to enhance the regular course material by permitting students to "get into the act." Grambs and Iverson describe the panel as a "trial by fire," serving two major purposes:

1. It helps the teacher to see the level of competence of his students in order to *train them further* in the necessary skills.

2. It brings the students into an active role in developing their own skills and setting their own standards for adequate performance.[21]

In order to avoid the disintegration of the panel into a dull series of short speeches, the teacher must play an active part in the organization and procedure; he cannot sit back and let the students "take over." Purposes of the method must be made clear, mechanics developed, and plans made for appraisal.

Wright, in the use of the panel discussion in a salesmanship class, gives these procedural steps:

---

[20] Virginia M. Belt, "The Businessman: A Help to the Instructor," *Collegiate News and Views* (December, 1955), p. 13.

[21] Jean D. Grambs and William J. Iverson, *Modern Methods in Secondary Education* (New York: The Dryden Press, 1952), p. 226.

Assuming a class size of thirty students . . . six groups of five members each are designated as separate panels. Dates for their joint effort are set, with care being exercised to separate the time of panel appearance and sales demonstrations of each student. Discussion topics are then assigned to each panel by the instructor, largely as a matter of expediency to get work started. There is no other reason why each panel could not arrive at its own subject for discussion.

Each panel is instructed to meet and elect a chairman whose responsibility it is to divide the research to be done. When panel day arrives, the chairman acts as moderator. The panel is seated at a table in front of the class. Each member is allotted time for short opening remarks, the chairman summarizes, and discussion follows. The last quarter of the hour should be reserved for questions from the class.[22]

Values of the panel discussion as a method for a change of pace for the nonskill business class are outlined briefly by Wright:

1. The panel is currently fashionable in business as a means of communication. . . . Thus, the student is receiving training in a technique he may be called upon to use in his business career.

2. Every opportunity a person has to express his ideas before a group is an enriching experience.

3. An opportunity to do research on a given problem is provided.

4. A challenge to think out some problem to its logical conclusion is likewise presented.

5. A greater fund of knowledge is possible, as each panel in a sense becomes the teacher for the entire class.

6. Members of the class obtain a "close-knit" feeling.[23]

---

[22] John S. Wright, "A New Idea for the Salesmanship Course," *Collegiate News and Views* (October, 1957), pp. 7-8.
[23] *Ibid.*, p. 8.

The Case Problem Method and the Incident Process

As a further variation of the use of group dynamics in nonskill teaching, the business teacher might want to experiment with the case problem method—a teaching technique whereby an actual "case" or incident, or circumstance, is used as a basis for class discussion and problem solving. The case method is not widely used in high school teaching, but it has become quite popular with industrial relations and management groups. The Incident Process, developed by Pigors and Pigors [24] and produced by the Bureau of National Affairs, Inc., is a technique using the case problem, or "incident," as an approach. The problems are taken from actual cases on file in Washington, D. C. under Labor Arbitration Reports—Dispute Settlements. Generally, it is a union-company dispute which has gone to arbitration. The student leader has all the facts, but he gives them out only as answers to questions by the students. The class is given the "incident" in a few words; and to get all the facts, questions must be asked to establish the real reason for the grievance. The incident is a short sketch of something that actually happened. The facts are brought out by group interview of the leader, who has all the information.

After learning all the facts of the grievance, each member of the class renders his decision as if he were the arbitrator of the case. Naturally, the decisions will be different. Usually about one half of the class decides that management is right and the other half favors the employee. Each side then is asked to back up its decisions by reasons. Finally, then, the decision of the arbitrator, who had the actual case, is read to the class. Before leaving this case, the group discusses how this grievance might have been avoided by proper management procedure.*

---

[24] Paul Pigors and Faith Pigors, *The Incident Process* (Washington, D. C.: Bureau of National Affairs, Inc., 1957).

* The description of the Incident Process was contributed by Mr. Ruben Dumler, Division of Business Administration, College of Guam.

Teachers who have used the case method are enthusiastic about it. All the elements of problem solving are there. The values of the case method become clear once the teacher begins to plan: recognition of a central problem, determination of possible solutions, selection of a solution most appropriate under the given circumstances, and relation of theory to the case elements. Satlow stresses a policy of *gradualism* in the use of the case method.

The attack on cases assumes three phases: In the *first phase*, pupils are trained to: (a) select from the facts stated in the problem those that are salient and organize them in their proper time sequence, (b) determine the point in dispute, and (c) settle the argument by ascribing a reason. . . . In the *second phase*, pupils are required to give their answers in terms of legal principles followed by one-word decisions. . . . Upon developing facility in isolating legal principles, the work advances to the *third phase*, in which pupils are introduced to a three-column tabular arrangement which calls for the headings: Principle of Law, Discussion or Application, and Decision. Once this form has been introduced, it is required on all homework, board-work, and tests.

Principle	Discussion	Decision
1. A contract in reasonable restraint of trade is legal.	Cook's promise not to open a grocery store in the entire state was unreasonable.	Yes. He may open a store three blocks away.
2. A contract for personal service terminates when the party who is to perform the service dies.	The painting of a portrait calls for personal services.	No. Mrs. Smith will not be required to sit for the portrait.
3. A promise to pay another person's debt must be in writing.	Clark's promise was an oral one.	No. Brown will not be able to collect.[25]

---

[25] I. David Satlow, "Handling Cases in the Law Class," *Business Education Forum* (November, 1956), p. 28.

Brainstorming

Present-day problems require boldness and imagination on the part of the instructor. A method certain to draw out ideas from the otherwise "quiet" student is known as brainstorming. Dumler gives a comprehensive explanation of the technique and its application:

> Brainstorming is a conference technique which has been used with a great deal of success by banks, schools, churches, the military services, civic organizations, and even political parties. New ideas are difficult to get, but this approach sometimes shakes them loose from the most unexpected sources. Generally, here are some of the basic rules for a successful brainstorming session:
>
> 1. No criticism or evaluation is permitted during the session. Everyone should pop out with *any* idea related to the problem which comes to his mind. No negative ideas are allowed.
> 2. The wilder the idea, the better it is; some of the "silly" solutions hit pay dirt.
> 3. Quantity—the greater the number of ideas, the more likely you are to get acceptable ones.
> 4. Ideas beget ideas. A suggestion of one person may stimulate the thinking of others.
> 5. *All* ideas should be recorded.
> 6. A time limit is set for each session; when the time is up, the meeting is over.
> 7. Later on, the ideas are put into categories and a regular conference is called for evaluation.

In the classroom, problems from the textbook or from everyday life situations can be treated by the brainstorming method. Situations of current importance to everyone offer the best possibilities for the use of the method.[26]

---

[26] This material was contributed by Mr. Ruben Dumler, Division of Business Administration, College of Guam.

The Buzz Group

The buzz group is a discussion technique wherein a problem is placed before the class or assembly as a whole. The topic is briefly explored. At conventions this is frequently done by means of a keynote address. The problem is then broken down into a series of logical subtopics. The class, or group, is divided into small groups. Each section is assigned a subtopic. The small groups organize themselves for action, discuss their assignment briefly and vigorously, then report back to the assembly or class. A statement covering the total solution is then formulated.

The buzz group technique can be applied successfully to nonskill business classes, particularly those influenced by the day's headlines, such as economics and consumer education. One of the best treatments of the buzz group is given by Grambs and Iverson.

> If the teacher wishes to use the "buzz group" idea, it is important that at first he plan it very carefully. The selection of a live issue is crucial. Find some topic that will excite most of the students to express an opinion. . . .
>
> After the issue has been clearly stated, the class can be divided; a group of four or five is about the maximum for this type of short discussion. It is a good idea to put on the board the question around which their discussion should center.
>
> The *time* element should be clear, for it keeps the group members vigorously at work. The time for a buzz group should be as short as possible, commensurate with allowing the members to explore the topic. It is better, however, to allow too little time than too much, because after a topic is exhausted, students easily turn to horseplay and noise. The teacher may have to "call time" before he planned if his prediction of the time necessary to discuss the topic is erroneous. He will then, of course, say to the class that he overestimated how long it would take them to get their ideas in order and that actually they did not need as long as he

had expected. It is also possible that the time will have to be revised in the opposite direction. If the teacher has given the groups five minutes to arrive at a statement of their position on a given issue, but discovers that there is too much to be said before group consensus can be reached, then he can announce, "This topic gets bigger all the time; let's take another ten minutes for the group discussion."

Each group should have a reporter who is appointed by the teacher or by the group. The use of a reporter from each group channels the group's thinking. It also adds the requirement that what the spokesman says is agreeable to all members, thus furthering the need for group consensus. In order to facilitate the choice of reporter when groups are still new to this technique, the teacher can follow this procedure. When the buzz groups are announced, the teacher can walk down the aisles, count off the class by fives, and hand to one student a small card or a sheet of paper on which the buzz-group topic has already been indicated. That individual then acts as the group reporter. Choosing at random helps to draw in some of the more silent and peripheral students. Sometimes it will be necessary to select as reporter some student who will help move the group along, but not dominate it by talking too much himself. In the first trials, the student reporter may need to be someone relatively secure in addressing the class.

To facilitate reporting, the teacher should designate the groups by number immediately after they are organized. "This five will be group 1, and this group of five here will be group 2," and so on. Then when the time comes to call for reports, the possibility of confusion is lessened. Sometimes it helps to place a seating chart on the blackboard and indicate what sections of the room will be used for each group.[27]

Role-Playing—Dramatic Skits

Dramatization may take many forms. The natural tendency of youth to imitate and to mimic suggests the use of

---

[27] Grambs and Iverson, *op. cit.*, pp. 210-211.

dramatic activity for certain nonskill courses. Grambs and Iverson describe the broad scope of dramatic activities for the classroom, regardless of subject area:

> When we were all very young, we used to play "Let's Pretend" and forthwith produced fascinating versions of school, family, cowboys, historical stories. This play acting can be seen among all young children; an observer may often gain new insights into the child's view of the world by hearing a group of four-year-olds "play house. . . ." Not only do the observers learn about the child's world, but the child is going through an interesting learning experience; he is trying out the various real-life or fantasy-life characters that he sees or dreams about. . . . Dramatic play of this sort, both creative and realistic, is utilized in the . . . schools to provide teachers with insight and to develop on the part of the young people a new dimension for learning.[28]

Role-playing differs from the planned play or drama in that emphasis is on individual performance and on the role itself. The classroom teacher who becomes skilled in the basic techniques enjoys a unique opportunity to help pupils explore their own problems. Since role-playing is unrehearsed, it is necessarily free from the restrictions and complications of the apprehensions developed in the course of extensive preparation and rehearsal. McKillop reviews the aims of the use of role-playing for a salesmanship class and illustrates an actual plan for such a class:

> The objectives of such a program (in a class in beginning selling) are three in number: (1) to create tools to aid the teacher in successfully applying theory studied in the classroom, (2) to obtain some measure of the individual's actual ability and progress in the sales situation, (3) to create an atmosphere as close to reality (on-the-job) as possible.

> Let us examine the plan in action. For the first three or four days the instructor created a series of artificial salesman-

---

[28] *Ibid.*, p. 187.

customer situations. The class acts as audience and critics. Then two students were assigned specific parts as in regular role playing. The person who was to play the salesperson was given specific merchandise information, which he could write down or memorize before he was sent out of the room. The salesperson having left the room, the "customer" was then instructed in the part he was to play. Since the customer's objection was the crux of the problem in almost every case, it was very important that he understand his part thoroughly. In that way he could play his part to the hilt. Before the "customer" left, the audience suggested various solutions to the problem and voted on the best solution. The stage had thus been set.

The two players entered and carried out their parts in the drama. As they were carrying on the dialogue, the instructor picked out specific points and jotted them down. When the sales presentation had been concluded, the instructor called these points to the attention of the salesperson and the customer.[29]

Role-playing is only one dramatic technique. Standard written and rehearsed skits are another form. When students are brought into the development and writing of the script itself, even greater values accrue to the learners. For example, the wide range of activities needed to prepare a skit involve the varying capacities of many students, as Claypool indicates:

> Before the skit is actually written, the committee chairman requires a written report listing the law principle involved, the subject matter of the case, and other ramifications. With the approval of the teacher, the teams work to construct the court case. Students use the business department library, the school library, and outside authorities in assembling their case. During the development of the case, an excellent opportunity is provided for a trip to a court of

---

[29] John McKillop, "Role Playing in Sales Classes," *Business Education Forum* (May, 1953), p. 39.

law and an interview with a local attorney, justice of the peace, or another legal official. The trial briefs, when completed, are submitted to the instructor for approval. At this point, the class is reorganized into committees consisting of six or seven members. These committees are the approval committees. They read the submitted manuscripts, check rules of law, and make a list of suggested changes and corrections. The approval committee is returned to members of the committee who wrote the skit; then they revise and revamp their skit. Approximately forty copies of the case brief are reproduced; one is given to each member of the class; and several are kept for our files. Each year the law class prepares approximately ten skits which are given in class. A vote is usually taken to determine the best skit.[30]

In the utilization of this method, the business teacher is cautioned, of course, that the place to develop dramatic techniques and to emphasize dramatic experience is the drama club or drama classes. Although the values of dramatic activity as a creative experience or of self-expression are recognized, these values remain secondary to those of instruction in basic business knowledge and concepts.

Class Report

The current events flavor of class reports on topics of immediate relationship to course subject matter need not restrict the subject fields in which this method is used. It emphasizes the art of reading and reporting, oral and written. For the purpose of giving the reader insight into the actual use of this procedure, the following statement by Davis is given below:

My favorite technique in teaching the nonskill subjects in business requires that students do a certain amount of outside reading in national publications such as *U. S. News*

---

[30] Donald G. Claypool, "Teamwork, Originality, and Understanding through Skits in the Business Law Class," *The Balance Sheet* (January, 1961), p. 211.

& *World Report, Time, Newsweek,* and *Business Week.* It is especially effective in teaching economics and related subjects. This technique can be used particularly well in the latter part of the semester or school term to perk up the group and let them get an idea of the practical application of the subject being studied.

On Mondays—this could be any day of the week for that matter—I ask the students to be prepared to discuss some article concerning economics that they have read during the past week in one of the current magazines or newspapers. At the beginning of the class, I quickly ascertain the topics included in the students' reports. Generally, subjects that are especially timely, such as gross national product, gold movement to and from the United States, government expenditures, are included in this list. After discussing with the group the scope of their articles and their application, one student is chosen to give his report.

I use two methods in promoting class discussion on the basis of this student's report. Sometimes the student completes his report and the class determines how economic theory applies to this situation, but very often I ask that the student let us discuss an issue right at the time it is contained in the report. For instance, if a student should give a report on the deterioration of the stock of gold in the United States, this could start a discussion on "What difference does this make since no one can transfer his money into gold anyway?" or "Why should European nations be interested in our gold supply?" and so on. As can be seen, just one statement taken from one of these reports can stimulate student thinking in many different areas of economics or related subjects.[31]

Maedke presents a further treatment of the value of this reading-reporting device in the nonskill subjects:

Many instructors in the social business area devote one class period, or part of a class period, each week to current

---

[31] This material was contributed by Dr. A. Reed Davis, Dean, West Virginia Institute of Technology, Montgomery, West Virginia.

events affecting the consumer. A good consumer information teacher will encourage the students to bring magazine articles to class. These articles can serve as a reference source of current beliefs, as a basis for drama in committee presentations, and for use in reports.[32]

Chapter VIII contains a procedure whereby the discussion leader can ascertain quickly the extent of reading done by the members of the group. Bahr also has developed an evaluation form for reviewing the reading of the class: [33]

ECONOMIC READING REPORT

By .... Date ....

INFORMATION

Name of Book, Magazine, or Pamphlet ....

....

Author or Authors .... Publisher .... Yr. ....

Topic in Economics to which reference applies ....

....

Number of pages read ....

FACTS

Brief Outline (this may be a summary in outline form, chapter headings, a paragraph on its content, etc.)

OPINIONS

Suitable for ... Freshmen-Sophomores, ... Junior-Senior, ... Adults

Interesting? Yes ... No ...

Compared to our text, Harder to understand ... Easier ...

Compared to Reader's Digest, As interesting ... Not as interesting ...

Evaluate the reading (give your own opinion)

---

[32] Wilmer Maedke, "The Contribution of Popular Magazines to Consumer Education," *Business Education Forum* (October, 1953), p. 37.

[33] Gladys Bahr, "Suggested Classroom Teaching Methods and Techniques in Basic Business Education," *Improved Methods of Teaching the Business Subjects*, Monograph 63 (Cincinnati: South-Western Publishing Company, 1945), p. 78.

Scrapbooks—Notebooks

The scrapbook, in the minds of some teachers, enjoys the dubious distinction as a busywork assignment. As in the case of many other classroom methods, this device has lesser or greater value in direct proportion to the awareness of the teacher as to its possibilities for enriching the learning experiences of children and to its effectiveness in weaving this pupil activity into the total program.

In basic business courses, the keeping of scrapbooks by pupils brings into use a number of fundamental skills—collection, classification, reading, selection, and so on. Heimerl lists the following uses for the scrapbook in a major nonskill subject:

> The consumer student can make analytical collections of advertisements, of labels, of kinds of fabrics and weaves, experiment reports, news clippings appropriate to a specific topic, such as the cost of living.

> Or he can make a notebook on any of a score of important topics such as: a buyer's guide for a particular product, the kinds of insurance, their purposes and costs, clippings about legal cases involving consumer interests, a diary of consumer experiences, an annotated personal budget history.[34]

As a product of committee activity, the scrapbook or notebook may extend the area covered by a unit of study, thereby enriching the total unit experience of the whole class. Rainey describes the use of the notebook technique for a class in economic geography:

> The teacher can have the class prepare an economic-geographic history of the county (or area) in which the school is located, complete with maps, illustrations, statistical tables, and so on. The completed history can then be mimeographed and bound. . . . Several periods should be

---

[34] Heimerl, *op cit.*, p. 17.

spent in conditioning the students for the project before assignments are given. Time spent in developing student interest and motivation will not be wasted. Once the students are motivated, the class can be divided into groups or committees and special assignments and procedural instructions given.[35]

The availability of duplicating equipment is a material aid to the scrapbook-notebook project device. Bahr points out the use of the duplicating machine in making supplementary materials available to the students:

> The duplicating machine may be used as a vital tool in a nonskill business subject. Its product serves as a learning guide to suit the needs of a basic business class as to its interests and abilities.
>
> In an investment unit, the class may need to study the *Wall Street Journal*. A worksheet which alerts the pupils to valuable features of this financial paper can be prepared.
>
> The pupils may need to know facts about basic business in their particular town, state, and the nation. It is well to reproduce the small loan law of the state, the revolving credit terms of a local department store, or comparative business indicators.[36]

Whether the scrapbook is of an individual-student nature, or the product of a committee, its development lends interest and motivation to the nonskill class. An individual-student scrapbook project of particular interest to most nonskill students is described by Arensman and Maxwell:

> 1. Direct students to design their own letterhead. Give them their choice of designing letterheads for (a) companies with which their fathers are affiliated, (b) companies for which students now work, (c) companies for which the

---

[35] Bill G. Rainey, "Economic Geography A'la Mode," *Business Education Forum* (May, 1960), p. 28.

[36] This material was contributed to the authors by Gladys Bahr, New Trier Township High School, Winnetka, Illinois.

students someday intend to work, (d) companies which the students know by national reputation, or (e) imaginary companies.

2. Have students bring in (for a scrapbook) and study letterheads from firms (particularly local) that reflect the nature of the firm and the impression to be created by letterhead content and layout.[37]

Motion Picture Films

A good motion picture film carefully selected, well timed, and skillfully presented is a profitable aid to instruction in nearly all classes. A film may be used to introduce the lesson, project, demonstration, or unit activity in order to stimulate interest and establish a common ground of readiness. When used to introduce a topic area, it can serve as a medium to illustrate the "whole," as, for example, in the study of banking and its related activities. Having once been shown, the film may be rerun as a terminal activity to refresh the memory and to clarify understanding. Timing is important! It is better not to use the film at all than to attempt to "patch it in" at an inappropriate time.

Previewing the film selected from catalog description is essential. It enables the teacher to ascertain specific details so that he can correlate the film content with the lesson, the text, supplementary reading materials, or other materials being used. Previewing shows the teacher how, when, and where it is best to use the film. Some films have decided advantage as introductory materials, such as *Productivity—the Key to Plenty*, which can be used to introduce the beginning course in economic principles, while others increase informational content or are best used for review. Previewing helps students to identify new words and concepts.

---

[37] Ray W. Arensman and Gerald W. Maxwell, "Twelve Motivational Vitamins for Business Correspondence Classes," *Collegiate News and Views* (December, 1959), pp. 5-6.

Much highly desirable class activity may result from the effective presentation of a good film. Class discussion and panel discussions may be more fruitful after the film viewing; optional reading or independent study may be stimulated by it; it may suggest new projects; or it may, and frequently does, evoke questions from the class which suggest the need for additional information or for review of certain areas.

The following suggestions by the Audio-Visual Center of the University of Connecticut for film selection are pertinent:

1. Have valid reasons in mind for using a particular film.

2. Make sure that content fits pupil needs, interests, maturity, and experience levels, subject matter areas being studied, and personal or group problems.

3. Determine the best means of developing student readiness. That is, give an introductory talk, raise questions, show how the film content is related to previous experiences and future plans, and direct attention to those parts of the film action which will reveal or clarify difficulties or issues.

4. Make advance preparation for room darkening and projector operation to avoid distractions and loss of time.

5. Be ready after the presentation to take appropriate action in guiding student reaction to or use of the film experience.[38]

Most classroom showings are conducted under conditions which provide enough light for students to take some notes. For this purpose, a film discussion sheet can be duplicated and distributed before the showing. This instrument can serve both as a means for evaluating the film and for "reminders" in later class discussion. An illustration of such a sheet is given on the following page.

---

[38] From *Films for Teaching*, University of Connecticut, 1956-57.

FILM REVIEW AND DISCUSSION SHEET

Course: _____

Student's Name _____

NAME OF FILM:

SPECIFIC POINTS SHOWN RELATED TO CLASS STUDY:

QUESTIONS ON FILM RELATED TO COURSE:

OTHER STUDY AREAS COVERED BY THE FILM:

REMARKS:

The film follow-up is a critical factor in obtaining full value from the time spent. Giffin lists several points of primary consideration on the follow-up:

1. Discuss the film after it is run. Rerun it if necessary to make certain things clear.

2. Draw conclusions from the story in the film.

3. Relate the story of the film to the lesson and move naturally back into the lesson or unit under consideration, or into the assignment for the following day.

4. Use the experience of the film in subsequent discussions for illustrative purposes.
5. Prepare and use questions based on the film. They should become part of the test used for the unit.[39]

Filmstrips—Slides—Transparencies

Although it may be expected that enthusiasm is greater for certain teaching aids than for others, the use of the motion picture to the complete exclusion of slides, filmstrips, and other projectible materials ignores many devices that are extremely adaptable to the nonskill subjects. The value of any one of these devices is determined by the teacher's method and by the instructional content. The teacher needs to be familiar with slides and other projectible materials in order to use them effectively in his classroom.

In terms of still projection, there is probably no single machine as useful to the teacher in the basic business subjects as the overhead projector. The overhead projector in contrast to the opaque projector, can be used in a fully lighted room. The overhead projector can be used without the necessity of a darkened room and without an expensive screen. Materials for this medium of projection can be tailor-made to fit the particular situation in the teaching plan. With the use of a ball-point pen, opaque carbon paper, cellophane, and a typewriter, readily usable materials can be prepared on the spot or in the teacher's office. For involved, intricate materials diazo transparency film in several colors is available, or one may use auto-positive film which can be processed in only a few minutes.

Instead of trying to place intricate drawings on the board between classes, these transparencies can be prepared in connection with the planning for the course. Artistic inability plagues many teachers with the result that last-minute reliance on the chalkboard reveals efforts of doubtful

---

[39] James F. Giffin, "To Teach Economic Literacy—Show Them!" *Business Education World* (February, 1960), p. 37.

clarity to the students. Types of materials that can be quickly copied for projection are illustrated below: [40]

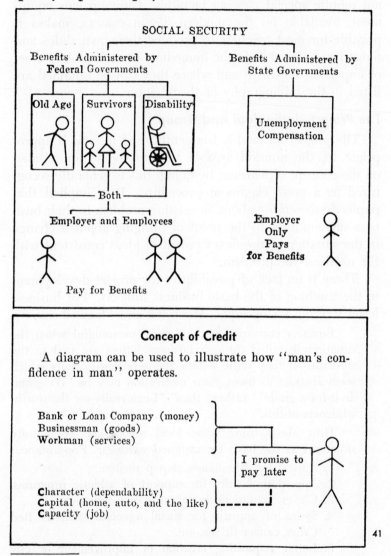

SOCIAL SECURITY

Benefits Administered by
Federal Governments

Benefits Administered by
State Governments

Old Age   Survivors   Disability

Unemployment
Compensation

— Both —

Employer and Employees

Employer
Only
Pays
for Benefits

Pay for Benefits

Concept of Credit

A diagram can be used to illustrate how "man's confidence in man" operates.

Bank or Loan Company (money)
Businessman (goods)
Workman (services)

I promise to
pay later

Character (dependability)
Capital (home, auto, and the like)
Capacity (job)

41

---

[40] Ted J. Boduch, "Developing Concepts in Basic Business," *Business Education Forum* (March, 1960), p. 15.
[41] *Ibid.*

Filmstrips play an important part, too, because they may be used under conditions of less than total darkness and do not require special viewing facilities. Close-up lens equipment, available on the modern 35mm camera, makes it possible for most teachers to produce their own slides and filmstrips, tailored to fit the immediate situation. A number of important filmstrips and where they can be obtained are listed in the bibliography of this chapter.

The Project—Individual and Group

The project method is frequently used in, and is appropriate to, the nonskill area of business education. Based on the concept of learning by doing, this is generally recognized as a good classroom procedure. It is implied that pupils *do something* about an existing problem in their business surroundings to the point of bringing about a change in the situation or the development of ideas consistent with the needs of the problem.

There is no lack of possibilities for project development in the teaching of the basic business subjects. For business letter writing, for example, Arensman and Maxwell say:

> Business correspondence is more meaningful when the situations handled through business letters are real to the students. If they write letters about business affairs which seem abstract to them, their motivation may be "We-gotta-do-it-for-a-grade" rather than "I-can-really-see-the-worth-whileness-of-this."

How about using some local school and community situations as the basis for assigned writings? For instance:

1. Appeal for attendance at pep session.
2. Appeal to faculty for support of athletic programs.
3. Clever invitations to school social activities.
4. Series of appeals for social agencies such as Red Cross, cancer drives, etc.
5. Letter requesting creation or improvement of city parks.

6. Letter turning down selected appeals and requests listed above.
7. Letter explaining why certain "uncomfortable" campus regulations (parking, no running in the halls, etc.) must be enforced.[42]

For organization of a small business Witherill suggests:

> The success of a project depends on careful counseling with each student before, and following, his particular project. In order to make the project as realistic as possible, actual available locations must be found; rental rates (or building costs) obtained; license applications must be obtained and filled out; tax and insurance rates should be obtained and figured; inventory lists prepared complete with costs and suppliers' names and addresses; organization charts must be made; diagrams made of plant or store layout; advertising programs planned. In short, everything should be done except actually spending money.[43]

For a unit in basic business Phelps suggests:

> For the culminating activity in consumer buying units, let each student plan a "dream" house. Such an activity helps bring together the learnings from previous units of study and gives the students an opportunity to see these units in a total perspective and in an applied form. . . . Timid students who have trouble getting started may need a suggested outline of requirements. The outline may include style of house (illustrated by pictures or drawings), a simple plot plan showing position of house on the lot, simple floor plan, special features, exterior features and landscaping, interior decoration and furniture for at least three rooms, estimated cost, method of financing, and insurance plans.[44]

---

[42] Arensman and Maxwell, *loc. cit.*

[43] Robert D. Witherill, "Course Projects Add Realism in Small Business Management," *Collegiate News and Views* (May, 1960), p. 7.

[44] Winona Phelps, "Planning a Home: A Summarizing Activity for the Consumer Buying Units," *Business Education Forum* (May, 1958), p. 29.

The committee technique can be employed in the use of this method. Not only does the pupil do something for himself and further his own development, but he can also become a member of group activity. McGill points out the value of the committee as an adjunct to the project method:

> The committee can be one of the most versatile of the multitude of teaching aids that should be used in the classroom. It is an organizational unit around which almost any kind of activity can be developed. Many different committees can be working simultaneously on different aspects of the same problem area.[45]

Evaluation of the project as a teaching device in the nonskill area is especially essential because it involves varied activities which are carried out over an extended period of time. Witherill presents a justification for the time spent in the use of this procedure:

1. The project stimulates and motivates student interest in the course.

2. Since the business is usually selected by the student, the project provides insight into costs and management problems of a business he may eventually face.

3. Projects tend to point out the validity (or invalidity) of principles taught through classroom lecture.[46]

The project method, despite the opportunity that it provides for learning by doing, is time consuming. It should not be the sole method of instruction when time allocations are sharply limited. In every instance, it should be supported by related reading, by discussion and demonstration, and by the use of well-selected visual aids.

---

[45] E. C. McGill, "How to Make Basic Business Alive," *Business Education Forum* (March, 1957), p. 12,
[46] Witherill, *loc. cit.*

Field Trips—Educational Tours

Educators have granted certain values to the field trip, such as: to enable students to see concrete illustrations of classroom theory; to reinforce understandings developed from reading and discussion; to see, smell, and touch or hear the objects or procesess previously described; to enter into conversation with the people who are actively engaged in business; to ask questions that might not arise in the classroom.

Some exponents of the field trip hold that there must be a "solid" preparation for the trip and the things observed should be carefully outlined and described by the teacher in advance. The students should not be concerned with the novelty of the situation; rather they should observe what is considered as relevant by the teacher. As opposed to this, there are those who say that the value in a trip is to be placed upon the exploratory element, where only the general objective is known, not the details, which the pupils discover for themselves. Whether the educational values to be derived are general or specific will be determined by the purpose of the trip.

Before field trips can be expected to yield benefits to the class beyond "a day off," careful consideration of certain guidepoints must be made:

1. *Purpose of the trip.* "Is this trip necessary?" This question was a common quip during the hectic days of World War II. It is *apropos* to the school class excursion or tour. Is the educational experience gained worth the trouble involved? Students will have to miss other classes; they will require special transportation; legal responsibility will have to be assumed or assigned; parents may have to be notified; advance and follow-up contacts need to be made. Is it worth it?

2. *Preparation for the trip.* If one believes in pre-trip preparation, the following elements are helpful for getting

"in the mood": annual reports of the firm to be visited, descriptive public relations materials about the company, 2 x 2 slides taken by the teacher or an assistant and shown to the class, products made by the company, photographs of the activities of the company.

In addition, advance preparations must be made with officials of the company. This can be done as a class project by letters, phone calls, or personal visits to the people to be visited. Many companies are well prepared for this type of activity as a part of their public relations program. They will have to know the principal objectives of the group, the age or grade level, and other similar details.

School officials will need to approve the trip, and parents must be aware that the pupils will not be in class attendance on the particular time involved. This usually makes necessary an official consent slip signed by the parents concerned and filed in the school administrative office.

3. *Appraisal of the trip.* As soon as possible after the completion of the tour, classes should appraise the results so that the maximum educational value can be derived from the trip. Committee appointments can be used for reports on certain phases of the activities observed. In addition, certain groups can be responsible for a follow-up letter to the firm, expressing thanks to the officials, guides, and others involved. At times, officials of the company are interested enough in seeing the results of the trip that they will consent to visit the classroom for a follow-up discussion. The instructional values of a visit to a company or plant do not terminate with the trip itself. To merely drop the subject or to ignore a follow-up is to leave questions unanswered and opinions unexpressed.

Callan developed a list that can serve well as a basis for a summary checkup device to ascertain the completeness of the trip planning:

1. Will the planned field trip contribute to the student's understanding and appreciation of the problems being studied?

2. Is the planned field trip of sufficient value to warrant the expenditure of time and effort?

3. Has the class assisted in the planning and arranging for the trip?

4. Is the purpose of the trip clearly understood by the members of the class?

5. Have the students been sufficiently prepared to take the trip?

6. Have arrangements been made with the business for the trip at a specific time?

7. Is the trip itinerary carefully planned and flexible?

8. Has the study guide been prepared and used by the class in planning for the trip?

9. Have provisions been made for possible "stragglers"?

10. Have signed consent slips been obtained for each student and filed in the office of the school principal?

11. Have plans been made for an evaluation of the trip? [47]

The Stunt

The stunt is used occasionally by teachers to relieve the monotony of the usual day-to-day routine of the class. It is best used when it fits in with the immediate class situation. If the reader is interested, he might read the article by Beckner [48] in which she presents an excellent stunt "for those tedious times." She suggests the use of the crossword puzzle to develop banking concepts. She has the puzzle all worked out, ready to use. Space does not permit including it here. F. Kendrick Bangs, United Services Editor for that issue of *Business Education Forum* added the following:

---

[47] John Henry Callan, *op. cit.*, p. 14.

[48] Caroline Beckner, "For Those Tedious Times," *Business Education Forum* (December, 1959), p. 24.

The reproduction of this crossword puzzle can be turned into a worthwhile duplicating activity for your students in typewriting, general clerical, or other business classes. The layout, shading, and numbering of the crossword puzzle can be reproduced either by the stencil process or the liquid process for use in your general business class.[49]

Bulletin Boards—Display Boards

So-called "bulletin" boards—tackboards—are found in most schools and classrooms. If these display boards are used only for memos from the administration, the use of a valuable teaching aid is lost.

The bulletin board may be considered an all-purpose board or medium to be used to the fullest possible advantage for many purposes within the school. When designed for entire school use, it serves as a display board for notices of a general nature. In the business classroom, however, it can be used as a unit-development plan board, for display of materials collected, and in connection with class activities. Pictures, maps and charts, graphs, clippings, and three-dimensional materials may be tacked or placed on it. Solid objects may be hung from it to give the illusion of depth. Pupil committees may be assigned the responsibility for providing these displays and for maintaining the board.

Emphasis should, of course, be placed on the *quality* of material for display rather than the *quantity*. A single piece arranged in an especially attractive way may bring greater rewards in conveying a message or concept than greater quantities and variety of material that require considerable time in reading for understanding. *The board that is of especial importance is one that conveys a single idea at a glance, much the same way as our modern billboard.*

The bulletin board is an excellent technique through which the nonskill business subjects can be enriched.

---

[49] *Ibid.*

Even the "first-day jitters" of students can be ameliorated through the use of the bulletin board. Witherow explains the application of this technique:

> Since students usually do not have textbooks the first day, the bulletin board display can be used as a springboard for a short introduction. Then have the class write two or three paragraphs on how business serves them.[50]

In Chapter X and in the bibliography of this chapter sources for free and inexpensive materials are listed. There is no shortage of excellent material for display. In some instances special display boards, such as those described by Lynott, add flexibility to the use of this device:

> The three boards I have are made of beaver board, 33 inches wide by 47 inches long. For all three the cost was less than four dollars. Each board was bound with masking tape for a smooth, neat finish. A wooden easel supports each board, or they can be placed against a blackboard. Portable boards are a valuable aid if you lecture away from your classroom.[51]

The textbook in the nonskill subjects is a source of basic information, but it is important that the teacher go beyond this primary source to make the concepts come alive.

Tape Recorder

One of the modern-day devices of considerable importance in its motivational impact in the nonskill courses is the tape recorder. This teaching aid has been emerging for a number of years, getting its first great impetus in business education in 1953, with Leslie's *Tape Recording in Business*

---

[50] Mary Witherow, "Using Visual Displays in Basic Business to See, to Know, to Remember," *Business Education Forum* (October, 1960), p. 31.

[51] Mary Louise Lynott, "Teaching Aids for Business Letter Writing Courses," *Collegiate News and Views* (October, 1954), p. 15.

Education,[52] and moving ahead rapidly with the establishment of more and more tape collections in libraries in the various states.

Now, with innovations in the manufacture of tape recorders so that high fidelity and precision in recording are made possible under ordinary room conditions, the tape recorder has come into its own. Taped recordings of such programs as "Face the Nation," "Meet the Press," and "American Forum of the Air" are excellent class material. Economics and general business classes respond immediately with the use of this medium of teaching. Current examples of the use of this teaching aid in the nonskill classes are described by Packer:

> In basic courses like business English, business mathematics, business economics, business law, and general business, the recorder is used to record panel discussions and to dramatize student reports. One business English teacher recorded casual conversations and used the playback as a test of his students' alertness to grammatical and pronunciation errors.[53]

Malahan gives more specific examples of today's use of the recorder in this area of business education:

> In sales classes the tape recorder can be used in connection with a term project. If this project is the development of a sales presentation, for example, the final presentation can be more effective and have more meaning when it is taped.
>
> Law classes usually make use of the case method of learning. As good as this method is, it becomes even more effective with the tape recorder. Dramatizing the cases, taping them, and then playing them back to the class helps

---

[52] Louis A. Leslie, *Tape Recording in Business Education* (St. Paul, Minnesota: Minnesota Mining and Manufacturing Company, 1953).

[53] Harry Q. Packer, "Audio-Visual Aids: Using a Tape Recorder to Enrich Instruction," *Business Education World* (December, 1953), p. 27.

the students. They hear the case twice, seem to listen more closely to the points involved, and tend to discuss the case more fully.

Freshman classes in general business, too, provide many opportunities for the use of the recorder. Oral reports that are to be taped are done more conscientiously, and the class will be more attentive to them. More reports will be made on a voluntary basis when students know they will be recorded.[54]

Television

Television, with its added visual element, appears to be enjoying more rapid and more general acceptance as an educational tool than did radio at a comparable stage of development. It appears to hold even greater promise than did radio despite the fact that it takes more time and is more expensive. This newcomer on the educational scene holds a strong potential for enriching the content and method in both the skill and nonskill business courses. Some of the critical problems in secondary education, and in business education in particular, may be resolved through the use of television.

Since television production costs are high, to the point of being prohibitive for many school systems, it is probable that dependence upon commercial stations will continue for years to come.

Current experiments show that a variety of approaches are possible for business education. Stella cites this point of view:

> Since television is a means of video and audio presentation, the traditional lecture class is in danger of "losing its audience" at the very beginning, for it has failed to utilize the video channel for effectiveness in television teaching.[55]

---

[54] Andrew J. Malahan, "Tapes are Tops," *Business Education World* (May, 1959), p. 27.

[55] Mary Stella, "Teaching Shorthand by Television," *Business Education World* (May, 1959), p. 15.

Other experiences indicate a preference for the lecture method through the medium of television, as compared with the classroom lecture:

> In the spring semester of 1954 . . . for the first time, accounting lectures were given on television (in Houston). . . . The favorable points emphasized by students were:
>
> 1. Students were not distracted by classroom noises.
> 2. The difficulty of "back seat" students not being able to see the instructor's work was eliminated.
> 3. Students experienced the psychological reaction that the instructor was talking to the individual watching him, which gave a greater intimacy to the lecture than could be accomplished in the classroom.[56]

The following suggestions are proposed for the teacher faced with the necessity for planning and preparing television programs for school and classroom business education subject matter:

1. Care must be taken that the program content fits the needs and interests of the viewing group.

2. When at all possible, pupil participation in the program should be anticipated and used.

3. Teaching competence and technical excellence in production should be assured.

4. Specific teacher planning and preparation are of primary importance to the success of the medium.

5. The program should fit into the framework of the unit activity, or be integrated rather than "patched in" or superimposed on the unit.

6. As with the use of other methods and devices television is only one of many teaching aids. It should not be used when other methods are more effective.

---

[56] I. E. McNeill, "Teaching Elementary Accounting on Open Broadcast Television," *Collegiate News and Views* (March, 1957), p. 2.

Miscellaneous Techniques

1. **Debate.** Development of the oral facility in the language arts is a part of the task of the business teacher. In the basic business subjects, this facet becomes a significant part of the planning. Students of business *must* be able to communicate effectively orally both in their occupational lives and as members of their community. Material for debate in the nonskills is plentiful.

Debate offers an excellent opportunity to develop points of view and to arouse thinking on facts and concepts that do not often lend themselves to "book" answers. Teams representing sides on such diverse points of view as "What difference does our gold supply make on the value of U. S. money?" arouse interest in certain subject content that might otherwise play second fiddle to a new rock-and-roll record.

Most students are familiar with basic debate techniques. A discussion using this method can be planned and organized on the spur of the moment.

2. **Term Papers.** A time-honored reporting device, the term paper, is still in evidence as a teaching device, particularly in those business subjects in which reading of resource materials is an important part of the course. Happily, the term paper, as a paper, is being rapidly supplanted by the more valuable term project or class report. In the latter methods, students are encouraged, and ultimately expected, to produce material that shows a command of the written word.

Expression of oneself through written communication is essential for all who plan to work in business occupations. Hildreth points out the importance of good written communication and gives suggestions on sound classroom practice for the business teacher:

> Clear, effective writing contributes to effective citizenship through facilitating communication from one person to

another. Good English expression is an essential for anyone who is going into a vocation or profession that demands a high level of skill in writing, e.g., secretarial work, newspaper reporting, teaching, advertising, and so on. . . . One recommendation (to help students organize their ideas in written form) is to eliminate formal theme writing. There are too many occasions in a live school program that require real writing to necessitate spending time on stereotyped compositions. In place of formal theme writing, there can be practice in everyday letter writing, written reports on reading done for class projects, or work on a project that calls for considerable writing, such as getting out an edition of the class paper. Another suggestion is not to demand formal book reviews; but those students who enjoy writing reports of interesting books they have read should be given every encouragement to do so.[57]

3. **The "Analytical Approach."** This method of helping students gain a realistic point of view as opposed to giving "right" answers to students in our business classes, is described by Leith:

Another of our serious problems is that our students have been taught by us to get the "right answer." They assume that there is such an answer to all problems. We "take off" for a strikeover and give full credit for a perfect copy; we use multiple-choice items on our examinations with only one correct answer; we debit cash and we credit sales when a cash sale is made. It is understandable, then, that our students want to know the right answers to business and economic problems. We are obligated, therefore, to help our students understand that in many areas of life there are no definitive right answers; there are only alternative courses of action. This is particularly true in the area of business and economics. A major purpose of the analytical approach in advanced basic business, then, is to help the

---

[57] Gertrude Hildreth, "Remedial Learning in Written Expression," *The Fundamental Processes in Business Education*, American Business Education Yearbook, Vol XII (New York: New York University Bookstore, 1955), p. 144.

student see that there are alternative courses of action—
that he must seek out these alternatives, evaluate them, and
then take that course of action which seems best in the light
of the evidence he is able to obtain.[58]

4. Team Teaching. This relatively new approach to
teaching the basic business subjects has come about, in part,
as a result of continuing teacher shortages in the face of
climbing secondary school enrollments. Experimental efforts
by the Evanston Township High School, Evanston, Illinois,
business department revealed the following factors:

> The use of the teacher-team is an effort to improve the
> quality of education for growing pupil enrollments despite
> a continuing teacher shortage. It is an effort to gain the
> maximum efficiency and effectiveness of personnel and facili-
> ties through optimum use of each.
>
> Team-teaching in basic business at our school means
> joint planning by a group of teachers who teach the same
> subject. The students of all the teachers of the team meet
> in one large group for some lessons and in smaller groups
> for others. Teachers best qualified in a particular phase of
> the subject teach that phase to the large groups; the other
> members of the team concentrate their share of the teaching
> load on their individual strong, specialty areas. . . .
>
> We believe that team-teaching increases the effectiveness
> of instruction. Teacher time is saved, for example, when one
> teacher who is especially qualified in specific area of basic
> business, lectures to the large group composed of four
> conventional-sized classes. The remaining three teachers
> need not be present during the lesson. While one is teach-
> ing, the other three may use the time for planning their
> lessons, grading papers, pupil conferences, parent confer-
> ences, etc. A team of four business teachers now teach a
> total class of 125 students.[59]

---

[58] Harold Leith, "An Advanced Course in Basic Business," *Business Education Forum* (March, 1961), p. 9.

[59] W. G. Carpenter, "Team-Teaching in Basic Business," *The Balance Sheet* (February, 1961), p. 279.

Putting Planning Into Action

The resource unit is a device through which methods and materials are tailored to suit the needs and interests of the particular class or course. In order to introduce the neophyte to this teaching aid, we are including a unit on investments and savings by Heimerl. Here is an excellent example of the meaning of the term "resource unit": [60]

SAVINGS AND INVESTMENT

(A Resource Unit)

The Problem

Good financial planning or budgeting should make provision for savings and investments. Saving money sometimes means that this money is left idle. Investing money implies that it is being used and will be earning a return for the owner as well. Most people do not have the information necessary to make good investments; young consumers should be encouraged to investigate this area of investments to make better use of their money in the future.

Young people are interested in money and probably will be interested in the field of investments if led to see the importance in their future lives. All areas of investments should be covered in this unit—insurance, real estate, stocks, bonds, savings, and investment trusts.

Objectives

1. Recognize the importance of a knowledge of business principles and procedures in individual success.

2. Understand the basic principles involved in investing money in the various possibilities.

3. Show growing strength in the use of a business vocabulary, especially in the area of investments.

---

[60] Ramon P. Heimerl, "Investments and Savings," *Business Education Forum* (March, 1961), pp. 21-23.

4. Realize the influence of business practices upon the general social and economic welfare of the individual.

5. Realize that planning for the future is an important undertaking for all individuals.

6. Provide a knowledge of business practices and principles as an introduction to specialized study of investments.

7. Understand the various methods of saving and investing money that is not used for immediate needs.

8. Evaluate the quality of the many different types of investments which are intangible.

9. Use competent investment information to the advantage of individual investors.

10. Appreciate the possibility of developing a personal philosophy of investment.

Activities to Introduce the Unit

1. Several good students or the teacher can present an oral report on "reasons for investing." Materials can be collected from various sources in the library for this report. Actual personal illustrations may also be given.

2. The film "Capitalism" or "What Is a Corporation" might be presented and then discussed to show the basic organization of business in the American economy. From this the teacher can easily lead into investments of various kinds.

3. A speaker from one of the local brokerage offices or a bank can present an inspirational talk on investments and their purpose in business.

4. Give a pretest on investments to find out just what students do know about this area. The New York Stock Exchange has prepared a pretest entitled "The World of Investing" which will be furnished free to teachers wishing to use this device.

5. A report might be presented on the "profits theory" of business. Materials for such a report might be obtained from various pamphlets published by the U. S. Chamber of Commerce or the National Association of Manufacturers. See the listing at the end of this unit under materials.

Developmental Activities

1. Have a class discussion on the meanings of savings, investment, and speculation. Perhaps for this discussion, readings should be assigned so that the discussion will proceed smoothly and effectively.

2. Reading and discussion on the criteria for investments—what guides do investors look for before making an investment?

3. Reports on the various methods of savings investments can be presented by individuals after careful study.

4. Discussion and analysis of the various methods of savings possible in the community. Perhaps the teacher can direct the discussion which may end with a graphic presentation on the chalkboard of advantages and disadvantages of each.

5. Each student will keep a graphic record of four investments for a period of one month. He may select stocks, bonds, insurance, a mutual fund, or other investment that can be plotted. This procedure will enable students to follow the financial reports in the daily newspaper.

6. A committee of students present a discussion on "How to Read a Financial Report." For the background, students may use a booklet by this title published by Merrill, Lynch, Pierce, Fenner & Smith, Inc., 70 Pine Street, New York 5, New York (28 pages, 1960, free).

7. Field trip to a brokerage office or stock exchange, if possible. Students should be prepared to look for the following things: explanation of quotation board, the buying and selling process, ticker tape or electronic board in operation, actual buying and selling of stocks or bonds.

8. Students present discussions of current events dealing with investments. The financial pages of daily papers can furnish much useful information concerning investments.

9. Students should become familiar with the *Wall Street Journal.* If possible, secure copies for all students.

10. Students can prepare skits on the sale of investments. The teacher might portray the part of the salesman in order to demonstrate the unscrupulous methods that may be used.

11. Guest speakers may be invited to the class and speak on the following topics: government savings bonds, investment trusts or mutual funds, investment counseling, insurance programs as a means of investment, postal savings.

12. Debate the various kinds of investments, such as mutual funds versus buying stock directly. Many other topics can be organized for the capable students. However, debate involves very careful preparation on the subject. Each participant should be prepared on both sides of the issue.

13. Purchasing a share of stock may be carried out. Usually the class members contribute a certain amount and the certificate of stock is purchased in the teacher's name. At the end of the unit or year, the share may be sold through a broker or to the teacher at the market price.

14. Show the New York Stock Exchange film "What Makes Us Tick." This film presents clearly in animated, cartoon form the workings of the stock exchange.

15. Present either "Working Dollars" or "Your Share in Tomorrow," two other films produced by the New York Stock Exchange. These present the process of investing using the monthly investment plan and the role of capital and investors in the growth of American industry respectively.

16. Students are to keep a complete notebook on the investment unit. Some of the materials that they should collect include class notes, reading notes, newspaper and magazine articles and summaries regarding financial matters, vocabulary, information on each type of investment, and operation of the stock market.

17. Committees can work on the collecting of advantages and disadvantages of each type of investment. These can be presented in graphic form to the entire class for discussion.

18. Individual students can bring in samples of various kinds of investments. These can be explained to the class by means of an opaque projector and a short talk by the student.

Summarizing Activities

1. Students may be divided into committees according to the various kinds of investments. Each committee will

present to the group an explanation of "Why we would invest money in _____." This explanation period may be followed by general questions from the class to further clarify the viewpoints.

2. Debates, forums, and symposiums can be conducted on various topics dealing with investments. These are effective only after sufficient study. Such a technique would indicate whether the better students in the class really understand the principles of investments.

3. Showing the New York Stock Exchange film "Your Share in Tomorrow" will summarize the place of investments in American economy.

4. Use case problems on investments. Good examples of cases may be found in some of the textbooks.

Evaluation Procedures

1. Give the New York Stock Exchange test on "The World of Investing" again and compare the results of those of the pretest given.

2. Problem cases can be devised to check on the application of investment principles to actual cases.

3. A vocabulary spell-down might be of help in clinching the meaning of terms used in the investment unit.

4. Essay tests on various kinds of investments will give the students an opportunity to demonstrate the extent of their understanding of investments.

5. Various kinds of tests can be given throughout the unit as activities are completed.

6. Teachers should evaluate all the activities of the unit and all the tangible work produced during the study.

Suggestions for Teachers

1. In this unit there is an opportunity to stimulate and challenge the good students in class. Certainly many of the phases of investments are rather involved and this should be a real opportunity to dig into more complicated materials.

2. The teacher should study the area of investments carefully beforehand so as to avoid unnecessary delay in getting the unit started.

3. Experiences of students and their families can be used to advantage in the classroom. However, avoid criticizing personal investments of members of the class or their families. The teacher must be very objective about this situation.

4. The community resources should be used extensively so that the students will understand how to use the services provided by business firms.

5. This unit is not intended to prepare experts in the field of investments, but stresses understanding the principles and seeing their application to actual situations. Knowing where to get expert help should also be an outcome of this unit.

Special Materials for Unit

1. Graph paper for charting progress of stock.

2. Copies of *The Wall Street Journal* or a daily newspaper to find the market quotations.

3. Actual stock certificates.

4. A kit containing materials for four presentations on "How Our Business System Operates" from National Association of Manufacturers, 2 East 48th Street, New York 17, New York.

5. Economics Chart Service for Educators, Educational Department, National Association of Manufacturers, 2 East 48th Street, New York 17, New York.

6. The National Industrial Conference Board, 460 Park Avenue, New York 22, New York. "Road Maps of Industry," series of graphs dealing with all phases and problems of American business.

7. Portfolio of Teaching Aids, New York Stock Exchange, P.O. Box 252, New York 5, New York. Teachers can secure copies for each student of "You and the Investment World."

Films

† *What Makes Us Tick?* 12 min., color, animated cartoon, 1952. Explains what stocks are and how the Stock Exchange works.

† *Working Dollars.* 13 min., color, animated cartoon, 1956. An engaging story of how an average man puts his dollars to work by investing in the Monthly Investment Plan.

† *Your Share in Tomorrow.* 27 min., color, 1957. Describes the role of capital and investors in the growth of American industry.

‡ *Capitalism.* 11 min., B & W or color, 1948. Important aspects of the capitalistic system are illustrated—private property, profit, competition, freedom of contract, free enterprise, and government regulation.

‡ *What Is a Corporation?* 11 min., B & W or color, 1949. Advantages and disadvantages of three types of business organizations are explained.

‡ *Work of the Stock Exchange.* 16 min., B & W or color, 1941. Part the Stock Exchange plays in economic structure is explained.

‡ *Understanding the Dollar.* 11 min., B & W or color, 1953. Shows how the changing value of a dollar affects the lives of people with various sources of income.

Pamphlets

About This Stock and Bond Business, 1960, 31 pages, free

How To Invest, 1960, 20 pages, free

Over-the-Counter Securities, 1961, 20 pages, free
Merrill, Lynch, Pierce, Fenner & Smith, Inc.
70 Pine Street
New York 5, New York

---

† Available on free loan from New York Stock Exchange, 11 Wall Street, New York 5, New York, or the nearest branch of Modern Talking Pictures.

‡ Available for purchase from Coronet Films, 65 E. So. Water Street, Chicago 1, Illinois, or perhaps on loan from a nearby film library.

Money Management, Your Savings and Investment Dollar,
  1959, 38 pages, 15 cents
  Money Management Institute
  Household Finance Corporation
  Prudential Plaza
  Chicago 1, Illinois

Regulations Governing U. S. Savings Bonds, Department
  Circular 530, eighth revision, 1957, 22 pages, free
  U. S. Treasury Department
  Washington 25, D. C.

* *Understanding the Modern Securities Market,* 1961, 32
  pages, 50 cents
  Commodity Research Publications Corporation
  82 Beaver Street
  New York 5, New York

* *Stock Exchange Paces U. S. Progress,* 1957

You and the Investment World, 1961, 6 pages, free

Types of Business Organizations, 1961, 6 pages, free

The American Corporation, 1961, 6 pages, free

Stocks: Common and Preferred, 1961, 6 pages, free

Bonds: Government, Municipal, and Corporate, 1961, 6
  pages, free

Buying and Selling Stocks, 1961, 6 pages, free

New York Stock Exchange, 1961, 6 pages, free

Capitalists: Investors in the Nation's Business, 1961, 6 pages,
  free

Investing for American Families, 1961, 6 pages, free

The Newspaper and the Investor, 1961, 6 pages, free

Sources of Information on Investments, 1961, 6 pages, free

The Investor in American History, 1961, 6 pages, free
  New York Stock Exchange
  11 Wall Street
  New York 5, New York

---

* Materials suggested for teacher use and for use by better students.

Over-the-Counter Trading Handbook, 1960, 26 pages, free to
  schools
National Association of Securities Dealers, Inc.
1707 H Street, N. W.
Washington 6, D. C.

Let's Look at Stocks and Bonds, 1959, 28 pages, 6 cents
San Francisco Division
Pacific Coast Stock Exchange
310 Pine Street

° *Profits—Something for Everyone,* 1957, 36 pages, 50 cents
San Francisco 4, California
Economic Research Department
Chamber of Commerce of the United States
Washington 6, D. C.

Books

° Clendenin, John C. *Introduction to Investments,* Third
Edition. New York: McGraw-Hill Book Company, Inc.,
1960, 689 p.

° Cohen, Jerome B., and Hanson, Arthur W. *Personal
Finance: Principles and Case Problems,* Revised Edition.
Homewood, Illinois: Richard D. Irwin, Inc., 1958. Chs. 12-15.

Cooper, Robert U. *Investments for Professional People,*
Revised Edition. New York: Macmillan, 1959, 342 p.

° Donaldson, Elvin. *Personal Finance,* Second Edition.
New York: The Ronald Press, 1956. Chapters 17-23.

Kamm, Jacob O. *Economics of Investment.* New York:
American Book Company, 1951, 547 p.

Livingston, J. A. *The American Stock Holder.* Philadelphia: J. B. Lippincott, 1958, 290 p.

Roussile, Gladys V. G. *What's a Good Investment?* New
York: Barron's Publishing Company, 1940, 98 p.

Scott, Edgar. *How to Lay a Nest Egg.* Chicago: John
C. Winston Company, 1950, 65 p.

Troelstrup, Arch W. *Consumer Problems and Personal
Finance,* Second Edition. New York: McGraw-Hill Book
Company, Inc., 1957. Chapters 12 and 13.

Wilson, W. Harmon, and Eyster, Elvin S. *Consumer
Economic Problems,* Fifth Edition. Cincinnati: South-
Western Publishing Company, 1961. Chapters 16, 18, and 19.

° Materials suggested for teacher use and for use by better students.

SUMMARY

Good teachers of the nonskill business subjects, as the reader has seen from the references given, have been rather successful in making their teaching effective. Their close alliance with the development of the motor skills and repetitive practice classes has not kept them from seeing value in providing a way of learning which enables the pupils to experience activity with all the senses.

One point of caution is evident in all that we have tried to present in this section of the book: excessive talking by the teacher, without reinforcement by other materials, robs the pupils of time and opportunity for more valuable experiences. Pupils either do not like the "talking" business courses or they become apathetic and let the discussion "bounce off" so that the teacher is conducting a one-man show. Sensory aids and group dynamics are challenging, realistic supplements to verbalized course material.

We hope that the techniques described will induce the new and inexperienced nonskills business teacher to utilize and refine methods of his own to fit his immediate classroom situation.

SELECTED BIBLIOGRAPHY

Business Education Forum. Washington, D. C.: The National Business Education Association (formerly The United Business Education Association), March issues.

Callan, John Henry. *Community Resources Handbook in Business Education,* Monograph 87. Cincinnati: South-Western Publishing Company, 1954.

Crabbe, Ernest H., Herman G. Enterline, and S. Joseph DeBrum. *Methods of Teaching General Business.* Cincinnati: South-Western Publishing Company, 1959.

Dale, Edgar. *Audio-Visual Methods in Teaching*, Revised Edition. New York: The Dryden Press, 1954.

Dodd, James Harvey. *Economics in the Secondary Schools*, Monograph 80. Cincinnati: South-Western Publishing Company, 1953.

Douglas, Lloyd V., James T. Blanford, and Ruth I. Anderson. *Teaching Business Subjects*. Englewood Cliffs, New Jersey: Prentice-Hall, Inc., 1958.

Enterline, Herman G. "Using Discussion Techniques in Teaching General Business," *The Balance Sheet*. Cincinnati: South-Western Publishing Company (October, 1955).

Evaluating Competence for Business Occupations, American Business Education Yearbook, Vol. VII. New York: New York University Bookstore, 1950.

Fickett, Lewis P., Jr., and Christobel M. Cordell. *Colorful Teaching of Business Law*. Portland, Maine: J. Weston Walch, 1954.

Freeman, M. Herbert. *Basic Business for Everyday Living*, Monograph 74. Cincinnati: South-Western Publishing Company, 1951.

Grambs, Jean D., and William J. Iverson. *Modern Methods in Secondary Education*. New York: The Dryden Press, 1952.

Hansen, Kenneth J. "What Every Young Business Teacher Should Know," *The Journal of Business Education* (December, 1951).

Hardaway, Mathilde, and Thomas B. Maier. *Tests and Measurements in Business Education*, Second Edition. Cincinnati: South-Western Publishing Company, 1952.

How to Teach Business Subjects. Washington, D. C.: The National Business Education Association, 1959.

How to Use Group Discussion, No. 6, How to Do It Series. Washington, D. C.: The National Council for the Social Studies, 1952.

Huffman, Harry. "Will Teaching Machines Make You Obsolete?" *Business Education World* (February, 1960), 11-13.

Improved Methods of Teaching the Business Subjects, Monograph 63. Proceedings of 1945 Business Education Institute,
Teachers College, University of Cincinnati. Ray G. Price,
ed. Cincinnati: South-Western Publishing Company, 1945.

Kuhns, Caroline. "Role-Playing in Classroom Selling Situations,"
Business Education Forum (May, 1959), 30-31.

Let's Educate Youth for Effective Business Life, Monograph 98.
Cincinnati: South-Western Publishing Company, 1959.

Lloyd, Alan C. "Student Projects in General Business," *Business
Education World* (April, 1954), 17-18.

Lomax, Paul S. "Vital Trends and Problems in the Administration and Supervision of Business Education," *The National
Business Education Quarterly* (May, 1960), 36.

"Make Youth Discussion Conscious!" *A Handbook on Discus-
sion Techniques for the Classroom, School Assemblies, and
Youth Forums.* Columbus, Ohio: The Junior Town Meeting
League, 1948.

National Council on Geographic Education. *Geography Via
Television.* Norman, Oklahoma: University of Oklahoma,
1958.

*Portfolio of Teaching Techniques (Including Tested Practices in
Group Dynamics for the Classroom Teacher).* New London.
Conn.: Educators' Washington Dispatch.

Stolurow, Lawrence M., and Leonard J. West. "Teaching Machines and Self-Instructional Programming," *Delta Pi Epsilon
Journal* (April, 1961).

*Teaching Economic Understanding through Secondary School
Business Subjects.* New York: Joint Council on Economic
Education, 1952.

Tonne, Herbert A. "Evaluation in the Social-Business Subjects,"
Business Education Forum (March, 1953).

——————, Estelle L. Popham, and M. Herbert Freeman.
Methods of Teaching Business Subjects, Second Edition.
New York: Gregg Publishing Division, McGraw-Hill Book
Company, Inc., 1957.

Tracy, Myles A. "Family Finance: Timely Topic for Television," *The Journal of Business Education* (January, 1960), 26-29.

Wood, Marion. "We Taught Better Office Procedures by TV," *Business Education World* (February, 1960), 18-20.

SUPPLEMENTARY MATERIALS

Films

How We Live in America, American Economic Foundation, New York, 1955.

What Makes Us Tick? Modern Talking Pictures, Inc., 3 East 54 Street, New York 22, New York.

The Story of Distributive Education, Modern Talking Pictures, Inc., 3 East 54 Street, New York 22, New York.

Using Bank Credit, American Institute of Banking, 629 South Hill Street, Los Angeles 14, California.

Understanding the Law, Business Education Films, 4607—16th Avenue, Brooklyn 4, New York.

Sharing Economic Risks, Business Education Films, 4607—16th Avenue, Brooklyn 4, New York.

Work of the Stock Exchange, Business Education Films, 4607—16th Avenue, Brooklyn 4, New York.

Introduction to Foreign Trade, Business Education Films, 4607—16th Avenue, Brooklyn 4, New York.

Wise Buying, Coronet Films, 65 East South Water Street, Chicago 1, Illinois.

Basic Court Procedures, Coronet Films, 65 East South Water Street, Chicago 1, Illinois.

Basic Elements of Production, Encyclopedia Britannica Films, Box 358, Wilmette, Illinois.

Your Money Is What You Make It, National Association of Manufacturers, 2 East 48 Street, New York 17, New York.

It's Everybody's Business, Chamber of Commerce of the United States, 1615 H Street, N. W., Washington, D. C.

Living Under Law, Michigan Bar Association, 300 Michigan National Tower, Lansing 8, Michigan.

Office Supervisors' Problems, Set I: *The Follow-Through, The Grapevine, How Much Cooperation, In the Middle, The Bright Young Newcomer, By-Passed,* Text-Film Department, McGraw-Hill Book Company, Inc., 330 West 42 Street, New York 36, New York.

Office Supervisors' Problems, Set II: *The Missing Interest, Danger—Work Improvement Ahead, The Short Circuit, The Sour Grape, The Popularity Contest, The Logical Mistake,* Text-Film Department, McGraw-Hill Book Company, Inc., 330 West 42 Street, New York 36, New York.

Filmstrips

Directing Your Dollars, Institute of Life Insurance, Educational Division, 488 Madison Avenue, New York 22, New York.

How Life Insurance Operates, Institute of Life Insurance, Educational Division, 488 Madison Avenue, New York 22, New York.

Your Money's Worth in Shopping, Money Management Institute of Household Finance Corporation, Prudential Plaza, Chicago 1, Illinois.

How to Stretch Your Food Dollars, Money Management Institute of Household Finance Corporation, Prudential Plaza, Chicago 1, Illinois.

Handling Difficult Employees, Variety Merchandiser Publications, Film Division, 192 Lexington Avenue, New York 16, New York.

Supervisory Problems in the Office, Set I: *Understanding of Employee Viewpoint, Error-Correction Talk, Motivating the Long-Service Employee, Orientation and Induction, Combatting Job Monotony, Excessive Supervision,* Text-Film Division, McGraw-Hill Book Company, Inc., 330 West 42 Street, New York 36, New York.

Supervisory Problems in the Office, Set II: *The Corrective Guidance Talk, Developing Team Spirit, Easing a Disappointment, Making Compliments Count, Overcoming Resistance to New Methods, Rating Employee Performance*, Text-Film Division, McGraw-Hill Book Company, Inc., 330 West 42 Street, New York 36, New York.

Selling with a Modern Touch, E. I. du Pont de Nemours and Company, Inc., Motion Picture Distribution, Wilmington 98, Delaware.

Behind Each Sale, Modern Talking Pictures, Inc., 3 East 54 Street, New York 22, New York.

Sources of Supplementary Materials for the Nonskill Subjects

100 Selected Films in Economic Education, Joint Council on Economic Education, New York, 1960.

Baited Bulletin Boards, Fearon Publishers, 2450 Fillmore Street, San Francisco 15, California.

Educator's Guide to Free Tapes, Scripts, and Transcriptions, Educators Progress Service, Randolph, Wisconsin, 1959.

Film Evaluation for Business Education, Volume I, Delta Pi Epsilon, North Texas State University, Denton, Texas, 1959.

Film Evaluation for Business Education, Volume II, Delta Pi Epsilon, North Texas State University, Denton, Texas, 1960.

The Incident Process, Bureau of National Affairs, Inc., Washington, D. C., 1957.

Suggestions for a Basic Economics Library for Secondary Schools, Joint Council on Economic Education, New York, 1959.

"The High School Business Library," *American Business Education*, Manchester Regional High School, Haledon, New Jersey, May, 1960.

Visual Aids for Business and Economic Education, Monograph 92, South-Western Publishing Company, 5101 Madison Road, Cincinnati 27, Ohio, 1956.

CHAPTER X

THE WORKING TOOLS OF THE MODERN BUSINESS EDUCATOR

"Know thyself" is an oft-repeated admonition from the scholar Socrates. Ideally, teachers should examine themselves periodically. Attempts at self-analysis are futile unless followed by real efforts of self-improvement. These efforts are varied. However, certain basic areas have been general targets for specific self-help: (1) interest in the profession of teaching, (2) attitudes toward students, (3) professional preparation, and (4) continued personal improvement.

It is the intent of the authors to assist in at least one of these significant areas by providing sources of instructional materials, or "working tools," in this chapter. One gains stature in his profession as he learns better ways of achieving desirable results. The teacher who has experimented with several techniques is more capable of handling a new situation. The teacher who has acquired a rich background in his field can make a better selection of material for his needs. The beginning teacher, however, has had little opportunity to practice the profession of teaching and therefore needs guidance in the selection and procurement of valuable teaching materials. Someone has said, "We do not know unless we know *something*." The credits filed in the registrar's office in our *alma mater* are of no use to us unless we can put this content to work for us. Mere exposure to content that leaves one unchanged is not education. One's personality must change, must grow. "Education is growth," said Dewey; and one continues to grow only as long as he feeds this growth through added social and educational experiences.

One of the factors that contribute to teaching success is a deep, abiding curiosity concerning interest-arousing materials. Files of procedures, methods, evaluative criteria, and general classroom materials should accompany the relatively brief notes used for the general outline of the course. It is our concern in this chapter to assist the beginning business teacher in familiarizing himself with sources of the materials for business education.

The materials of business education are those which most readily prepare youth for business. Materials are aids to learning which increase the effectiveness of the teacher. They stimulate interest, simplify, clarify, increase understanding, and motivate the student to learn. Materials are the tools of the teacher and are the agents which assist in transforming the natural interest, curiosity, and talent of the pupil into knowledge and understanding. The teacher uses these materials to achieve the objectives set for the course. This apparent emphasis on the use of materials, or tools ("gimmicks," to some), is not intended to deny the importance of words in teaching and learning. Many of the tools in this chapter *are* words. It is through words that the world's culture is transmitted. Seldom do we find adequate substitutes for words and their abstract meanings.

The difference between the slow and fast learner is not merely in understanding abstractions. Indeed, it is the extreme variation in learning capacities, coupled with problems of the English language and its complexities, which makes imperative the use of a wide variety of teaching aids to support the meaning of the spoken word. *All of us who teach must finally accept this fact.*

In certain instances extra-textbook materials must be considered as substitutes for words; in others, as supplementary materials which further enrich and strengthen learning. The following diagram, patterned greatly after a graphic device which illustrates the economic concept of supply, demand, and price intends to show the range between the concrete and the abstract and the part that supplementary tools play in lessening this tremendous gap:

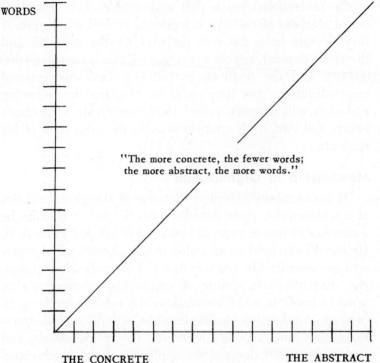

WORDS

"The more concrete, the fewer words; the more abstract, the more words."

THE CONCRETE   THE ABSTRACT

The extent to which the enrichment of courses is necessary is indicated by Hoban and his associates:

> If varied experience has already developed wide and manifold differentiation and integration from the concrete through the intermediate levels of experience to the meaningful use of words (verbalization), further visual aids are unnecessary for the development of progressive abstraction.[1]

[1] Charles F. Hoban, Charles F. Hoban, Jr., and Samuel B. Zisman, *Visualizing the Curriculum* (New York: The Dryden Press, 1937), p. 23.

Since the use of supplementary aids has relative value in developing otherwise abstract concepts, the teacher must use every source wisely. All subjects do not lend themselves to the same teaching aids. Judicious choice making is part of the professional touch that makes a *teacher*. Inexperienced teachers often have a tendency to feel inadequate if they deviate from the sure path set by the textbook and therefore depend largely upon the lecture, occasional discussion, and the textbook in fulfilling their instructional responsibilities. Any time spent in adapting the following materials will simplify rather than complicate a teacher's efforts and enrich his contributions to the education of his students.

Membership in Organization

It is commonly accepted that one of the characteristics of a wide-awake, up-to-date business teacher is that he be a member of one or more associations in his particular field. He should also hold membership in organizations that represent community-life participation: Parent-Teacher, Lions, etc. Executives in charge of employing teachers usually want to know in what associations the teacher holds membership. Application blanks almost universally include questions that endeavor to ascertain the professional- and community-mindedness of the applicant. Teacher-education institutions tend to stress the importance of professional alertness.

The reason for urging teachers to become members of professional and community organizations is that no man is sufficient unto himself. Trade associations can be traced back almost to the beginning of business history. Business education must constantly keep up with developing conditions in business and industry. Unless the clearinghouse of ideas in business education is kept open and unless all business teachers become active in the operation of this clearinghouse, business will continue to step out ahead of education, and many teachers will unknowingly develop in their students skills and personality factors that fail to function in actual practice.

All business teachers should be members of a national and a local association in business education. Department heads, committee chairmen, and others holding leadership positions should consider affiliating themselves with some of the other associations and groups listed on the following pages.

1. Professional associations in business education.

    a. National

        National Business Education Association (a department of the National Education Association), 1201 Sixteenth Street, N. W., Washington 6, D. C. (Formerly United Business Education Association)

        National Association for Business Teacher Education (NBEA Division), Research Foundation for the NBEA International Society for Business Education (U. S. Chapter), Administrators Division of the NBEA

        American Vocational Association, Inc., 1010 Vermont Avenue, N. W., Washington 5, D. C.

        Catholic Business Education Association, Duquesne University, Pittsburgh, Pennsylvania

        Delta Pi Epsilon, North Texas State University, Box 6402, NT Station, Denton, Texas

    b. Regional

        Commercial Education Association of the City of New York and Vicinity

        Eastern Business Education Association

        Eastern Business Teachers Association

        Mountain-Plains Business Education Association

        North-Central Business Education Association

        Southern Business Education Association

        Western Business Education Association

c. State and local

State and local business teacher organizations have either separate or nationally-affiliated units directed toward improvement of business education.

2. Professional education associations

National Education Association
National Association of Secondary School Principals
American Association of School Administrators
National Society for the Study of Education
State units affiliated with NEA
Local units affiliated with NEA

3. Associations of persons not directly connected with business education or professional education but valuable to business teachers.

American Accounting Association
National Secretaries Association International
American Management Association
National Office Management Association
American Psychological Association
Local civic organizations (Rotary, Kiwanis, Lions, etc.)

Teachers' Reference Materials

The critical nature of the times requires in-service training now more than ever. The need for in-service growth is perhaps greater for the business teacher than in any other area of teaching. The constantly changing methods and materials of business, the new ways of doing things, and the constantly evolving technological changes are reasons for the business teacher to continue to grow after the completion of his "formal" training.

One of the most common ways, and perhaps the least involved, of continuing in-service growth is through the constant review of new methods and developments as reflected through published materials. It's true, of course, that one cannot begin to read everything printed, even for a small segment of a profession. The listed items that follow are the nucleus of regular reading materials that are up to date and important in terms of today's practices in business and in education.

1. Publications of professional associations and organizations.

a. Business education periodicals:

ABWA Bulletin, The American Business Writing Association, 1007 West Nevada Street, Urbana, Illinois

American Business Education, Eastern Business Teachers Association, Manchester Regional High School, Haledon, New Jersey

Business Education Forum, National Business Education Association, 1201 Sixteenth Street, N.W., Washington 6, D. C.

Business School Executive, National Association and Council of Business Schools, 2400 Sixteenth Street, N. W., Washington 9, D. C.

Catholic Business Education Review, Catholic Business Education Association, Duquesne University, Pittsburgh, Pennsylvania

EBTA Journal (Successor to *American Business Education*), The Eastern Business Teachers Association, 1368 Commonwealth Avenue, Brighton 34, Massachusetts.

International Review for Business Education, International Society for Business Education, Samuel Schaffner, Ed., Kirchlistr. 59, St. Gall, Switzerland

NABTE Bulletin, National Association for Business Teacher Education, National Business Education Association (formerly United Business Education Association), 1201 Sixteenth Street, N. W., Washington 6, D. C.

National Business Education Quarterly, National Business Education Association, 1201 Sixteenth Street, N. W., Washington 6, D. C.

The Secretary, The National Secretaries Association, 10214 Crane Road, Kansas City 34, Missouri

b. Monographs and yearbooks:

American Business Education Yearbook, Joint Publication Commission of the Eastern Business Teachers Association and the National Business Teachers Association, New York University Bookstore, 18 Washington Place, New York 3, New York.

EBTA Yearbook, Eastern Business Teachers Association.

The Delta Pi Epsilon Journal, Delta Pi Epsilon, North Texas State University, Box 6402, NT Station, Denton, Texas

Yearbook of the CEA, Commercial Education Association of New York and Vicinity, New York University Bookstore, 18 Washington Place, New York 3, New York

c. Other professional publications useful to the business teacher:

Accounting Review, American Accounting Association, School of Commerce, University of Wisconsin, Madison 6, Wisconsin

American Vocational Journal, American Vocational Association, Inc., 1010 Vermont Avenue, N. W., Washington 5, D. C.

Bulletin of the National Association of Secondary-School Principals, National Association of Secondary-School Principals, 1201 Sixteenth Street, N. W., Washington 6, D. C.

Journal of Higher Education, Ohio State University Press, Columbus, Ohio

Journal of the National Education Association, National Education Association, 1201 Sixteenth Street, N. W., Washington 6, D. C.

Junior College Journal, American Association of Junior Colleges, 1785 Massachusetts Avenue, N. W., Washington 6, D. C.

2. Publications of private organizations.

   a. For business education:

      The Balance Sheet, South-Western Publishing Company, 5101 Madison Road, Cincinnati 27, Ohio

      Business Education Newsletter, Educational Book Division, Prentice-Hall, Inc., Englewood Cliffs, New Jersey

      Business Education World, Gregg Publishing Division, McGraw-Hill Book Company, Inc., 330 West 42 Street, New York 36, New York

      The Business Educator, Allied Publishers, Inc., 645 S. E. Ankeny, Portland 14, Oregon

      The Business Teacher, Gregg Publishing Division, McGraw-Hill Book Company, Inc., 330 West 42 Street, New York 36, New York

      Collegiate News and Views, South-Western Publishing Company, 5101 Madison Road, Cincinnati 27, Ohio

      Journal of Business Education, Trethaway Publishing Company, Inc., 512 Brooks Building, Wilkes-Barre, Pennsylvania

      The Pitmanite, Pitman Publishing Corporation, 2 West 45 Street, New York 36, New York

      Systems for Educators, School Department of Remington Rand Division, Sperry-Rand Corporation, 315 Fourth Avenue, New York 10, New York

      Today's Secretary, Gregg Publishing Division, McGraw-Hill Book Company, Inc., 330 West 42 Street, New York 36, New York

      Typewriting News, South-Western Publishing Company, 5101 Madison Road, Cincinnati 27, Ohio

   b. For general use:

      Administrative Management (formerly *Office Management and American Business*), Geyer-McAllister Publications, 212 Fifth Avenue, New York 10, New York

Advanced Management—Office Executive, National Office Management Association, 1927 Old York Road, Willow Grove, Pennsylvania

Nation's Schools, Modern Hospital Publishing Company, Nation's Schools Division, 919 North Michigan Avenue, Chicago 11, Illinois

The Office, Office Publications, Inc., 232 Madison Avenue, New York 16, New York

3. Publications of state organizations and institutions.

The Ball State Commerce Journal, Department of Business Education, Ball State Teachers College, Muncie, Indiana

Beacons on Business Education, Department of Business Education, Central Connecticut State College, New Britain, Connecticut

The Kansas Business Teacher, Kansas Business Teachers Association, Abilene High School, Abilene, Kansas

Michigan Business Education Association News Bulletin, Michigan Business Education Association, 26565 Midway, Dearborn, Michigan

The Ohio Business Teacher, Ohio Business Teachers Association, Miami University, Oxford, Ohio

Virginia Business Education Bulletin, Business Education Service, State Department of Education, Richmond 16, Virginia

4. Special reference materials.

Business Education Index, Delta Pi Epsilon, Gregg Publishing Division, McGraw-Hill Book Company, Inc., 330 West 42 Street, New York 36, New York

"The High School Business Library," *American Business Education,* May, 1960

How to Use the Business Library, Second Edition, Johnson and McFarland, South-Western Publishing Company, 5101 Madison Road, Cincinnati 27, Ohio

Major Textbook Publishers in Business Education

The textbook has long been a basic material of instruction and one which has strongly influenced the curricula in American schools. It has been and remains the teacher's most important tool. Its use cannot be easily overlooked.

That there are disadvantages in the use of a textbook to the exclusion of most other teaching-learning materials is not denied. A textbook is used to advantage or disadvantage depending upon the experience of the teacher and his skill in using other materials. Where schools do not provide other appropriate materials, its use is not a matter of choice. In certain subject areas, it remains the *only* major tool of instruction, as in accounting where the sequential order of material is necessary and where standardized procedures are the rule. This does not mean that the instructor does not introduce concrete and realistic illustrations or that supplementary materials are not used; it does mean that instruction is along specific lines and that the textbook furthers instruction.

It is important to recognize in the consideration of textbooks for business classes that social and technological changes are continual and progress at a rapid pace. Obsolete textbooks may do more harm than good. For this reason, those responsible for the selection, and for the publication, of textbooks must be cognizant of progress and seek to be as up to date as possible.

Several criteria for careful selection of textbooks follow. Both publishers and users of the books need to consider these points carefully:

1. The contents of a book should be as up to date as possible in terms of today's business world.

2. A book should be constructed so as to recognize the different age groups in terms of reasonable standards and levels of learning.

3. Contents of a book should be such that pupil interest is aroused and stimulated. There should be provision for intelligent self-direction.
4. Type size, materials, vocabulary, and material format should be consistent with age group reading ability and comprehension.
5. The contents should be organized so that they lend themselves to various teaching methods.
6. Authorship should reflect experience and competence for writing in the field.
7. A textbook should be written in an interesting style and should contain attractive and appropriate illustrative materials.

Publishers in the field of business education have in general distinguished themselves in providing not only useful textbooks but also supplementary aids in the form of workbooks, practice materials, and evaluative instruments.

Test Materials in Business Education

The words "measurement" and "evaluation" have been defined in a number of ways and used in such a pattern that they mean the same thing to some and are completely opposite in meaning to others. Evaluation implies the assignment of values to stated quantities or qualities and the appraisal of achievement in terms of these values. Measurement implies the use of a measuring device or instrument with the objective of determining a quantitative or qualitative achievement. Since the purpose of measurement, or testing, is to aid in evaluation, these two concepts are tied together and enable the teacher to accomplish both in a single action. Evaluation, however, is a broad concept that goes far beyond the giving of a test.

It is evident that the more effective the utilization of measuring and evaluating procedures during the period of instruction, the more effective will be the ultimate evaluation or final mark. Every business teacher should consider the use of a variety of measuring and evaluating procedures to help determine final judgments. The tendency of many teachers to limit evaluation to commonly used procedures— quizzes, written tests—is an indication of denial of accuracy and refinement which greatly handicap good appraisal of the finished product. We have attempted to outline in the preceding chapters some of the techniques of good evaluation.

The selection, administration, and use of various tools of measurement are important functions of the classroom teacher. The items that follow provide information on sources and types of measuring instruments in business education.

Testing instruments fall into two categories: (1) those for measuring achievement in a subject field and (2) those used for prognostic or vocational aptitude testing. It is not possible in the space of this chapter to list the extensive catalog of these tests. However, there are available to the teacher two significant sources of this information:

> *Tests and Measurements in Business Education*, Second Edition, Hardaway and Maier, South-Western Publishing Company, 1952.
>
> Achievement Tests—Chapter 11
>
> Prognostic Tests—Chapter 16
>
> *A Summary of Clerical Tests*, Bennett and Cruikshank, The Psychological Corporation.

Hardaway and Maier [2] list 130 achievement tests for business subjects in the following areas: accounting, bookkeeping, business arithmetic, business English and correspondence, business law, business management, consumer

---

[2] Mathilde Hardaway and Thomas B. Maier, *Tests and Measurements in Business Education* (2nd ed., Cincinnati: South-Western Publishing Company, 1952), pp. 243-256.

economics, economics, economic geography, filing, general business, introduction to business, office machines, office practice, record keeping, shorthand, stenographic proficiency, spelling, transcription (machine), typewriting.

The tests are listed by the following guides: (1) text for which designed; (2) edition; (3) authors; (4) publisher; (5) tests in series; and (6) cost.

A sampling of the Bennett and Cruikshank [3] compilation show the following:

Stenographic Proficiency Test—The Psychological Corporation

SRA Dictation Skills—Science Research Associates

Test of Clerical Competence—Science Research Associates

Shorthand Aptitude Test—World Book Company

Clerical Perception Test—Educational Test Bureau

Because the sources of these studies may not always be readily available, we are including the following list of publishers of both the achievement and vocational aptitude tests: [4]

American Book Company, 55 Fifth Avenue, New York 3, New York

American Institute of Records Administration, Remington Rand Building, 315 Fourth Avenue, New York 10, New York

Bureau of Educational Measurements, Kansas State College, Emporia, Kansas

Bureau of Tests, Manchester College, 1108 North Sycamore Street, North Manchester, Indiana

California Test Bureau, 5916 Hollywood Boulevard, Los Angeles 28, California

---

[3] George K. Bennett and Ruth M. Cruikshank, *A Summary of Clerical Tests* (New York: The Psychological Corporation, 1949).

[4] Hardaway and Maier, *op. cit.*, pp. 257, 259.

Dictaphone Corporation, 420 Lexington Avenue, New York 17, New York

George Washington University, Washington, D. C.

Ginn and Company, 72 Fifth Avenue, New York 11, New York

Gregg Publishing Division, McGraw-Hill Book Co., Inc., 330 West 42 Street, New York 36, New York

Industrial Psychology, Inc., 105 West Adams Street, Chicago 3, Illinois

Richard D. Irwin, Inc., 1818 Ridge Road, Homewood, Illinois

Lyons and Carnahan, 2500 Prairie Avenue, Chicago 16, Illinois

Management Service Company, 3136 North 24 Street, Philadelphia, Pennsylvania

Martin Publishing Company, 690 Market Street, San Francisco 4, California

McGraw-Hill Book Company, Inc., 330 West 42 Street, New York 36, New York

Pitman Publishing Corporation, 2 West 45 Street, New York 36, New York

Prentice-Hall, Inc., Englewood Cliffs, New Jersey

The Psychological Corporation, 552 Fifth Avenue, New York 18, New York

The Psychological Institute, 3506 Patterson Street, N. W., Washington, D. C.

Public School Publishing Company, 509-513 North East Street, Bloomington, Indiana

H. M. Rowe Company, Inc., 624 North Gilmore Street, Baltimore 17, Maryland

Royal McBee Corporation, Westchester Avenue, Port Chester, New York

Science Research Associates, 57 West Grand Avenue, Chicago 10, Illinois

Smith-Corona Marchant, Inc., 410 Park Avenue, New York 22, New York

South-Western Publishing Company, 5101 Madison Road, Cincinnati 27, Ohio

State High School Testing Service for Indiana, Purdue University, Lafayette, Indiana

C. H. Stoelting Company, 424 North Homan Avenue, Chicago 24, Illinois

J. C. Winston Company, 1006 Arch Street, Philadelphia 7, Pennsylvania

University Publishing Company, 239 Fourth Avenue, New York, New York

World Book Company, 317 Park Hill Avenue, Yonkers 5, New York

Audio-visual Materials in Business Education

There is today an overwhelming abundance of educational material available in nearly every field in business education. Professional journals, film guides, and commercially distributed catalogs list materials in the audio-visual field. The acceptance and use of audio-visual media in American schools was given a tremendous impetus by the experience gained in training personnel during World War II. The various branches of the armed forces with almost unlimited funds at their disposal developed areas of service and efficiency of instruction not anticipated up to that time. This effort has brought about changes in teaching methods and enrichment of learning—all to the advantage of the pupils. Visual illustration of what were once problems for the imagination has brought understanding of fact and principle. Time and experience in the application of the principles of psychology of learning to the use of audio-visual material have brought improvement and greater effectiveness in utilization.

The need for evaluating all materials in their perspective of the whole learning picture is assumed. The degree of appropriateness is always a factor. The writers voice the feelings of many learned business educators on the subject when they maintain that the outcome is the important factor; if the "gimmick" gets in the way of real learning, then it should not be used.

These observations obligate the teacher to evaluate, both before and after using, all materials that are a part of the instruction. The following criteria are helpful in evaluating the effectiveness of audio-visual materials:

1. Are the materials in tune with sound psychological principles relative to their particular use?

2. Do the materials provide an added degree of realism to the regular instruction?

3. Does the time required for preparation and evaluation after use justify their use?

4. Do the materials draw out the desired pupil participation?

5. Do they stimulate interest in the particular lesson or unit under study?

6. Do the materials fulfill the purposes of instruction and contribute to the achievement of the overall business education objective?

7. Are the materials up to date and in tune with the times in relation to business and economic practices?

8. Do they contribute to the concreteness that is a desired end product of their use in the development of a concept; that is, are they really a help or an added boost to the "telling" done by the teacher?

The listings that follow are relatively restricted in scope. They are intended to provide a selection of representative materials that will enable the beginning teacher, or the experienced one for that matter, to become familiar with general sources and to become oriented to the possibilities of enriching class instruction.

The chart below is a composite listing of the various possibilities open to the teacher for course enrichment:

AUDIO-VISUAL MATERIALS

Advertisements	Films, motion picture	Posters
Bulletin boards	Filmstrips	Radio
Flannel boards	Maps	Recorders
Brochures	Magazines	1. Wire
Booklets	Models	2. Tape
Charts	Monographs	3. Records
Courses of study	Newspapers	Samples, specimens
Clippings	Projectors	Television
Diagrams	1. Moving picture	Workbooks
Displays	2. Filmstrip	Tachistoscope
Drawings	3. Overhead	Field trips
Exhibits	4. Opaque	Globes

Sources of Projectible Materials

Because information on sources of materials tends to become obsolete, only the most standard distributors are listed below:

Association Films, Inc., 347 Madison Avenue, New York 17, New York

Business Education Films, 4607 Sixteenth Avenue, Brooklyn 4, New York

Business Education Visual Aids, 330 West 72 Street, New York 23, New York

Coronet Instructional Films, Coronet Building, Chicago 1, Illinois

DeVry Technical Institute, Film Service Department, 4141 Belmont Avenue, Chicago 41, Illinois

Encyclopedia Britannica Films, Inc., 1150 Wilmette Avenue, Wilmette, Illinois

General Electric Company, Film Library, One River Road, Schenectady 5, New York

Ideal Pictures, 233-239 West 42 Street, New York 36, New York

International Business Machines Corporation, Film Library, Division of Education, Endicott, New York

McGraw-Hill Book Company, Inc., Film Department, 330 West 42 Street, New York 36, New York

Modern Talking Picture Service, Inc., 3 East 54 Street, New York 29, New York

Remington Rand Division, Sperry Rand Corporation, 315 Fourth Avenue, New York, New York

Teaching Aids Exchange, Modesto, California

Underwood Corporation, One Park Avenue, New York, New York

United World Films, Inc., Government Department, 1445 Park Avenue, New York 29, New York

Young America Films, Inc., 18 East 41 Street, New York 17, New York

In addition to these standard sources, there are a number of corporations and organizations that distribute free or low-rental films. Sources of these valuable items can be found through use of the following catalogs:

A *Directory of 2,660 16 mm Film Libraries*, U. S. Department of Health, Education, and Welfare, Washington, D. C.

Directory of Public Service Training Films, Civil Service Assembly, 1313 East 60 Street, Chicago 37, Illinois

Educational Film Guide, H. W. Wilson Company

Educators' Guide to Free Films, Education Progress Service, Randolph, Wisconsin

The Film Book, Prentice-Hall, Inc., Englewood Cliffs, New Jersey

3,434 United States Government Films, Bulletin No. 21, Superintendent of Documents, Washington, D. C.

Sources of Free and Inexpensive Printed Materials

Commercial and governmental agencies provide informative materials, literature, and other services that will prove useful to the business teacher. They make available pamphlets, posters, bulletins, charts, and a variety of free and inexpensive materials. Although it is impossible to list the many sources where these materials can be obtained, the following are among those sources:

American Association of School Administrators, 1201 Sixteenth Street, N. W., Washington 6, D. C.

Automobile Manufacturers Association, 320 New Center Building, Detroit 2, Michigan

Business Education World, 330 West 42 Street, New York 18, New York

Business Teachers Guide, Dept. W., Box 114, Conway, New Hampshire

Educational Press Association, 1201 Sixteenth Street, N. W., Washington 6, D. C.

Free Teaching Aids Company, Harrisburg, Illinois

George Peabody College for Teachers, Division of Surveys and Field Services, Nashville 5, Tennessee

Government Printing Office, Superintendent of Documents, Washington 25, D. C.

Institute of Life Insurance, Education Division, 488 Madison Avenue, New York 22, New York

Joint Council on Economic Education, 2 West 46 Street, New York 36, New York

Junior Town Meeting League, 356 Washington Street, Middletown, Connecticut

National Association of Manufacturers, 2 East 48 Street, New York 17, New York

National Association of Secondary-School Principals, 1201 Sixteenth Street, N. W., Washington 6, D. C.

National Education Association, 1201 Sixteenth Street, N. W., Washington 6, D. C.

South-Western Publishing Company, 5101 Madison Road, Cincinnati 27, Ohio

University of Illinois, Business Management Service, College of Commerce, Urbana, Illinois

University of Texas, The Visual Instruction Bureau, Division of Extension, Austin 12, Texas

The Wall Street Journal, The Educational Service Bureau, 44 Broad Street, New York 4, New York

In addition to the sources listed, perhaps the most valuable single aid in the selection and finding of materials is the special issue of *American Business Education,* "The High School Business Library." [5] This issue supplies complete references on materials for 12 areas of business teaching, including textbooks for students, references for teachers, pamphlets and booklets, magazines, published tests, and audio-visual materials.

Community Resources

If there is one thing that is outstanding in recent developments in education, it is the emphasis that is being placed on the community relationship with the school. The community can furnish the business teacher with many valuable tools. Field trips and excursions offer means of access to

---

[5] "The High School Business Library," *American Business Education* (May, 1960).

instructional aids that cannot be duplicated in the classroom—a picture of business in action from first-hand
observation.

We see at the present time a state of constant interaction
in the relationship of the community and the business classroom. It is evidenced by the interest shown by business
leaders in the educational program. To encourage the
interchange of ideas and business understandings, more use
is being made of Business-Education Days.

The field trip in business education holds a world of
possibilities for enriching instruction in almost every course.
These opportunities serve to extend the range of interests,
to provide new experiences, and to make understandings
meaningful in terms of real application. As high school and
post-high school students visit factories, private business
offices, and government departments, they see occupational
services which provide vocational information and guidance.

Office managers and personnel directors can frequently
be prevailed upon to talk to business classes or to student
assemblies. Much valuable first-hand information can be
obtained this way.

In order to develop skill in handling business forms and
papers, actual forms are important. These may frequently
be obtained from local offices.

Many local business firms and industrial organizations
have sound films that are often as instructive as a trip
through the plant. As a rule, a representative will be glad
to show a film at school when requested to do so.

In general, the use of resource personnel drawn from
business and industry brings into focus for the students
many of the intangibles of the subject matter. These persons, by virtue of specialized training and experience, are
able to make a significant contribution to the vocational
and general business education of youth.

INDEX

A

Abilities, accommodating goals to students' ranges of, 40
Accuracy, concept of, 88-93; in typewriting, 64, 88-94; relaxation important for, 90
Accuracy builder, an effective, 118; Page Club as an, 93
Adjusting entries, in bookkeeping, 332
Advanced typewriting, 71-74; evaluation of, 77
Arithmetic, in bookkeeping, 393
Assignments, bookkeeping, 323, 346, 348, 386-391; materials for office practice, 264; office practice, 231, 234, 297; scoring, 371; shorthand, 148, 183; typewriting, 125
Audio-visual materials, 512
Awards as motivating devices, 38

B

Battery plan, of organization, in office practice, 246
Bookkeeping, adjusting entries, 332; arithmetic in, 393; assignments, 323, 348-351, 386-391; complete-cycle approach, 362-370; demonstration in, 319, 344-347, 379; evaluation in, 328, 370; Gestalt approach in, 330, 394; individual differences in, 322, 355, 380-384; learning blocks, 351, 391; lesson planning, 377; neat handwriting in, 327, 394; planning and organizing in, 334-344; practice sets in, 357-362, 371, 397; recording transactions in, 395; tests, 371; theories in teaching, 319
Bookkeeping equipment, 315, 345
Bookkeeping machines, 259
Bookkeeping transactions, 330
Bookkeeping vocabulary, 326
Bulletin boards, 474
Business education, aims of, 24; departments, evaluative criteria for, 12-17; modern, 7-10; motivation in, 30-36; programs, 8-11
Business education associations, 501
Business educator, can use community resources, 517; membership of, in professional organizations, 500; working tools of, 497-518

Business training program, work experience, 268-271

C

Calculators, kinds of, 259
Calling-the-throw drill, as speed builder, 118, 121
Case problem method, 451
Chalkboard illustrations, with the straight lecture, 439
Classroom, appearance of office practice, 299; democratic, 148
Classroom organization, for office practice, 245-248; in bookkeeping, 318; in typing, 69
Classroom procedures, in office practice, 245; in shorthand, 147, 163-167, 181
Community resources, 445-449, 517
Compatability, 237
Complete-cycle problems, 362-369
Composing, at the typewriter, 78, 100
Computing machines, 259
Conditions for learning, 29
Conference leader, 419
Conference members, duties of, 419
Control, in typewriting, 88-94, 110
Cooperative occupational experiences, forms of, 269
Cooperative office practice program, organizing a, 270

D

Democracy in classroom, 3
Demonstration, 443; as a teaching method, 265; in bookkeeping, 319, 344-347, 379; in typewriting, 81
Dictation, office-style, 211-214; selecting material for, 150
Discipline, 322
Duplicating, stencil, 252
Duplicating workshop, 253
Duplicators, 254

E

Education, modern, 4-7; role of the teacher in, 17
Efficiency, multiple-job, 74
English, 217
Emotional factors, in nonskill subjects, 411-416
Equipment, for office practice classes, 290-293; physical layout and, 260